TRAVELLING THE KOROSKO ROAD

SUDAN ARCHAEOLOGICAL RESEARCH SOCIETY
PUBLICATION NUMBER 24

TRAVELLING THE KOROSKO ROAD

Archaeological Exploration in Sudan's Eastern Desert

edited by

W. Vivian Davies
and
Derek A. Welsby

with contributions by

Alfredo Castiglioni
Angelo Castiglioni
Mahmoud Suliman Bashir
Andrea Manzo
Serena Massa
Francesco M. Rega
Philippe Ruffieux
Donatella Usai

SARS

LONDON

2020

ARCHAEOPRESS PUBLISHING LTD
Summertown Pavilion
18-24 Middle Way
Oxford OX2 7LG

www.archaeopress.com

Sudan Archaeological Research Society
Publication Number 24
Editors of this volume: W. V. Davies and D. A. Welsby

http://www.sudarchrs.org.uk

ISBN 978-1-78969-803-9
ISBN 978-1-78969-804-6 (e-Pdf)

Front cover: *Alamat* on the southern approaches to the pass in the Bab es-Silik
along the Korosko Road (photo: D. A. Welsby)
Back cover: Top – Angelo and Alfredo Castiglioni (photo: CeRDO)
Bottom – The SARS Survey team (photo: D. A. Welsby)

Available direct from Archaeopress or from our website www.archaeopress.com

TRAVELLING THE KOROSKO ROAD

Archaeological Exploration in Sudan's Eastern Desert

Contents

List of Tables

List of Plates

4. The Tracks of Egyptian Penetration

5. Traces of the Past – First Expedition

6. Traces of the Past – Second Expedition

7. The Journey to Onib Crater (el-Hofra)

10. Preliminary study of the macro-lithic tools collected by CeRDO in the Sudanese Eastern Desert

11. The Korosko Road as a major cross-desert route: a brief overview

12. Gazetteer of sites

List of Figures

panels below the rim from site R 57; f) rim sherd of a large closed bowl with thickened and pointed rim, decorated by a band of impressed comma-shaped notches from site R16; g) wall sherd decorated with a pattern of impressed comma-shaped motifs from site U14; h) wall sherd decorated with a pattern of framed bands of crossing lines associated with other geometric zoned incised decorations from site U19; i) sherd with a pattern of incised multiple superimposed "waves" from site R26 (scale in cm).

15. Securing the Gold of Wawat: pharaonic inscriptions in the Sudanese-Nubian Eastern Desert

Preface

W. Vivian Davies and Derek A. Welsby

This volume publishes accounts of archaeological exploration carried out during the last 30 years or so in the Sudanese Eastern Desert. It is divided into two related parts.

The first and foremost covers results from the work of the Centro Ricerche sul Deserto Orientale (CeRDO), which is based at Varese in northern Italy. Between 1989 and 2006, CeRDO, directed by the brothers Alfredo and Angelo Castiglioni, ran a pioneering programme of expeditions, which traversed the so-called 'Korosko Road' (the main desert route connecting Egypt and Sudan) and followed multiple other tracks throughout the Eastern Desert. They encountered in the process a rich archaeological landscape, hundreds of previously undocumented sites, many frequented over millennia, prominent among them gold-production areas and their associated settlements.[1] The CeRDO record, the photographic database, the material retrieved, to which several of the papers published here are devoted, are now all the more valuable, in that many of these sites have since been badly disturbed and some entirely destroyed by recent gold-mining activities (an alarming state of affairs highlighted in the Introduction below).

The second part, introduced by a concise account of the historical usage of the Korosko Road, reports in full on a single, short season of documentation, organized in 2013 under the auspices, and with the support, of the Sudan Archaeological Research Society. Its main aim was detailed recording of a group of pharaonic rock-inscriptions discovered by CeRDO expeditions, most located along the Korosko Road and almost all related to the colonial gold-working industry. The project included also a degree of investigation and mapping of the wider context, as well as the recording and study of associated archaeological material, in particular of ceramic remains. The results complement and usefully extend in part those of CeRDO.

We are grateful to the several colleagues who agreed to write reports for this volume and for the editorial assistance received during its preparation (see below). We acknowledge, of course, the core role of the National Corporation for Antiquities and Museums (NCAM) of the Sudan, for having permitted the expeditions to take place and for the ever helpful participation of its staff.

On a final sad note, we much regret the unexpected loss of Alfredo Castiglioni (1937-2016), a grievous blow to his family, friends, and the wider archaeological community. This book, to which he had already made a significant contribution, is dedicated to his memory.

Contributors

Part I: the CeRDO expeditions (1989-2006)

Alfredo and **Angelo Castiglioni**: Centro Ricerche sul Deserto Orientale, Varese, Italy.

Andrea Manzo: Università degli Studi di Napoli "L'Orientale", Naples, Italy.

Serena Massa: Università Cattolica del Sacro Cuore, Milan, Italy.

Francesco Michele Rega: Università degli Studi di Napoli "L'Orientale", Naples, Italy.

Part II: the SARS Korosko Road Project (2013)

Derek A. Welsby: c/o Sudan Archaeological Research Society, London, UK.

Phillipe Ruffieux: Service cantonal d'archéologie (Genève), Versoix, Switzerland.

Mahmoud Suliman Bashir: National Corporation for Antiquities and Museums, Khartoum, Sudan.

Donatella Usai: Centro Studi Sudanesi e Subsahariani, Treviso, Italy.

W. Vivian Davies: c/o Griffith Institute, Oxford, UK.

Editorial Assistance

Patricia Spencer, c/o Sudan Archaeological Research Society, London, UK.

---

[1] One should also note here the complementary field-research carried out in the Sudanese Eastern Desert over a three-season period (1996, 1997 and 1999) by Dietrich and Rosemarie Klemm, the results included in their impressive *Gold and Gold Mining in Ancient Egypt and Nubia: Geoarchaeology of the Ancient Gold Mining Sites in the Egyptian and Sudanese Eastern Deserts*. Berlin; Heidelberg. 2013.

Part I

The CeRDO expeditions
(1989-2006)

1. Explorations in Sudan's Eastern Nubian Desert, 1989 to 2006

Alfredo and Angelo Castiglioni

Introduction

When we requested authorization from the National Corporation for Antiquities and Museums (NCAM) in Khartoum, Sudan, in the second half of the 1980s, to carry out research in Sudan's eastern Nubian Desert, the reply was, "What do you hope to find in the desert? It is an archaeological void." Yet, that was not true. Over about 25 years of travel, we discovered and documented a vanished world centred on gold: mines and vast settlements where this precious mineral was mined, processed, stockpiled and defended.

At least from the fourth millennium before Christ until the 13th century of our era, the desert mines were exploited first by the Egyptians of the Pharaonic period, and in succession by the Ptolemies, the Romans, the Byzantines and the Arabs. This exploitation has continued in times closer to us: during the British colonial period, and, unfortunately, even today, by a multitude of improvised miners who are "sifting" the desert with modern technical means (metal detectors, excavators, etc.) and often destroying archaeological finds that have lain hidden for thousands of years in the solitude of the desert. We documented routes spanning vast distances also in terms of time, travelled by Egyptian caravans marching to conquer Nubia, by pilgrims going to Mecca, by spice and gold merchants bringing these precious goods to the rich and mighty of each succeeding generation.

The Nubian Desert in Sudan is huge. In this immensity, the area explored by the Research Centre on the Eastern Desert (referred to in this volume by its Italian acronym CeRDO.) covers more than 90,000 square kilometres, about the size of Ireland. Before we started our research, knowledge of the past of the Nubian Desert was based on historical documents written mostly by medieval Arab travellers and over the last two centuries on records of European scholars, travellers and explorers, such as Linant de Bellefont, A. E. P. Weigall and G. W. Murray.

The purpose

The aim of our research was to continue and extend these explorations, contributing with full documentation, including photographs, to raise awareness and keep alive the memory of a world that, just over these last years, is undergoing profound changes. We designated our first expeditions in the Sudan's Eastern Desert by means of letters: Expedition A, between January and March 1989; Expedition B, between February and March 1990; Expedition C, between December 1990 and February 1991; Expedition D, between January and February 1993; and Expedition E, between January and March 1994 (see Plate 1.1 and the summary catalogue with detailed site designations and brief descriptions in Castiglioni, Castiglioni and Vercoutter, *L'Eldorado dei Faraoni: alla scoperta di Berenice Pancrisia*, Novara, 1995, 177-186).

During these early expeditions, our research and interests were focused on the area of 'Wawat', the Egyptian name for Lower Nubia. According to the texts from Pharaonic Egypt, the immense gold producing region between the 25° and 18° north parallels was divided into three major distinct areas. The northernmost produced the 'gold of Coptos', extracted from the mines of the Wadis Hammamat, Silsila and Abbad; the southernmost area provided the 'gold of Kush', extracted from the mines of Upper Nubia, the closest to the Nile, from Buhen to Kerma, south of the Third Cataract. But it was, above all, the area of Wawat (mines of the Wadis Allaqi and Gabgaba and their tributaries) that produced most of the gold that flowed into the coffers of the pharaohs during their millennia of history. For example, in the 41st year of the reign of the Eighteenth Dynasty pharaoh Thutmose III (1479-1425 BC), the region of Wawat supplied the pharaoh with 3144 *deben* and 3 *kedet* of fine gold, i.e. more than 286kg of precious metal, whereas the mines of the land of Kush had produced only about 18kg in the same period (Castiglioni *et al.* 1995, 18-19). It is this fabulous region that our investigations initially covered.

The research

What factors and elements directed and guided our research? A frequent element comprised the traces of ancient caravans that by treading on rocky areas or compact crushed stone over the many centuries had left indelible marks of their passage on the ground. The pack animals travelled in a line, especially when moving through narrow passages between mountain chains. In these areas, the tracks are clearer: the hooves of generations of pack animals (donkeys first, and camels later) cut into the ground and marked the rocks. Once we had identified a route, we needed to locate the bivouacs of the caravans because the spot where men and animals spent the night was an important factor for us. It allowed us, in fact, to estimate the campsite of the next leg, bearing in mind that a caravan covered about 25 to 30km in a day, depending on the ground conditions, and that it proceeded where possible in a straight line to optimize both distance and time.

In the desert with camels

We wanted to have this experience to assess whether our hypotheses were well founded. Hassan, an old camel driver of few words but who knew all the "secrets" of a desert journey, served as our guide.

From the expedition diary: 12 February 1990: "Since a few hours, we have been travelling on our teetering rides across an immense stony plain towards Jebel Maqran, a tiny outcrop that looms in the void and fades into nothingness. We realize that Hassan is following the trail of an old caravan route without losing sight of the jebel rising ephemerally before us. The track runs straight to our destination, which, like a lighthouse, shows us the shortest path. When we climb over the low hills and the jebel disappears from our view, we know by the marks left by countless animals that travelled the same route that we are going in the right direction. When the track disappears, erased by a sudden sandstorm, Hassan rides on confidently into the emptiness of the desert using Jebel Maqran - now floating in the overheated air and seemingly farther and farther away - as reference point. "How many kilometres?" we ask Hassan, who slows down and looks at us with surprise. "You mean how many days or hours!" he exclaimed. And so we learn our first lesson of the desert: distances are calculated in time and not kilometres. At some point, we realize that our guide is no longer following the direct route that we had travelled until then. We question him with a look. He does not answer but the explanation comes after a few kilometres. A well stands before us and Hassan, still silent, draws water for his camels. Perfectly adapted to the desert climate, a camel can withstand a weight loss of up to 40% from dehydration and quickly restore its water balance by consuming an amount of water equal to half of its weight. A thirsty camel can drink 100 litres of water in a few minutes. Watering our animals takes little time and we continue on our way.

The second lesson of the desert comes at sunset, when Hassan stops to set up the night camp under the shelter of a sandstone slab that covers us like a roof. You do not travel at night in the desert and, usually, you stop at a place sheltered from the wind. The rock is engraved with graffiti of different periods. We see prehistoric signs, a barely visible hieroglyphic inscription erased by time and, scattered on the ground, pottery fragments. There is also Hassan's name, scratched on the rock when he camped there the first time - a timeless place and tradition. We calculate the day's travel: our camels covered about 27km in ten hours. It is a customary distance if the terrain is flat and unobstructed." It is the confirmation of distances we already know: the Darb el-Arba'in, a track of 1200km, can be covered in 40 days at 30km a day. The Muheila track, 160km long, takes instead only six days at a little more than 25km a day.

Final considerations

Karim Sadr, the archaeologist who shared the efforts and emotions of our first five expeditions, wrote (Castiglioni *et al.* 1995, 147): "The Sudanese Nubian desert is huge. How much archaeological research will be necessary for an adequate reconstruction of the past of such a vast territory? Archaeologists believe that a representative sample of 20% of the sites can provide a sufficiently clear framework of an area's history. They also believe that there is an average of one archaeological site per square kilometre; therefore, knowledge of about 18,000 sites is needed before the Nubian Desert bares the secrets of its past to us. At the end of the fifth expedition (March 1994), about 200 sites had been located. Not many compared to the theoretical number of 18,000, but if one takes into account that the Nubian Desert was considered an archaeological void only a few years before the Castiglionis obtained their concession, the progress made is not negligible. Actually, with 200 out of 18,000 sites, it is little more than a glimpse at the history of this extraordinary desert, but no less important therefore". The research continued from March

1994 to April 2006, broadening knowledge of this immense desert significantly.

The Nubian Desert in danger

In the past

The surveys and excavations carried out by the CeRDO allowed for the recording of a large number of ancient mining villages, various kinds of tombs, forts and settlements for defence, rock carvings, and hieroglyphic inscriptions spanning a period of at least 7000 years. A single factor, however, clouds the perspectives and the archaeological potential of the Nubian Desert: the sacking of its sites and the incalculable damage this has caused. For example, among the hundreds of huge circular platform mounds that we found, only ten were still intact. In these cases the majority of the plundering is very old and probably dates back to the gold rush in medieval times, when Arab miners descending from the banks of the Nile swarmed over the Nubian Desert. The tombs were certainly the easiest source of gold. The arduous task of crushing and pulverizing the quartz to win the precious material was probably started once the tombs near the mines had been systematically plundered for their grave goods.

In the present

The results of our first campaigns and the accompanying images had immediately preceded a new gold rush already back in the early 1990s. Unfortunately, our foreboding at the time became reality. It seems that this rush started in 2008, north of the city of Abu Hamed. The latest generation of metal detectors capable of identifying the type of buried material is the main tool of the illegal treasure hunters who start hacking away with picks and shovels only when the device has signalled the certain presence of nuggets. The stories (and photographs taken with mobile phones) of exceptional finds have fuelled the gold fever.

The news of a lucky gold seeker who arrived at Khartoum's market with some 60kg of the precious mineral was published by the Sudanese newspaper *al-Sahafah* in December 2010. In 2011, the Sudanese government estimated that there were more than 200,000 illegal gold seekers scattered across the Nubian Desert. The damage caused by these improvised "miners" to the fragile archaeological structures is difficult to quantify. The photos we took in Jebel en-Nigeim and the descriptions of the three correspondents, Massimo De Benetti, Marco Grassini and Paolo Nannini of the journal *Archeologia Viva*, who travelled through the Nubian Desert in early 2014 to document the damage caused by this frenetic and destructive gold rush, suffice to assess it.

From the journal *Archeologia Viva*, issue no. 163, January-February 2014:

'The desert is a bustle of activity with trucks carrying men, supplies and bags of precious mineral. Groups of gold seekers on old Bedford trucks are heading towards the deepest and unexplored areas. In their hands, the metal detectors point to the sky like flags. The gold seekers do not crush the stones; they follow the sand moved by bulldozers and tractors. It almost seems that there is not even a small patch of unspoiled desert left and our land rovers struggle to find a usable path…

Holes everywhere, on the hillsides, even on the hilltops. Not only gold, but also archaeological evidence has been dug up and taken who knows where. Confirmation comes in the afternoon, when among the remains of a necropolis we find numerous bronze fragments that had been discarded and thrown into the pits. We hope that the archaeological research on the past has limited the damage".

Entire pages of history are torn out each day from the great book of Nubian archaeology. Areas where silence reigned supreme until a few years ago are now awash with the deafening noise of excavators and the gold seekers' cries. The peace and immutability of the desert that had fascinated us during our first journeys are irretrievably lost.

The following account of our work is divided into six sections, each dealing (not necessarily in chronological order) with significant areas of exploration and the presentation of the more important discoveries: 2. Wadi Terfowi; 3. The gold mines of Kerma; 4. The Nubian Desert: The tracks of Egyptian penetration; 5. Traces of the past, first expedition; 6. Traces of the past, second expedition; 7. The Onib Crater (el-Hofra).

Appended here is a select bibliography of CeRDO reports. Other papers in this volume concentrate in depth on certain aspects of the work and on the material recovered and include detailed bibliographies.

Bibliography

Castiglioni, A. and A. Castiglioni 1994. 'Discovering Berenice Panchrysos', *Egyptian Archaeology* 4, 19-22.

Castiglioni, A. and A. Castiglioni 2003, 'Pharaonic Inscriptions along the Eastern Desert Routes in Sudan', *Sudan & Nubia* 7, 47-51.

Castiglioni, A. and A. Castiglioni 2006. 'The new discoveries along the route Korosko-Kurgus', in I. Caneva and A. Roccati (eds), *Acta Nubica: Proceedings of the X International Conference of Nubian Studies, Rome, 9-14 September 2002*. Rome, 401-410.

Castiglioni, A. and A. Castiglioni 2006. *Nubia, Magica Terra Millenaria*. Firenze.

Castiglioni, A. and A. Castiglioni 2007. 'Les pistes millénaires du désert oriental de Nubie', *Bulletin de la Société Française d'Égyptologie* 169-170, 17-49.

Castiglioni, A., A. Castiglioni and C. Bonnet 2010. 'The gold mines of the Kingdom of Kerma', in W. Godlewski and A. Łajtar (eds), *Between the Cataracts. Proceedings of the 11ᵗʰ Conference for Nubian Studies. Vol. 2*. Warsaw, 263-70.

Castiglioni, A., A. Castiglioni and G. Negro 1999. 'The ancient gold route from Buhen to Berenice Panchrysos', in S. Wenig (ed.), *Studien zum antiken Sudan. Akten der 7. Internationalen Tagung für meroitistische Forschungen von 14. bis 19. September 1992 in Gosen/bei Berlin*. Meroitica 15. Wiesbaden, 501-510.

Castiglioni, A., A. Castiglioni and K. Sadr 1997. 'Sur les traces des Blemmis: les tombes Bejas au premier millénaire après J.-C. dans les collines de la Mer Rouge', in *Actes de la VIIIᵉ Conférence Internationale des Études Nubiennes 1994*, Vol. II. (*Cahier de Recherches de l'Institut de Papyrologie et d'Égyptologie de Lille* 17/2). Lille 163-167.

Castiglioni, A., A. Castiglioni and J. Vercoutter 1995. *L'Eldorado dei Faraoni*. Novara.

Sadr, K., A. Castiglioni, and A. Castiglioni 1995. 'Nubian desert archaeology: a preliminary view', *Archéologie du Nil Moyen* 7, 203-235.

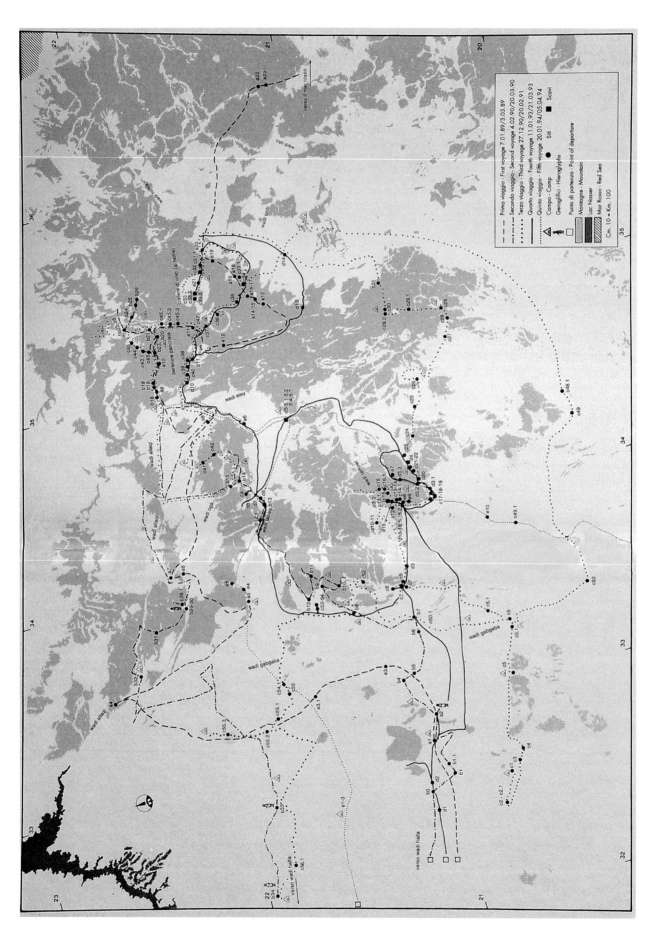

Plate 1.1. *Itineraries of the five CeRDO expeditions in the Sudanese-Nubian Desert (1989-1994). The map shows the locations of the explored mining sites, excavations and hieroglyphic inscriptions. They are about 100 identified settlements.*

4

2. Wadi Terfowi

Alfredo and Angelo Castiglioni

A wooded wadi

During our first archaeological expeditions in the Nubian Desert of Sudan, from 1989 to 1994, we passed several times through Wadi Terfowi (Latitude 21° 00.283' N; Longtitude 34° 03.217' E) (Plate 2.1). A few dozen kilometres long and 100m wide, the wadi is a green oasis surrounded by vast stretches of

When the fibre is stripped off, it secretes a whitish liquid that he rubs on his teeth. "It's like your toothpaste", he tells us flashing a bright smile. "Twenty centimetres of *arak* are worth a Sudanese pound at the Khartoum market", he says collecting a large bunch. This is a wadi with climatic and environmental conditions favourable for human life, now as in the past.

The Beja well

We come upon a campsite of the Beja Bisharin. A nearby well (site C16.1) about 10m deep provides water to the community. It is probably ancient, as the skilful stonework seems to confirm (Plate 2.2). On the rocks, at the side of the well, we see many graffiti depicting battle scenes. Men face each other holding long swords and protecting themselves with round shields (Plate 2.3). It is hard to date these representations: they could be quite ancient, as the patina in the grooves suggests. It is impossible to make any assumptions based solely on the types of weapons represented: over the centuries, the customs of the desert people have re-

Plate 2.1. View of Wadi Terfowi.

sand and red-hot rocks. It concentrates in a limited space many of the arboreal elements found in the Nubian Desert. Driving along the wadi is not always easy: the palms and acacias are so numerous that we have to change constantly the itinerary of our 4x4s. After sporadic rains, many flowers sprout up. This is an environment that would benefit from more in-depth botanical studies. It is also the realm of the Dorcas gazelle, a shy animal and very difficult to approach. There are many kinds of insects; the most common are locusts and mantises.

In some areas, where plants are sparser, colocynth (*colocyntis vulgaris*) grows on the sandy soil: vast stretches covered by these cucurbits that branch out by creeping on the ground. Our Sudanese archaeologist colleague called them small pumpkins that "know how to travel". In fact, when these light fruits ripen and drop from the plant, they cover long distances rolling along blown by the wind. Then, when they dry out and crumble because of the intense heat, the seeds are scattered around and generate new plants. The Sudanese archaeologist picks up a few of them. Their juice mixed with sugar, he tells us, "serves as antidote against snake and scorpion bites. Best to be prepared".

A little further on we stop again. Our Sudanese travel companion sees a thick bush with small light green leaves, called *arak*. He breaks off a small branch and chews on it slowly.

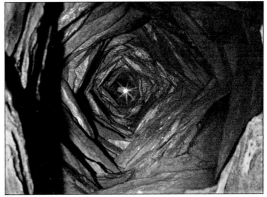

Plate 2.2. Interior of the well by the Beja Bisharin campsite.

mained amazingly unchanged. The depiction is perhaps a memorial of the fights engaged in to defend or capture that precious water point, the only one we came upon for many kilometres.

The mining settlements

Almost in the middle of Wadi Terfowi, we find many mining settlements set up to extract the gold from the auriferous

Plate 2.3. The graffiti next to the well, probably depicting battles for control of the well.

Plate 2.6. Mine D 16, grinding mills.

quartz (Plate 2.4). It is immediately apparent that the auriferous area was long exploited.

In mine D15, there is the outline of a mosque and rotating millstones (Plate 2.5). In the small settlement E9, we note the outline of another mosque, fragments of medieval pottery and again rotating millstones. In mine D16, a few kilometres north of mine D15, there are instead many grindstones; the oldest could be of Egyptian origin (Plate 2.6). In mine C13, we find fragments of what might be Pharaonic pottery. It is possible that this gold-rich area was mined over a very long time, from the Pharaonic era to the Arab medieval period.

Plate 2.4. Wadi Terfowi, mine settlement D15.

Plate 2.5. Mine D15, rotating millstones.

The Terfowi mining villages are concentrated in an area of just a few square kilometres (a rectangle of approximately 4.5 by 3.5km). Some are located on the eastern, others on the western, side of the wadi. The settlements consist of rectangular and circular structures made of dry-stone walls with internal dividers, often still well preserved (Plate 2.7). These are generally aggregated hovels, located at the foot of the hills or at the entrances of secondary wadis for protection against the wind.

On the hills overlooking the settlement there are numerous ceramic fragments. An intact pot was probably used to bring water to the miners. Nearby, in fact, extensive excavations testify to a long process of digging. Close to mine C13, we notice some geometric structures (Plate 2.8). As we did not carry out excavations, it is not possible to classify them. However, by comparison with the nearby cemetery we suggest that they are tombs. A large settlement (site C11- Kabeseit mine, Plate 2.9) is located to the north-northwest at some 20km from the mining group of Wadi Terfowi.

The Kabeseit mine

This is a wide and partially sand-covered mine at the foot of naturally degraded hills, in an area devoid of vegetation. There are numerous buildings with circular or rectangular plans and dry-stone walls, usually aggregated. Some walls, about 1m high, are still in good condition, and between the huts we note the outline of a mosque with the *mihrab*, the niche indicating the direction of Mecca, visible on one side. Our Sudanese colleague takes advantage of the rest to perform the ritual prayer.

The work areas are obvious, littered with many rotating millstones, both intact and broken, some of considerable size. There is quite a bit of Islamic medieval ceramic, ranging from the 9th to the 10th century AD (W. Y. Adams, pers. comm.), while some fragments seem to be of Egyptian origin. Extensive trenches, especially on the hilltops overlooking the mining settlement, confirm the intense exploitation of the quartz veins.

We fasten a camera to a helium-filled balloon and shoot some photos at a height of 150m by remote control. The images give us a detailed view of the central area of the mine. We can see the huts of the miners with the entrances facing downwind (Plate 2.10).

*Plate 2.7. Wadi Terfowi,
nucleated buildings.*

Plate 2.8. Wadi Terfowi, mine C13.

Plate 2.9. Kabeseit mine, site C11.

Plate 2.10. Kabeseit mine, bird's-eye view (from aerial balloon) of the central sector.

dieval times, during the first gold rush as recorded by the historical sources (Plate 2.13).

The distance between the Wadi Terfowi mining area and these tombs is about 20km, feasibly covered in a one-day caravan trip. It is, therefore, conceivable that during the search for the precious metal in medieval times the Arabs directed their attention to these burial places that, like treasure chests, contained rich funeral ornaments, often made of gold, before starting on the hard work of extracting gold from the mines. Unfortunately, the same consideration holds true today: thousands of improvised miners routinely violate the graves in search of gold, sieving the Nubian Eastern Desert attracted by a golden mirage.

A large rectangular structure seems to have no entrance (probably because of a collapsed wall that concealed the opening) and contains some rotating millstones. It is the likely area where the auriferous quartz was crushed. The smallest building on the left side was possibly used to store and safeguard the sacks of auriferous dust. Behind the building, in fact, we see the probable guardroom that housed the soldiers stationed there to protect the precious product. When we carry out a survey, we find some sack fragments and a small amount of auriferous dust inside the storeroom, which seems to confirm our hypothesis.

The circular platform mounds

There are many circular platform mounds, generally located on the hilltops north of the Terfowi mining area (site C14.1). They probably date to the pre-Islamic Beja period. We follow a left bank tributary of Wadi Terfowi and after about 5-6km we find a circular platform mound, isolated (site C12). The burial place has been disturbed (Plate 2.11). Among the scattered stones, we find the fragments of a probable ceramic support. We restore and draw the support and, at its centre, we notice an engraving that recalls a Christian cross (Plate 2.12). Whether the pre-Islamic Beja accepted the Christian faith is a question that still lacks a clear answer. Some texts, such as that of John of Biclaro, claim that the Beja became Christians in the Roman era. Engravings on their ceramics often include the cross motif. Although there is no certainty, one cannot fail to remember the Beja's role in counteracting Islam's advance into what was then Christian Nubia.

At about 20° 50' N latitude and 34° E longitude, Wadi Terfowi flows into Wadi Gwanikam, which, with its right bank tributaries, encompasses a triangle of about 160 square kilometres, where we identified 14 isolated graves, possibly a small necropolis. Here, too, almost all the inhumations with a circular platform had been violated, perhaps in the Arabic me-

Just north of the confluence of the two wadis, we find a large mound of soil and pebbles about 17m in diameter and 2m high, site C18. The photographs taken from the balloon indicate that it could be a man-made structure, perhaps a tomb. A test excavation at the top revealed instead a compact rock layer at a depth of

Plate 2.11. Site C12, circular platform mound, disturbed.

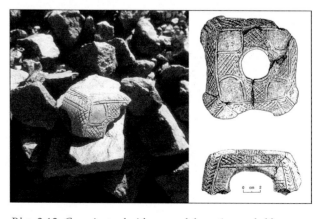

Plate 2.12. Ceramic stand with engraved decoration, probably a cross.

Plate 2.13. Wadi Gwanikam, disturbed burial places.

Four kilometres east of site D24, we find a large isolated stone circle, site C23, about 25m in diameter: almost in the centre stands a circular platform mound. Excavated in 1993, it revealed fragments of a leather blanket that allowed us to date the skeleton of the deceased to around the 7th century AD. It was the body of a youth, laid in a foetal position with five small golden discs as funerary ornaments (Plates 2.16 and 2.17). The grave had been built on a much older burial structure. In fact, in the stone circle that surrounded it, we found traces of an ancient hearth and bone fragments of cattle and sheep. The charcoal was dated to *c.* 3100 BC. Outside the circle, on the south side, we unearthed the articulated skeleton of a dog and other sheep and cattle bones, perhaps offerings to the long ago deceased individual. A few metres from site C23, we

350mm, but no archaeological deposits; the excavation was consequently abandoned (Plate 2.14).

We excavated a number of circular platform mounds during our archaeological expeditions, which furnished chronological information and, in many cases, important grave goods (Plate 2.15). Site C19, excavated during the fifth expedition, revealed the remains of a 21-25 year old individual, probably a young male. Some leather fragments on which the body lay, allowed us to date the remains to the later 7th century AD. Site D4, excavated during the 1993 expedition, held a child's skeleton. The dating of organic material gave us a date in the mid 8th century AD. These dates seem to confirm that the Eastern Desert was still fully controlled by the Beja at that time. The Arabs of Egypt discovered the gold mines (which had been abandoned for centuries and long forgotten) only between AD 820 and 830. It was during a punitive expedition against the Beja, guilty of having attacked the peaceful Nile Valley villages, that the Arabs, driving into the heart of the desert, encountered a previously unknown mining world.

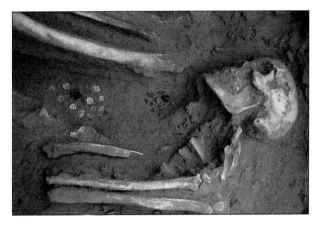

Plate 2.15. Site C19, inhumation of a young individual with precious ornaments.

find another case of a grave built over an inhumation of a previous period. On a collapsed circular platform mound, we find an Arabic grave, marked by two large stelae, according to Islamic burial customs.

We bypass a sandy plain, where we know from experience that discoveries are unlikely, and head south following the wadis between the mountains. After 6km, we find the last circular platform mound in the area we explored. It is site C24, standing isolated on a hill overlooking a wooded wadi (Plate 2.18). The organic substances that we recovered confirmed that the grave dated to the 8th century AD, further evidence that these monumental structures belong to the pre-Islamic Beja period, between the 7th and 8th century, before the medieval Arabs conquered the gold-rich lands of the Nubian desert. Perhaps other mounds belong to earlier periods. It is impossible at this stage to assess how much older they might be. Further research is required for a definitive answer.

Plate 2.14. Aerial view of the large mound C18. Probable burial place, though excavation revealed no finds.

Plate 2.16. Site C23, large stone enclosure with a central mound, aerial view.

Plate 2.17. Site C23, inhumation, 7ᵗʰ century AD.

Plate 2.18. Site C24, burial dated to the 8ᵗʰ century AD
through the analysis of organic remains.

3. The gold mines of Kerma and exploration of the South-Eastern Nubian Desert

Alfredo and Angelo Castiglioni

The purpose of the CeRDO archaeological expedition carried out between January and March 2006 was to search for and, if possible, locate the gold mines that provided the precious metal for the Kingdom of Kerma during its millenium of history and to explore the vast mountainous region that extends between the northern latitudes 20° 10' and 21° 20'.

The journey

We start from the town of Abu Hamed on the Nile, constantly heading to the east-southeast, on a bearing of 110°. We cross a vast plain of gravel areas interspersed with sandy stretches dotted with low jebels. We come upon the first villages of the Bisharin Umm Nagi, the ethnic group that inhabits these places. Numerous palaeosols testify to a region once rich in plants and animals. There are several Mesolithic sites with incised pottery-fragments on the ground. We come across numerous ruts of recent and ancient caravan routes and, in an area almost bare of vegetation, the first outcrops of auriferous quartz.

The mines of Jebel en-Nigeim

The Jebel en-Nigeim, bordered on the north by the eponymous wadi and on the south by the Wadi Halbob, rises in a location about 100km from Abu Hamed. To our surprise, we find on this jebel 15 Bisharin, who obtain gold from the quartz using extraction techniques not unlike those described by Diodorus Siculus nearly 2000 years ago. We decide to stay in the region for a few days because we wish to document an activity rooted in ancient times that we thought had long disappeared. Above all, we want to check whether the work to extract the auriferous quartz has harmed ancient structures.

In 2006 the "gold rush" that has since destroyed so many of the ancient archaeological sites had not yet begun. Nonetheless, initial damage (discussed further on) was already evident, fortunately limited to the Jebel en-Nigeim area and not spread across the entire eastern Nubian Desert as is now the case. We made a thorough photographic documentation, well aware, even then, of the irreversible harm caused by uncontrolled excavations, and submitted a report to the Sudanese authorities.

The gold mining process according to Agatharchides

The gold mining process was described more than 2000 years ago by Agatharchides of Cnidus, a geographer of the mid-2nd century BC appointed by Ptolemy VI (or Ptolemy VIII) to visit the Atbay gold mines. In the fifth book of his *On the Erythraean Sea*, a work quoted by Diodorus Siculus, he relates in detail the technical methods for extracting this precious mineral, which we found were used almost unchanged to this day in the Jebel en-Nigeim area. The mining area chief is an old Bisharin

who, we are told, was the first to discover the gold that still existed in the jebel, despite the uninterrupted exploitation over hundreds of years by the ancient miners: pre-Islamic Beja, medieval Arabs and perhaps even the inhabitants of Kerma. The most important work, namely the crushing of the auriferous quartz blocks, is carried out among the ruins of an ancient defensive building (Plate 3.1). This activity was

Plate 3.1. Jebel en-Nigeim, current exploitation of the auriferous quartz inside ancient structures and reuse of lithic tools.

most likely performed under the supervision of designated overseers even in ancient times. Each miner is given a certain amount of quartz that must be crushed during the day.

The area contains several veins of auriferous quartz, which, as Diodorus emphasized, "... *is a white stone*" that stands out against the dark colour of the surrounding rock. At the Jebel en-Nigeim mine, the quartz is broken by heating the vein with fire. The fragments are accumulated at the base of tunnels, dug by generations of miners (Plate 3.2). The method is the

Plate 3.2. Ancient Jebel en-Nigeim mine, with an accumulation of quartz fragments in the foreground.

same as that reported by Diodorus: "... they first burn (the auriferous quartz) with a hot fire ..." Since there are no trees in the area, the miners now use old car tyres as fuel; we see their metal skeletons transported by camel from the Nile Valley. Having cracked the vein with heat, the quartz is then broken into smaller fragments. Diodorus described the process, "... Then the men over thirty take this quarried stone ... and pound an allotted amount in stone mortars with iron pestles until the pieces are no larger in size than a lentil."

The miners of Jebel en-Nigeim assigned to the crushing process are young men at the peak of their strength and they perform this hard work using the old tools recovered from the mines as anvils. It takes a long time and a lot of physical effort to reduce the quartz fragments to 'the size of a lentil', as Diodorus related. A ring of straw and cloth surrounds the quartz pieces to prevent the splinters, shooting off under the hammer blows, from injuring the miners, especially in the eyes. Diodorus continued, "And the entire operations are directed by a skilled worker who studies the stone and points out the vein containing the metal (the gold) to the labourers." This task is performed also in the Jebel en-Nigeim mine by a man who visually evaluates the gold content in the quartz. Then a quartz powder sample is washed in a pan with water to separate the gold flakes, and from this the specialist estimates whether the amount of gold recovered is enough to begin the hard excavation work (Plate 3.3).

Plate 3.3. Jebel en-Nigeim, separation of gold from quartz powder.

The descriptions of Diodorus relate to the Ptolemaic period. However, as Jean Vercoutter pointed out, one can reasonably believe that the same extraction techniques were used in earlier or later times, as evidenced by the fact that they are still employed today, albeit with changes because of the use of modern tools. In fact, the last process, the pulverization of the quartz, is now carried out with a mechanical grinder driven by an old combustion engine. As described by Diodorus, the effort required for this work was quite different in ancient times: "This work is done by the women, either alone or helped by their husbands or relatives, locked up in enclosures. Several millstones are aligned here .... these women, using a wooden handle ... spin the grinders until the entire amount of stones given to them has been reduced to the consistency of the finest flour."

On the top and along the slopes of the jebel we see the trenches dug out in antiquity where the quartz veins were exhausted, along with more recent excavation works. This activity is performed more often by groups of miners who, by singing, try to alleviate the fatigue of long hours under the sun. There are also single miners assigned by the mine chief to test a new auriferous zone.

Archaeological damage caused by these uncontrolled works

Our long stay allowed us to ascertain the damage caused by clandestine excavations in the archaeological area. We discovered that "test" excavations are conducted also within archaeological structures, frequently causing significant damage. In Mesolithic settlements, deep holes are dug inside the perimeter of the dwellings. Machines are used to dig close to the defensive settlements, churning the soil and quartz with no concern for any underlying structures. In some ancient working areas, the millstones were moved and the soil dug out to search for auriferous quartz blocks abandoned by the miners (Plate 3.4). The worst damage can be seen inside the masonry structures. Excavations carried out at the base of the walls caused them to collapse, destroying buildings that have stood for centuries (Plate 3.5). Fortunately, as we were told, this auriferous area is exploited for only about one month a year.

Plate 3.4. Jebel en-Nigeim, lithic mills removed by recent excavations using machines.

Plate 3.5. Jebel en-Nigeim, damage to masonry structures caused by mechanical excavators.

Life in the en-Nigeim mine

The mine (site F20) is organized very precisely, following work patterns and rhythms that are repeated day in day out. The miners use shafts that penetrate tens of metres into the mountain as resting places. Those not working in the mines help in other ways, such as by filling goatskins with water drawn from a nearby well. This precious liquid is used only for the water needs of the community, certainly not for washing the auriferous powder.

Again as Jean Vercoutter observed, "Considering that water was scarce in almost all mines, only the crushing of the mineral was carried out on site, while the quartz dust was transported to the Nile."

At the en-Nigeim mine, the mineral is first collected in sacks and then transported by camel to the Nile located about 100km away, following the Wadi Senateb and Wadi 'Amur. At Abu Dis, on the banks of the Nile, some 20 Nubians separate the gold flakes from the raw mineral by panning (Plate 3.6).

Plate 3.6. Nile, Abu Dis. Miners separate the gold flakes from the raw mineral.

The work is carefully organized here as well. The bags with the pulverized quartz are carried to the riverbank where a man distributes the dust to the gold panners standing in the water to eliminate the lost work time that would be caused if each worker had to pause and get a new supply of dust. Each panner carefully examines the result of his work: a few grams of gold mixed with iron oxides. Only at the end of the day may the more lucky ones boast a nugget of the precious mineral. The documentation that we had the opportunity to realize shows a single, surprising historical continuity that reaches from the present day far back in time.

The mine of Jebel en-Nigeim (en-Nigeim means "star" according to the Bisharin) is divided into four quarters and the main mining area is located on the top of the jebel. Despite careful searching, we find only a few pottery-fragments that were probably unearthed by the extensive excavation operations that disturbed the ground. In the other three quarters, we find numerous rotating millstones and cubic strikers with hollows to facilitate gripping (Plates 3.7 and 3. 8).

The shelters of the ancient miners are circular or rectangular, sometimes isolated, sometimes aggregated into a few units. On the top of the jebel, rectangular structures with massive dry-stone walls more than 1m high made of granite

Plate 3.7. Jebel en-Nigeim, rotating millstones.

Plate 3.8. Jebel en-Nigeim, cubic strikers.

blocks suggest a building used for defence or to store the auriferous dust (Plate 3.9).

We leave Jebel en-Nigeim and head east-northeast. Four kilometres from the settlement, we find ten tombs shaped like truncated cones with a diameter of 5-6m and about 1m high, probably of pre-Islamic Beja date. All had already been violated (Plate 3.10). After about 90km, we reach Jebel Kamotit where the *bir* (well) of the same name provides abundant and potable water. We take the opportunity to supplement our scarce water supply. We head north, bordering the west side of the jebel, and after 25km we find the mine

Plate 3.9. Jebel en-Nigeim, probable defensive or guard structure on the hilltop.

Plate 3.10. Burials of probable pre-Islamic Beja period close to the mining area.

long period. At Jebel Komotit, there are no defensive constructions or quartz veins; we see only vast expanses of sand and gravel removed superficially in search of alluvial gold. The few shelters, with a scarcity of tools, suggest temporary settlements.

In the present state of the research, it is not possible to state with certainty that Kerma merchants went directly to the mines to buy the gold, especially as no ceramic fragments from Kerma were found. It can be proposed instead that trade in the precious metal with the Nile Valley settlements took place through the Beja. It remains uncertain who worked in the mines. It is hard to imagine the Beja (who lived off caravan trade and often made forays to the Nile to plunder the wealthy villages) as miners.

The Arab historian Maqrizi wrote in this regard in the 15th century, "Before and after the advent of Islam they (the Beja) often wrought havoc in the eastern part of Upper Egypt where they destroyed a multitude of villages. The Pharaohs fought them often in their country, making peace soon after because of their need for gold. When the Rum (i.e. the Ptolemies) took over Egypt, they acted in the same way ...". The Romans also fought the Beja, under the Emperor Diocletian (AD 284-305), yet negotiated with them at the same time. According to the Byzantine historian Procopius, Diocletian had in fact apparently "ordered for a fixed contribution in gold to be delivered yearly to the Blemmyae (as the Beja were called in Roman times) provided they no longer plundered the land of the Romans". Quite a paradox: the Romans had always been used to collect taxes from the subjected populations, yet here instead they paid a contribution to the Beja.

Discarding, therefore, the hypothesis that the Beja, who lived as shepherds and robbers, worked the mines, it is likely that the mining was carried out by indigenous peoples subjected by the Beja and under their control. A few years ago, we documented a situation that lends some support to this hypothesis. In the Gobeit mine, we saw a Nubian mining gold for a Beja under the latter's careful supervision (Plate 3.11).

The most important auriferous zone (Jebel en-Nigeim)

F18 (Wadi Tesa) where surface excavations, dug in search for alluvial gold, are evident. On the top of a hill, we notice some isolated shelters for miners, rectangular in plan. The area around Wadi Eidukal and Wadi Tesa is rich in grass, but with few other plants. Immediately to the north, in an extremely arid environment, we find three other settlements: the mine F19 (Amtinedit), the F17 (Kiriu) and the mine F16. Here as well, there are surface excavations on the hillsides. There are neither houses nor grinders and hammers. We continue the exploration of the western side of Jebel Komotit and we note that again the bottom of the wadi has been dug superficially for several kilometres. We calculate that the area of alluvial gold prospecting extends for about 25km².

The Precambrian metamorphic rocks of the mountains that separate the Nile from the Red Sea contain auriferous quartz veins that erosion caused by winds and ancient rivers has ground down over the millennia, transporting the gold contained in them downstream where it accumulated as tiny flakes in the sand of the foothills. In ancient times, gold seekers did not have to dig tunnels and shafts, nor grind the hard quartz to extract the gold. It was easy to obtain just by sifting and washing the sand. It must, therefore, be assumed that the search for alluvial gold was the first mining activity conducted in the desert.

Conclusions

Although the existing structures of the mining settlements seem to date to the medieval Islamic period, one can reasonably believe that the same areas were exploited in previous periods to provide gold for the Kingdom of Kerma. The region lies between 19° 25' and 19° 50' latitude north and 34° 10' and 35° 10' longitude east; the auriferous zones are concentrated around Jebel en-Nigeim and Jebel Komotit. In the first location, gold was extracted from auriferous quartz; in the latter, it came from alluvial mining.

The differences between the two mining regions are immediately evident. At Jebel en-Nigeim, there are defensive constructions and the settlement is planned, consisting of shelters built near the quartz veins. The extensive excavations and numerous tools testify to an activity that lasted for a

Plate 3.11. Gobeit Mine, current search for gold controlled by a Beja warrior.

is located about 90km from the Nile and so at 2-3 days of caravan travel. Trade with Kerma could, therefore, occur either by sailing down the Nile or by travelling through the desert, a 250-300km trip taking about ten days by caravan. The Jebel en-Nigeim mines lie in fact on the same latitude as Kerma, along tracks still travelled by caravans that cross flood plains lacking any elevations. The absence of Egyptian hieroglyphic inscriptions and ceramic may indicate a degree of Kerma control over the region.

Exploration of the auriferous zone of Jebel Abu Dueim, February-March 2006

A plain dotted with low hills opens to the north of Jebel en-Nigeim and Jebel Komotit. The plain separates these two auriferous zones from the vast northern mountainous region with Jebel Abou Dueim at its centre. Located 100km from Jebel Komotit, Abou Dueim is rich in gold: 15 mining settlements are concentrated in a rectangle of about 50 x 100km. It was probably a gold mining area free from the influence of Kerma and the Egyptians, so the native population could sell the gold at profitable prices. Fortified settlements protected the region from invasions from the south (Kerma's area of influence) and the east (the Egyptian realm). After the first few days of travel, we find out how difficult it is to travel into the heart of the Abou Dueim massif. The wadi that we are following is not always free of obstacles. Sometimes an ancient waterfall cuts across the route, forcing us to find an alternative way.

A search in the mountains requires, therefore, an experienced guide who knows the passages and connections between the wadis. We find such a guide in a village, right at the beginning of the mountain area. His name is Bàfatil and he is a Bisharin who knows the region perfectly having crisscrossed it with his camel in search of pastures.

Bisharin is the generic term currently used to define the various Beja tribes, divided into four groups in Sudan: the Ababdeh (Ababda), the Hadendoa, the Bisharin and the Beni Hamer. It should be noted that these desert nomads were known by different names over the centuries. In the third millennium BC, they were the Medjay of Egyptian sources. In the Greek era, they became the Cadoi ophiophagi (snake eaters); the late Romans called them the Blemmyae; Arab writers of the Middle Ages identified them as the Buja, which gave rise to the current appellation of Beja - an ancient people, then, who have always considered themselves the owners of the Eastern Nubian Desert and its riches.

Bàfatil, our Bisharin guide

From the expedition diary: "It's five-thirty, dawn reddens the peaks. A rhythmic noise rips us from the warmth of our sleeping bags. Bàfatil prepares coffee for everyone after having ground in a wooden mortar the beans just roasted on a perforated metal sheet. The aroma is pleasant and we gather around our guide who offers us the coffee in silence: in the desert you economize on everything, even words".

Bàfatil knows the area well, especially the Jebel Abou Dueim and the wadis descending from this massif. Littered with stones, they are a true test for our vehicles. During the

journey, he points to the mountains and tells us their names, frequently not recorded on the maps of the early 20th century British prospectors. He calls the highest mountain *horba*, the hills *tokùsh* and the wadis *aba*.

He was received with some suspicion by the Sudanese team, who call him *adarob*, a term used to identify those who, like him, barely speak Arabic and, while professing the Islamic creed, are not considered true believers. *Adarob* is a generic term, like *khawadja*, used for all white foreigners regardless of their nationality. Bàfatil enables us to deepen our understanding of this ancient but still poorly studied ethnic group. He tells us that he has three wives and five children, and that he paid three camels, five *karuf* (rams) and four *atut* (goats with thick black fur) as bride price to the relatives of his last wife. Around his neck hang black leather bags (*tuktàb*) and on his arm, above the elbow, he wears *amrab*, his inseparable amulets. He says they contain *suras* of the Koran, but the Sudanese overseer believes that there are also feline teeth and claws, and snake-skin pieces, objects linked to persistent pre-Islamic beliefs.

Bàfatil's knowledge of the region proves immediately valuable and allows us to carry out the expedition with more and more discoveries. The first settlements we come across as we enter the Jebel Abou Dueim mountain range are the mines of Tamiam (Site F14) and Barkshap (site F1), the latter being the largest. They are located in a transitional region between the wide plain that opens to the south and the mountain range that extends to the north, in an extremely windy area. The miners' dwellings, aggregated into groups of three or more units, are built in narrow wadis mainly to protect them from the *habub*, the wind that blows from the south for several months a year.

We notice a fence protected by walls with a construction that is still in good condition (Plate 3.12). It could have been

Plate 3.12. Barkshap, Site F1. Buildings with drystone-wall, a probable guard room for the auriferous dust.

the home of an overseer in charge of controlling the bags of the auriferous quartz powder kept in the warehouse. In a small work area, used to crush the quartz in ancient times, we note some recent excavations, a sign suggesting that the illegal search for gold is extending northwards from Jebel en-Nigeim.

The fortified mining settlements

We explore the region up to latitude 21° 20', finding 17 mines and four settlements with small strongholds. Three of these (Keyau en-Nafaab, Kamba and Avai) are in a straight line.

Running from west to east, they are nearly on the same latitude and stand at a distance of about 10 to 15km from each other (10km between Kamba and Avai; 15km between Avai and Keyau en-Nafaab). They are most likely a fortified line designed to defend the rich auriferous zones of Jebel Abu Duheim and control the movements of the miners arriving from the north (the region of Onib and of the upper Wadi Allaqi) and south (the region of Komotit and en-Nigeim).

Keyau en-Nafaab (site F7) is the most important settlement in the region. It lies in a vast plain at the confluence of Khor Kiau and Wadi Rebeide. At the centre of the settlement stands a fort with two towers at the corners that were probably built to control the southern valleys and those that open to the north (Plates 3.13 and 3.14). In front of the defensive structure, there is an area for working the auriferous quartz. The south tower is in good condition, while the north tower has partially collapsed. Maybe it was the more important tower, designed to control the caravans heading to or arriving from the north, the regions with the most gold mines (Plate 3.15). Far away against the horizon loom the mountains behind which Berenice Panchrysos lies hidden, more than 120km as the crow flies. The perimeter walls of the building are built with interlocking stones bonded with mud. The largest and best-preserved construction is at the centre of the complex with one side against the outer wall of the fort. Probably it was the home of the manager of the mine or the depositary for the auriferous dust.

The old houses of the miners and inhabitants of Keyau

Plate 3.13. Keyau en-Nafaab, Site F7. Defensive structure.

Plate 3.14 Keyau en-Nafaab, Site F7. Defensive structure, perimeter wall made of stones bonded with clay.

Plate 3.15. Keyau en-Nafaab, Site F7. Defensive structure, south tower.

en-Nafaab are located in different areas. The most numerous buildings are located about 500m from the fort, along the north side of Wadi Kebeide. The settlement, in poor condition and apparently the oldest one, is located slightly higher than the course of the wadi and is shaded by large trees. We note rectangular structures divided by a main road axis crossed at right angles by secondary streets littered with stones from the collapsed houses. The settlement of Keyau, divided into quarters, is very extensive and complex. One quarter is located east of the main settlement and consists of completely destroyed rectangular huts. To the west, about 10m above Wadi Kiau, we see the ruins of a long building divided into rectangular rooms, perhaps a second collapsed fortress, overlooking the course of the wadi. In a valley, wedged between low hills, stands a small residential cluster (Plate 3.16).

The long occupation of the site is also evident from the town's great necropolis, which contains various types of

Plate 3.17. Keyau en-Nafaab, necropolis.

square metres; there are numerous rotating millstones, including some large ones (Plate 3.19). The walls are made of carefully assembled slabs of schist and stones. On the periphery, we find the outline of a large mosque dating to the medieval Islamic period, perhaps the last phase of occupation of the settlement. At the exit of the village, we notice a partially collapsed tower facing the wadi. A group of dwellings equipped with loopholes are perhaps depositaries where the auriferous dust was safeguarded. A small fort with the ruins of two towers stands at the centre of the wadi, evidently positioned to control the caravan routes from the north and the south (Plate 3.20).

In the settlement of Avai (site F3) the miners' dwellings are built with stones without binder, set one against the other. Large spaces enclosed by walls suggest that these are the common work areas (Plate 3.21). A fort, still in good condition, is situated at the cross roads of two wadis, again placed in a

Plate 3.16. Wadi Kiau, ruins of a probable fortification.

tombs, some recent. The necropolis is in fact still used by the Bisharin shepherds who live in the villages around Keyau (Plate 3.17). Not far away is a deep well of large diameter, perhaps ancient, which is still used by the Bisharin shepherds to draw water for their herds, especially goats. On the mountains looming over the town stand several isolated and large truncated cone mounds, almost always positioned on the peaks. The dark patina of the stones confirms the antiquity of these inhumations that probably date back to the pre-Islamic Beja period.

The settlement of Kamba (site F4) is located about 25km from Keyau. The miners' dwellings are located on the sides of the wadi (Plate 3.18). They are usually aggregated, with a rectangular or circular plan enclosing a living space of a few

Plate 3.18. Kamba mine, site F4. Buildings at the sides of the wadi.

Plate 3.19. Kamba mine, site F4. Large rotating mills.

Plate 3.21. Avai settlement, Site F3.

Plate 3.20. Kamba mine, site F4. Small fort
in the middle of the wadi.

Plate 3.22. Avai settlement, Site F3, fortified
structure at the intersection of two wadis.

controlling position (Plate 3.22). A little further on we see the outline of another fort, probably more ancient, which has completely collapsed (Plate 3.23). All around we see many workplaces, also eroded by time. Deep excavations on the mountains indicate that gold mining activity was carried out here over a long period of time. We find many inhumations of different types and ages in the area, prehistoric tombs (probably Mesolithic), circular platform mounds, conical mounds and an Islamic cemetery, all testifying to the long occupation of the site.

Under the guidance of Bafàtil, we travel from one mine to another following the wadis between the mountains. We often come across pastures for the Bisharin's camels. "I discovered this area", Bafàtil tells us proudly. "Now everyone comes here."

The last fortified mine, the settlement of Duara en-Nafaab (site F1), is located about 20km north of Keyau en-Nafaab. Here, most of the miners' houses are located along the wadi's banks, standing slightly higher to protect them from possible floods. Although rare, sudden storms on the

mountains can in fact channel the rainwater into the wadis with devastating effects. Other buildings wedged between the hills are located along the paths leading to the mines. Equipped with loopholes they controlled the excavation areas normally located on the upper slopes of the mountains. A probable control structure stands at the base of a hill: the massive walls

Plate 3.23. Avai settlement, Site F3, another fortified structure probably
more ancient than the preceding.

18

facing the centre of the wadi controlled the caravans coming from the north (Plate 3.24). Some imposing and articulated buildings in the settlement might have been the command post and storage depositary for the auriferous quartz (Plate 3.25); a structure without windows and with a single door was perhaps intended for this latter purpose. Not far away, a

Beja in the past. The location of the graves in clearly defined areas (at the entrance of the major wadis, in grazing areas or on the top of an important jebel) suggests that the entombed belonged to clans or family groups, separated from other groups by several miles of desert, according to the custom still followed by the Beja. An example is provided by the large circular platform mound, possibly undisturbed, standing isolated and located in a very specific area, on a hill overlooking a grassy wadi (site C31, Plate 3.27). Circular platform mounds are rare in the Jebel Abu Dueim region, whereas conical mounds are frequent, especially in the Orshab and Sifia craters, two geological formations worthy of in-depth studies.

Plate 3.24. Duara el-Nafaab, Site F1. Buildings among the hills.

The Orshab Crater

At the crater's entrance, we see an isolated conical mound about 600mm high and 1.2m in diameter (site C29, Plate 3.28). It does not appear to have been violated like the other mounds of this type that we found. Our need to keep moving in order to explore as much of the area as possible did

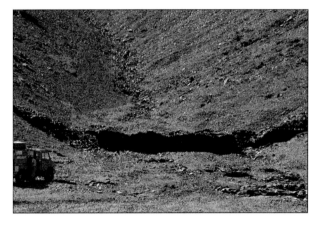

Plate 3.25. Duara en-Nafaab, Site F1. Probable fortified building or guard room for the auriferous dust.

Plate 3.26. Duara en-Nafaab, probable water-retaining wall near the settlement.

few hundred metres from the settlement, a wadi is closed by a wall that crosses it completely (Plate 3.26), perhaps a barrier to retain rainwater descending from the mountaintops. At the foot of a hill, a huge heap of crushed auriferous quartz, most likely the waste from working the mineral, is further evidence of the long period of mining activity in the region.

The graves of Jebel Abu Duheim and of the western region

Tombs of different types are found on Jebel Abu Duheim and in the region located directly west of the mountain massif. The conical tombs and large circular platform mounds are usually isolated and not grouped in cemeteries, still the custom among the nomadic tribes today and among the pre-Islamic

Plate 3.27. Jebel Abu Duheim, Site C31. Large circular platform mound.

Plate 3.28. Orshab Crater, Site C29. Isolated conical tumulus.

the vast plain heading south and find only small tombs, an indirect confirmation that the big tombs were destined only for high-ranking persons. We enter the Sifia crater, which is home to some Beja families. The well is the area where the women gather to draw water and serves as the meeting and resting place for the men and the animals.

About 15km from Sifia, we notice a circle of stones about 15m in diameter that enclose a mound (site C25, Plate 3.30). We head south. After about 90km, we find another isolated stone circle, about the same size as the first. The difference lies in the stones used, which are white and do not occur in this area (site C49.1, Plate 3.31). Continuing to explore the vast plain that stretches up to the Abu Siha mountain group, after about 120km we find the only palaeosol in a region that once certainly offered favourable conditions for human settlement. Among the sand, we recover a perfectly

not allow us the opportunity of performing systematic excavations. During our expeditions, we opened only two conical mounds, which provided little information. We found no organic material useful for dating or any artefacts in these tombs and, therefore, nothing to establish their cultural and chronological attribution. Just past the crater's entrance lies a vast plain of sterile sand and gravel, topped by a crown of mountains. We strike camp at sunset. Nearby, the only Beja family we meet pitched its tent close to the mountains, in a position protected from the wind.

The Sifia Crater

We leave the Orshab crater and head to the Sifia crater, about 45km to the north west. In the

Plate 3.30. Site C25, large circular enclosure (about 15m in diameter) with a central tumulus.

space of a few kilometres we come across three large conical mounds, C28, C27 and, on a rise, C26 (Plate 3.29). These four tombs (C26-28 and the previously cited C29), positioned between the two craters, suggest the possibility that it was a place for the burial of socially important persons. We cross

Plate 3.29. Sifia crater. Large conical tumulus in an elevated position.

Plate 3.31. Site C49.1, Large circular structure with white stones not available locally.

preserved hand-axe and some ceramic fragments (site E10, Plate 3.32).

Our expedition ends in view of the Abu Siha mountain chain shimmering against the far horizon. We leave Jebel Abu

Plate 3.32. Site E10, hand-axe.

Duheim and the south-eastern Nubian Desert bringing with us a small contribution to knowledge of this hitherto almost completely unknown region.

4. The Tracks of Egyptian Penetration

Alfredo and Angelo Castiglioni

The Korosko Road

During several expeditions, from 1989 onwards, we explored sections of the 'Korosko Road', one of the tracks, perhaps the main one, of Egyptian penetration southwards across the desert, from Korosko on the Nile in Lower Nubia (now submerged under Lake Nasser) towards Abu Hamed situated on the great bend of the Nile between the Fourth and Fifth Cataracts, a distance of about 500km (over two weeks by caravan), as compared to 1,200km by the river and its many cataracts. The desert route might have been used during the early Eighteenth Dynasty to reach Kurgus, just south of Abu Hamed, identified by royal stelae at the site of the southern boundary of the Egyptian empire.

The 'road' starts from the mouth of Wadi Korosko, heading south, the first section of the journey running through mountains, not without difficulty. After about 50km, the route crosses a region dotted with low hills and sandstone pinnacles and becomes easier. We travel another 35km and reach the border between Egypt and Sudan, signalled by a row of oil barrels that fade in and out of view amidst the wind-blown sand (Plate 4.1). We continue southwards, following the "logic" of a caravan travelling through the desert, namely to cover as much territory as quickly as possible. Where the route allows, we proceed sheltered by hills to protect us from the wind, searching for caves or crevices to spend the night and for "*ghelte*", natural basins of water accumulated at the base of groups of hills. Where the ground is solid, we find traces of ancient caravan routes.

The narrow passage of Khashm el-Bab

We are about 100km from Korosko and the caravan routes fan out. Further south, they come together again before entering a narrow passage that the Arab camel drivers call Khashm el-Bab ('the door lock'). In fact, this pass leads to

Plate 4.1. Border between Egypt and Sudan.

a wide plain about 100km in extent (north-south) that ends again in a mountainous area, the Umm Nabari massif. From the direction of Korosko it is quite easy to find the narrow passage, marked by the hoof prints of thousands of pack animals. One need just follow them. The same cannot be said for caravans coming from the south. Each can take a different path, creating a maze of overlapping tracks that widen out in every direction. For this reason, the entrance of the valley leading to the pass is marked by "*alamat*" (acting as sign-posts) and low dry-stone walls. A crude arrow of stones with the tip pointing towards the passage indicates the shortest path. We see the remains of a low tower, still in fairly good condition. It is built in a strategic position, guarding the valley entrance on the south side and controlling the path to the Khashm el-Bab pass and its entrance on the north side (Plate 4.2). It

Plate 4.2. Pass of Khashm el-Bab ("the door lock").

is part of a system for monitoring caravan movements that was possibly developed when, after the military conquest by the Egyptians, trade routes were opened up and gold began to be mined in the region.

The hieroglyphic inscriptions of Khashm el-Bab

From the expedition diary: "It is almost noon when we reach the summit of the Khashm el-Bab pass.

We note a natural sandstone shelter that juts out towards the valley. An ideal place to rest and hide from the sun. A harsh light erases any depth. We do not see immediately the hieroglyphic inscriptions engraved on the bottom of the shelter and in the shade. We are about to continue the journey when the Bisharin guide who accompanies us tells us with some emotion, "look at the rock, it speaks". Hieroglyphic inscriptions, the first that we find since the beginning of the expedition. In silence we observe those signs that have reached us from the dawn of time: a few lines of history that thrill us like an old fairy tale."

They are inscriptions left by "gold accountants", scribes

sent to the mines to keep the tallies (Plates 4.3 and 4.4). It is difficult to take good photographs. The inscriptions merge with the cracks and fissures of the rock.

Plate 4.3. Pass of Khashm el-Bab, hieroglyphic inscriptions.

Plate 4.4. Pass of Khashm el-Bab, hieroglyphic inscriptions.

We are able to take good pictures only during later expeditions, when we have time to wait for the best light conditions. We must emphasize the difficulties of searching for graffiti. Many times, an incision is nearly invisible when time has "glazed" it over with a patina that takes on the colour of the rock. It is often a slanting ray of sunlight that highlights a graffito we had not noticed before. Another circumstance makes these signs of human presence precious. Smooth surfaces and soft sandstone, which allowed the execution of a graffito, are rare in the heart of Nubia. Moreover, the caravans stopped only for a night or for a short rest of a few hours, hardly enough time to carve even the simplest incision. One can also assume that many of the ancient and skilled navigators of the desert did not know how to write and these dangerous expeditions were not always accompanied by scribes or persons of a certain rank who could carve their name in the stone. Whatever the reasons, there is one obvious fact: the rarity of hieroglyphic inscriptions found so far, despite careful and systematic investigation (for a more detailed account of the inscriptions encountered, see W. V. Davies, this volume).

We examine carefully the graffiti discovered at Khashm el Bab. Some appear very ancient: the grooves have taken on the colour of the rock; others stand out more clearly and suggest that the shelter was also used in later times. The execution technique is that of incising, sometimes superficial, other times deeper, made possibly with a metal tool. Sometimes the grooves are well finished and the incision is sharp and precise. We explore the area and find some bivouacs. Many are recent; others seem ancient. One in particular attracts our attention. It may be Egyptian.

Beyond Khashm el-Bab

We leave the mountainous region behind. A vast plain that reaches Jebel Umm Nabari opens in front of us. To the east, a chain of low sandstone hills runs south. We travel along its base taking as a reference point two hills silhouetted on the horizon about 30km from Khashm el-Bab, a distance of one day's travel. Among the hills, we seek traces of the next bivouac area. We explore thoroughly but our search is fruitless; there are no suitable caves or surfaces at the base of the jebels. Graffiti, if they existed, might have been eroded away by wind-blown sand. We continue southwards, the route winding between low scattered hills. After about 30km, a day's march by caravan, we resume our search.

The second inscription

From the expedition diary: "We drive slowly with our vehicles from one jebel to the next, looking for traces of ancient human presence. The heat is oppressive. The rays of a pitiless sun hit the motionless desert expanse, bouncing on the stones and the air vibrates animating the ground and creating illusory stretches of water. There is no horizon, erased by the whiteness of the sand that blends into the washed-out sky. It seems that the sun wants to claim its absolute domination. We stop, switch off the engines to lower the temperature of the radiators, and we are immediately enveloped by silence. The desert is not just emptiness, nothingness; it is also the reign of silence, and when the wind dies down, it becomes overwhelming. We open the bonnets to cool the engines, running them at idle, and check the water and oil levels. These tasks take several minutes and do not interest Suleiman, the Arab expedition mechanic accustomed, as he says, to tougher jobs. We see him climbing a sandstone hillside and disappearing into a small cave, half hidden by a boulder that conceals the entrance. He calls us. That insignificant-looking recess has a surprise in store for us. We enter."

On the left side, just after the entrance, we can clearly see a hieroglyphic inscription on the rear wall dedicated to the god 'Horus, lord of the desert' (Plate 4.5). It was initially thought

Plate 4.5. Hieroglyphic inscription discovered south of Khashm el-Bab on the way to Jebel Umm Nabari.

to include the name of an Egyptian scribe, but we now know that it refers to a native Kerma ruler. Once again, we had a stroke of luck. If it had not been for that unexpected stop, we would have passed right by the cave without noticing it. We take notes and several photographs. It is an important site. In the narrow shelter next to the hieroglyphic inscriptions, we also notice prehistoric graffiti depicting goats (Plate 4.6). At the base of the hill, in a lateral khor, we find the remains of a bivouac with ceramic fragments. We have travelled from Khashm el-Bab for about 60km without finding any water and there are still 50km left before we reach Jebel Umm Nabari, where we hope to restock our water supply. The Egyptian caravans heading south probably had the same problem.

Plate 4.6. Prehistoric graffiti at the side of the inscription.

Nubian camel driver

The unexpected meeting with a Nubian leading a herd of camels to Egypt provides us with valuable information. He informs us that the well of Hatab lies north of Jebel Umm Nabari and that there is water to the south as well, at the railway station no. 6 (on the track between Wadi Halfa and Abu Hamed). To his knowledge, water can also be found in reservoirs among the rocks, natural basins that fill up during the rainy season between August and November. The news is of considerable interest. These reservoirs could give us a chance to find other traces of Egyptian penetration. Hoping to get more information, we accept the invitation of the Nubian camel driver to share the evening meal with him.

From the expedition diary: "It is dusk, when we sit down in a circle on a mat, put a few tins of food in the centre: fruits in syrup, mackerel, tuna fish, various vegetables, carefully avoiding corned beef that would not be accepted because it is not made according to the dictates of the Koran. In turn, the Nubian brings a steaming pot of stewed Dorcas gazelle, cooked with canned tomatoes and "*ful Sudani*" ("Sudanese beans" = peanuts). The meat is fresh; he tells us that he shot the gazelle at first light, and making suitable faces to accompany his words, plays out the various moments of the hunt.

Early in the morning, when the gazelles are still grazing, he approached the animals with the sun behind him. A few dozen metres from the prey, he had launched the "*trombash*", a piece of wood curved like a boomerang, rotating it at ground level. The precise shot had broken the animal's legs. He shows us the *trombash*, a weapon used already in the Badari era and

by the Egyptians for bird hunting. The conversation lasts at least two hours but, at the end, we get the information we need. "Keep along the left side of the jebel ("where the sun dies") – he says – and follow the road that opens among the rocks." It is probably Wadi Tonaidba.

The third inscription.

We spend the night near the cave and at first light, we continue toward Jebel Umm Nabari, heading south-southeast. After about 30km, we follow Wadi Tonaidba and immediately discover a hieroglyphic inscription standing out clearly against the dark rock. It reads, "The mayor Hornakht, son of Penniut deputy commander of the troops of Miam (Aniba)". It is a very exciting moment. This inscription confirms that an Egyptian military force had been present in this desert region. Below the inscription, the wall is covered with prehistoric graffiti. They show mostly herds of goats (Plate 4.7). There

Plate 4.7. Wadi Tonaidba, prehistoric graffiti and hieroglyphic inscriptions.

are only a few cattle, some with great horns. Five kilometres from there, we find the basin for collecting rainwater indicated by the Nubian camel driver (Plate 4.8), a natural deposit that induced people to stop. The walls are eroded and there is no sufficiently flat sandstone surface to carve an inscription.

Plate 4.8. Ghelta in the Wadi Tonaidba.

24

The fourth inscription.

Ten kilometres further south we reach a cave. It is about 60m long and on average about 6m high, excavated by an ancient long-disappeared river that opened an almost straight tunnel through the hill. We enter. The shade and the slight current of air created by the opposite opening bring us unexpected relief. We advance in the penumbra. Then, when our eyes have become accustomed to the dim light, we see a hieroglyphic inscription on the right wall, almost at the entrance of the cave. It reads, "Chief of Tehkhet (Debeira) Paitsy" (Plate 4.9). Facing it, on the opposite wall, there is another inscrip-

Plate 4.9. Wadi Tonaidba, hieroglyphic inscription 10km south of the previous one.

tion referring to the same personage (Plate 4.10). We crowd in: words are superfluous and the Sudanese inspector's face opens into a bright smile. It is a simple graffito but for us it is very important. It is further evidence that the Egyptians came here through the desert.

Plate 4.10. Wadi Tonaidba, hieroglyphic inscription opposite the previous one.

We drive along the western side of Jebel Umm Nabari looking for other traces. It is cluttered with boulders that do not allow us to skirt it closely. We observe the mountain carefully, using also a telescope, but we do not notice any caves or crevices. We reach the mine of Umm Nabari without stopping since we had already visited. Continuing to follow the west side of the jebel, we reach Jebel Mandara where we hope to find more traces of Egyptian military penetration. Our hopes are disappointed: the walls are eroded and the jebel has no caves suited for a stopover. After the jebel, a plain devoid of shelters opens for about 50km up to Jebel Abu Siha. To keep

as straight a route as possible, instead of driving around the mountain chain, we cross it. Here, too, there are no smooth walls or caves so we do not find any engravings. After Jebel Abu Siha, the expedition encounters no further history. In front of us opens a vast plain that extends for about 160km, with no major elevations, up to the Kurgus stelae, that mark the limit of Egyptian penetration in Africa as well as the end of our expedition.

Search for the Gold Mines

The Egyptian military penetration into Nubia probably led to the exploitation of the gold mines and intensive extraction of the 'gold of Wawat' cited in Egyptian texts (see Introduction). Thus, the central region of the mines of Wawat, around Jebel Umm Nabari and Wadi Gabgaba, had been the first area we explored at the very beginning of our expeditions in the eastern Nubian Desert in early 1989.

From the expedition diary: "We have been searching for days for traces of the work and toil of thousands of men who, in this inhospitable corner of the world, extracted from quartz and sand the gold that would adorn far away temples and palaces. For centuries, they faced the same void that opens before us. They felt the indefinable anguish and superstitious terror that invades those who live and work in these infinite spaces. They faced a difficult environment that does not forgive the slightest mistake and defends the treasures kept in the sands of the plains and in the rocks of the mountains. Unknown regions swept by sudden sandstorms, mountains burning during the day and swept by cold winds at night. Men who listened with anguish to the voice of the desert: the whistle of the wind that blows through the valleys, the moan of the overheated rocks that crumble and break because of the huge temperature swings. We will search for the old mines with shafts open in the mountains; the incredible excavation works that sometimes dug out entire areas modifying them; the precarious refuges that sheltered men; the millstones and stone tools used to extract a few grams of gold out of tons of quartz. All traces of a long-gone life, which will allow us to revive a world of which only an evanescent, unclear memory remains".

The mining settlements

We attempted to group the settlements into categories and, despite the differences found in each, we were able to determine common and recurring elements.

Extended settlements: villages that could accommodate several dozen people, not only miners. They are usually built at the foot of hills (Plate 4.11) or along wadis.

Temporary settlements, perhaps seasonal: they represent the majority, scattered in areas of alluvial auriferous quartz extraction or gold prospecting. All built very simply, they present common characteristics. The shelters, about 500-600mm high, consist of walls made by accumulating large stones. A light covering of mats supported by a wood frame, long gone, served as a roof. They are normally round and stand isolated or aggregated (Plate 4.12). The rarer rectangular shelters also stand isolated or in groups. The location of the settlements is dictated mostly by the need for protection against the climate.

Plate 4.11. Umm Fit-Fit, extended mining settlement.

Plate 4.12. Probable temporary settlement.

Plate 4.13. Probable external area for quartz processing.

The shelters are often built in narrow valleys to protect them from the cold north winds or in khors that flow into the main wadi. In general, the living space varies from 5-10m², sufficient for a small team of two to three people, without any regard for comfort (stone seats, niches for storing water or food vessels are absent), simple shelters, with only space for sitting or lying down. The entrance faces downwind. Although we found millstones in some dwellings, the auriferous quartz was crushed and pulverized outside the shelter, usually in a space bounded by stones arranged in a circle (Plate 4.13).

Complex settlements, often equipped with defensive systems: these date to the medieval Islamic period. It is clear that the buildings, very complex and massive, were not built at random but according to a predetermined plan. In fact, the size ratios between the different structures and a logical arrangement in relation to their intended purpose are quite evident. Some of the miners' dwellings are wide, protected from the wind by high dry-stone walls. Inside there are niches for storing food or other items (Plate 4.14). Much larger buildings were perhaps used as warehouses or as housing for the mine chiefs. In some settlements, we find areas where working tools, hammers and millstones are accumulated. One can, therefore, assume that their management was entrusted to an overseer. The auriferous quartz was crushed and pulverized collectively in an area designed for this purpose.

In some settlements, there is a main road intersected by secondary streets that define the various zones of the inhabited area (Plate 4.15). The massive defensive structures

Plate 4.14. *Wadi Nesari, dwelling with niches formed in the inner wall.*

Nabari (Plate 4.16) is surely the most important and longest exploited mine. It was reopened at the beginning of the last century during the Anglo-Egyptian Condominium. First excavated by the Egyptians (pottery fragments and numerous grindstones confirm this), it was later re-used in the medieval Islamic period. It is now abandoned. From the expedition diary, 1990, late in the afternoon: "We left Station 6 and as we head west, the massif takes shape, rising darkly above the dazzling expanse of sand. The scenery is unreal, as are the structures that stand out against a bleached sky at the foot of the hills. The buildings with a rectangular plan, some built with stones, others, taller, with sun-dried bricks, cast their shadows on the sand that the sun, now low on the horizon, stretches and deforms into fantastic geometric shapes. On the slopes, well shafts that plunge into the heart of the hills, deep chasms from which tons of auriferous quartz were extracted.

Plate 4.15. *Alar, an example of mining settlement organised at the sides of the main axial road.*

are normally positioned at the intersection of wadis and near caravan routes and had a control and defence function. Other constructions with the same purposes are located at the entrance of khors that led to the excavation areas. Walls or towers equipped with slits seem to validate the defensive hypothesis.

The mines of the Umm Nabari region.

Our research has established that the area with the most mining settlements is concentrated east and west of Jebel Umm Nabari. Here we found and catalogued several important mines and other less important ones. These settlements almost certainly date to the Egyptian period. Site A1 at Umm

The processing waste, the quartz powder washed to separate it from the gold, is accumulated at the bottom of the valley, an impressive deposit of tons of very white and fine powder" (Plate 4.17). At Umm Nabari, the new and ancient overlap with striking contrast: grindstones of probable Egyptian origin used to pulverize the auriferous quartz lie next to rusted mining carts; lithic mills consumed by use are scattered near cement basins used to wash the auriferous dust. We reach the most imposing building, erected on a hill that overlooks the entire mining complex: two columns define the steps that lead to the entrance and the large interior rooms. It is probably the home of the mine chief, as confirmed by the material accumulated in a heap next to the building, fragments of

Plate 4.16. Umm Nabari, A1. Ancient mine reopened at the beginning of the last century during the Anglo-Egyptian Condominium.

Plate 4.17. Umm Nabari, accumulation of quartz powder, remains of the extraction process.

finely decorated pottery and glass from English liquor bottles, overshadowed by the astounding remains of a piano: precious finds for archaeologists of future generations."

Though not planned in our programme, we encounter and document graffiti found 25km west of Jebel Umm Nabari. Two representations on the same sandstone surface record two moments of prehistoric activity. The first shows two cows, one of which, in the foreground, has distinctive udders, presumably an animal that was bred. In the second, a hunter armed with bow and arrow is shooting a gazelle. The two graffiti have the same patina and execution technique and are presumably contemporary (Plates 4.18 and 4.19).

Plate 4.18. Prehistoric graffiti, 25km west of Jebel Umm Nabari.

Plate 4.19. Prehistoric graffiti, 25km west of Jebel Umm Nabari.

At about 20km east of Jebel Umm Nabari, an "*alama*", situated on the top of an isolated hill, is a marker that can be seen from a great distance in a flood plain with almost no obstacles. It directed the caravans to the mines of Mosei and Nabi. There are many grindstones in the Mosei mine, while extensive trench-type surface mining excavations are evident in the Nabi mine, all signs of ancient gold mining exploitation. The *alama* also indicates a vast auriferous region with large quartz monoliths almost completely dismantled by the miners and large areas of surface excavations in search of alluvial gold (Plate 4.20). In addition to the gold contained

Plate 4.20. Excavations in search for alluvial gold, area of the Mosei and Nabi mines.

in the quartz, the miners searched for this precious metal in a form freed from the rock as a result of wind and river erosion over the millennia, mineral accumulated in the foothills and recoverable as small flakes and auriferous sand. It was easy to obtain, just by washing and sifting the sands. The satellite image shows the auriferous region related to Wawat as well as probably to that of Amu (Plate 4.21).

The quantity of alluvial gold extracted in ancient times has certainly been underestimated. Jean Vercoutter, in the 1980s, reported on a desert area not far from Semna. He found that "the sandy bottom had been turned over from east to west, as from north to south in search of gold. Not a single square meter had been left intact". Before him, in 1920, the English geologist T. A. Rikard had discovered another similar region in the Eastern Desert of Sudan, about 100 square miles (260km²) of land "ploughed" by ancient gold

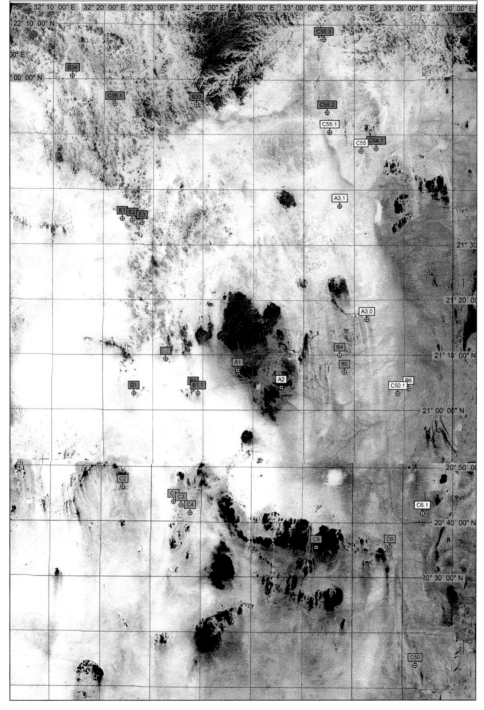

Plate 4.21. Auriferous regions of Wawat and Amu.

The Medieval Mines

The mining region of Wawat ends nearing longitude 33° 30' east, at the beginning of the vast mountainous region that extends eastwards. From here up to longitude 33° 50', we found 13 mining settlements with no traces of Egyptian presence. There is instead copious evidence for a long medieval Islamic occupation. We list the main settlements, from the north:

B31: many well preserved circular buildings made of dry-stone walls. They have a diameter of about 4m and the openings face north. No millstones. Extensive trench-type surface excavations.

B28.1: many dozens of dry-stone constructions with circular plan. A single rotating circular millstone, broken and then abandoned. The other tools were probably transported to other mines.

A7, Abu Fas: an extensive mining centre active since ancient times (Plate 4.24). Re-opened during the Anglo-Egyptian Condominium as evidenced by abandoned materials. Numerous traces of the past: dry-stone constructions of circular and rectangular plan. The quartz crushing areas are bounded by stone circles. Many circular rotating millstones and cubic strikers. Chutes for washing the auriferous powder (Plate 4.25). Paths from the valley miners. Other mines, probably exploited in pharaonic times, are three settlements in Egyptian territory, mines A4, B32 and Umm Qarayat, all located along the lower Wadi Allaqi. A4: numerous circular and rectangular dry-stone buildings scattered along the edge of the wadi; on the hills, traces of excavations "in trenches" (Plate 4.22).

B32: the mine is indicated by an "*alama*"; there are numerous dry-stone constructions of circular plan and a chute for washing. Near a building, we find two vessels (Plate 4.23).

Umm Garayat: the mine was in recent use by the Egyptians, as documented during January to March 1989. The area is greatly compromised by digging. No traces of previous occupation are visible.

Plate 4.22. Lower Wadi Allaqi, mine A4.

Plate 4.23. Mine B32, ceramic vessel in situ.

Plate 4.24. Abu Fas mine (A7).

Plate 4.25. Abu Fas mine (A7),
chute for washing the auriferous dust.

bottom led to the mining areas in the hills. Trench-type mining excavations. A dry-stone wall bars the wadi, perhaps a dam to store rainwater or a bulwark to defend the goldfields. Islamic tombs at the entrance of the wadi.

E5, Bir Tawil: about 15 constructions. Maybe a mining village even if the characteristic structures of mining settlements, millstones and washing-tables are absent. Brown wheel-turned ceramics, not decorated, with thick sides.

A5, Ismat Omar: about 50 dry-stone constructions with circular plan. Many circular rotating millstones and cubic strikers. Chutes for washing the auriferous powder. Trench-type mining excavations about 100m long. Painted and plain ceramics, probably Islamic.

B12, Abu Baraga: about 30 dry-stone constructions with circular plan, isolated and aggregated. Fragments of circular rotating millstones. Engraved pottery, perhaps medieval Islamic.

C54, Wadi Abaraga (Plate 4.26): some dozens of dry-stone constructions of circular plan, generally isolated. Wheel-turned Aswani pottery dating to AD 700-850 (W. Y. Adams, pers. comm.). No circular rotating millstones. Trench-type mining excavations, almost completely silted up.

Plate 4.26. Wadi Abaraga mine.

C53, hills of Wadi Abaraga: four fortifications built probably to defend the mines. The buildings, well preserved, are made of dry-stone walls. The walls of the main fort, with a square plan, are 10m long and equipped with loopholes. Inside the construction, there is a small rectangular room, perhaps the depositary for the auriferous quartz dust (Plate 4.27).

Plate 4.27. Wadi Abaraga, fortified structure
probably of the medieval period.

C52, Telat Abda: dry-stone constructions of circular plan, isolated or aggregated. Quartz crushing area enclosed by stone circles. Circular rotating millstones of large diameter (Plate 4.28). Two tables for washing the auriferous powder. Wheel-turned pottery, medieval Islamic of the 11th and 12th century AD (W. Y. Adams, pers. comm.). Outline of a mosque. Large area of shaft-type excavations on the hillsides.

C8, Nabi Tana: large settlement composed of dry-stone constructions of circular plan. Some are divided internally by walls; one still has the lintel above the entrance. Work areas bounded by stones. Circular rotating millstones close

Plate 4.28. Telat Abda (C 52) mine, rotating mills of remarkably large diameter.

Plate 4.30. Idarib, site B7.

to the dwellings. Trench-type mining excavations (about 1m deep) on the hilltops. Rotating millstones near the excavation. Wheel-turned pottery dating to medieval Islamic period, 8th and 9th centuries AD (W. Y. Adams, pers. comm.). Outline of a mosque and some Islamic burials.

C7.1: some poorly preserved dry-stone buildings of circular plan. Islamic burials.

C9: About a dozen well preserved constructions with circular plan at the confluence of Wadi Naba and Wadi el-Ku. Some external walls are 800-900mm high. No millstones (Plate 4.29).

Plate 4.29. Site C9 (confluence of Wadi Naba and Wadi el-Ku).

B7, Idarib: covering an area of 2-3km², a large settlement consisting of dry-stone structures of circular plan, isolated or aggregated (Plate 4.30). Many circular rotating millstones, whole and broken, and several cubic strikers. Outline of a small mosque and small Islamic cemeteries. Medieval Islamic ceramic. Trench-type mining excavations, almost completely silted up.

The problem of gold smelting

As noted in almost all the mines which we visited, certain tools (millstones, cubic hammers, mortars etc.) and facilities (washing slides) were required to crush the auriferous quartz and subsequently wash the quartz dust on the inclined tables in order to recover the tiny gold particles.

While these operations, described by Agatharchides of Knidos, a geographer of the second half of the 2nd century

BC, are confirmed by archaeological discoveries, the exact process of melting the auriferous dust to transform it into bars must be considered carefully. Agatharchides wrote: "The 'washer' deliveries the quartz dust to the 'melters' who put it into a ceramic vessel and, in proportion to the quantity received, add a piece of lead, a pinch of salt, and even a little alloy of silver and lead and barley bran. The mouth of the container is hermetically sealed with clay. The melters then let the container heat for five consecutive days and nights. (After this period) the next day, when the heated content has cooled, they pour it in another container: they no longer find the added products, but a mass of molten gold weighing slightly less than the weight of the starting material". As may be noted, the melting has magical connotations with the addition of substances that certainly do not affect the result of the operation. Our search to find the furnaces where the auriferous dust was "heated for five consecutive days and nights" was fruitless, even though the melting was probably done at the mines. The Arab historian al-Yakoubi wrote in the late 10th century referring to the Allaqi mines, "Here the gold nuggets are transformed into bars" (obviously by melting the ore). However, in January 1989, in a khor that flowed into the Wadi Elei, which we were exploring, we found a small furnace that might represent a first, limited example. The structure was a low tunnel with a wider inlet facing the prevailing wind and a narrower outlet on the opposite side. It was located on a hill where the wind blows constantly during certain hours of the day. One can assume that the melters would have made a funnel using mats and branches to direct the wind into the rear opening of the small tunnel. This created the so-called "Venturi effect", which could raise the temperature of the fuel up to 1063° C, indispensable for melting the gold. These are only suppositions: more research will be needed to solve the problem definitively. During the 1994 expedition, in a tributary of the Wadi Nesari, about 20km as the crow flies from Berenice Panchrysos and not far from another hieroglyphic inscription (Plate 4.31), we found what looked like another furnace (Plate 4.32), also located on top of a hill, with the rear opening facing south to take advantage of the winds blowing constantly from the south from April to June, but other interpretations are possible (for example, it could be a 'tunnel-grave', a type of structure well known from the Fourth Cataract area).

The gold, melted into bars or stored as powder in pots, had

Plate 4.31. Wadi Nesari, hieroglyphic inscription.

Plate 4.32. Wadi Nesari, probable furnace with mouth facing south.

protects the residential settlement consisting of rectangular dry-stone buildings (Plate 4.33), some of which are massive. They wind along the bed of a khor, a tributary of the Wadi Murrat. During the 1993 expedition, at the centre of the wadi, we find a stela almost completely covered with sand: an Arabic inscription, dating from 1897, bearing the name of two Anglo-Egyptian soldiers and the number of the well, 14. Some cartridge casings, perhaps of a machine gun, testify that the fort was inhabited during the Anglo-Egyptian conquest of Sudan. Narrow paths run through the hilltop overlooking the complex. We note several buildings, probably guard posts, and a low tower, perhaps a watchtower (Plate 4.34). Fragments of pottery of different types are scattered everywhere; there are no millstones to grind and pulverize auriferous quartz.

Below us is a wonderful view of the Wadi Murrat, which runs north west to south east and flows into the nearby Wadi Gabgaba. We reach the bushes close to the cliff that borders the north side of the wadi. We make our way through the thick tangle of branches and leaves realizing that we are sweating profusely; the water that is almost certainly not far below the sand emerges by capillary action and increases the humidity of the place.

The old well has now disappeared: we find no trace of it despite our search. Our disappointment is lessened by a certainly more important discovery: on a vertical wall of stone, concealed by a thick bush, are engraved some signs that we cannot make out at first sight. The sun, penetrating through the branches, draws intricate arabesques on the wall confounding the graffiti. Only by moving some branches and fully illuminating the wall can we see the various hieroglyphic signs, perhaps left by Egyptian caravan drivers who stopped to rest and water their animals. The most remarkable figure, about 300mm high, is the schematic representation of Horus depicted with a solar disc over his head (Plate 4.35).

To the left of and below the graffito, we read the name of "Herunefer", priest of Horus, repeated several times. The hard stone allowed only a superficial incision, obtained by

to be safeguarded. This is most likely the reason for the many forts and defensive complexes built during the medieval Islamic period. Almost all the mines found during the expeditions in the eastern Nubian Desert were located a few kilometres from a large centre, often equipped with a defensive system.

Fort Murrat

The complex of Fort Murrat, which we visited for the first time in March 1989, was also built with a defensive purpose: to protect the wells of Wadi Murrat, vital sources of water. A wall equipped with narrow slits

Plate 4.33. Fort Murrat.

Plate 4.34. *Fort Murrat, tower of a probable guard post.*

Plate 4.35. *Wadi Murrat, hieroglyphic inscription near a probable well.*

before sunset, the wind stopped blowing: the dust-free air is clearer and the sight extends far. On the horizon, a hill higher than the others stands out. At its centre, we can see the dark opening of a large cave. For travellers coming from the plain, the cave appears as a point of arrival, a safe shelter for the night. We drive over to examine it".

A few metres from the entrance of the cave, some near-intact amphorae, one four-handled, emerge from the sand (Plate 4.36). We pass by them without stopping, our eyes

Plate 4.36. *"Cave of Heqanefer", finds in front of the entrance.*

pattering the contours, perhaps with a metal tool. Neverthe-less, the incision stands out clearly with a light patina against the dark brown rock. Next, we notice other hieroglyphic inscriptions and representations of the god Horus. The re-petitiveness of the graffiti, of both Horus and the name of the priest Herunefer, suggests the existence of an ancient area of worship. On the near-by rocks, we also notice graffiti of oxen with long horns and, perhaps, the faint representation of an elephant, engravings that date the human presence further back in time, even to prehistory.

The graffiti with Horus are located about 6km from the auriferous area of Umm Nabari, the same distance from the two major mines of Mosei and Nabi. It is, therefore, likely that these three locations were connected by the Wadi Murrat and that the representation of Horus, about halfway, indicates an area of worship dedicated to this deity.

The Cave of Heqanefer

Another route taken during the 1989 expedition connected Buhen (Wadi Halfa) on the Nile with the area of Jebel Umm Nabari. From the expedition diary: 3 March 1989. "The area that we are travelling along, en route from Wadi Halfa, is characterized by outcrops of friable Nubian sandstone that make the landscape even more pleasant in the light of the approaching sunset. Soft sandy hills that the sun low on the horizon colours a deep orange follow one another endlessly, interspersed with large golden plains. As so often happens

fixed on the end of the cave where, with incredible clarity, a hieroglyphic inscription over a metre and a half long stands out (Plate 4.37). We sit on the soft and clean sand and look carefully at the graffito. The patina is ancient, dark yellow, and stands out sharply against the smooth ochre-orange sandstone wall. The engraving is perfect, the corners sharp, and the groove precise, perhaps executed by incising with a metal tip. The writing is ancient, dating to the New Kingdom. We immediately recognize the importance of the discovery: the inscription we are looking at does not carry the name of an otherwise unknown traveller but that of an important, well attested personage, a Nubian prince, "Chief of Miam

Plate 4.37. *Heqanefer inscription.*

(Aniba), Heqanefer", who served under the viceroy of Kush, Huy, during the late Eighteenth Dynasty (*c.* 1350 BC).

From the hill above the cave, the plain leading to the region of Wawat opens up. Perhaps Heqanefer was travelling along the track that connects Buhen to Umm Nabari or perhaps he was headed to Berenice Panchrysos to inspect for his viceroy the extractive activities in those remote districts. However, the itinerary could have also been another. It is likely that Heqanefer lived in Toshka (his tomb is located in Toshka East) about 70km as the crow flies from the cave and that he had come from this town to inspect the mines of the Eastern Desert. Perhaps the shelter was not a place found accidentally – to spend a night or to take cover from a sudden dust storm – but a regular staging area used by this high dignitary during his journeys through the desert: from Toshka/Aniba to Umm Nabari; from Buhen to Berenice Panchrysos. The cave is in fact about three caravan days from both settlements, an ideal place for a stop, before facing the hard and inaccessible areas of the Eastern Desert. We spend the night in the "cave of Heqanefer" as we called it, sheltered from the wind, enjoying a pleasant sense of protection and well-being.

The Arab Route towards the East

Perhaps the same route followed by Heqanefer to reach the mining region was travelled more recently by the medieval Arabs during the great "gold rush", the first in recorded history. The itinerary crosses a plain free of obstacles. Often, the sand raised by the wind that blows constantly in the area squeezes between the sandstone hills hiding them from view. Owing to the relative lack of clear reference points, it was necessary to build "*alamat*" to help indicate the right direction for caravans, still useful for travellers today (Plate 4.38). Where possible, the "*alama*" is built on an elevation to make it visible from afar.

The "*alamat*" are about 4-5m high, made with a clever accumulation of stones without binding that have withstood the wind and survived in good condition. Often they are made of heavy sandstone blocks transported from far away because there are no quarries in the area. It should be noted, however, that there is no standard form of construction; any available material was used to build the *alama*. The distance between one "*alama*" and the other is a few kilometres except on flat and uniform ground, where they are erected at a distance of few hundred metres to make

Plate 4.38. Along the track towards Wawat, alama positioned in the direction of Jebel Umm Nabari.

them clearly visible when the terrain is obscured by wind-blown sand. Their form and style seem to be attributable to the medieval Arabic period, testified to also by Arabic writing incised at the base of some of them (Plate 4.39)

Plate 4.39. Along the track towards Wawat, Arabic writing.

The remains of the houses of the workers who built these "*alamat*" are still often visible as are the outlines of mosques. Where the first mountains rise over the plains and the direction can be identified more easily, the pyramid-like structures are replaced by simple piles of stones placed on the mountain top. The track ends in sight of Jebel Umm Nabari, confirming that the route led to Umm Nabari and the gold-mining region (Plate 4.40).

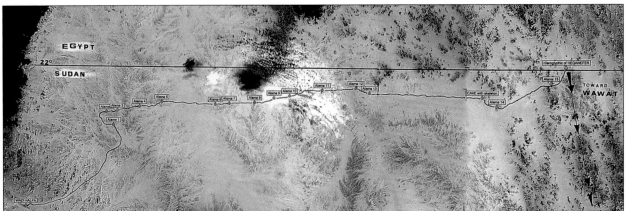

Plate 4.40. Satellite image with the track towards Wawat indicated by the alamat.

The Land of Amu

According to Egyptian sources, Wawat was the main source of gold during the Pharaonic period. But we must not forget another region that supplied the precious metal, that of 'Amu', mentioned in a list, inscribed in Luxor temple, of the mines of the period of Ramesses II (1279-1213 BC). The Egyptians classified the main places of interest identifying them by different names, places, however, that are often difficult to identify with accuracy. The toponym also appears to occur in an Eighteenth Dynasty rock-inscription of a scribe called 'Userhat of Am(u)' at the site of Sabu, near the Nile in Nubia, just downstream of the Third Cataract, which we visited between November 2007 and January 2008 (Plate 4.41).

Plate 4.41. Hieroglyphic inscription at Sabu downstream of the Third Cataract.

After a careful study of the satellite photos and the course of the wadis that penetrate into the desert, we believe it possible that the land of Amu is located in the mountain chain of Abu Siha, 250-300km from the Nile: a succession of mountains oriented east to west, rich in auriferous quartz, a location that could be reached by caravan in 10 to 12 days. In this case, we suggest that the gold of Wawat and Amu might have been obtained respectively from two clearly distinct auriferous areas, separated by about 50km of desert (Plate 4.42).

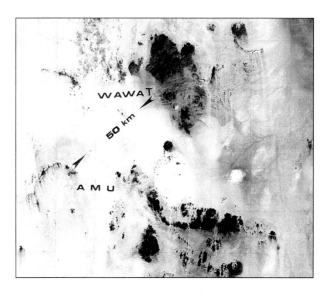

Plate 4.42. Satellite photograph of the mining areas of Wawat and Amu.

From the Nile to Amu

At Sabu, the Nile flows peacefully, an easy landing-place for boats, in both antiquity and today, and an ideal starting point for caravans heading east. From the expedition diary: "We leave the Nile valley on 10 November 2008. We have drawn on a satellite photo the shortest and easier travel route that, by following the wadis, will lead us to the mountains of Abu Siha" (Plate 4.43).

Following the hypothesized itinerary, we find the rut of a track dug into the rocky ground by pack animals. It is a "fossil" track, perhaps ancient, now long abandoned, but a clear confirmation that the area was travelled by numerous caravans. A short distance away, we see an *"alama"*. Along the way, we find other *"alamat"*, some built on hilltops and, therefore, visible from afar. They are all oriented towards the mountain chain of Abu Siha. The stones used to build them, blackened from the surfacing of salts, show their age.

About halfway, the route crosses sandy areas where progress is not always easy. There is an increasing number of *"alamat"*. Placed on the hilltops, they allow one to keep the direction in

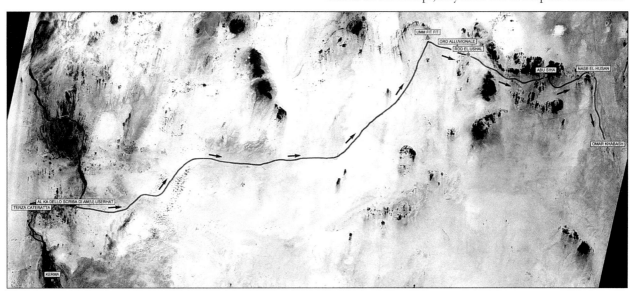

Plate 4.43. Itinerary of the expedition from the Nile to Abu Siha following the easiest way along the wadis.

a region that is uniform and without landmarks.

After three days of travel, we see a dark line that cuts the horizon and shimmers in the strong heat. We have reached the mountain chain of Abu Siha. Several tracks reappear among the blackish stone chips, probably made by ancient caravans. Maybe we have reached the land of Amu, the land of gold.

As we get closer to the auriferous area, the traces of ancient caravans increase and overlap. Following them, we reach the mine of Umm Fit-Fit, the largest in the area, located in the western part of the mountain massif (Plate 4.11). The buildings are wedged in an amphitheatre of low hills of flaky sandstone and granite boulders.

There are numerous millstones, probably dating to the Pharaonic period (Plate 4.44), but no rotating mills, which were probably introduced into Nubia during the Ptolemaic period and also used in the Islamic period. The sole presence of grinding mills suggests that these mines were exploited mainly in Egyptian times and then abandoned in the early Islamic period, perhaps due to the exhaustion of the auriferous quartz. Some dwellings are located along the banks of a now dry wadi.

Plate 4.44. *Rubbing millstones in the mine of Umm Fit-Fit, probably of the Pharaonic period.*

Not far from the main settlement, we find the quarry of the granite blocks for the grinders. Isolated on a hillside is the outline of a square construction, more massive then the others and with only one opening facing the valley. The walls are made of two parallel rows of stones. Between them, the stone chips are packed and compressed and make the enclosure solid (Plate 4.45). Maybe it was a repository for the auriferous dust. There are ceramic fragments throughout the mining area. Some date to the Pharaonic era, perhaps the New Kingdom. After some 20km, we find a large flat area, where there are traces of excavations for alluvial gold (Plate 4.46).

At 25km east of Umm Fit-Fit, we come across another mining settlement. It is located a few kilometres from Jebel Kefayeb, the highest peak in the area. It is the mine of Rodel Ushal. The buildings are scattered over a sandy plain without hills. We do not find any millstones. We reach the mine of Abu Siha, almost in the centre of the massif that bears its name (Plate 4.47). A little further to the east lies the mine of Nasib el-Husan, west of the eponymous jebel (Plate 4.48). We find no millstones in either of these mines. Perhaps the working tools were moved to another area of auriferous exploitation once the veins were exhausted, a hypothesis that is confirmed

Plate 4.45. *Umm Fit-Fit mine, masonry technique that distinguishes one of the buildings, likely deposit for the auriferous powder.*

Plate 4.46. *Terrain dug up to search for alluvial gold about 20km east of Umm Fit-Fit.*

Plate 4.47. *Abu Siha mine.*

by the mine of Omar Khabash (Plate 4.49), 40km south of Nasib el-Husan. It is the gold-bearing area most distant from the Nile, at the south-eastern end of the mountain chain.

Plate 4.48. Nasib el-Husan mine.

Plate 4.49. Omar Khabash mine.

There are numerous millstones here (Plate 4.50). They are evidence of a centuries-long mining exploitation, confirmed by pottery fragments of the Pharaonic era and medieval Islamic period. After more than a month we return to the Nile hoping to have found the land of Amu.

Plate 4.50. Omar Khabash mine, numerous millstones.

The Mountains of Irtjet

Many scholars hold that the region around the ancient town of Kerma, on the Nile, is the mythical land of Iam. From Iam, one might reach the Nile again through the Nubian Desert towards the north. After crossing a mountainous region, one would reach the Wadi Allaqi, the shortest way to get back to the great river. In our view, it is the likely route followed by the celebrated Harkhuf, a governor of the Sixth Dynasty, during his third trip to Iam on behalf of Pharaoh Pepi II (2246-2152 BC), as recorded in his tomb-inscriptions at Qubbet el-Hawa,

Aswan. It is the longest and most interesting of Harkhuf's journeys, not least because of the inclusion of place names, like the 'mountains of Irtjet', which historical and archaeological research have not yet certainly identified.

In early October 1996, following what we believe might have been Harkhuf's route, we head east-northeast across the Atmur desert, an immense plain without natural reference points. Numerous remains of mummified animals that had died from thirst and heat lie scattered along the way. This region, now so sterile, once hosted prehistoric communities.

Plate 4.51. Desert of Atmur.

Millstones, often accompanied by their crusher (Plate 4.51), are clear evidence that grains, wild or cultivated, grew in this area thousands of years ago. The petrified remains of trees date back even further in time, perhaps millions of years. From Kerma, we cover about 250km (a ten-day caravan's march) without finding a well, a problem that Harkhuf would also have had to face. We travel another 100km before reaching Bir Hatab in the homonymous wadi, the only well in the area. It is very old, built with masterly interlocking dry-stone walling (Plate 4.52). Perhaps the caravan of Harkhuf stopped right here to replenish its water supply before resuming the journey.

Plate 4.52. Wadi Bir Hatab, well.

The route through the mountains

About 70km from the well, Wadi Hatab flows into Wadi Hesmet Omar. Here, at about longitude 33° 40', starts the mountain range, perhaps the Irtjet chain which Harkhuf had to cross to reach the Nile. In his tomb-inscription we read:

"When the king of Irtjet ... saw how strong and numerous was the troop of Iam coming down with me to the Residence (Memphis) ... then this ruler escorted me, gave me cattle and goats, and guided me on the roads of the mountains of Irtjet". The route, evidently a wadi system, would have needed to be relatively wide and free of obstacles to allow the transit of such a large caravan with pack-animals and other stock.

In the search for this route, we relied on the information of the Beja living in the region. Herders, always looking for new pastures for their livestock, know the area perfectly and show us the easier passages and the wells for replenishing the water supply. We explore numerous wadis that cross the mountains before finding a wide path that passes from Wadi Hesmet Omar into Wadi Tawil and from there into Wadi Umm Gat. The Beja also point out two wells (Bir Hesmet Omar and Bir Tawil) situated a short distance from each other. In the end, at the spring of Wadi Umm Gat, we discover a feasible passage, a shortcut that leads to the Allaqi and then to the Nile, a route (a camel driver tells us) still followed to bring camels for sale to Egypt, avoiding border problems. We mark what might have been the route of Harkhuf, including the 'mountains of Irtjet', on a map (Plate 4.53).

Supportive evidence is provided by the presence in the region of a Sixth Dynasty inscription (Plate 4.54), located on a rock-face next to an old well, Bir Umm Gat. It names an Egyptian dignitary, Sabni, probably a contemporary of Harkhuf, who also probably travelled the route. The translation (by Alessandro Roccati) runs: "(1) The sole friend, lector-priest, whose good name is Khenementi, Sabni. (2) Functionary of the king, director of foreigners, Qar. (3)

Plate 4.54. Hieroglyphic inscription, Bir Ungat.

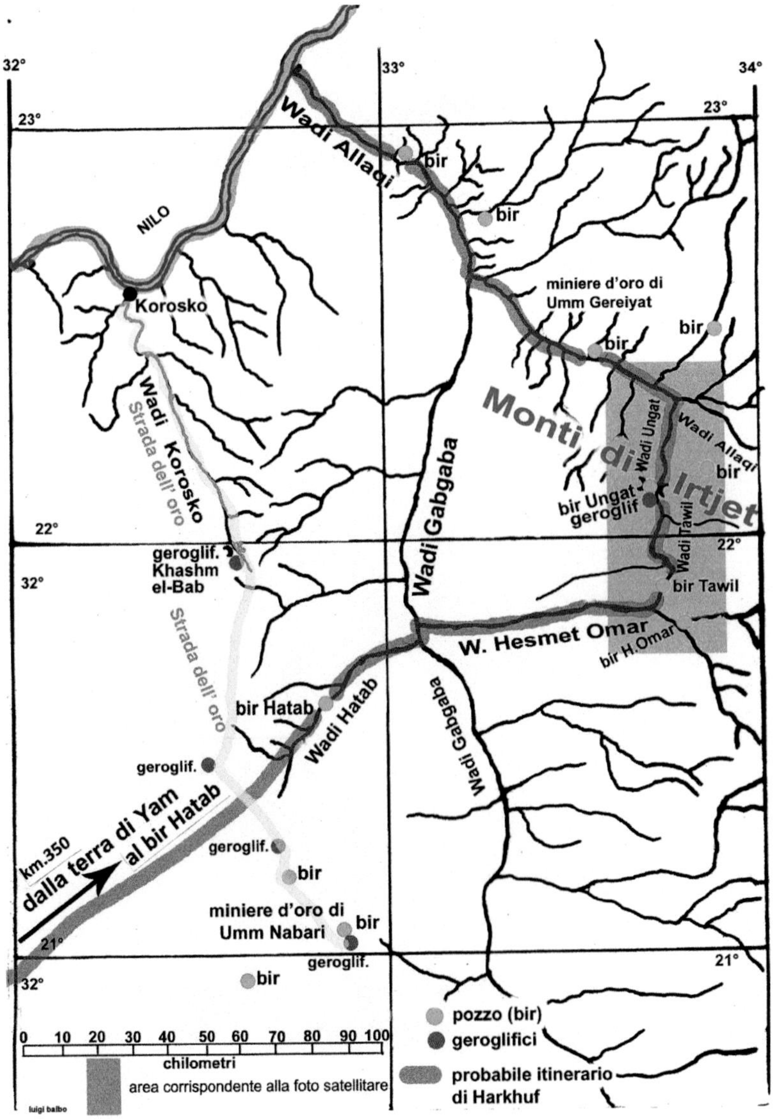

The scribe Antef, Iri (is?) his good name ... (?)". It seems possible that this Sabni could be the Sabni (also a known traveller), whose tomb is located at Qubbet el-Hawa (not far from that of Harkhuf), his alternative name, Khenementi, unknown until now.

The "Southern Road" of the Pilgrims

In the 11th and 12th centuries, Palestine was occupied by the Crusaders. The track of the pilgrims that passed through the Sinai Peninsula to reach Mecca was no longer viable: "... in Sinai the Franks (the Crusaders) have a garrisoned fort", wrote Ibn Jubayr (1145-1217), an Arab traveller and geographer.

To reach the holy places of the Muslim faith, therefore, pilgrims had to start from Aswan (Egypt) and cross the eastern Nubian Desert to the port of Aidhab, on the Red Sea, one of the most important points of embarkation for the Holy City. During this long and dangerous journey across more than 500km of desert, they stopped at the upper Wadi Allaqi to obtain the gold needed to pay the fee required at the port.

The pilgrims started from Aswan heading constantly 40-50 degrees east-southeast and faced a flat and barren region during the first part of their journey.

We travelled along this route during various expeditions through a land now empty but once inhabited, as confirmed by the many prehistoric millstones encountered during the journey. The risks for the pilgrims were con-

Plate 4.53. Possible itinerary of Harkhuf.

siderable. During the1989 expedition, about half way along the route, we found a silted up and long abandoned well. One could see still the grooves on the beams where the ropes ran. A few kilometres away, some skulls and bones peeked out of the sand, perhaps the remains of a small group of pilgrims who had died of thirst having found the well dry. The Arab traveller Ibn Jubayr, who travelled this route to the Red Sea and to Mecca in the 12th century wrote: "... we came to the well and found that sand had fallen inside and covered the water: the camel drivers tried to dig it up to replenish the water supply but failed, so the caravan had no more water ...."

The gold of the upper Wadi Allaqi

Pilgrims eventually reached the mountainous region of the upper Allaqi, where gold was of exceptional quality, as al-Maqrizi wrote, "... the whole country...is full of mines and, where the terrain rises, the gold is more pure and abundant." It is an auriferous area of about 85 by 95km, set approximately between 21° and 22° 10' latitude north, and 34° 50' and 36° longitude east. In this area, we found about 12 mines for the processing of the gold-bearing quartz.

The wealthiest pilgrims could buy small gold bars directly at the most important mines. Al-Yaqubi wrote in the late 10th century: "(In the mines) the gold nuggets ... are made into bars." The poorest, those who did not own goods to trade, were forced to work in the mining settlements or to extract gold from the quartz veins. This was probably the most common way of obtaining the precious metal. The limited number of people able to carry out this activity is evident from the work places, where only one man could operate. In areas where the quartz outcrops were more abundant, although smaller, the work was carried out by just a few men. They were probably pilgrims who mined auriferous quartz that was economically worthless for the major mining settlements. They left behind only small amounts of production waste. During our expedition, we encountered groups of improvised miners who, as in the past, were seeking gold. The ceramic fragments we found date to the medieval Islamic period (Plate 4.55), as does a mosque, the outline of which is visible near a small work place.

The hard work, together with the difficulties posed by the long journey to reach the mine, caused numerous deaths, marked by the Islamic burials of the Upper Allaqi. Fourteen isolated tombs have been documented in this area, some on

Plate 4.55. Islamic medieval ceramics, Upper Wadi Allaqi.

the hills, others, in greater numbers, along the course of the Allaqi and at the side of the tracks that led to the mining areas. Next to some mounds, we found offerings to the dead in the form of steatite jugs or earthenware containers (Plate 4.56).

Plate 4.56. Upper Wadi Allaqi, funerary offerings at an Islamic burial.

The journey with camels

Along the Wadi Allaqi, there are numerous graffiti depicting camels, probably left by pilgrims as mementos of the long and dangerous journey. They stand out clear and distinct against the blackish patina of the rock. Some confirm what was written by the Arab traveller Ibn Jubayr about desert travel: "... the only way to travel in these deserts is by camels, given their resistance to thirst. The best way to travel, used by wealthy people, is in a *saqadif*, a sort of sedan chair ... because these ... are covered with leather and comfortable." Some graffiti show this way of travelling: one can see two paired camels supporting the sedan chair (Plate 4.57). The poor, however, travelled quite differently. Ibn Jubayr continues: "... They sit atop the loads, suffering discomfort from the burning wind that pains and torments them ...".

Plate 4.57. Upper Wadi Allaqi, graffiti with depiction of camels.

When they reached the port of Aidhab, the suffering of the pilgrims was not necessarily over. At Aidhab, they had to pay a toll in gold. The Muslim geographer Idrisi wrote in the 12th century, "...this tax amounts to 8 dinars each, in raw or minted gold. The pilgrims cannot cross (the sea) to Jeddah if they do not prove the payment (of this tax)". If a pilgrim could not pay, wrote the Arab historian Abul-Fida

(1273-1331), "a terrible punishment awaits him, ... among the punishments... they used to suspend him by the testicles or other such horrible things".

The crossing to Jeddah

The boats (*gilad*) carrying pilgrims to the Arabian coast were built without nails and held together only by ropes. Ibn Jubair goes on to write: "They coat (the boat) with fat and castor oil, or *qirs* (shark) oil which is of better quality.... The reason they coat the boat is to make the wood pliable and soft because of the many rocky shores of this sea". Only a few years ago, there was still a small boatyard near Port Sudan, where boats were built using the same old techniques. The builder did not use nails but wooden pins, and they coated the plating and ropes with shark fat to make the plating resilient and capable of absorbing the impacts against the reef.

If crossing the Red Sea to the Arabian coast was hard and dangerous for pilgrims, sailing back after visiting the Holy Places could be even worse owing to the headwinds that according to Ibn Jubayr, "... throw (the boats loaded with pilgrims) off course into desert places to the south, away from the destination (the port of Aidhab). Then the Bugah (the Beja), a clan of Sudanese who live in the mountains, come down to them and hire them camels and guide them along routes with no water, so that often most pilgrims lose their way and die of thirst".

The Beja and the Battle of the Bells

The Beja considered themselves to be the sole masters of the desert for centuries. They attacked the Arab caravans, the mining settlements and quite often the Nile Valley villages. The Arabs often fought them, with uncertain results. In AD 854, General Mohammed al-Qummi won a decisive battle. At the head of 20,000 soldiers, he faced the more numerous Beja troops of men on camels. The battle was fought at Wadi el-Allaqi near the city of Allaqi (Berenice Panchrysos), then the capital of the Beja kingdom.

As the Arab traveller, Ibn Hawqal, reports, the 'battle of the bells' has this name because of a stratagem devised by al Qummi. He had hundreds of metal bells tied to the necks of his horses. During the battle, their tinkling sound, unfamiliar to the camels, drove them to panic; they unsaddled the Beja, who, once on foot, were massacred. The Beja king, Ali Baba, surrendered to General al Qummi, pledging not to attack the pilgrim caravans, to pay tribute, and to cease preventing the Arabs from exploiting the desert gold mines. A graffito we discovered probably reflects the "battle of the bells". One sees soldiers on horseback facing Beja warriors on foot (Plate 4.58). The graffito, about 5m long and very eroded, is engraved on a rock formation in the upper Wadi Abu Dila, a tributary of Wadi Allaqi, about 70km from the town of Berenice. Two other graffiti, much smaller, are located to the south west (Plates 4.59 and 4.60). In both engravings, one sees a Beja warrior with a characteristic round shield facing on foot a mounted soldier

The end of the south road

The "south road" gradually lost its importance in the 13th century, when the pilgrims were again able to take the land

Plate 4.58. Wadi Abu Dila, graffiti depicting a scene probably referring to the famous "Battle of the Bells" fought by al-Qummi.

Plate 4.59. Graffito depicting Beja warriors facing cavalry.

Plate 4.60. Graffito, a Beja warrior faces a cavalryman.

route to Medina and Mecca, passing through the Isthmus of Suez and the Sinai Peninsula. Slowly, the memory of this once important pilgrim-track faded away.

Berenice Panchrysos

One of the main routes into the heart of the eastern Nubian Desert is the Wadi Allaqi which, after a distance of 250km, reaches an area extremely rich in auriferous quartz. Here, between the mountains, lies Berenice Panchrysos, "the Berenice all made of gold ", mentioned by Pliny the Elder in his *Naturalis Historia* (VI, 170), an ancient town, the memory of which had been lost in the mists of time. Only Arab legends testified to its existence.

At the end of the 19th century, a curious story circulated in the maze of Cairo's alleys: in the depth of the desert, there was a ghost town that could be seen only once because a malicious genie (the *jinn* of the Arabs), who was its jealous keeper, made it disappear before the eyes of those who, having found it once, wanted to see it again. It was not just a legend; the town really existed. This is the chronicle of its discovery, which we made on 12th February 1989.

Plate 4.61. Remains of a possible guard tower in the middle of Wadi Allaqi, near Berenice Panchrysos.

The discovery

From the expedition diary: "We wake up at dawn and dismantle the camp in a few minutes. We have been travelling for several days with Giancarlo Negro and Luigi Balbo along Wadi Allaqi. We are looking for old gold mines that are supposedly present in the wadi as claimed by medieval Arab travellers and geographers. We proceed slowly between stones and debris covering the path. The sun sets quickly behind the mountains and shortly the cone of shadow thrown by the peaks will obscure the valley. Suddenly, a pile of stones rises in front of the vehicles (Plate 4.61). More than three meters high, it is certainly artificial."

As always, the unexpected discovery of man's work in such a hostile and lonely place excites us. They are the ruins of a building that must have been impressive, perhaps a tower, erected in the middle of the wadi for defensive purposes or to control the transiting caravans. Some 80m ahead, we notice two parallel rows of stones partially buried by the sand (Plate 4.62), maybe the foundations of a wall that cut across the wadi. The ground is strewn with fragments of pottery of different types and ages. Then, after another 100m, we reach the base of a construction with a rough rectangular plan, not very visible because it is also buried in sand; a few stones in a line define living spaces, faint traces of an impressive building. On the western side of the wadi, we notice low dry-stone walls running parallel to the banks, probably built to support an old trail that ran along the river.

After about 4km, we reach "Deraheib" ("buildings" in Beja), as this settlement is called by the Arab caravans passing down the Allaqi (Plate 4.63), a tiny spot on an old English map of 1932. Suddenly this name is materialized in the incredible ruins of a dead city. Two impressive castles form the background to a sequence of collapsed buildings, scattered along the eastern side of the valley (Plate 4.64).

Plate 4.62. Remains of the probable foundation of a wall crossing the Wadi Allaqi near Berenice Panchrysos.

Is it the ghost town of the Arab legend? We observe the astonishing view that the sunset light renders even more magical, similar to the shimmering images of a mirage. The dimmed brightness and suffused glimmers of the twilight

Plate 4.63. Beja transiting in front of the fort of Berenice Panchrysos, which in their language they call Deraheib, i.e. "buildings".

Plate 4.64. The two imposing forts of Berenice Panchrysos.

transform the wadi into an enchanted world. The old buildings gain depth and unexpected relief, through an unending gamut of colours. We pass through streets that separate the houses, inadvertently stepping on broken glass and potsherds; we feel as if we are profaning a sacred place. Then the cold evening colours take over, sliding down the mountain sides. The wind falls, and the silence weighs on us advancing incredulously among collapsed walls and still intact arches.

On the next day, the morning light brings us back to reality: we have little time for photographic documentation and survey. Our water supplies are running out.

The town comprises a vast residential settlement located on the east side and scattered buildings along both sides of the Allaqi for about 1.5km. The buildings are separated by a main axial road, 6m wide in some places (Plate 4.65), and

often surmounted by arches that seem to defy the laws of gravity (Plate 4.66). At the large loop formed by the wadi, which runs from the east and then turns to the north, there are two imposing forts. The complexity of the town obliges us to make a choice: we decide to focus on the two castles.

Plate 4.66. Rounded arches at the entrance of Berenice Panchrysos.

The most important fort is in fairly good condition (Plates 4.67 and 4.68). The walls, 25m long on the north side, are over 6m high at some points. On the north-west wall are three rows of open windows that reveal an internal arrangement on three floors (Plate 4.69). Passing through a large portal at the foot of a partially collapsed semi-cylindrical tower, we cross the arched entrance that leads into the interior of the castle, protected by a "trapdoor" open in the tower, at a height of a few metres. The carbon 14 analysis of a piece of wood taken

Plate 4.65. Main axial road of Berenice Panchrysos.

We leave the castle and 50m further south reach the second fort. It is a classic example of a Greco-Roman *praesidium* (Plate 4.72). Two towers, one of which is largely intact, rise at the end of the massive wall through which the entrance opens. Walking through the walls, a staircase of bare stones gives access to a rampart walk, oriented south east. The rooms, built against the walls, surround a large courtyard, in the centre of which there perhaps stood a well, now long gone. Almost in the centre of the town there is a large rectangular enclosure of about 30 x 15m. There are some arched windows in the east wall (Plate 4.73). They are almost certainly the remains of an ancient mosque. At the north-east

Plate 4.67. Berenice Panchrysos, main fort.

Plate 4.68. Berenice Panchrysos, main fort. The figure in the foreground highlights the monumentality of the structure.

Plate 4.69. North-west wall of the main fort, preserved to a considerable height on several floors.

from the entrance lintel will reveal the date of construction of the tower to be around AD 740. Just inside, we find semicircular arches that lead into spaces with open sides, small rooms probably used by the garrison (Plate 4.70). Outside, in front of the entrance, defensive works emerge from the sand. We notice a wall with narrow loopholes (Plate 4.71).

corner, we can glimpse the ruins of a tower and, inside, a few steps of a spiral staircase.

We take various aerial photographs with two helium-filled balloons. The camera attached to the balloons is sent up and activated from below with a radio control unit. The photographss show the structure of the two forts (Plate 4.74) and

Plate 4.70. Berenice Panchrysos, interior of the fort.

*Plate 4.73. Remains of a probable mosque
at the centre of Berenice Panchrysos.*

*Plate 4.71. Exterior of the main fort, remains of defensive
structures probably related to an earlier period.*

the main settlement of Berenice Panchrysos (Plate 4.75). One can see the main road axis crossed by smaller streets.

Using a metal detector, we make a brief search in some dumps, unearthing a tetradrachm of Ptolemy I Soter (Plate 4.76), a plate from scales used to weigh the auriferous dust and some small cubical copper weights.

With limited time available, we explore the mining area. Here we find, indicated by *alamat*, extensive excavations in the form of trenches, shafts and deep wells (Plate 4.77). The mountains have been carved out by incredible works of excavation, bone-breaking endeavours carried out over centuries, levelling the top of some hills.

The research

Archaeological excavations carried out over the following years enabled us to propose that these ruins of Wadi Allaqi are those of Berenice Panchrysos. The identification was endorsed by a special commission that met in Milan in 1990,

Plate 4.72. Berenice Panchrysos, second fort.

44

Plate 4.74. Berenice Panchrysos, the two forts photographed from the balloon.

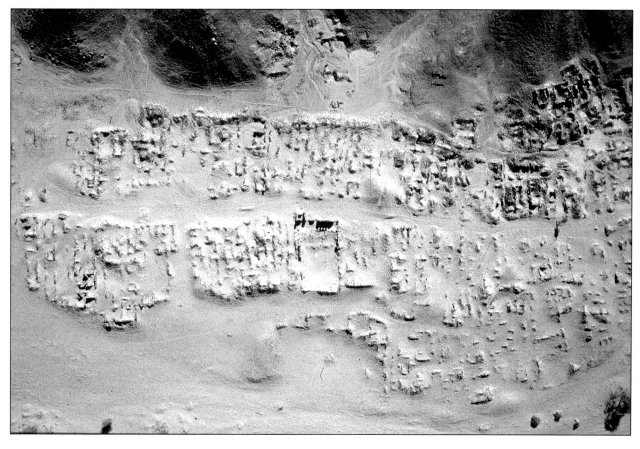

Plate 4.75. Berenice Panchrysos, main urban nucleus, organized at the sides of the road axis (photograph by balloon).

Plate 4.76. Tetradrachm of
Ptolemy I Soter
found at Berenice Panchrysos.

Plate 4.78. Milan, 1990. Scientific meeting with the international academic committee that
endorsed the identification as Berenice Panchrysos of the site found by the Castiglioni Expedition (from left to right: Isabella Caneva, Charles Bonnet, Jean Vercoutter, Sergio
Donadoni, Anna-Maria Roveri Donadoni, Alfredo Castiglioni,
Giancarlo Negro and Angelo Castiglioni).

Plate 4.77. Mining excavations in the
mountains surrounding Berenice Panchrysos.

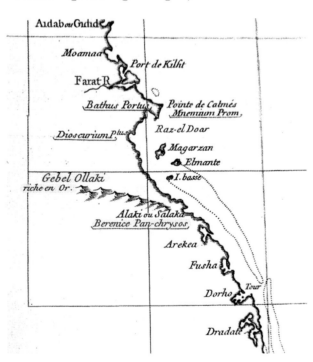

Plate 4.79. Map of Jean-Baptiste d'Anville (1768)
with the wrong location of Berenice Panchrysos.

chaired by Jean Vercoutter, Academician of France, which also included Sergio Donadoni, Academician of the Lincei, Anna-Maria Donadoni Roveri, then director of the Egyptian Museum of Turin, Charles Bonnet, a Geneva scholar, Isabella Caneva and other experts of the Nubian region (Plate 4.78).

Historical investigations also supported the hypothesis. The scholar who first tried to give a geographical location for Berenice Panchrysos was the French geographer Jean-Baptiste d'Anville who, in his book *Géographie Ancienne Abrégée* (Paris 1768), placed the town near a "mountain with mines from which the Ptolemaic Dynasty mined much gold, the mountain that the Arab geographers call Alaki or Ollaki" (Plate 4.79). On his map, D'Anville erroneously marked Jebel Allaki and Berenice Panchrysos as lying near the Red Sea. Actually, those hills of Wadi Allaqi rich in auriferous quartz are located about 250km from the coast. A medieval map preserved in Strasbourg, drawn by the Arab geographer and astronomer al-Khuwarizmi (before AD 833), indicates the location of Ma'din ad-Dahab, i.e. the "gold mine", probably referring to Berenice Panchrysos (Plate 4.80). The town lies on the map at latitude 21° 45' north, with an error of little more than 20km as the crow flies from the present ruins of Berenice.

Towards the end of the 12th century, the gold mines of Wadi el-Allaki were abandoned when the production proved insufficient to cover the extraction costs. The memory of these mines and of Berenice Panchrysos was lost. Only a mischievous jinn remained to remind us of their existence.

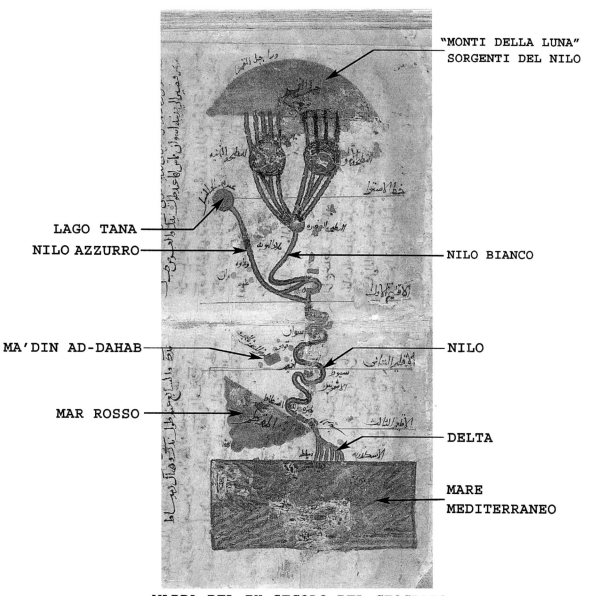

"MONTI DELLA LUNA"
SORGENTI DEL NILO

LAGO TANA

NILO AZZURRO

NILO BIANCO

MA'DIN AD-DAHAB

NILO

MAR ROSSO

DELTA

MARE
MEDITERRANEO

MAPPA DEL IX SECOLO DEL GEOGRAFO
ASTRONOMO ARABO AL-KHUWARIZMI

*Plate 4.80. Ninth century map of the Arab geographer and astronomer Al-Khuwarizmi
with the location of Ma'din ad Dahab, 'the golden mine'.*

5. Traces of the Past – First Expedition

Alfredo and Angelo Castiglioni

The expedition began on 10th February 2004 and travelled more than 2,000km in the Atmur Desert. The research area is located west of Jebel Umm Nabari, crossed by a dense network of khors. It is a flat region, dotted with low hills where wind erosion has carved out the fragile Nubian sandstone, creating caves that served caravans as shelters protected from wind. We decided to search these caves precisely for this reason, to see if there were any signs of possible ancient occupation. About 30% of the shelters we visited produced positive results. We identified prehistoric and historic traces carved on the sandstone walls. The graffiti on walls exposed to the west and east had been preserved in good condition. However, the engravings on walls facing north (and thus exposed to the *khamsin* wind that blows from the north during the dry season) and on walls facing south (exposed to the *habub* wind that blows from the south during the rainy season) were almost completely unreadable.

The journey

After having left Lake Nubia/Nasser, the expedition skirts a low band of sandstone hills running south-southeast. Numerous ceramic fragments abandoned by recent and ancient caravans lie on the ground along the first few kilometres of the route; they could be campsite remains, confirming that our expedition was following ancient tracks (see, for example, site AE (Plate 5.1). At the foot of a hill, about 3km south east

Plate 5.1. Atmur Desert, ceramic fragments documented in site AE.

of Jebel Enat, we discover substantial traces of occupation (mills, pestles, ceramic fragments) in an area of about 150-250m². We document mills of different sizes, made of quartz and granite, evidence of ancient farming activity (site RD 18).

One kilometre north of the previous site, the plain is crossed by a narrow wadi. It is the bed of an ancient river that allowed the development of a prehistoric community. Some graffiti of cattle with long arched horns represent animals still bred by the Peuls Bororo of the "Sahel" (Plate 5.2). North of this wadi, in a lateral khor, we find a large tomb 5m in

Plate 5.2. Graffito of cattle with long curved horns,
1km north of site RD 18.

diameter (site AG). We photograph the ceramic fragments discovered. After 10km, we see numerous cupels carved into boulders in horizontal or vertical positions. They are almost all the same size and positioned at different distances from each another. Their function has not yet been clarified (Plate 5.3). About 150m to the north, half hidden by stones, lies

Plate 5.3. Boulder with numerous
cupels, site AI.

an intact amphora with two handles, which we are able to recover intact (Plate 5.4) (see further Ruffieux and Mahmoud Bashir, this volume, 168-9, Plate 13.31). We photograph the ceramic fragments collected (site AI). At about 6km from this site (direction 32°), at the base of a jebel, we find numerous prehistoric settlements, as evidenced by several mills. One of these, recovered in a shelter against a wall and, therefore, protected from the weather, has traces of a white powder that

Plate 5.4. Two-handled amphora found intact about 150m north of site AI.

Plate 5.5. Millstone with traces of white substance, site AK.

should be analysed (Plate 5.5). We photograph the pottery fragments recovered (site AK). Four kilometres north west of Jebel Nasb Enat, near the end of the mountain chain, we catch a glimpse of a dozen eroded and almost illegible graffiti, engraved on a rock face exposed to the wind. We also find some hieroglyphic inscriptions, partially erased but still legible. They are arranged in two lines, located a few metres apart, both about 3m above the wadi floor (Plate 5.6), (site RD20) (see further W. V. Davies, this volume).

The discoveries made and routes taken in this first hilly chain are highlighted on the satellite image (Plate 5.7). The sites that we have described above are shown in blue; other less important sites are marked in yellow.

A second group of hills, 50km from the first, stretches for about 30km running east to west. Jebel Nahoganet is the highest peak. The exploration of the new area begins south of the mountain chain in a region characterized by low flaky sandstone hills.

In a large shelter at the south-east edge of the jebel, we find some cattle graffiti of good quality. The coats of the animals depicted have been highlighted by scraping away the dark part of the rocky mass (Plate 5.8); those to the side are engraved in the Nubian sandstone with precise strokes - two differing execution techniques, perhaps dating from different periods

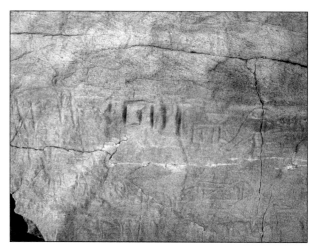

Plate 5.6. Hieroglyphic inscription, site RD20.

(site RD1). Three kilometres away (direction 300°), a duel between two Beja is depicted: the round shield is characteristic of this population. It probably represents a struggle for the possession of a well or spring. The graffiti are realized by pecking and the light-coloured patina suggests a rather recent execution (Plate 5.9) (site RD2).

At about 14km straight ahead and taking an approximate heading of 290°, we reach a small prehistoric site 250 x 250m in extent (site S) that contains a large concentration of stone materials, especially fine-grained mills (Plate 5.10). Circular structures are scattered all around, probably graves and the walls of prehistoric shelters. We photograph the pottery finds. North west of Jebel Nahoganet, a smooth rock wall on the side of a low hill features some coarsely executed graffiti of prehistoric giraffes. The incision was made by pecking the surface patina to bring out the red colour of the rocky mass. The deeply incised contours characterize the oldest period of rock art (Plate 5.11). We photograph some of the many fragments of pottery scattered on the surface (site RD5).

Three kilometres away on a bearing of 100° lies an ample shelter on top of a Nubian sandstone jebel. We notice some enigmatic graffiti on the wall. The high relief carvings are coloured with red ochre (Plate 5.12). Another graffito, also executed in high relief and painted pale violet, is just as difficult to interpret as the other graffiti. It could be representations of boats. In fact, at the end of the cave we see a lateen-rigged sailboat, although seemingly executed more recently (site RD6).

Again in the satellite image, the most important settlements are indicated in blue, while the less interesting sites are marked in yellow (Plate 5.13).

Heading east, we reach an open plain crossed by the Wadi Hatab, a left bank tributary of the Wadi Gabgaba that once flowed into the Nile, a hydrographic system that had created the necessary conditions for the development of a pastoral economy in prehistoric times. In a cave, at 4m from the bottom of a wadi, we find several overlapping graffiti. At the entrance, two boats are carved next to each other. Just below there is a hieroglyphic inscription of an Egyptian priest (Plate 5.14) (see further W. V. Davies, this volume). The cave walls are completely incised with mysterious inscriptions, wavy lines and engravings of cattle that prove the long frequentation of the site (site RD9).

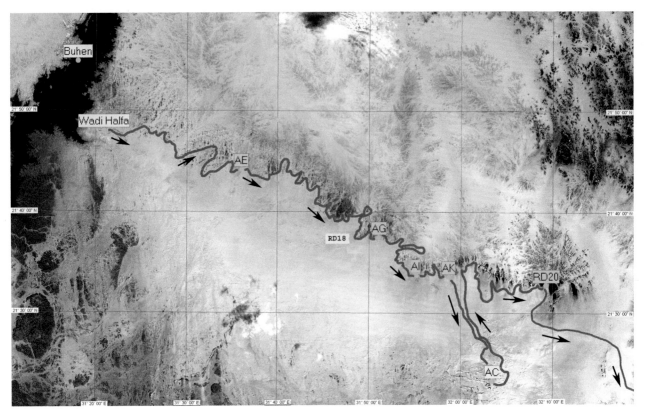

Plate 5.7. Satellite photo with location of sites mentioned in the text.

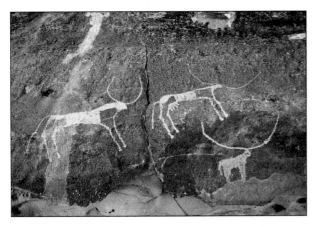

Plate 5.8. Jebel Nahoganet, site RD1. Graffiti with depiction of long-horned spotted cattle.

Plate 5.10. Site S, lithic and ceramic fragments.

Plate 5.9. Site RD2. Graffiti with a scene depicting a duel between Beja, identified by the round shield.

Plate 5.11. Site RD5, graffiti with depiction of giraffes realised with pecking technique.

Plate 5.12. Site RD6, rock-drawings with traces of red colour.

*Plate 5.14. Site RD9, depiction of boats; below,
a hieroglyphic inscription.*

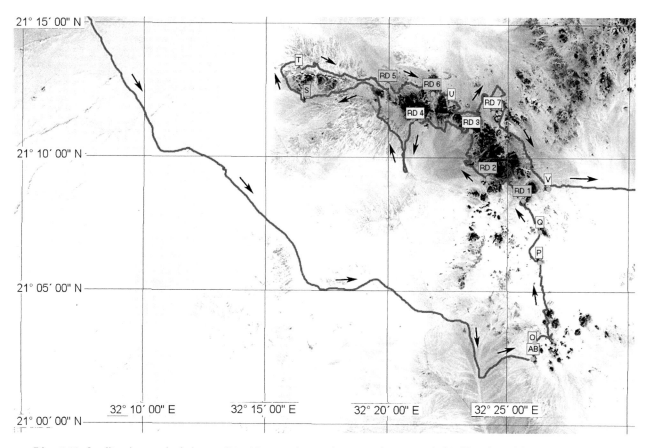

Plate 5.13. Satellite photograph of the expedition itinerary; the most important sites are marked in blue, those of lesser interest in yellow.

Further north, on a horizontal rock, we find some small cavities, perhaps used as millstones (site RD10). At about 12km (approximate direction 140°), a very low cave retains a red ochre painting, showing a bovine and mysterious drawings. Some hollows still contain pigment traces (Plate 5.15) (site RD11). At about 5km (direction 53°) stands a shelter opening on the west side of Jebel Abu Merek that preserves graffiti depicting goats. The animals are represented in a row as they head toward the pasture (Plate 5.16). Nearby, another graffito also shows several goats. Some are recent and, therefore, have a lighter patina, and overlap the older and better-executed graffiti. This representation is at the centre of a slightly con-

cave wall, in a higher position with respect to the bottom of the wadi. It could have been an area of worship dedicated to these herbivores (Plate 5.17) (site RD13).

About 6km from the previous site (direction 335°), we notice a pastoral scene on a sandstone surface. It depicts two cows being led to pasture by a cowherd and behind them a feline about to leap on the last animal from the top of a rock. It is most likely a lioness as evidenced by the fur on its back and the absence of mane. It should be noted that following the herd while waiting for the chance to pounce on the last animal is a hunting tactic frequently adopted by these felines (Plate 5.18) (site RD14). After about 5km (direction 58°), we

51

Plate 5.15. Site RD11, rare representation in red: long-horned cattle.

Plate 5.16. Jebel Abu Merek, carvings depicting a herd of herbivores.

Plate 5.17. Site RD13, graffiti representing herbivores, probably made at different periods.

Plate 5.18. Site RD14, probable scene of a feline attacking cattle being led to pasture.

Plate 5.19. Site RD15, graffiti outside the shelter.

Plate 5.20. Site RD17, next to the depiction of cattle and goats, antelope with long spiral horns – perhaps addax – are also depicted.

find a cave opening into a sandstone hill. There are no graffiti inside, although we see some on a rock at the entrance. The representation highlights two execution techniques: some graffiti have a pecked surface, others only the carved outline (Plate 5.19) (site RD15).

After 5km (direction 55°), we come across a collection of graffiti carved on a wall protected by two boulders from the north and south winds. Next to the depiction of cattle and goats, we notice carvings of antelopes with highly

emphasized spiral horns. They could be addax antelopes, herbivores that were bred (Plate 5.20) (site RD17). Four kilometres to the south, the sand accumulated by the wind has partially submerged a shelter and with it a group of graffiti. A detail shows two herders with bows, represented schematically behind the animals; they seem to guide and protect them as they are about to enter a shelter (Plate 5.21)

Plate 5.21. Site RD16, graffiti partially submerged in the sand; one can see two schematized human figures, possibly herders armed with bows.

Plate 5.22. Site RD24, carvings of goats on an elevated rock, perhaps a place of worship dedicated to these animals.

(site RD16). Not far away, numerous goats are depicted on a sandstone wall. At the centre of a slightly concave wall, we notice a very well executed carving of this herbivore. The site might perhaps have been a place of worship dedicated to these animals (Plate 5.22) (site RD24). The satellite image highlights the most important discoveries (in blue) and the route taken (Plate 5.23).

Jebel Umm Nabari, with the Rafit peak rising to 780m above sea level, stands out a few kilometres to the east. Our expedition ends near this mountain range.

Addendum: other likely areas of worship dedicated to goats

During the expedition of the following year (early 2005), we explored the region south west of Jebel Umm Nabari, finding and classifying many prehistoric sites. We also noted several sites probably dedicated to the worship of goats. We describe the most important ones.

The first site is located about 150km as the crow flies from Jebel Umm Nabari. The graffito shows a group of goats carved at about 3m from the bottom of the wadi (Plate 5.24), a situation very similar to that found in other areas. There are many animals in the representation and one of these in the

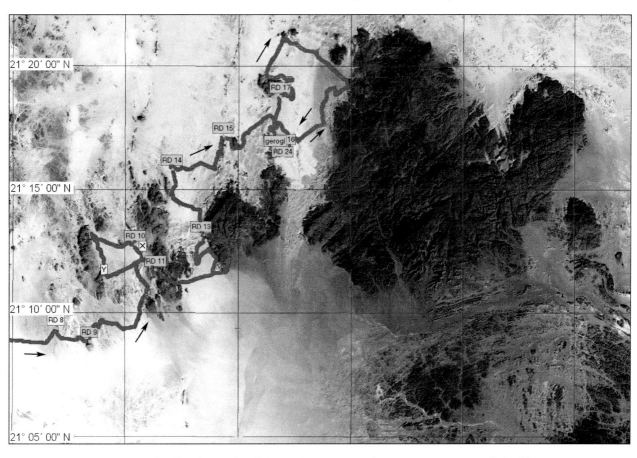

Plate 5.23. Satellite photograph with the expedition itinerary, the most interesting sites marked in blue.

Plate 5.24. Site RD25 (not marked on the satellite photo), probably a place of worship dedicated to goats. The depiction is located about 10m from the bottom of a wadi.

Plate 5.25. Site RD27, probable drinking trough.

centre is highlighted (site RD25, not marked on the satellite map). Another possible place of worship lies 10km north-northwest from the previous. Here, too, a group of goats is represented on a compact, slightly concave sandstone block about 3-4m from the bottom of the wadi. A detour of about 10km to the south west leads us to a small wadi where we find many large stone basins, carved out of compact granite blocks. They were possibly drinking troughs to save the scarce water in a region that was rapidly desertifying (Plate 5.25) (site RD 27, not marked on the map).

During the expedition, we carried out a thorough cataloguing of the ceramic finds. The information obtained will perhaps allow us to establish the movements of the prehistoric populations who inhabited this region.

6. Traces of the Past – Second Expedition

Alfredo and Angelo Castiglioni

In early 2005, we carry out another exploratory journey, this time in the vast desert region north east of Jebel Umm Nabari: an area of 160 x 70km, more than 11,000km². The north-eastern Nubian Desert is a realm of contrasts and extreme conditions. During the middle of the day, the temperature reaches and often exceeds 40° C in the shade, while in the middle of the night it falls, approaching zero.

Vast plains, where the horizon blurs and blends into the heat-whitened sky shimmering with blinding light, alternate with dark mountains crossed by narrow khors, the realm of twilight and soft lighting. Natural water-basins (the *ghelte*) that reflect the blue of the sky and provide animals with the element indispensable for life are surrounded by barren sandy areas, often dotted with carcasses of camels and animals that died of thirst. Long periods during which the wind covers and whips away every word alternate with equally long silences and the desert becomes the realm of tranquillity and peace.

So for us, who face the nothingness of the desert, it is difficult to imagine that thousands of years ago a place so full of contradictions could accommodate a world alive with people and animals crossed by perennial watercourses that made it fertile. Ancient humans lived along rivers that have long since disappeared, where it was easy to hunt the game that came to drink or, in later periods, the cattle and caprids that man had learned to breed. They rested in small circular enclosures built with dry-stone walls or in caves and ravines to protect themselves from attacks by predators and often from bad weather. They manufactured stone tools, for use in peacetime and in war, and ceramic containers for food, abandoning any broken or unusable ones.

Research must, therefore, take into account these changed climatic and human conditions. If a wadi retains some thorny bushes or a few stunted acacias, it could be a possible, albeit tenuous, indication of a region once rich in vegetation and, therefore, favourable to human and animal life. A cave at the basis of a jebel and located in a place protected from the weather might have been a sheltered prehistoric dwelling. Quite often, the discovery of a stone cropping out from the sand, which at first glance seems natural, turns out to be a man-made tool: a grindstone, a crusher, a hand-axe, a spear or arrow tip: tools used by women to grind grain or by men for hunting or defence. A crest of rocks sticking out of the ground and arranged in a circle could be the perimeter of an old shelter or grave, hidden by the sand.

The desert covers and uncovers everything continuously. What is now hidden may surface tomorrow after a sandstorm. In consequence, there are often many artefacts scattered around on the surface, mostly incised pottery fragments. In the region we explored, these traces of a distant past that amaze us with the fantasy of their decorations are very frequent. Drawings, often elaborate, incised on the clay, embellish the poorest material and the vessel becomes a valuable container. They are fragments of globular pottery ware and the incisions were obtained by impressing, on the still unhardened surface,

fish bones, seeds, cords, shells or any other objects dictated by the creativity of women who have long since disappeared. It is among the oldest pottery in the world, produced in the Mesolithic period, between 9,000 and 6,000 years ago. There are also numerous graffiti of cattle and other herbivores on external sandstone walls or preserved in caves and crevices. These representations cannot be precisely dated, but probably belong to a period between the oldest traces of domestication (4500 BC), when domestic animals first appeared in Nubia, and about 2000 BC, when the increasing aridity made breeding impossible. These drawings, often finely executed and sometimes quite sizeable with dozens of animals, indicate that these barren regions could once host large herds. The multiplication of the herds accelerated the desertification, having a major impact on both the natural and the human environment.

The diet and activities of these populations and the social relations within each group and among groups changed, since the resulting concept of ownership had to be dealt with for the first time. In our explorations we found very few graffiti in the Red Sea hills, which are instead frequent in the areas closest to the Nile and along the wadis, suggesting that the shepherds also used the river resources in their seasonal cycles in search of pastures.

The prehistoric sites documented during the expedition

During two months of travel, we found about 40 prehistoric sites; we highlight only those which we consider most important. Each site is marked with a progressive number; the missing numbers refer to places of little interest that are consequently not marked on the satellite map.

The expedition begins with the exploration of the hill chain, of which Jebel Daweig is the most prominent hilltop, running north to south. We classify the following sites discovered along the way:

Site 03: a shallow cave opens on the north side of an isolated jebel. At the entrance, many graffiti are carved in low relief, almost completely erased by the quartz sand driven inside by the khamsin, the wind that blows from the north. Two graffiti with maces and one of a goat remain at the bottom of the cave (Plate 6.1). We head east across a group of low sandstone hills.

Site 04: in front of the entrance to a cave, carved out by the wind in a low flaky sandstone hill, we find some lithic tools including an axe head, a grindstone and several mills (Plate 6.2). In the wadi below, we discover settlements and some prehistoric graves. We explore the area of low hills heading in a south-western direction.

Site 05: the graffito of a cow and two goats is carved on a sandstone wall facing east and, therefore, protected from the wind that blows from either north or south according to the seasons. The animals are not proportionate and the outline of

Plate 6.1. Massif of Jebel Daweig, site 03.
Graffiti depicting a mace and a goat.

Plate 6.2. Massif of Jebel Daweig, site 04. Lithic finds.

the incision made by hammering speaks of a recent realization. We continue eastwards.

Site 07: at the entrance of a small cave, sandals with evident strings are carved on the sandstone wall. Slightly further down, some cows are depicted on a vertical rock. The deeply executed incisions suggest that they were made in the same period (Plates 6.3 and 6.4).

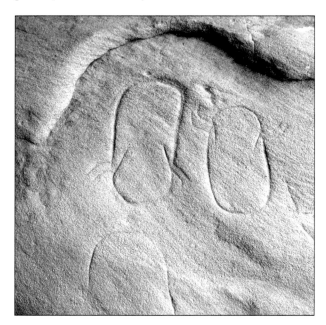

Plate 6.3. Massif of Jebel Daweig, site 07, deep incisions
on sandstone wall depicting sandals with laces.

Plate 6.4. Massif of Jebel Daweig, site 07. Schematic representation
of cattle next to the carving of sandals.

We leave the hills, skirting Jebel Daweig, and cross the wide plain that opens to the east.

Site 12: in a small wadi at the base of low hills, there are about ten prehistoric graves mostly covered with schist slabs cut out from the nearby mountains. The circular walls of the houses are also built with blocks of this rock. A mysterious structure, built partly with flakes and partly with blocks of schist, is located at the mouth of the wadi (Plate 6.5). From the hilltop, we can clearly see a circular structure about 12m in diameter, perhaps a tumulus (Plate 6.6).

Plate 6.5. Massif of Jebel Daweig, site 12,
structure difficult to identify.

Plate 6.6. Massif of Jebel Daweig, site 12. Circular structure
about 12m in diameter, perhaps with a funerary function.

We reach Jebel el-Hatan Atshan (Plate 6.7). It rises isolated from the plain. A compact sandstone mass of about 36km², numerous prehistoric settlements are concentrated along its base. The jebel in fact offered favourable environmental conditions for human and animal life. It was surrounded to the north and east by Wadi el-Hatab, now dry, but which once flowed with sufficient water to allow lush plant growth. Of the abundant water in the past, only a well, the Bir Hatab south of Jebel el-Hatan Atshan, survives today, yet that, too, is slowly running dry.

Site 18: 2km east from the previous site, at the beginning of a low hill chain running parallel to Jebel el-Hatan Atshan, we find a small prehistoric settlement. There are some fences built with dark stones that stand out against the yellow sand. In a lateral khor, a few hundred metres away, we see an inhumation burial similar to others we had already found in the desert. It consists of a number of mounds built over a circular structure (in this case with a diameter of about 8-10m). There are no clear reasons for these overlaps, which show that recent burials are located over earlier graves (Plate 6.11). There is

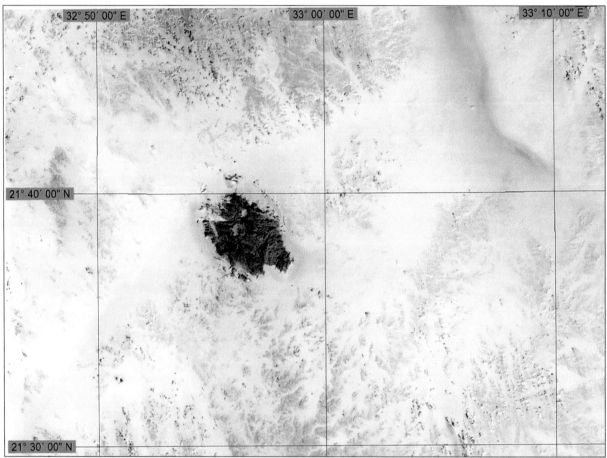

Plate 6.7. Satellite photograph of Jebel el-Hatan Atshan, with a large concentration of prehistoric sites at its base.

We explore the area along the base of the jebel and find five sites.

Site 14: on the western side of the jebel, an overhanging rock has protected a sandstone slab that features an interesting composition. The scene depicts some cowherds grabbing cattle by the horns, perhaps to drive them out of the enclosure (possibly symbolized by an ovoid) and lead them to pasture (Plate 6.8).

Site 15: in a narrow valley along the western side of the jebel, we find some 20 prehistoric dwellings. The whole area is crossed by several khors, which ensured fertility for the region (Plate 6.9). We recover a grindstone and two hand-axes (Plate 6.10).

Site 17: in the extreme northern tip of the jebel, we find a few settlements and prehistoric graves scattered over a large area. Many other structures are covered by sand as evidenced by the many outcropping rocks that signal the top of buried structures. We carry out a long survey, stopping to set up camp at sunset.

Plate 6.8. Jebel el-Hatan Atshan, site 14.
Graffiti depicting cowherds and cattle.

58

Plate 6.9. Jebel el-Hatan Atshan, Site 15. Structures presumably of prehistoric times.

A khor runs from the jebel. We walk along the khor and, not far from the entrance, we find another settlement with five dwellings (Plate 6.12). Wanting to check whether prehistoric life had developed also at the centre of the jebel, we follow the khor for some kilometres. Our search is entirely unsuccessful and the track is littered with stones forcing us to turn back. We head east.

Site 22: an imposing circular earthwork (Plate 6.13) is located on the western side of a dried lake that stretched from north to south for a length of about 10km and from west to east for approximately 2-3km. It was a lake formed by the Wadi Gabgaba, an important Nile tributary; its ancient course, almost completely submerged by sand, is still visible today. This was once a particularly fertile area, crossed by another river, the Hismat Omar, now also waterless. What reason drove prehistoric men to build such an extensive and massive con-

Plate 6.10. Jebel el-Hatan Atshan, site 15. Hand-axes.

Plate 6.12. Jebel el-Hatan Atshan, site 20. Probable housing units.

Plate 6.11. Jebel el-Hatan Atshan, site 18. Tumulus within a circular structure of around 10m in diameter; other small burials presumably of a more recent period.

Plate 6.13. Jebel el-Hatan Atshan, site 22. Circular mound about 30m in diameter and 3.5m high positioned at the centre of a reservoir.

little ceramic material. We recover a scraper.
Site 20: on the extreme southern tip of Jebel el-Hatan Atshan, we reach a small hollow where we find the outline of an isolated prehistoric dwelling.

struction – about 30m in diameter and 3.5m high – remains a mystery. It might have been a place of worship (some graves around the building would seem to confirm this). The imposing structure was erected at the centre of the settlements established on this bank. From the top of the earthwork, one can see the bed of the dried lake: communities lived along its shores whose inhabitants ate, among other things, freshwater mussels. In fact, we find a considerable amount of shells among the dwellings. Fragments of ostrich eggs are also scattered over a large area. Eggs and shellfish were

There are numerous pottery fragments, although we also find a few larger pieces buried under a few centimetres of sand (Plate 6.15).

Site 27: on the hills to the east of the lake, we find a large settlement of about 20 units. The dwellings are located on a

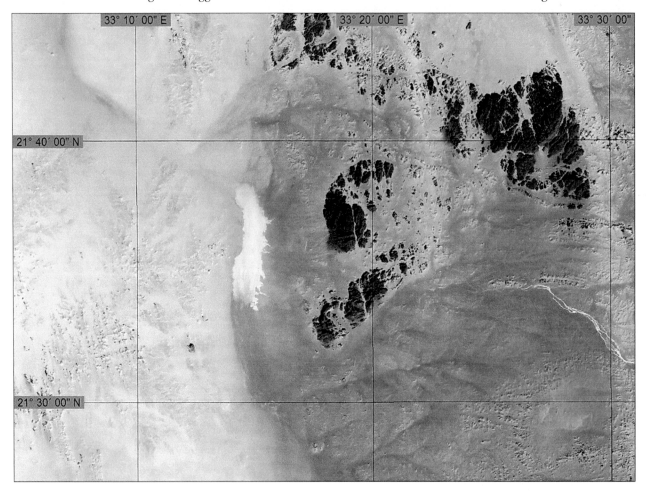

Plate 6.14. The white bottom of the lake, today dried up, stands out on the satellite photograph.

most likely the primary food staples of these populations. The whitish colour of the bottom of the dried lake stands out on the satellite photo (Plate 6.14).

Site 24: north of the lake and a few hundred metres from the shore, we find several prehistoric graves. We count about ten, some isolated, others grouped to form small cemeteries.

Plate 6.15. Ceramics in situ *near the necropolis, site 24.*

hill overlooking the reservoir. Some are isolated; others are grouped together. On the ground, we can see the slight traces of an ancient path.

Site 29: continuing westwards, the land rises gradually. A prehistoric settlement of some ten shelters is located about 20km from the lake, between low hills of degraded sandstone. Almost all dwellings are rectangular. We head south along the base of isolated mountain groups.

Site 31: this is a large settlement and a large necropolis scattered across hills formed like an amphitheatre and overlooking a valley crossed by a wadi. It was surely a fertile region in the past, in which a large human community was able to survive. The necropolis is concentrated on a plain of blackish pebbles (Plate 6.16), while the dwellings are scattered throughout the hills. Few ceramics and no lithic tools were found. We retake the route to the east and cross a vast plain lacking any settlements.

Site 32: at the foot of low hills that flank a narrow valley, we notice about ten tombs unlike any found so far: they are conical mounds about 1.5-1.8m high made of superimposed blocks. We find no settlements nor any pottery or lithic tools. They could be tombs of nomadic herders who crisscrossed the valley in search of pastures.

Plate 6.16. Jebel el-Hatan Atshan.
The necropolis of the extensive site 31.

Plate 6.18. Jebel el-Hatan Atshan, site 33. Probable Islamic burials.

We head northwards. We cross a plain entirely devoid of palaeosols and after about 50km we reach the dry bed of an ancient river. Its course is shown by a slight track that stands out on the satellite photo (Plate 6.17).

Site 33: on low hills we find several shelters located on the left bank of the wadi where some acacias still survive, evidence of a once luxuriant region suitable for human and animal life. On a hill overlooking the settlement, we find a small cemetery. One of the six tombs has two standing stones, which suggest that the necropolis could be dated back to the medieval Islamic period (Plate 6.18). We find no pottery fragments or lithic material that might help to establish conclusively the period of frequentation of the site. We follow the dry bed of the river that heads towards the west and the mountains.

At longitude 33° 37.50', the course of the wadi forks and the two branches penetrate into the mountains. We follow them up to longitude 33° 40'; past that point, the route becomes extremely difficult and dangerous. The expedition ends.

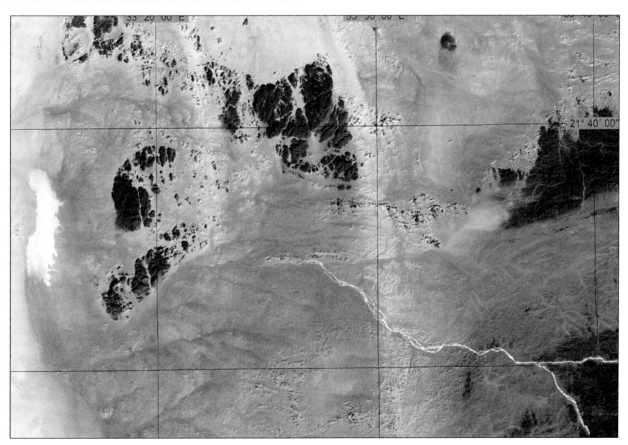

Plate 6.17. Between sites 32 and 33, the satellite photograph shows the dry bed of a river, presumably flowing into the lake.

7. The Journey to Onib Crater (el-Hofra)

Alfredo and Angelo Castiglioni

The route

In March 1990, arriving from the west, we cross the wide plain of the Wadi Elei, along the Wadi Komotit and up to the Wadi Nesari, which we meet at about lat. 21° 52' and long. 34° 53'.

We follow the Wadi Nesari, taking the south-southeast direction, and after 5km, we reach the mine, site C40. Here there is a large rectangular building of dry-stone walls, with partition walls that separate the various rooms (Plate 7.1). The vast central space is strewn with numerous fragments of quartz,

Plate 7.1. Wadi Nesari, site C40. Mining village for the exploitation of the auriferous quartz.

tion, with partition walls (Plate 7.2). Other buildings of the same type are located in the lateral wadis. Circular structures are rare. Despite being an extended mine, we do not find grindstones. The intensive mining, developed in the medieval Islamic period, must have resulted in the full exploitation of the quartz veins and the abandonment of the settlement. Extensive trench excavations on the sides of the mountains show there was intense activity at the site over a long period. Islamic tombs (Plate 7.3) surrounded by low stelae, scattered on the hills around the wadi, also testify to long use of the site by the Arab miners.

It is probable that the lithic tools for working the auriferous quartz were transported to the nearby mine C38, about 4km away, where there are many grindstones, some of them large. About 20km further south, we find a small mining area (sites C47a and C46a). All the mines of the wadis and of the khors show signs of long exploitation followed by abandonment, with only a few grindstones left behind. One assumes that the mining activity, with the requisite tools, had been moved to the nearby mine, site A11. Here there are constructions of rectangular plan made of dry-stone walling with some external walls about 2m high (Plate 7.4). In the walls, there are niches perhaps to store food

perhaps the area where the mineral was collectively crushed. We find many rotating mills and a limited number of grinding mills: it may signify that the mine was used briefly in Egyptian times and for a longer period in the Islamic era. Some confirmation comes from the pottery scattered on the site. We do not find, despite careful research, fragments of Egyptian pottery, while ones dating to the medieval Islamic period are abundant. Nearby, a vast cemetery seems to confirm the hypothesis of a long period of Arab exploitation.

Continuing to the east-southeast, after about 5km we find the mining settlement, site C39. It consists of a large rectangular building of dry-stone construc-

Plate 7.2. Wadi Nesari, mining settlement C39.

Plate 7.3. Wadi Nesari, Islamic graves on the hills surrounding the mining settlement C39.

Plate 7.5. Wadi Nesari, mining settlement of Alaar (C37). Wall preserved in elevation with entrance door.

Plate 7.4. Wadi Nesari, mining settlement A11. Remarkably well preserved structures, some up to 2m in height.

Plate 7.6. Site C37, the different colours of the millstones highlight the supply of materials of various origins.

and/or hold water containers. A highly articulated construction suggests a defensive complex with towers, the bases of which are visible. The zones of quartz crushing are also clearly visible, with the presence of cubic strikers. There are clear signs of mining excavations in the hills above the settlement, with several circular rotating grindstones still on site. About 10km to the south, the Wadi Nesari flows into the Khor Oar, where we find the vast mining settlement of Alaar, site C37.

Alaar, dating also the medieval Islamic period, contains two groups of rectangular buildings made of dry-stone construction (granite and schist), divided by an axial road. The buildings are partially collapsed. However, there are external walls, about 2m high, with entrance doors (Plate 7.5). Circular structures, perhaps the oldest on site, are rare. There are mills for crushing the quartz, both inside the housing and along the main roads. Heaps of the single rotating part of the millstone suggest there was management and control of these tools by the administrators of the mine. The grinders, if moistened, reveal different colours, indicative of the various stones of which they were made. Such stones do not exist locally and must have been transported from elsewhere (Plate 7.6). Quartz fragments are scattered over the entire surface, excavations and trenches in the hills above denoting the intensive exploitation of the quartz veins. There are also fragments of wheel-thrown pottery dating to the medieval Islamic period (8th and 10th century – W. Y. Adams, pers.

comm.) and small ceramic pieces, possibly Egyptian. The presence of some metal structures indicates more recent occupation of the site, probably dating to the Anglo-Egyptian Condominium. Some blocks of stone bearing graffiti appear to have been removed from their original location, perhaps at the time of the re-opening of the mine. Towards the south west, about 16km from Alaar, lies the site A12, marked by a large rectangular building of dry-stone construction. Inside, some walls delimit rooms and large central open spaces (Plate 7.7). On the surrounding hills, there are remains of circular

Plate 7.7. Wadi Nesari, site A12. Large building with a rectangular plan and walls enclosing rooms and large spaces, perhaps for collective use.

structures, but no grinding mills or pottery fragments. Continuing southwards, we encounter the flank of a crater, 10km in diameter. Near the northern entrance of the feature there rises a quartz outcrop of pyramidal shape, site C36.0. Nearby are tombs of different types. We find no traces of dwellings inside the crater, but there are numerous mounds along its eastern perimeter.

At the crater's southern tip is site C35, where traces of different periods may coexist. The site is located at the intersection of the Khor Haderat, which runs from west to east, with the Khor Mirdieb coming from the north. There are large circular platform mounds, probably of the pre-Islamic Beja period (average diameters: 17-20m; average heights: 1.25-1.3m). At the foot of a low hill overlooking the cemetery are the remains of rectangular buildings (Plate 7.8), possibly once shelters for ancient miners (perhaps Egyptian); a number of grinding millstones are also present.

Plate 7.10. Islamic necropolis near site C35, probable mosque with delimitation of stones marking the mihrab.

Plate 7.8. Site C35, circular platform mounds of probable pre-Islamic Beja period and the remains of rectangular constructions.

Plate 7.11. Site C35, millstones of different types.

Continuing 250m to the east, we meet a second group of tombs, around which are Islamic inhumations. Between the two groups of platform mounds, we find a small Muslim cemetery, close to a circular construction of dry stone (Plate 7.9). This structure, equipped with a small window and a narrow entrance door, is probably a place of worship, perhaps a mosque. Noticeable is a row of stones that seems to mark the *mirab* facing towards Mecca (Plate 7.10). There are numerous grinding mills and lithic anvils spread around and between the inhumations (Plate 7.11). Rotating millstones are completely lacking. All the circular platform mounds, probably belonging

to pre-Islamic Beja, were desecrated in ancient times. Ceramic fragments, which would aid dating, are rare. Other mounds of the same type are scattered along the wadi. Although the whole area is littered with fragments of quartz, we do not find the gold mines.

We head south east, following the Khor Haderat which penetrates between high hills. After 5km, we encounter a *ghelta* (site A17), a natural basin of water where some curious insects live. Numerous circular platform tombs are scattered around. One and a half kilometres north from the *ghelta* is site C34, a large rectangular building, made of stones and clay (Plate 7.12). From here, to the south, the auriferous area of Jebel

Plate 7.9. Islamic necropolis near site C35.

Plate 7.12. Site C34, large building made of stones and clay.

Onib opens up, the area so called because it is located around the mountain of this name. At site A14, a building, with a rectangular plan, constructed with dry schist slabs is near to collapse. At A15, the date "1907", incised on the stone of a building, indicates recent interest in the site (Plate 7.13).

Plate 7.13. Site A15, the date marks a recent visit.

About 5km eastwards is site A16, marked by a number of circular platform mounds built with an annex with an opening at their extreme end (Plate 7.14). The superstructures, in

Plate 7.14. Site A16. Mound with entrance corridor.

several cases, incorporate grinding mills. In the adjacent mining settlement – consisting of circular constructions, almost completely destroyed – there are many grinders of this type (Plate 7.15), together with abundant fragments of quartz. Eight kilometres further east, we reach site A18, a building of rectangular plan made of schist splinters, superimposed on one another without the use of a binder (Plate 7.16); its location, with openings facing the wadi, suggests a sighting or defensive function.

The Onib crater

Onib crater (el-Hofra) (Plate 7.17), about 40km in linear distance from the town of Berenice Panchrysos, is a true natural fortress, where the larger tombs of the pre-Islamic Beja are located (Plate 7.18). Photos taken with a balloon (Plate 7.19) highlight a vast necropolis built on a raised plateau, of about 700 x 400m, consisting of more than 50 circular platform mounds, ten of which have a diameter of 10m and more (site C33). Possibly it was the necropolis of the kings of the Beja, who lived in Berenice.

Plate 7.15. Site A16, millstone with two crushing areas.

Plate 7.16. Site A18, building of rectangular plan, probably with defensive and/or observation function.

In fact, Olympiodorus (*c.* AD 425) informs us that, though the Blemmyes had four cities in the Nile Valley, the king did not reside on the river but in the interior of the desert and that Allaqi (Berenice Pacrisia) was the capital. The same statement is expressed by Ibn Sa'id al-Andalusi "... In the desert, lies the town of Allaqi, which is the royal city of the Beja kings".

Some graves are isolated and located in the centre of the crater, near a pyramid of natural quartz which assumes different colours depending on the hours of the day (Plate 7.20). From the top, formed of large blocks of quartz (Plate 7.21), you have the view of the valley below, surrounded by the hills that enclose the crater, whose colour varies with the height of the sun on the horizon. Unfortunately, the inhumations have been desecrated over the centuries (Plate 7.22), and it is, therefore, impossible to evaluate the offerings that they might have contained. Certainly they were very important tombs. Smaller Beja graves (3-5m in diameter), dug in the crater, have often returned rich funerary objects.

From the extent and nature of the necropolis, it is reasonable to deduce that the pre-Islamic Beja had a kingdom with

Plate 7.17. Satellite Image of el-Hofra (Onib crater).

Plate 7.18. Interior of the crater, Beja pre-Islamic grave of monumental size.

Plate 7.20. Natural quartz pyramid at the centre of el-Hofra (Onib crater).

Plate 7.19. El-Hofra (Onib crater), photograph taken from a balloon. You notice the vast necropolis on the plateau.

Plate 7.21. Summit of the quartz pyramid.

Plate 7.22. Disturbed grave inside the Onib crater.

some scholars, similar to those used in ancient Egypt." The walls of the huts are made with acacia trunks (Plate 7.23). Of

Plate 7.23. Hut of a Beja village at the entrance of the Onib crater.

truncated-conical shape, the buildings have a diameter ranging from 2-5m and a height of between 1m and 2.5m, built with a tangle of branches that lets in a little light, but prevents the wind from carrying too much sand into the interior. They enclose a circular area always kept very clean, which is accessed through a door that is sometimes closed with mats or woven branches. The cover is finished with pieces of cortex, placed so as to prevent the sun's rays from penetrating the interior. Hanging from the ceiling, the straw mats are protected from the voracity of the goats. "They live in houses that look like tombs", says our Arab guide. Indeed the inhumations of the pre-Islamic period are of conical truncated shape, very similar to the current Beja homes. Before leaving, we make a survey with a hang glider, to document from above a world fixed for centuries that is slowly disappearing. Our route through the region of the Onib crater is indicated in the satellite image (Plate 7.24).

political structure and social stratification. The marked differences in the size of the tombs suggest a division of the population into individuals of higher and lower status, also highlighted by the presence of sacrificed dogs, symbols of high social position in this period in the history of Sudan, which are only found in the larger tombs.

A Beja village

From the diary of the mission, March 1990: "At the entrance of the Onib crater, we encounter a Beja village (site A 21), a few huts, where only some tens of people live. Of closed and lonely character, the Beja do not like large groupings. In front of a house, we note an oblong millstone with its crusher, identical to those found in Neolithic sites. We also find two pots of steatite. Carved with a knife in this soft stone, these containers are considered, by

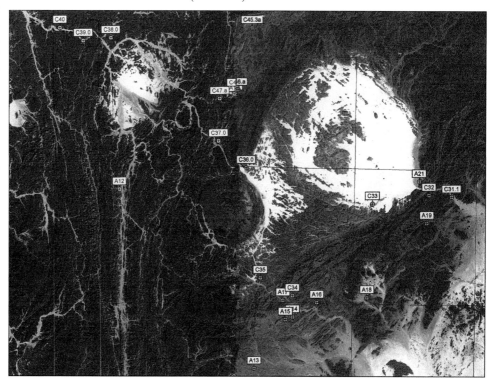

Plate 7.24. Satellite photograph with location of the sites mentioned.

8. The Nubian and Pharaonic Ceramic Materials

Andrea Manzo

Introduction

The investigations conducted by CeRDO in the Eastern Desert of Sudan resulted in the discovery of a large number of archaeological sites, and in the collection of a large amount of archaeological material, lithics and ceramics, which complement the data on the ancient peopling of the region provided by textual sources, rock inscriptions and rock art. Some of the ceramic material was already published in reports of the first campaigns up to 1994 (Sadr *et al.* 1994; 1995; 2004). Other ceramic material going back to Mesolithic and Neolithic times collected in more recent fieldwork was more extensively published by Maria Carmela Gatto and Simone Lanna (Gatto and Lanna 2010; Gatto 2012), while some preliminary insights into the Middle Nubian and Eastern Desert Ware finds, were provided by the author (Manzo 2012a; 2014a). In this chapter a more extensive overview of the ceramic finds based on a study of the material presently kept in Varese in the newly established Castiglioni Museum is provided. In the light of what was said before, more space will be devoted to the material dating to post-Neolithic times, although the available data on the earliest phase will be summarized and also some new remarks will be made on them. Finally, it should be mentioned that in this chapter, the material imported from Late Antique and Medieval Egypt will not be dealt with, as this is described and discussed separately by Serena Massa elsewhere in this volume.

Before starting the description of the material, it should be stressed that this material certainly provides a relevant contribution to the reconstruction of the history of the region, together with other data discussed elsewhere in this volume. Nevertheless, with the only exception of a few sherds collected in limited excavations, it should be noted that all of them were collected on the surface of the sites, and that the collections conducted were unsystematic. Therefore, while the ceramic material may give important chronological, cultural and historical clues, for the moment these are subject to verification, that can only be provided by more prolonged and systematic investigation in the Eastern Desert.

The ceramic finds in the collections of the Castiglioni Museum can be ascribed to four main phases, Prehistoric, Late Prehistoric, Protohistoric and Late Antique. The main features of the ceramic assemblages of each phase are described below.

Prehistoric phase

The ceramic assemblages of this phase were hitherto the more thoroughly studied and published, thanks to the already mentioned efforts of M. C. Gatto and S. Lanna (Gatto 2012, 47-50; Lanna and Gatto 2010, 326-327). They consisted of fragments of closed or open bowls sometimes bearing clear traces of pinching or coiling technique (Figure 8.1a), with rounded (Figure 8.1b) or pointed bases (Figure 8.1c). Two main types of sand-tempered fabrics were recorded, one finer and the second coarser (see also Lanna and Gatto 2010,

Figure 8.1. a) wall sherd of an open bowl with traces of coiling technique from site RD8; b) rounded base of a vessel from site RD22; c) pointed base of a vessel from site AP; d) rim sherd of a bowl with wavy incised decorative pattern from site U2; e) rim sherd of a bowl with impressed wavy decoration from site U9 (scale in cm).

325). The decoration mainly consisted of wavy line patterns, both impressed and incised, sometimes forming true waves (Figure 8.1d-e), and other times arches (Figure 8.2a-d). The application of alternated pivoting stamp technique, results both in herringbone patterns (Figure 8.3a), and lines of dots which can be in turn more or less densely packed (Figure 8.3b-c). All these patterns apparently covered most, if not all, the external surface of the vessels and were often associated with rim bands consisting of larger notches, sometimes on the lip (Figures 8.2b, e; 8.3d, e). A very typical decoration is represented by densely packed lines of bosses possibly obtained by the application of alternately pivoting stamp with return technique (see Gatto 2012, 50; Lanna and Gatto 2010, 327) (Figure 8.2e).

Interestingly, in association with sherds characterised by these very distinctive patterns, some sherds with scraped surfaces were also occasionally collected as, for example, at sites ED20, RD16 and Y. While the scraping of both the internal and external surfaces from the 5th millennium BC became a distinctive marker of the ceramic tradition of Eastern Sudan

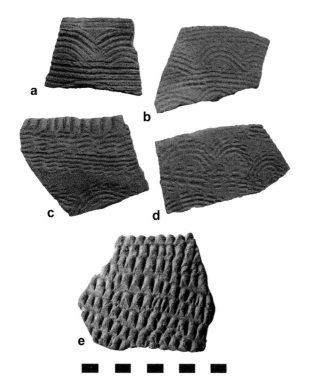

Figure 8.2. a-b) body sherds decorated with incised arches from site U14; c-d) body sherds decorated with impressed arches from site U14; e) body sherd decorated with densely packed lines of bosses from site V (scale in cm).

(Fattovich *et al.* 1984, 176-178; Fattovich 1990, 10-11; Marks and Fattovich 1989, 453; Marks and Sadr 1988, 71), and its association in some of the later collections from the Eastern Desert will be duly taken into consideration, also the association with earlier material may not be causal, as scraped sherds were recently collected in Mesolithic assemblages also in the Nile Valley (see Salvatori 2012, 416).

Relations between the assemblages of the Eastern Desert and those of Upper and Lower Nubia, the Butana and the Khartoum region, and especially with the Khartoum Variant and the tradition of the Kerma region, have already been noted on stylistic grounds (Gatto 2010, 50; Lanna and Gatto 2010, 327).

The absolute chronology of this phase, suggested on the basis of the comparisons of the ceramic assemblages can range from 7500 to 6000 BC (see Gatto 2012, 50-51; Lanna and Gatto 2010, 328).

Assemblages to be ascribed to this phase were recorded on the following sites:[1]

2, 6, 7, 8, 12, 13, 15, 16, 17, 18, 19, 20, 21, 22, 23, 24, 25, 26, 33, 35, 41, 42, 61, 63, 64, 67, R10, R12, R13, R14, R16, R17, R19, R26, R28, R29, ED2, ED8, ED9, ED12, ED13, ED15, ED16, ED17, ED18, ED19, ED20, ED21, ED22, ED23, ED24, ED25, ED26, ED33, ED35, ED41, ED42, ED61, ED63, ED64, ED65, ED67, ED69, R35, R36, R45, R46, R48, R49, R56, R57, R60, R61, R65, R68, R72, R85, R87, AC, AG, AH, AI, AJ, AK, AL, AM, AN, AO, AP, AQ, D, E, F, H, J, I, L, O, P, Q, S, T, U, V, W, Z, Y, RD1, RD4, RD5, RD7, RD8, RD12, RD15, RD16, RD17, RD19, RD21, RD22, Mine 1,

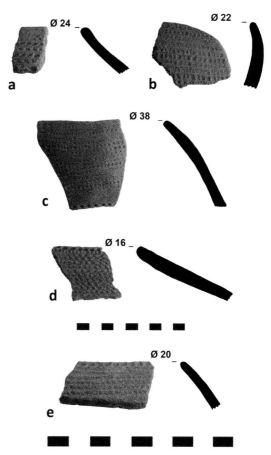

Figure 8.3. a) rim sherd of a bowl with a pivoting stamp technique decoration resulting in a herringbone pattern from site R65; b) rim sherd of a bowl decorated with a rim band and a packed pattern of dots obtained with pivoting stamp technique from site R35; c) rim sherd of a bowl decorated with pivoting stamp technique resulting in a more spaced pattern of dots from site ED22; d) rim sherd of a jar decorated with a rim band and a packed pattern of dots obtained with pivoting stamp technique from site U2; e) rim sherd of a bowl decorated with a rim band and a packed pattern of dots obtained with pivoting stamp technique from site AQ (scale in cm).

Mine site D14, D2, U1,[2] U2, U3, U4, U5, U6, U7, U8, U9, U10, U11, U12, U13, the sites of the Wadi Tonaidba (U18), and site U14 associated with a troncoconical tomb. Other sites going back to this phase were previously noted at D1, B0.1, B1.0, D2, D4, D15, C18 and B20 in the upper Wadi Allaqi and upper Wadi Gabgaba areas (see Sadr *et al.* 1993, 7-20; 1995, 205-207).

Late Prehistoric phase

The ceramic assemblages of this phase were characterised by sand-tempered fabrics more or less depurated. The recorded forms are bowls and cups with closed or open shape and presumably rounded or slightly pointed base. Noteworthy amongst the decoration is the occurrence of rippled ware (Figure 8.4a; see also Sadr 1997, 67, fig. 3), also recorded by a French mission in the lower Wadi Allaqi (Paris *et al.* 2006, fig. 8): this is a well-known decorative technique in Late Neolithic

---

[1] It should be stressed that the list presented by Lanna and Gatto 2010 was integrated with further material dating back to this phase which were identified in the collections in the Castiglioni Museum.

[2] Sites with a U prefix were not named by the survey team but were recorded by their co-ordinates. For a concordance between the new names assigned by the author and the co-ordinates see Appendix 1.

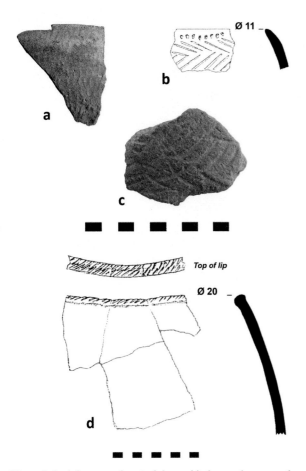

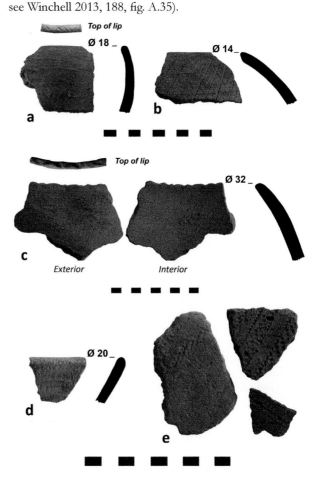

Figure 8.4. a) fragment of a rippled ware black topped ware cup from site RD19; b) rim sherd of a closed cup with rim band of notches and herringbone incised pattern from site D3 (drawing by K. Sadr, see Sadr et al. 1993, fig. 4.3); c) fragment of the body of a vessel with rocker plain pattern from site AH; d) rim sherd of a closed bowl with thickened rim decorated with rocker plain pattern from site D5 (drawing by K. Sadr from CeRDO 1994) (scale in cm).

cultures in the Nile Valley, but here apparently only used on red ware and not on black-topped vessels, which is a feature of the Upper Nubian Neolithic and Pre-Kerma assemblages (Gatto 2012, 52; see also Honegger 2004, 40, Types 11-12, figs 4-6).

Herringbone incised and rocker patterns obtained with tools with a plain continuous edge also occur (see Figures 8.4b and c respectively, see CeRDO 1994, fig. 4.3; Sadr 1997, fig. 3; Sadr *et al.* 1993, fig. 4.3). Similar patterns are widely occurring Late Neolithic features both in the Lower (see Nordström 1972, 76, pl. 25, Group 1, 14, 16, pl. 36, 15, 23, pl. 63, 2, 5-6, 15, pl. 132, 4, 6, 9, pl. 137, 6, pl. 139, 1, 2, pl. 141, 6, 7, pl. 170, 2, pl. 171, 2, pl. 173, 1) and Upper Nubian Nile Valley (Honegger 2004, 40, Types 3-4, figs 5-6) and in Eastern Sudan (Winchell 2013, 164, fig. A.14, item in the bottom row on the right).

Similar comparisons can also be proposed for the vessels whose rims are characterised by impressed notches and continuous edge rocker impressions on the lip from the village D5 and the tombs nearby (Figure 8.4d; see Sadr 1997, fig. 7, 8, j; Sadr *et al.* 1995, 208, fig. 8, e; CeRDO 1994), reminiscent of the Lower (Nordström 1972, 75, pl. 24, pl. 63, 9, 20, pl. 132, 1, 2, 4, pl. 141, 1, 2) and Upper Nubian Neolithic and Pre-Kerma (Honegger 2004, 40, Types 2, 9-10, figs 4-6), as well as of Butana Group types (Winchell 2013, 173-177, fig. A.22-23,

177-182, fig. A.28; Manzo *et al.* 2012, 52, fig. 73, b-c, fig. 74).

Certainly related to the Atbai Ceramic Tradition of Eastern Sudan, and more precisely to the 4th-early 3rd millennium BC Butana Group, are the bowls with wiped surfaces and notches on the lip from site R43 (Figure 5a and for comparisons Winchell 2013, 169-170, fig. A.18-19), the vessels decorated with patterns of spaced parallel shallow lines (Figure 5b; see Winchell 2013, 159-161, fig. A.10-12; Manzo 2017a, 22, fig. 15, c; Manzo *et al.* 2012, fig. 73, a) from the sites of the Wadi Tonaidba (U18), the scraped vessels sometimes characterised by regular notches on the lip (Figure 5c; see Manzo 2017a, 22, fig. 15, e; Manzo *et al.* 2012, 52, fig. 76; Winchell 2013, 169-170, fig. A.18-19) whose fragments were collected in sites of the Wadi Tonaidba (U18) and at site RD3, the cups with spaced rows of very regular light notches on the external surface from D5 village and from site RD3 (Figure 5d, and CeRDO 1994; for comparisons see Winchell 2013, 182, fig. A.31; Manzo 2017a, 22, fig. 15, d; Manzo *et al.* 2012, 52, fig. 75), and the vessels decorated with bands of parallel spaced comb impressed notches framed by incised lines always from sites in the Wadi Tonaidba (U18) (Figure 5e; for comparisons see Winchell 2013, 188, fig. A.35).

Figure 8.5. a) rim sherd of a bowl with wiped surfaces and notches on the lip from site R43; b) rim sherd of a jar decorated with patterns of spaced parallel shallow lines from a site in the Wadi Tonaidba (U18); c) rim sherd of a scraped bowl with regular notches on the lip from site RD3; d) rim sherd of a cup with spaced rows of very regular light notches on the external surface from site RD3; e) body sherds of vessels decorated with bands of parallel spaced comb impressed notches from a site in the Wadi Tonaidba (U18) (scale in cm).

A pierced ceramic disk usually associated with the Clayton rings, a ceramic device of unknown use, although certainly related to the strategy of adaptation to an arid environment, was collected on site 42 near Jebel Umm Nabari (Figure 8.6; see also Gatto 2012, 52), and may well be ascribed to the very end of the 4th millennium BC (Riemer 2004, 976-979, 984-986). Interestingly, this is the fourth site in the Eastern Desert that has yielded this kind of finds, and the southernmost, as the other three are all in the Egyptian Eastern Desert (Lassányi 2010, 289; see also Riemer 2004, 973-975).

Figure 8.6. Pierced ceramic disk usually associated with Clayton rings, from site 42 near Jebel Umm Nabari (scale in cm).

On the basis of the above remarked similarities, possible relations were suggested for this phase between the Eastern Desert, Upper and Lower Nubia as well as Eastern Sudan (Gatto 2012, 52; Sadr 1997, 74). The absolute chronology of this phase is based on a few C14 dates ranging between the mid-5th and the end of the 4th/early 3rd millennium BC (see Sadr 1997, 73-74; Sadr *et al.* 1995, 227), and it is basically confirmed on comparative grounds, if the above described similarities with assemblages in Nubia and Eastern Sudan are taken into consideration.

Assemblages to be ascribed to this phase were recorded on the following sites: AH, D3, H, I, ED23, ED28, ED66, RD1, RD3, RD19, R42, R43 and the sites of the Wadi Tonaidba (U18). Moreover, tumuli associated with material of this phase were recorded at site D5, as well as an occupation phase of the village nearby (CeRDO 1994; Sadr *et al.* 1993, 21-32).

Protohistoric phase

The ceramic material dating to this phase is characterised by sand-tempered fabrics and is handmade, except for a few sherds imported from Egypt (see below). The recorded types are the following:

1. Rim sherds of small dark brown, reddish brown or grey ware from closed bowls with direct or slightly everted rim decorated with horizontal incised lines on the body and sometimes small impressed notches on the top of the rim (Figure 8.7a).

Vessels with this kind of decoration are widespread in First Intermediate Period-11th Dynasty assemblages at Ele-phantine (Seidlmayer 1991, 343-344, Abb. 1, 8; see also Raue 2012, 52, fig. 7), in Middle Kingdom assemblages at Mersa/

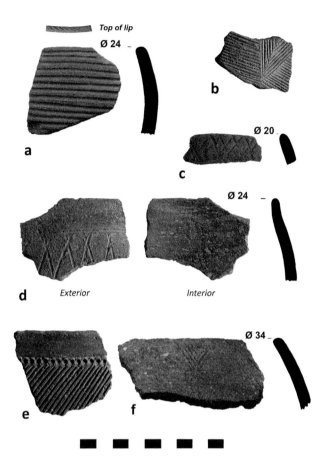

Figure 8.7. a) rim sherd of a bowl decorated with horizontal incised lines on the body and small impressed notches on the top of the rim from site U19 in the upper Wadi Elei; b) body sherd of a bowl with the body covered by incised lozenges or triangular sectors filled with parallel oblique incisions from site AL; c) rim sherd of a bowl with a band of incised crossing lines covering the upper part of the body from site R65; d) rim sherd of a black topped bowl with a slightly "S" profile, and with crossing bands of oblique lines covering the upper part of the vessel from site U5; e) wall sherd of a bowl with a band of oblique incisions framed by accurate horizontal bands of notches covering the upper part of the body from site R49; f) rim sherd of a bowl with a rim band of oblique crossing incisions forming triangles from site U16 (scale in cm).

Wadi Gawasis (Manzo 2012 b, 214-215, fig. 2, a), but also in Second Intermediate Period-early New Kingdom Pan-Grave cemeteries in Lower Nubia (Bietak 1968, Taf. 16, type P 13), in late Second Intermediate Period assemblages of the Second Cataract fort of Askut (Smith 1992, 33, fig. 2, c), in *Kerma Classique* assemblages in the fort of Mirgissa (Gratien 2006-2007, 155-158, fig. 2, a-b)' and in other Lower Nubian sites such as Scandinavian Joint Expedition cemeteries 18 C and 176 (Säve-Söderbergh 1989, 261-262, pl. 163, 6 and 200-205, pl. 37, 8, 176/76:0 respectively). They also occur in C-Group domestic contexts (Bietak 1979, 123, fig. 8). At Wadi es-Sebua East, this type dates from the very end of the 12th Dynasty to the Second Intermediate Period and has been regarded as a possible Pan-Grave element (Gratien 1985a, 52-55, type NT 8, fig. 12).

In Upper Nubia this kind of vessel was collected at Kerma, in the sector of the Western Deffufa, in assemblages dating from the second half of the 3rd millennium BC (Privati 2004, 174, fig. 137, 15, 178, fig. 139, 8) and in *Kerma Moyen* cemeteries in the Fourth Cataract region (Kołosowska and el-Tayeb 2006-2007, 212, fig. 8, b, fig. 9, b, see also Braddock 2003, 53, fig. 3.4, 29 and possibly Emberling and Williams 2010, fig. 26, d).

In the Eritrean-Sudanese lowlands this type of vessel is considered as an import and/or imitations of Nubian types characteristic of both the Middle and the Late Gash Group (Manzo 1997, pl. 4 c, 2014 b, 1151, pl. 1, b, 2017b, fig. 5, e) as well as the Jebel Mokram Group assemblages (Sadr 1990, fig. 5, v).

Sherds to be ascribed to vessels of this type were recorded at mining sites D5, D3 and at D18.1, near a tumulus, in the Wadi Allaqi and Wadi Gabgaba areas (see also Sadr *et al.* 1993, 33, 37, fig. 4.2, 4.4, 1995, fig. 10, upper row left), at AC, AN, ED6, R10, R12, R13, R14, R28, R46, R49, R56, RD14, RD15, RD19, in the sites of the Wadi Tonaidba (U18), in the Wadi Elei (U19), and in site U16 associated with a tumulus.

2. Body sherds of dark brown or grey ware bowls with the body covered by incised lozenges or triangular sectors filled with parallel oblique incisions, quite often crossing other parallel oblique incisions (Figure 8.7b).

Although this kind of vessel was recorded since late Old Kingdom times in Elephantine (Raue 2012, 50, 52, fig. 1-4, 6), and occurs in Middle Kingdom assemblages at Mersa/Wadi Gawasis (Manzo 2012b, 215-216, fig. 2, b), it was mainly typical of Second Intermediate Period-early New Kingdom Pan-Grave cemeteries in Lower Nubia (Bietak 1968, Taf. 16, type P 10; see also Säve-Söderbergh 1989, 166-174, pl. 20, type PI b2 47/B and 47/1:2). In Egyptian sites, like Qasr el-Sagha (Śliwa 1992, Abb. 3, 3), in the Kharga Oasis (Manassa 2012, 135, fig. 5, a, d, fig. 6, d) or in the Second Cataract fort of Askut, this type of vessel was recorded in Second Intermediate Period assemblages and is considered typical of the Pan-Grave culture (Smith 1992, 33, fig. 3, d). Vessels with this type of decoration were discovered in C-Group settlements, but considered as a Pan-Grave related element (Bietak 1979, 123, fig. 8; Gratien 1985 a, 51-52, type NT 7, fig. 11, 314).

This kind of vessel was also recorded in *Kerma Moyen* cemeteries and *Kerma Moyen* and *Classique* assemblages in Upper Nubia (Welsby Sjöström 2001 a, 327, fig. 5.59, decoration D 21.1-3) and in the Fourth Cataract region (Kołosowska and el-Tayeb 2006-2007, 212, fig. 9, a; Sidebotham *et al.* 2010, 97, fig. 23, 7; Braddock 2003, 53, fig. 3.4, 5; Phillips and Klimaszewska-Drabot 2005, 118, fig. 5 see also Emberling and Williams 2010, fig. 26, c, e; El-Tayeb and Kołosowska 2005, 54-55, fig. 5, a, c; Paner 2014, pl. 21), where they can be ascribed to the group of ceramic types sharing decorative features with the Pan-Grave culture (Welsby 2008, 37).

Finally, similar vessels were also collected in the Eritrean-Sudanese lowlands in Middle to Late Gash Group assemblages, where they are considered exotic objects of Nubian origin (Manzo 1997, pl. 4 c), and are part of the Pan-Grave component of the Jebel Mokram Group culture (Sadr 1987, 273, fig. 5).

In the Sudanese Eastern Desert, sherds of vessels of this type were recorded at sites AL, ED16, ED17, R26, R49 and R65.

3. Body sherds of brown or grey organic and/or mineral tempered ware, sometimes black topped from open or slightly closed bowls with bands of oblique incised or of incised crossing lines covering the upper part of the body (Figure 8.7c).

Sherds of vessels with this decoration, always interpreted as cooking-pots, were discovered in Egypt at Memphis in late Middle Kingdom assemblages (Bourriau 2012, 150-151, 153, fig. 1, fig. 4, b-f, fig. 5, d-f), at Ezbet Helmi in early New Kingdom assemblages (Aston 2012, 172, fig. 2, 8964J), at Ballas, near Thebes, in a domestic context associated with *Kerma Classique* and Egyptian pottery going back to the late 17th to early 18th Dynasty (Bourriau 1991, 131, fig. 1, 2), at other sites like Qasr el-Sagha, in assemblages dating from the late 12th Dynasty and Second Intermediate Period (Arnold 1979, 34-36, Abb. 21, 1, 2; Śliwa 1992, Abb. 3, 3), and at Tell Edfu in late Second Intermediate Period to early 18th Dynasty assemblages (Ayers and Moeller 2012, 111, fig. 8, ED 2547.N.1, ED2547.N.2). This kind of vessel also occurs in the Pan-Grave cemetery at Hierakonpolis (Giuliani 2001, 41-43, fig. 11, a-e, i, fig. 12, a-b, e). At Wadi Kubbaniya, north west of Aswan, similar vessels, always considered as cooking-pots, were associated with Egyptian pottery dating from the very beginning of the Second Intermediate Period if not to the late Middle Kingdom (Gatto and Giuliani 2006-2007, 123-124, fig. 7; Gatto *et al.* 2012, 94-95, fig. 9, 3, 5, 7, 9, 10), while at Sheikh Mohammed, in the same region, they date to the 17th Dynasty (Gatto *et al.* 2012, 95, fig. 11, 1, 5). At Elephantine this kind of vessel may date from the mid-12th Dynasty to the New Kingdom (Raue 2012, 52, 55, fig. 8, 12), and a New Kingdom chronology is also ascribed to this material at Aswan (Forstner-Müller 2012, 78, fig. 14, 29). At Mersa/Wadi Gawasis this kind of vessel occurs in Middle Kingdom assemblages (Manzo 2012 b, 217-218, fig. 2, c). In the Kharga Oasis they date to the Second Intermediate Period (Manassa 2012, 135, fig. 6, a-c).

Both in the Second Cataract fort of Askut, where this kind of vessel was collected in Middle Kingdom (late 12th-13th Dynasty) and late Second Intermediate Period-New Kingdom assemblages (Smith 1992, 28, 33, fig. 1, b, fig. 3, a-b; 1995, fig. 3.16, B, fig. 4.10, A-B), and at Mirgissa, where sherds of this type were ascribed to the *Kerma Moyen-Kerma Classique* culture (Gratien 2006-2007, 155-158, fig. 2, h), the links with the Pan-Grave culture were stressed. Vessels of this type were of course recorded also in Pan-Grave assemblages dating to Second Intermediate Period-early New Kingdom in Lower Nubia at Sayala (Bietak 1966, Taf. 27, Grab B/3, #76015/b, Taf. 31, Friedhof B; Säve-Söderbergh 1989, 166-174, 218-219, pl. 20, type PI c2, 47/A, and type PI b4 47/1:1, 47/121:1, 47/51:1 and 193/3:1). Similar vessels were also recorded in the early 18th Dynasty assemblages at Sesebi (Rose 2012, 24, fig. 7, 39-40).

Similar vessels, often characterised by black topped treatment, occur in *Kerma Moyen* assemblages at Kerma and in other Upper Nubian sites (Privati 1999, 47, fig. 14, 4, 2004, 166, 178, fig. 130, 13, 170, fig. 133, 8, fig. 140, 11; Welsby Sjöström 2001b, 350, fig. 6.2, BU 5.2, fig. 6.3, BU 5.8; 2001a, 330, fig. 5.62, decoration D40.1, D40.9), and in the Fourth Cataract area (Emberling and Williams 2010, fig. 25, a-i; Paner 2014, pl. 30).

In the Eritrean-Sudanese lowlands this kind of vessel was recorded among the Nubian imports in Classic and Late Gash Group assemblages (Manzo 1997, 79, 2014 b, 1151, pl. 1, a, c-e), and in the Pan-Grave component of the Jebel Mokram Group culture (Manzo 2017a, 43, fig. 37, a-b, 2017b, Fuig. 6, b; Manzo *et al.* 2012, 60, fig. 87; Sadr 1987, 273, fig. 5, fig. 10; 1990, fig. 5, u).

In the Sudanese Eastern Desert, sherds from vessels of this type were recorded at sites AC, AL, AN, ED16, RD14, RD15, R65, R72, U3, and U9, in the Wadi Tonaidba (U18), and in site D9.

4. Fragments of brown mineral tempered ware bowls with a slightly 'S' profile, black topped and characterised by crossing bands of oblique lines covering the upper part of the vessel (Figure 8.7d).

Similar vessels are quite typical of *Kerma Moyen* pottery (Privati 1999, 47, fig. 12, 12), but they may appear earlier, already at the end of the *Kerma Ancien*, in the settlement of Kerma (Privati 2004, 164, fig. 128, 12, 166-168, fig. 130, 7, 180, fig. 140, 11).

In the Sudanese Eastern Desert, sherds from vessels of this type have been recorded at site U5.

5. Fragments of brown mineral-tempered bowls with bands of oblique, often crossing, incisions framed by precise horizontal bands of notches covering the upper part of the body (Figure 8.7e).

This kind of vessel, although not unknown, is very rare in the Egyptian Nile Valley, where it dates to the Second Intermediate Period-early New Kingdom (see e.g. Forstner-Müller 2012, 78, fig. 14, 29; Gatto *et al.* 2012, fig. 10, 3; Manassa and Darnell 2012, 124, fig. 8).

Similar vessels are apparently more common in Pan-Grave assemblages in Lower Nubia (Bietak 1968, 120, Taf. 16, P 8 β) and in Kerma sites in Upper Nubia (see e.g. Privati 1999, 47, fig. 13, 5; Welsby Sjöström 2001a, 273, fig. 5.45, Type BO 11.2), especially in the region of the Fourth Cataract, in assemblages dating from the first half of the 2nd millennium BC (Kołosowska *et al.* 2003, pl. 6; Kołosowska and Mahmoud el-Tayeb 2006-2007, 212, fig. 8, c; Paner 2014, pl. 21; Wolf 2004, pl. 4, see also Emberling and Williams 2010, figs 26, i-j and 28, e-f; Sidebotham *et al.* 2010, 95, fig. 21, 17).

This kind of vessels also occurs in the sites in the Eritrean-Sudanese lowlands, especially in the region of Agordat, ascribed to the Gash Group and to the Jebel Mokram Group (Arkell 1954, pl. VI, 6, VII, 4, VIII, 5; Manzo 2014, 1151, pl. 3; Manzo *et al.* 2012, 64, fig. 92).

In the Sudanese Eastern Desert, sherds of these vessels were collected at sites ED16 and R49.

6. Fragments of rims or close to the rim of dark grey or brown organic and/or mineral-tempered bowls with a rim band of oblique crossing incisions forming triangles (Figure 8.7f).

At Mersa/Wadi Gawasis, on the Egyptian Red Sea coast, sherds of similar vessels occur in Middle Kingdom assemblages (Manzo 2012b, 218-219, fig. 2, d). In the Pan-Grave cemetery at Hierakonpolis similar vessels were associated with Egyptian pottery dating from the very beginning of the Second Intermediate Period if not to the late Middle Kingdom (Giuliani 2001, 41-43, fig. 11, c), like at Askut (Smith 1992, 28-33, fig. 1 a; 1995, fig. 3.16, A), while in Elephantine they date to the First Intermediate Period-11th Dynasty (Seidlmayer 1991, 343-344, Abb. 1, 16). At Wadi es-Sebua East, this type dates from the very end of the 12th Dynasty to the Second Intermediate Period and has been regarded as a possible Pan-Grave element (Gratien 1985 a, 53, type NT 10, fig. 13, 221, 223, 232, 251, 265). In the same phases the type also occurs at Mirgissa (Gratien 2006-2007, 155-158, fig. 1, e).

This type was discovered in the Kerma assemblages dating from the first half of the 2nd millennium BC at Sai (Gratien 1982, 30, fig. 3, c, 1985b, 420, fig. 313, a; Gratien and Olive 1981, 77, fig. 3, c), in *Kerma Moyen* funerary assemblages at Ukma (Vila 1987, 196, fig. 221, V), in the Dongola Reach (Welsby Sjöström 2001b, 351, figs 6.4, BU20.12, 6.5, BU6.6, BU6.9, 6.8, BU13.5; Welsby Sjöström 2001a, 270 decoration D41.1, D.41.6, fig. 5.40, Types BU 6.6, BU 6.7, BU 11.5, 330, fig. 5.62) and at Kerma itself (Privati 1999, 46-47, fig. 9, 10, fig. 14, 7; 2004, 166, fig. 130, 3, 172, fig. 134, 13). Apparently, it should be regarded as typical of the *Kerma Moyen* phase (Gratien 1978, 175, Type KM 4, fig. 49, 4).

In the Sudanese Eastern Desert, sherds of vessels of this type were recorded at site AK, at site D18.1, near a tumulus in the Wadi Gabgaba area (see Sadr *et al.* 1993, 37, fig. 4.4), and in a small scale excavation at site U6.

7. Fragments of rims of grey mineral-tempered ware, black-topped cups with a horizontal red band interrupting the black one below the rim (Figure 8.8a).

The black-topped vessels characterised by silver or red/

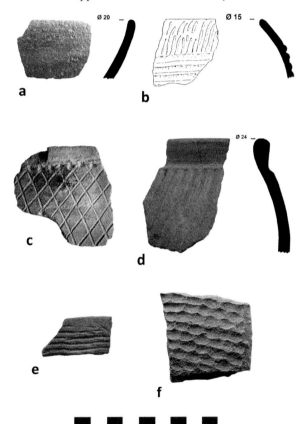

Figure 8.8. a) rim sherd of a black topped cup with a red band interrupting the black one below the rim from site AH; b) rim sherd of a jar with horizontal grooves covering the body and multiple rim bands of oblique incised irregular notches from site D3 (drawing by K. Sadr, see Sadr et al. 1993, fig. 4.3); c) sherd of a bowl with slightly everted thickened triangular in shape rim with oblique crossing incised lines from site ED16; d) rim sherd of a bowl with slightly everted, thickened, triangular in shape rim and lightly oblique grooves from site ED16; e) body sherd of a vessel decorated with almost horizontal irregular roughly parallel lines on the external surface from site U14; f) wall sherd of a bowl with rounded base reinforced by a stratum of clay from site U9 (scale in cm).

yellow horizontal bands interrupting the black band below the rim are a typical feature of the Kerma culture in Upper Nubia and they occur both in Kerma and on other Kerma sites (Gratien 1978, 210-213; 1985b, 430, 432).

In the Sudanese Eastern Desert, a sherd of a vessel of this type was found at site AH.

8. Fragments of mineral-tempered brown ware vessels, characterised by horizontal grooves covering the body and by multiple rim bands of oblique, incised, irregular notches (Figure 8.8b).

Although rare, sherds of vessels of this type were found in assemblages dating back to the end of the *Kerma Ancien*-early *Kerma Moyen* at Kerma (Privati 2004, 170, fig. 133, 9).

In the Sudanese Eastern Desert, several sherds of vessels of this type were recorded at site D3, in the Wadi el-Ku, and in the Wadi Gabgaba basin (Sadr *et al.* 1993, 37, fig. 4.3).

9. Grey ware rim sherds of bowls or cups, with smoothed grey surfaces and small and medium-sized mineral inclusions. The lip is set-off and thickened, triangular in shape. The external surface is characterised by vertical or oblique incised lines often crossing other horizontal to slightly oblique parallel lines sometimes associated with an irregular horizontal band of notches under the rim (Figure 8.8c).

The decoration and shape recall Pan-Grave types from Egypt (see e.g. Ayers and Moeller 2012, 109-111, fig. 6, ED 2659.N.1; Giuliani 2001, fig. 11, c and d; Manzo 2012b, 222, fig. 3, b) and Lower Nubia (Bietak 1966, 54-55, Taf. 25-26 Grab B/1 # 76001, 76002, and 76003/a, Taf. 30, Grab B/11, 76047/c, 1968, 120, Taf. 16, P 8 α), some fragments in domestic C-Group assemblages at Wadi es-Sebua dating from the late Middle Kingdom-Second Intermediate Period (Gratien 1985a, fig. 14, 260) and some at Mirgissa in assemblages dating to the same phases (Gratien 2006-2007, fig. 2, g).

In Eastern Sudan, this class is typical of the Jebel Mokram Group assemblages (Manzo 2017b, fig. 6, a, c; Manzo *et al.* 2012, 60, fig. 88; Sadr 1987, 272-273, fig. 5).

In the Sudanese Eastern Desert, sherds with similar decorations were collected at site ED16 and in the Wadi Tonaidba (U18), perhaps a very fragmentary one in site U8.

10. Grey ware rim sherds of bowls or cups, with smoothed grey surfaces and small and medium-sized mineral inclusions. The lip is set-off and thickened, triangular in shape. The external surface is characterised by vertical or lightly oblique grooves (Figure 8.8d).

The decoration and shape recall Pan-Grave types from Egypt (Ayers and Moeller 2012, 109, fig. 6, 2659.N.3) and Lower Nubia (Bietak 1966, 55, Taf. 27, Grab B/3, # 76020, 76015/b, Taf, 30 Grab B/10, 76046/b, Taf. 31, Grab B/12, 76052/a, 1968, 120, Taf. 16, P 9).

In Eastern Sudan this class is typical of the Jebel Mokram Group assemblages (Manzo 2017a, 43, fig. 37, e, 2017b, fig. 6, d-e; Manzo *et al.* 2012, 60, fig. 86; Sadr 1987, 273, fig. 5).

In the Sudanese Eastern Desert, sherds of this type of vessel were collected at sites AL, ED16, R49 and in the wadi.

11. Brown ware body sherds of vessels decorated with almost horizontal, irregular, roughly parallel incised lines on the external surface (Figure 8.8e).

These sherds recall incised patterns on sherds from sites in Egypt, like the ones from the First Intermediate Period-11th

Dynasty assemblages at Elephantine (Seidlmayer 1991, 343-344, Abb. 1, 13), from Middle Kingdom assemblages at Mersa/Wadi Gawasis (Manzo 2012b, 222, fig. 3, d), and from Qasr el-Sagha, dating from the late 12th Dynasty and Second Intermediate Period (Arnold 1979, 34-36, Abb. 21, 3). In Lower Nubia similar sherds were collected in the C-Group II settlement 18 C, in the concession of the Scandinavian Joint Expedition, whose pottery was also considered to be characterised by similarities with the Pan-Grave (Säve-Söderbergh 1989, 261-262, pl. 163, 11). Vessels with a similar decorative pattern also characterised *Kerma Moyen* assemblages in the Fourth Cataract region (Kołosowska and el-Tayeb 2006-2007, 212, fig. 9, b; see also El-Tayeb and Kołosowska 2005, fig. 5, b).

In the Sudanese Eastern Desert, sherds with similar decoration were collected in site U14 associated with a tumulus.

12. Brown mineral-tempered fragments of bowls whose rounded base was reinforced by a layer of clay also bearing some rough impressions (Figure 8.8f).

Similar vessels are well known in C-Group settlement sites like Wadi es-Sebua East (Gratien 1985a, 53, type NT 9), in Kerma cemeteries (see Gratien 1985b, 419-420, fig. 313, b, d, f; Vila 1987, 196. fig. 221, V-3) and domestic assemblages (Gratien and Olive 1981, 77, fig. 4, a), where they were interpreted as cooking pots, and also in the Fourth Cataract region (see Emberling and Williams 2010, fig. 30, f). Vessels with reinforced base also characterise the *Kerma Classique* assemblage in the Second Intermediate Period fort at Askut (Smith 1992, 28-33, fig. 4, D).

In the Sudanese Eastern Desert, fragments of similar vessels were collected at sites R28, R46 and (characterised by very regular impressions) at site U9.

13. Brown mineral-tempered black-topped ware bowls with a rim band, consisting of a double zig-zag line obtained by impressing a double-toothed stamp and notches on the lip (Figure 8.9a).

Similar vessels are well known in Kerma, where they occur in *Kerma Ancien* assemblages in Upper Nubia (Privati 1999, 44, figs 3, 4, 14; Welsby Sjöström 2018, 79, pl. 3.9, n-o), in the Wadi Howar in the 3rd millennium BC assemblages (Keding 1997, 163, Taf. 17, 2-3), and in the Gash Group of Eastern Sudan (Manzo 2014b, 1151, pl. 2 a).

In the Sudanese Eastern Desert, a rim sherd of this type was collected in the Wadi Tonaidba (U18).

14. Brown to reddish-brown mineral-tempered ware sherds of rim-banded bowls and cups (Figure 8.9b).

Rim-banded bowls and cups are a very distinctive marker of the Gash Group culture of Eastern Sudan (Capuano *et al.* 1994, 114; Fattovich 1990, 16-17; 1991a, 104; Manzo 2017a, 33, fig. 22, a, c, e; Manzo *et al.* 2012, 56, figs 79 b, 80, 83) also surviving – although less frequent – into the later Jebel Mokram Group (Manzo 2017a, 43, fig. 37 f, 2017b, fig. 5a-c, fig. 7, g; Manzo *et al.* 2012, 60, fig. 90 b; Sadr 1987, 272-276, fig. 5; 1990, 69-70, fig. 5 p-z"; 1991, 45). In Eastern Sudan, the rim bands consist of impressions or of crossing incisions not extending to the rest of the body of the vessel.

In the Sudanese Eastern Desert, fragments to be ascribed to this type have been collected on the following sites: R35, R43, RD7 and in the Wadi Tonaidba (U18).

Top of lip

Ø 22

Ø 26

a

b

c

d

e

f

Figure 8.9. a) rim sherd of a black topped bowl with rim band consisting of a double zig-zag line and notches on the lip from site U18 in the Wadi Tonaidba; b) rim sherd of a bowl with rim band consisting of impressed notches from site U18 in the Wadi Tonaidba; c) scraped body sherd from site RD18; d) body sherd with finger nail decoration from site RD15; d) body sherd of a Marl A3 jar from site U13; e) fragment of body of Marl A3 vessel from site U13; f) (scale in cm).

15. Fragments of mineral-tempered reddish-brown scraped or of lightly scraped/wiped vessels (Figure 8.9c).

This kind of surface treatment on both surfaces of the vessels should be regarded as a regional feature of the ceramic tradition of Eastern Sudan (Atbai Ceramic Tradition) since the 5th millennium BC (see above), and widely occurs in the Gash Group (see e.g. Manzo 2017a, 33, fig. 22 g-h; Manzo *et al.* 2012, 56, fig. 81) and, although less frequently, in the Jebel Mokram Group assemblages (Sadr 1987, 273, fig. 5). For this reason the scraped and wiped sherds from the Eastern Desert, when associated with other protohistoric types, may well date to the 3rd-2nd millennia BC.

In the Sudanese Eastern Desert, sherds of scraped or wiped ware, were found in protohistoric sites R35, RD18 and in the Wadi Tonaidba, as well as in site U13, and in small scale excavation at site U16.

16. Brown to reddish-brown ware sherds of vessels, decorated with finger nail impressions on the external surface (Figure 8.9d).

Finger nail impressed vessels occur in the Butana, in the mid-3rd - very beginning of the 2nd millennium BC assemblage of Shaqadud rock shelter (Robertson 1991, 160-161, fig. 7-13 a-d, f). Finger nail decoration also occurs in the same phases in

Gash Group assemblages of the Eritrean-Sudanese lowlands (Manzo *et al.* 2012, 56, fig. 79 a).

In the Sudanese Eastern Desert, sherds to be ascribed to this type have been collected on the following sites: H and RD15.

17. Fragments of pharaonic pottery rarely occur on the sites of this phase in the Sudanese Eastern Desert.

They are represented by fragments of body of Marl A3 vessels (Figure 8.9e), as in the case of the sherds from the group of sites R10, R12, R13 and R14, from RD18, or from site U13. Their chronology can only be suggested on the basis of the type of ware, as this fabric was apparently used since the First Intermediate Period, while the rarity of mineral inclusions characterising this fabric before the Second Intermediate Period should be remarked upon (Rzeuska 2011, 462-468).

On the contrary, site AF and again site U13 yielded fragments of a well-known type of New Kingdom Marl D handled amphorae (Figure 8.9f) (Wodzińska 2010, 69, 71, Types New Kingdom 22, 24), of which more complete examples are also known from site KRP8 (see Ruffieux and Suleiman Bashir 2014; this volume, 168).

Moreover other fragments of handmade protohistoric vessels whose dimensions are too small to be ascribed to specific classes of vessels were recorded at the following sites: ED6, ED17, ED22, R10-12-13-14, R26 and R46.

On the whole, the chronology of the mid-3rd to 2nd millennium BC suggested for this phase is supported by the similarities of the ceramic assemblage with the Nubian Nile Valley and Eastern Sudan.

Late Antique phase

The ceramic material dating to this phase is characterised by sand-tempered fabric and is handmade except for a few sherds imported from Egypt (see Massa, this volume). Given the generally poor state of preservation of the finds from surface collections, it was very rarely possible to identify the original shape of the vessels and sometimes the sherds could be ascribed to the Eastern Desert Ware only on the basis of their decoration and – but not always - the associated surface treatment. Moreover, in some cases the original surface may have been damaged by erosion. The recorded types are the following:

1. Fragments of brown mineral-tempered ware multi-footed vessels with a squared platform supported on four (?) feet, decorated with framed bands of crossing oblique incisions forming a kind of 'griddle', with panels of notches framed by incised lines or with triangles filled by crossing incisions forming an 'X-motif' (Figure 8.10a, b).

The 'X-motif' decorative pattern is not unknown in Eastern Desert Ware assemblages in the Egyptian Eastern Desert and in Lower Nubia (Barnard 2006, 61, 2008, 147-148, fig. 11-1, EDW 4, table 10-3; Lassányi 2010, 287, 91; Magid *et al.* 1995, pl. IV, b, lower row left; Sadr 1994, fig. 3, lower row left; Strouhal 1982, figs 9, 12; 1984, fig. 126, P 185, fig. 128, P 1278), although in the case of the sherds from the Sudanese Eastern Desert a specific feature is that the pattern was obtained exclusively with incisions and not, as often happens elsewhere, with the combined use of incision and impression.

Figure 8.10. a) fragment of multi-footed vessel decorated with triangles filled by crossing parallel incisions forming an "X-motif" from site R37; b) fragment of multi-footed vessel decorated with panels of notches framed by incised lines from site R37; c) rim sherd of a cup with rim band consisting of alternatively oblique incised parallel lines associated with oblique bands of parallel incised lines apparently covering a large portion of the vessel from site R68; d) rim sherd of a cup characterized by a pattern of bands of notches framed by parallel incised lines associated with a rim band of alternatively oblique incised parallel lines from site R38; e) rim sherd of a cup characterized by incised "X-motifs" forming a band of panels below the rim from site R 57; f) rim sherd of a large closed bowl with thickened and pointed rim, decorated by a band of impressed comma-shaped notches from site R16; g) wall sherd decorated with a pattern of impressed comma-shaped motifs from site U14; h) wall sherd decorated with a pattern of framed bands of crossing lines associated with other geometric zoned incised decorations from site U19; i) sherd with a pattern of incised multiple superimposed "waves" from site R26 (scale in cm).

As far as the panels of notches are concerned, although more rarely, they are also occurring in other Eastern Desert Ware assemblages (see Barnard 2008, 151, 163, figs 11-4 EDW 47, 11-14 EDW 225). Finally, the 'griddle' incised pattern, is also well known in other Eastern Desert Ware assemblages (Barnard 2006, 59, 2008, 146, table 10-3 see also 150, 164, figs 11-3 EDW 31, 11-4 EDW 33 and 35, 11-15 EDW 240; Lassányi 2010, 285, 287, 92; Sadr 1994, fig. 3 lower row right).

In the Sudanese Eastern Desert, sherds of this type of vessels were collected at sites R37, R68 and near the cylindrical low tumuli in the Wadi Allaqi and Wadi Gabgaba area (Castiglioni et al. 1997, 164-166, fig. 1, pl. 15 b; Sadr et al. 1993, 109,

fig. 6.20 and 6.21; 1995, 221, figs 25 lower row right, and 26).

2. Fragments of large brown mineral-tempered ware bowls or cups, characterised by rim bands consisting of alternately oblique incised parallel lines often associated with oblique bands of parallel incised lines, framed bands of crossing lines apparently covering a large portion of the vessel (Figure 8.10c).

The band parallel to the rim was labeled as 'zig-zag' pattern and also occurs in other Eastern Desert Ware assemblages in the Nile Valley and in association with Late Antique or Early Byzantine finds in the Egyptian Eastern Desert (Barnard 2006, 61, 2008, 147, table 10-3 see also 166, fig. 11-17 EDW 256; Lassányi 2010, 285-286, n. 82; Sadr 1994, fig. 3 upper row left).

In the Sudanese Eastern Desert, sherds of this type of vessels were collected at sites R68, R38, in the the upper Wadi Elei (U19) and the sites in the region of the Wadi Allaqi and Wadi Gabgaba (Sadr et al. 1995, 221, fig. 25 upper row left; Sadr et al. 1993, 106, fig. 6.20).

3. Fragments of brown mineral-tempered ware bowls and cups, characterised by geometric decorative patterns consisting of bands of notches framed by parallel incised lines which sometimes cross each other, often associated with rim bands or other decorative patterns like the previously described 'zig-zag' pattern (see above) (Figure 8.10d).

The decorations and surface treatment characterising these sherds recall well known Eastern Desert Ware decorative patterns formed by such bands and burnished surfaces (see e.g. Barnard 2008, 148, fig. 11-1, EDW 4; Strouhal 1984, fig. 129, P 849).

In the Sudanese Eastern Desert, sherds of this type of vessels were collected at sites R37, R38, R68, at in the upper Wadi Elei (U19).

4. Fragments of brown mineral-tempered ware bowls or cups, characterised by the previously described 'X-motif' (see above) forming a band of panels alternated with other incised geometric or empty panels immediately below the rim (Figure 8.10e; see also Sadr et al. 1995, 221, fig. 25, centre).

Similar vessels were recorded in association with Late Antique or Early Byzantine finds in the Egyptian Eastern Desert (Barnard 2008, 152, fig. 11-6, EDW 63; Lassányi 2010, 287-288, n. 95).

In the Sudanese Eastern Desert, sherds of this type of vessels were collected at sites R55 and R57.

5. Sherds of large closed bowls with a thickened and pointed rim, decorated with bands of impressed comma-shaped notches (Figure 8.10f, g).

This is a well know type in the Eastern Desert Ware corpus recovered in association with Late Antique or Early Byzantine finds in the Egyptian Eastern Desert and in Lower Nubia (Barnard 2008, 149-150, fig. 11-3 EDW 26; see also Lassányi 2010, 285-286, n. 84). The decorative pattern labeled as 'running dogs' is also well known (Barnard 2006, 60, 2008, 147, tab. 10-3, see also 148-149, figs 11-1 EDW 5, 11-2 EDW 12, 11-3 EDW 21 and 159, 11-11 EDW 168 and 161, 11-12 EDW 191 and 164-165, 11-15 EDW 239, 11-16 EDW 244, and 252; Lassányi 2010, 285-286, n. 85; Sadr 1994, fig. 3, middle row right; Strouhal 1982, fig. 9, 13; 1984, figs 127 P 799, 128 P 1126, 130 P 842 and 852).

In the Sudanese Eastern Desert, sherds of this type of vessel were collected at sites R16 and R28 and in the region of the Wadi Allaqi and Wadi Gabagaba (Sadr *et al.* 1995, 221, fig. 25, upper row right).

6. Fragments of large brown mineral-tempered ware bowls, characterised by horizontal bands along the rim, consisting of framed bands of crossing lines associated with other geometric zoned incised decorations on the body (Figure 8.10h).

Such bands parallel to the rim are also characteristic of some bowls occurring in Eastern Desert Ware assemblages in the Nile Valley and in the Egyptian Eastern Desert (see e.g. Barnard 2006, 58, 2008, 146, 150, figs 11-3 EDW 31, 11-4 EDW 33).

In the Sudanese Eastern Desert, sherds of this type of vessels were collected in the Wadi Elei (U19).

7. Sherds with impressed or incised, single or multiple 'waves', located on the body or forming rim bands (Figure 8.10i).

This is a very distinctive and common feature of the Eastern Desert Ware corpus widely occurring at several sites in the Eastern Desert and in the Nile Valley (Magid *et al.* 1995, pl. IV, lower row center and right; Barnard 2006, 61, 2008, 147, tab. 10-3, 148-168, figs 11-1 EDW 7, 11-2 EDW 16-20, 11-4 EDW 37, 11-5 EDW 51, 55, 57 and 60, 11-6 EDW 61 and 75-77, 11-7 EDW 79, 83-84, 86 and 89-90, 11-8 EDW 99, 102, 105, 108 and 114, 11-9 EDW 132, 11-10 EDW 150, 11-11 EDW161, 164, 166-167, 170-171 and 176-177, 11-12 EDW179-182, 185, 188-190 and 192, 11-13 EDW 194-195, 199, 202-204, 207 and 210, 11-14 EDW 213, 217, 222 and 225-227, 11-15 EDW 230, 234-236, 238 and 241, 11-16, EDW 243, 246-247 and 249-250, 11-17 EDW 267 and 271, 11-18 EDW 281-282, 286-288 and 290; Lassányi 2010, 286, 83, 88, 90, Sadr 1994, fig. 3; Sadr 1994, fig. 3, middle row right; Strouhal 1982, figs 1, 2, 5, 7-12, 14 and 16; 1984, figs 125 P 810, 126 P 802, 813 and 896, 127P 798, 128 P 958, 1202 a, 1278, 1303 and 1391 a, 130, P 840, 841 and 891, 132, P 959 and 1237; see also Barnard and Strouhal 2004, pl. 1).

In the Sudanese Eastern Desert, sherds with this kind of decoration occur at sites R26, R28 and R72 and near a conical tumulus at site U14.

The absolute chronology of this phase, suggested on the basis of comparisons with the ceramic assemblages of dated sites in the Nile Valley, on the Egyptian Red Sea coast and in the Egyptian Eastern Desert, can range from the 3rd to the 6th centuries AD. Radiocarbon dates from structures associated with material of this phase in the Sudanese Eastern Desert range from the 7th to the 8th century AD (Castiglioni *et al.* 1997, 163-164; Sadr *et al.* 1995, 227).

Other sherds bearing typical Eastern Desert Ware decoration, although not ascribable to a specific type of vessel due to their small size, were recorded at sites R10-12-13-14, R16, R17, R26, R28, R35, R37, R38, R39, R43, R45, R46, R55, R57, R61, R62, R68, R72, U14, in site U15 associated with a tumulus and in the mining site D14.

Final remarks

Despite the bias affecting the data, stressed in the Introduction, some preliminary interpretative remarks on the ceramic material collected by CeRDO in the Sudanese Eastern Desert can be proposed.

Firstly, if the absolute chronology proposed mainly on a comparative basis for the four phases to which the collected material can be ascribed is considered, it is immediately apparent that there is a big gap between the Protohistoric phase and that of the Late Antique period, in the 1st millennium BC and in the early 1st millennium AD. Nevertheless, it is highly unlikely that at that time the Eastern Desert was abandoned, as Napatan texts (see e.g. Eide *et al.* 1994, 221-222, n. 34, lines 16-20; 1996, 407, n. 71, line 46, 448-450, 492, n. 84, line 61) as well as Hellenistic and early Roman sources (see e.g. Eide *et al.* 1996, 559-60, n. 109; 1998, 830, n. 190, 859, n. 198) refer to several groups inhabiting the region. The lack of ceramic finds also contrasts with the discovery of objects of Napatan-Meroitic type in a tumulus in the Wadi Allaqi region (Sadr *et al.* 1995, 218, fig. 23). The lack of ceramic finds going back to this specific phase may be due precisely to the fact that the absolute chronology of the ceramics from the Eastern Desert was mostly established through the cross-dating with materials and sites of the Nile Valley. Actually, the absolute chronology of certain types and stylistic traits in the sites of the valley and in the Eastern Desert may be a bit different: some ceramic classes typical of the Eastern Desert, and also occurring in the Late Antique sites of the Nile Valley in the mid-late 1st millennium AD may have emerged earlier in the Eastern Desert, while other classes occurring in the early 2nd millennium BC sites in the Nile Valley may have continued to be produced longer in the Eastern Desert than in the valley itself. Finally, perhaps some of the sites characterised by atypical material may also go back to the 1st millennium BC-early 1st millennium AD.[3] Moreover, the difficulty of ascribing material to this specific phase may be related to the lack of material regarded as originating in the Eastern Desert in the sites of the Nile Valley in the 1st millennium BC and early 1st millennium AD. This fact may be meaningful in itself, as it may mark a different pattern of relations between the Eastern Desert and the Nile Valley compared with the earlier and later phases, when, for example we have evidence of settlement of groups from the Eastern Desert in specific sectors of the Nile Valley (Barnard 2012a, 15-16; 2012b, 180). Was this related – at least in the case of the Nubian Nile Valley – to the rise there of the Kushite state?

Of course, the surveys conducted by CeRDO were unsystematic, and this did not guarantee a proportional sampling of the different topographic sectors in the Eastern Desert, such as valleys, plains, slopes and top of hills and crests, as well as of the different regions of the Eastern Desert itself. This clearly affects the reliability of any remarks on the spatial distribution of sites.

On the other hand, some quantitative remarks can be proposed on the occurrence of sites of different phases in the surveyed areas (Figure 8.11). The dominance of sites with material going back to the Prehistoric phase is perhaps related to the more humid conditions prevailing in the first half of the Holocene in the whole of Northeast Africa (Bubenzer *et al.* 2007; Nicoll 2001; 2004; Williams 2009). As in the Western Desert, this may have favoured the occupation of the Eastern Desert by quite a large number of groups, perhaps

---

[3] Atypical materials were collected on sites AD, AF, AJ, AL, D9, E3, ED07, ED27, ED28, RD1, RD11, R28, R39, R63, R60, R12, R17, R85, RD18, X, Mine 1, D, J, U7, and in the Wadi Tonaidba (U18).

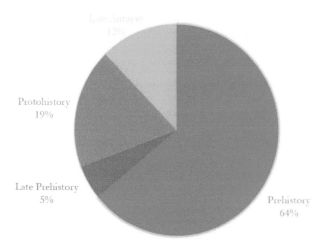

Late Antique
12%

Protohistory
19%

Late Prehistory
5%

Prehistory
64%

Figure 8.11. Graph showing the frequencies of sites of the different phases recorded in the CeRDO explorations in the Sudanese Eastern Desert.

exploiting the resources available in the internal basins (see e.g. Kuper and Kröpelin 2006). In the 5th and 4th millennia BC the decreasing number of sites may be explained by the impact of more arid conditions, while the fact that the economy of the inhabitants of the Eastern Desert may have increasingly relied on the breeding of cattle, sheep and goats (see Lesur *et al.* 2013, 152-154), resulting in them becoming highly mobile, will certainly also have resulted in the decreasing number of archaeological sites recorded. On the contrary, a higher number of sites characterises the following phases, Protohistoric and Late Antique. As it is very likely that the economy of the inhabitants of the Eastern Desert continued to be based on cattle and sheep-goats breeding, perhaps the increasing number of sites - or maybe just their increased visibility compared with the Late Prehistoric phase – may have been favoured by the emphasis placed on the exploitation of mineral resources in this phase, mostly gold. This may have already started in the 5th-4th millennium BC (see below) and increased in later phases, as more and more of these commodities were required by the fledging states in the Nile Valley (Wengrow 2006, 138-140, 166-167). As the need for these kinds of commodities did not end in the following centuries, this pattern never changed up to the Late Antique and Islamic times (Barnard 2012b, 176-77; Klemm and Klemm 2013, 609-621).

A further remark that can be proposed on the basis of the available evidence is that in all the four phases, ceramic finds collected in the Eastern Desert can be compared with materials from sites in the Nile Valley, and this is certainly related to contacts between the two regions. In the earliest Prehistoric phase this may be explained by the easier movements of human groups in more humid conditions. In the Late Prehistoric phase, also due to the above referred emergence of increasingly arid conditions, it is very likely that the groups inhabiting the Nubian-Sudanese Eastern Desert contributed both from a demographic and cultural point of view to the rise of the Neolithic and Bronze Age cultures in the valley itself, as was demonstrated for the inhabitants of the Western Desert (see Barnard 2012a, 11; Kuper and Kröpelin 2006). In the later Protohistoric and Late Antique phases, the interactions between the Eastern Desert and the Nile Valley may be explained by the seasonal mobility of the groups of herders inhabiting the desert, as well as by the

contacts favored by the indirect and direct exploitation of the mineral resources of the desert by the groups inhabiting the Nile Valley, and by the symbiotic economic relations between the inhabitants of the Eastern Desert and those of the Nile Valley (Barnard 2012a, 16-17).

Since at least the 4th millennium BC if not earlier, the exploitation of resources such as gold was likely started by the inhabitants of the Eastern Desert and this continued to be crucial also in the following phases of history, as suggested by the discovery of gold objects in Neolithic tombs and by the occurrence of 3rd-2nd millennium BC materials in mining villages (see Sadr 1997, 73; Sadr *et al.* 1993, 32, 44-47). Of course, this involvement may also have continued in later periods, as suggested by the occurrence of Eastern Desert Ware in the Late Antique and Islamic period sites (see Sadr *et al.* 1993, 111-112; 1995, 210-211). In the Late Antique phase the involvement of the inhabitants of the Eastern Desert in the exploitation of the mineral resources, as well as in the symbiotic economic activities with the groups of the Nile Valley, continued (Barnard 2012b, 176; Manzo 2014a, 247-248). At that time, the contacts between the inhabitants of the Eastern Desert and the groups living in the Nile Valley were certainly enhanced by an even more marked mobility due to the adoption of the dromedary. This, together with the crisis affecting the states based in the valley, not only favoured the penetration of the valley itself by groups originating from the desert, but also made them a crucial factor in the regional scenario (Barnard 2012a, 1; 2012b, 176-177; Manzo 2004, 81; Updegraff 1988, 89).

The interaction with the groups inhabiting the Nile Valley certainly favoured the presence of material imported from, or stylistically related to, the cultures of that region in the sites of the Eastern Desert. The occurrence of such exotic vessels may be explained by their use as containers for commodities from the Nile Valley, perhaps exchanged for the mineral or pastoral resources of the Eastern Desert; otherwise they may have contained supplies for groups of people from the Nile Valley temporary or permanently settled in the desert, possibly to exploit its resources. Alternatively, some of these exotic vessels may have been produced in the Eastern Desert itself, as a consequence of the adoption of stylistic traits originating in the Nile Valley by the local people or even directly by people from the Nile Valley, settled temporary or permanently in the region. Of course, when the material is clearly imported from the valley and consist of necked jars, like, for example, the above described Egyptian Middle and New Kingdom types, both explanations, i.e. the exchange of commodities with groups of the Eastern Desert, and supplies for groups from the Nile Valley exploiting resources in the Eastern Desert, remain possible. On the contrary, when the imported material consist of open shaped types such as cups and bowls, it is likely that they are traces of movement of individuals or groups from the Nile Valley. In turn, the local production of vessels characterised by traits originating in the Nile Valley may be explained by the settlement of Nile Valley potters in the Eastern Desert, also for example, through the practice of exchange by women, as is the case in traditional cultures elsewhere in Africa, since in those contexts pottery production is often a female task (Gosselain 1998, 103, see also Manzo 1997, 81), or again by the settlement in the Eastern Desert of groups from the Nile Valley. Unfortunately, a more precise assessment of which of these explanations is more likely each time exotic material from the Nile Valley is found on sites located in the Eastern Desert is not possible, until more precise data on the context from which these exotic materials were collected, and on the associated finds, are available, i.e. until systematic and extensive excavations are conducted on those sites. Moreover, laboratory analysis may also show if some of this exotic material was produced in the Eastern Desert or imported from the Nile Valley.

The fact that the Eastern Desert in antiquity may have been a kind of ethnic melting pot, as it is still today (Barnard 2012b, 182-188), very clearly emerges in the Islamic phase, when, starting at least in the 8th century AD, the groups using Eastern Desert Ware may have been interacting with groups of Arabs penetrating the region, and mentioned in the written sources (Vantini 1975, 71-72, 151-52), which are perhaps archaeologically represented by some types of late wheel-made pottery (see Massa, this volume). In the Protohistoric phase, the occurrence of Kerma, Pan-Grave and Egyptian elements may again suggest the co-existence of different groups in the region and perhaps in the same places (Table 8.1). Among the different ceramic types, the ones related to the inhabitants of the desert may be represented by those of the Pan-Grave. Of course also the ceramics of the inhabitants of the Eastern Desert may have been part of the shared Middle Nubian tradition characterising the C-Group, Kerma and Pan-Grave cultures in the first half of the second millennium BC and mainly emerging in the domestic assemblages from settlement sites (Gratien 2006-2007, 152, 154, 158-159; Hafsaas 2006-2007, 171; see also Säve-Söderbergh 1989, 262; Gratien 1985a, 54-55). As previously noted, some of the shared Middle Nubian types also occur in the collections of CeRDO.

TABLE 8.1. DISTRIBUTION OF GENERIC MIDDLE NUBIAN (MN), KERMA (K), PAN-GRAVE (PG), GASH GROUP (GG) AND EGYPTIAN (EG) MATERIALS IN THE SITES GOING BACK TO PROTOHISTORIC PHASE. TO BE NOTED IS THE FREQUENT CO-OCCURRENCE OF DIFFERENT CULTURAL COMPONENTS AT THE SAME SITE.

Site	1 MN	2 MN	3 MN	4 K	5 K/PG	6 MN	7 K	8 K?	9 PG	10 PG	11 MN	12 K	13 K/GG	14 GG	15 GG	16 GG	17 EG
D5	X																
D3	X							X									
D9			X														
D18.1	X				X												
AC	X		X														
AD	X																
AH							X										
AK					X												
AL		X	X								X						
AN		X															
ED6	X																
ED16		X	X		X				X	X							
ED17		X															
H																X	
R10	X																X
R12	X																X
R13	X																X
R14																	X
R26		X															
R28	X											X					
R35														X	X		
R43														X			
R46	X											X					
R49	X	X			X					X							
R56	X																
R65		X	X														
R72		X															
RD7														X			
RD14	X		X														
RD15	X		X													X	
RD18																X	X
RD19	X																
U3			X														
U8									X								
U9			X									X					
U13																X	X
U14	X											X					
U15					X												
U16						X									X		
Wadi Tonaidba U18	X		X						X	X			X	X	X		
Wadi Elei U19	X																

79

It should be emphasized that the identification of Pan-Grave materials in the region is a very important achievement of the explorations conducted by CeRDO, relevant for the reconstruction of the history of the whole Northeast Africa, as Pan-Grave material also occurs in Egypt, Nubia and Eastern Sudan (Bietak 1966, 64-71). Actually, just after the beginning of the CeRDO fieldwork in the Eastern Desert, in 1993, in an unpublished report submitted to NCAM, the disappointing paucity of the 3rd-2nd millennia BC remains, was stressed mainly as far as the Pan-Grave culture is concerned, and it was also remarked that this fact cast some doubts on the identification of this archaeological culture with that of the inhabitants of the Eastern Desert and perhaps with the Medjay mentioned in the Egyptian texts (Sadr *et al.* 1993, 5, 154; see also Näsr 2012, 81). Now, the occurrence of clearly Pan-Grave material in some of the sites recorded by CeRDO in later expeditions fills a gap between the Pan-Graves sites in Egypt and Nubia, and the roughly contemporary sites of the Jebel Mokram Group in Eastern Sudan (Manzo 2012a, 80-81; 2017a, 51-53, 2017b), filling a spatial gap in what Bietak called the '*aktionsradius*' of the Pan-Grave culture (Bietak 1966, 70). In the meantime, also the presence of sites with Kerma material is very intriguing, suggesting that Kerma groups may have had links with the Eastern Desert (Manzo 2012a, 81-82; 2017a, 52-54), perhaps, as was already suggested, related to the exploitation of gold resources in some areas (Castiglioni *et al.* 2010, 267-268). The fresh ceramic evidence from the sites surveyed by CeRDO in the Eastern Desert may also support the hypothesis of a more direct involvement in that area of the Kingdom of Kush (Davies 2014, 35-36) and may confirm the links with the inhabitants of the Eastern Desert perhaps emerging from the mention of the Medjay among the allies of Kush in the Second Intermediate Period inscription of Sebenakht from ElKab (Davies 2003, 52).

Bibliography

Arkell, A. J. 1954. 'Four Occupation Sites at Agordat', *Kush* 2, 33-62.

Arnold, Do. 1979. 'Die Keramik', in Di. Arnold and Do. Arnold, *Der Tempel Qasr el-Sagha*. Mainz am Rhein, 29-40.

Aston, D. 2012. 'From the Deep South to the Far North: Nubian Sherds from Khatanᶜa and ᶜEzbet Helmi (Tell el-Dabᶜa)', in Forstner-Müller and Rose (eds), 159-179.

Ayers, N. and N. Moeller 2012. 'Nubian Pottery Traditions during the 2nd Millennium BC at Tell Edfu', in Forstner-Müller and Rose (eds), 103-115.

Barnard, H. 2006. 'The macroscopic description of Eastern Desert Ware (1935-2002)', in I. Caneva and A. Roccati (eds), *Acta Nubica. Proceedings of the X International Conference of Nubian Studies.* Rome, 51-62.

Barnard, H. 2008. *Eastern Desert Ware: Traces of the Inhabitants of the Eastern Deserts in Egypt and Sudan during the 4th-6th Centuries CE.* BAR Int. Ser. 1824. Oxford.

Barnard, H. 2012a. 'Introduction to Part 1: From Adam to Alexander (500.000-2500 Years Ago)', in H. Barnard and K. Duistermaat (eds), *The History of the Peoples of the Eastern Desert.* Cotsen Institute of Archaeology Monograph 73. Los Angeles, 3-23.

Barnard, H. 2012b. 'Introduction to Part 2: The Last 2500 Years', in H. Barnard and K. Duistermaat (eds), *The History of the Peoples of the Eastern Desert.* Cotsen Institute of Archaeology Monograph 73. Los Angeles, 176-188.

Bietak, M. 1966. *Ausgrabungen in Sayala-Nubien 1961-1965. Denkmaler der C-Gruppe und der Pan-gräber-Kultur, Akademie der Wissenschaften in Wien,* (Phil.-Hist. Klasse, Denkschrift, 92). Wien.

Bietak, M. 1968. *Studien zur Chronologie der Nubischen C-Gruppe Kultur, Akademie der Wissenschaften in Wien,* (Phil.-Hist. Klasse, Denkschrift, 97). Wien.

Bietak, M. 1979. 'Ceramics of the C-Group Culture', in F. Hintze (ed.), *Africa in Antiquity. The Arts of Ancient Nubia and the Sudan.* (Meroitica 5). Berlin, 107-127.

Bourriau, J. 1981. 'Nubians in Egypt During the Second Intermediate Period: An Interpretation Based on the Egyptian Ceramic Evidence', in D. Arnold (ed.), *Studien zur altägyptischen Keramik, des Deutschen Archälogischen Instituts.* Cairo, 25-41.

Bourriau, J. 1991. 'Relations between Egypt and Kerma during the Middle and New Kingdom', in W. V. Davies (ed.), *Egypt and Africa. Nubia from Prehistory to Islam.* London, 129-144.

Bourriau, J. 2012. 'Nubian Pottery from Memèhis, Kom Rabia', in Forstner-Müller and Rose (eds), 149-158.

Braddock, P. 2003. 'The Pottery', in D. A. Welsby (ed.), *Survey above the Fourth Cataract,* SARS Publication 10, London, 51-72.

Bubenzer, O., A. Bolten and F. Darius (eds) 2007. *Atlas of cultural and environmental change in Arid Africa.* Africa Praehistorica 21. Köln.

Capuano, G., A. Manzo and C. Perlingieri 1994. 'Progress Report on the Pottery from the Gash Group Settlement at Mahal Teglinos (Kassala), 3rd-2nd mill. BC', in C. Bonnet (ed.), *Études Nubiennes. Conférence de Genève, Actes du VIIᵉ Congrès international d'études nubiennes 3-8 septembre 1990, Vol. II.* Genève, 109-115.

Castiglioni, A., A. Castiglioni and C. Bonnet 2010. 'The gold mines of the Kingdom of Kerma', in W. Godlewski and A. Łajtar (eds), 263-270.

Castiglioni, A., A. Castiglioni and K. Sadr 1997. 'Sur les traces des Blemmis: les tombes Bejas au premier millénaire après J.-C. dans les collines de la Mer Rouge', in *Actes de la VIIIᵉ Conférence Internationale des Études Nubiennes 1994, Vol. II.* (Cahier de Recherches de l'Institut de Papyrologie et d'Égyptologie de Lille 17/2). Lille 163-167.

CeRDO 1994. *Field Report of CeRDO's Activities in 1994,* Varese (unpublished report).

CeRDO 2004. *Survey 2004 in the Eastern Sudanese Desert,* Varese (unpublished report).

Davies, W. V. 2003. 'Kush in Egypt: a new historical inscription', *Sudan & Nubia* 7, 52-54.

Davies, W. V. 2014. 'Recording Egyptian Inscriptions in the Eastern Desert and elsewhere', *Sudan & Nubia* 18, 30-44.

El-Tayeb, M. and E. Kołosowska 2005. 'Burial Traditions on the Right Bank of the Nile in the Fourth Cataract Region', *Gdańsk Archaeological Museum and Heritage Protection Fund African Reports* 4, 51-74.

Eide, T., T. Hägg, R. H. Pierce and L. Török (eds) 1994. *Fontes Historiae Nubiorum 1: From the Eighth to the Mid-Fifth Century BC.* Bergen.

Eide, T., T. Hägg, R. H. Pierce and L. Török (eds) 1996. *Fontes Historiae Nubiorum 2: From the Mid-Fifth to the First Century BC.* Bergen.

Eide, T., T. Hägg, R. H. Pierce and L. Török (eds.) 1998. *Fontes Historiae Nubiorum 3: From the First to the Sixth Century AD.* Bergen.

Emberling, G. and B. Williams 2010. 'The Kingdom of Kush in the 4th Cataract: Archaeological Salvage of the Oriental Institute Nubian Expedition 2007 Season. Part I. Preliminary Report on the Sites of Hosh el-Guruf and El-Widay', *Gdańsk Archaeological Museum and Heritage Protection Fund African Reports* 7, 7-38.

Fattovich, R. 1990. 'The Peopling of the Northern Ethiopian-Sudanese Borderland between 7000 and 1000 BP: A Preliminary Model'. *Nubica* I/II, 3-45.

Fattovich, R. 1991. 'Ricerche archeologiche italiane nel delta del Gash (Kassala), 1980-1989, un bilancio preliminare'. *Rassegna di Studi Etiopici* 33 [1989], 89-130.

Fattovich, R., A. E. Marks and A. Mohammed Ali 1984. 'The archaeology of the Eastern Sahel, Sudan: preliminary results', *African Archaeological Review* 2, 173-188.

Forstner-Müller, I. 2012. 'Nubian Pottery in Aswan', in Forstner-Müller and Rose (eds), 59-82.

I. Forstner-Müller and P. Rose (eds) 2012. *Nubian Pottery from Egyptian Cultural Contexts of the Middle and Early New Kingdom*. Wien.

Gatto, M. C. 2012. 'The Holocene Prehistory of the Nubian Eastern Desert', in H. Barnard and K. Duistermaat (eds), *The History of the Peoples of the Eastern Desert*. Cotsen Institute of Archaeology Monograph 73. Los Angeles, 43-57.

Gatto, M. C., C. Gallorini and S. Roma 2012. 'Pan-Grave Pottery from Nag el-Qarmilla and Sheik Mohamed Cemeteries in Gharb Aswan', in Forstner-Müller and Rose (eds), 83-102.

Gatto, M. C. and S. Giuliani 2006-2007. 'Nubians in Upper Egypt: Results of the Survey in the Aswan-Kom Ombo Region (2005-2006)', in B. Gratien (ed.), *Mélanges offerts à Francis Geus*. (Cahier de Recherches de l'Institut de Papyrologie et d'Egyptologie de Lille 26). Lille, 121-130.

Giuliani, S. 2001. 'Pottery from the Nubian Cemeteries', *Sudan & Nubia* 5, 40-45.

Godlewski, W. and A. Łatjar (eds) 2008. *Between the Cataracts. Proceedings of the 11th Conference of Nubian Studies, Part 1*. Polish Archaeology in the Mediterranean Supplement Series 2, 1. Warsaw.

W. Godlewski and A. Łatjar (eds) 2010. *Between the Cataracts. Proceedings of the 11th Conference of Nubian Studies, Part 2, 1*. Polish Archaeology in the Mediterranean Supplement Series 2, 2, 1. Warsaw.

Gosselain, O. P. 1998. Social and Technical Identity in a Clay Crystal Ball, in M. T. Stark (ed.), *The Archaeology of Social Boundaries*. Washington – London, 78-106.

Gratien, B. 1978. *Les cultures Kerma. Essai de classification*. Lille.

Gratien, B. 1982. 'Les fouilles de la partie méridionale de l'île de Saï 1977-1979', in P. Van Moorsel (ed.), *New Discoveries in Nubia. Proceedings of the Colloqium on Nubian Studies, The Hague 1979*. Leiden, 29-35.

Gratien, B. 1985a. 'Le village fortifié du Groupe C à Ouadi es-Séboua Est, typologie de la céramique', *Cahier de Recherches de l'Institut de Papyrologie et d'Egyptologie de Lille* 7, 39-56.

Gratien, B. 1985b. *Saï I. La nécropole Kerma*. Paris.

Gratien, B. 2006-2007. 'Au sujet des Nubiens au Moyen Empire et à la Deuxième Période Intermédiaire dans les fortresses égyptiennes de la deuxième cataracte', in B. Gratien (ed.), *Mélanges offerts à Francis Geus*. (Cahier de Recherches de l'Institut de Papyrologie et d'Egyptologie de Lille 26). Lille 151-161.

Gratien, B. and M. Olive 1981. 'Fouilles à Saï: 1977-1979', *Cahier de Recherches de l'Institut de Papyrologie et d'Egyptologie de Lille* 6, 69-159.

Hafsaas, H. 2006-2007. 'Pots and People in an Anthropological Perspective. The C-Group People of Lower Nubia as a Case Study', in B. Gratien (ed.), *Mélanges offerts à Francis Geus*. (Cahier de Recherches de l'Institut de Papyrologie et d'Egyptologie de Lille 26). Lille 163-171.

Honegger, M. 2004. 'The Pre-Kerma: a cultural group from Upper Nubia prior to the Kerma civilization', *Sudan & Nubia* 8, 38-46.

Keding, B. 1997. *Djabarona 84/13. Untersuchungen zur Besiedlungsgeschichte des Wadi Howar anhand der Keramik des 3. Und 2. Jahrtausends v.Chr.. (Africa Praehistorica* 9). Köln.

Klemm, R, and D. Klemm 2013. *Gold and Gold Mining in Ancient Egypt and Nubia. Geoarchaeology of the Ancient Gold Mining Sites in the Egyptian and Sudanese Eastern Desert*. Heidelberg – New York – Dordrecht – London.

Kołosowska, E. and M. el-Tayeb 2006-2007. 'Old Kush II Burials in the Fourth Cataract Region', in B. Gratien (ed.), *Mélanges offerts à Francis Geus*. (*Cahier de Recherches de l'Institut de Papyrologie et d'Egyptologie de Lille 26*). Lille, 205-218.

Kołosowska, E., M. el-Tayeb and H. Paner 2003. 'Old Kush in the Fourth Cataract Region', *Sudan & Nubia* 7, 21-25.

Kuper, R. and S. Kröpelin 2006. 'Climate-Controlled Holocene Occupation in the Sahara: Motor of Africa's Evolution', *Science* 313, 803-807.

Lanna, S. and M. C. Gatto 2010. 'Prehistoric Human Occupation in the Nubian Eastern Desert: An Overview', in Godlewski and Łajtar (eds), 319-328.

Lassányi, G. 2010. 'Pottery', in U. Luft (ed.), *Bi'r Minayh. Report on the Survey 1998-2004*. Budapest, 271-290.

Lesur, J., E. A. Hildebrand, G. Abawa and X. Gutherz 2013. 'The advent of herding in the Horn of Africa: New data from Ethiopia, Djibouti and Somaliland', *Quaternary International* 343, 148-158.

Magid, A. A., R. H. Pierce and K. Krzywinski 1995. 'Test Excavations in the Southern Red Sea Hills (Sudan): Cultural Linkages to the North', *Archéologie du Nil Moyen* 7, 163-190.

Manassa, C. 2012. 'Middle Nubian Ceramics from Umm Mawagir, Kharga Oasis', in Forstner-Müller and Rose (eds), 129-148.

Manzo, A. 1997. 'Les tessons 'exotiques' du Groupe du Gash: un essai d'examen statistique', in *Actes de la VIIIe Conférence Internationale des Études Nubiennes 1994*, Vol. II (*Cahier de Recherches de l'Institut de Papyrologie et d'Égyptologie de Lille 17/2*). Lille 77-87.

Manzo, A. 2012a. 'From the sea to the deserts and back: New research in Eastern Sudan', *British Museum Studies in Ancient Egypt and Sudan* 18, 75-106.

Manzo, A. 2012b. 'Typological, Chronological and Functional Remarks on the Ceramic Materials of Nubian Type from the Middle Kingdom Harbour of Mersa/Wadi Gawasis, Red Sea, Egypt', in Forstner-Müller and Rose (eds), 213-232.

Manzo, A. 2014a. 'New Eastern Desert Finds from Sudan and Ethiopia', in A. Lohwasser and P. Wolf (eds), *Ein Forscherleben zwischen den Welten. Zum 80. Geburtstag von Steffen Wenig*, Sudanarchäologische Gesellschaft, (*Der antike Sudan. Mitteilungen der Sudanarchäologische Gesellschaft zu Berlin* e. V.). Berlin, 237-252.

Manzo, A. 2014b. 'Beyond the Fourth Cataract. Perspectives for Research in Eastern Sudan', in J. R. Anderson and D. A. Welsby (eds), *The Fourth Cataract and Beyond. Proceedings of the 12th International Conference for Nubian Studies*. British Museum Publications on Egypt and Sudan 1. Leuven – Paris – Walpole, MA, 1149-1157.

Manzo, A. 2017a. *Eastern Sudan in its Setting. The archaeology of a region far from the Nile Valley*. Cambridge Monographs in African Archaeology 94. Oxford.

Manzo, A. 2017b. 'The Territorial Expanse of the Pan-Grave culture thirty years later', *Sudan & Nubia* 21, 98-112.

Manzo, A. (with contributions by Alemseged Beldados, A. Carannante, D. Usai and V. Zoppi) 2012. *Italian Archaeological Expedition to the Sudan of the University of Naples 'L'Orientale'. 2011 Field Season*. Naples.

Marks, A. E. and R. Fattovich, 1989. 'The later prehistory of the Eastern Sudan: a preliminary view', in L. Krzyżaniak and M. Kobusiewicz (eds), *Late Prehistory of the Nile Valley and the Sahara*. Studies in African Archaeology 2. Poznań, 451-458.

Marks, A. E. and K. Sadr 1988. Holocene Environments and Occupations in the Southern Atbai, Sudan: A Preliminary Formulation, in J. Bower and D. Lubell (eds), *Prehistoric Cultures and Environments in the Late Quaternary of Africa.* BAR Int. Ser. 405, Cambridge Monographs in African Archaeology 26. Oxford, 69-90.

Näsr, C. 2012. 'Nomads at the Nile: Towards and Archaeology of Interaction', in H. Barnard and K. Duistermaat (eds), *The History of the Peoples of the Eastern Desert.* Cotsen Institute of Archaeology Monograph 73. Los Angeles, 81-89.

Nicoll, K. 2001. 'Radiocarbon chronologies for prehistoric human occupation and hydroclimatic change in Egypt and Northern Sudan', *Geoarchaeology: An International Journal* 16 (1), 47–64.

Nicoll, K. 2004. 'Recent environmental change and prehistoric human activity in Egypt and Northern Sudan', *Quaternary Science Reviews* 23, 561–580.

Nordström, H.-Å. 1972. *Neolithic and A-Group* Sites. Scandinavian Joint Expedition 3, 1-2. Uppsala

Paner, H. 2014. 'Kerma Culture in the Fourth Cataract of the Nile', in J. R. Anderson and D. A. Welsby (eds), *The Fourth Cataract and Beyond. Proceedings of the 12th International Conference for Nubian Studies.* British Museum Publications on Egypt and Sudan 1. Leuven – Paris – Walpole, MA, 53-79.

Paris, F., H. Barakat, and D. Laisney 2006. 'Les sépultures du wadi Gabgaba et du wadi Seiga dans la region du wadi Allaqi. Premiers résultats', in I. Caneva and A. Roccati (eds), *Acta Nubica. Proceedings of the X International Conference of Nubian Studies.* Rome, 189-196.

Phillips, J. and E. Klimaszewska-Drabot 2005. 'Saffi Island, 2004: An Overview of the Ceramics', *Gdańsk Archaeological Museum and Heritage Protection Fund African Reports* 4, 117-123.

Privati, B. 1999. 'La céramique de la nécropole orientale de Kerma (Soudan): essai de classification', *Cahier de Recherches de l'Institut de Papyrologie et d'Egyptologie de Lille* 20, 41-69.

Privati, B. 2004. 'Le matériel céramique', in C. Bonnet (ed.), *Le temple principal de la ville de Kerma et son quartier religieux.* Paris, 162-189.

Raue, D. 2012. 'Medja vs. Kerma at the First Cataract – Terminological Problems', in Forstner-Müller and Rose (eds), 48-58.

Riemer, H. 2004. 'News about the Clayton Rings: Long-distance Desert Travellers during Egypt's Predynastic', in S. Hendrickx, R. F. Friedman, K. M. Ciałowicz and M. Chłodnicki (eds), *Egypt and Its Origins. Studies in Memory of Barbara Adams.* Orientalia Lovaniensia Analecta 138. Leuven-Paris-Dudley, MA, 971-989.

Rzeuska, T. 2011. 'Grain, Water and Wine: Remarks on the Marl A3 Transport-Storage Jar from Middle Kingdom Elephantine', *Cahiers de la Céramique Egyptienne* 9, 461-530.

Robertson, R. 1991. 'The Late Neolithic Ceramics from Shaqadud Cave', in A. E. Marks and A. Mohammed-Ali (eds), *The Late Prehistory of the Eastern Sahel. The Mesolithic and Neolithic of Shaqadud, Sudan.* Dallas, 123-172.

Rose, P. 2012. 'Early 18th Dynasty Nubian Pottery from the Site of Sesebi, Sudan', in Forstner-Müller and Rose (eds), 13-29.

Ruffieux, P. and M. Suleiman Bashir, 2014. 'Preliminary report on some New Kingdom amphorae from the Korosko Road'. *Sudan & Nubia* 18, 44-46.

Sadr, K. 1987. 'The Territorial Expanse of the Pan-Grave Culture'. *Archéologie du Nil Moyen* 2, 265-291.

Sadr, K. 1990. The Medjay in Southern Atbai. *Archéologie du Nil Moyen* 4, 63-86.

Sadr, K. 1991. *The Development of Nomadism in Ancient Northeast Africa.* Philadelphia.

Sadr, K. 1994. 'Preliminary Report on the Archaeological Reconnaissance in the Eastern Desert, Southeast Egypt', in C. Bonnet (ed.), *Études Nubiennes. Conférence de Genève, Actes du VIIe Congrès international d'études nubiennes 3-8 septembre 1990, Vol. II.* Genève, 7-11.

Sadr, K. 1997. 'The Wadi Elei Finds: Nubian Desert Gold Mining in the 5th and 4th millennia BC?', in *Actes de la VIIIe Conférence Internationale des Études Nubiennes 1994, Vol. II.* (Cahier de Recherches de l'Institut de Papyrologie et d'Égyptologie de Lille 17/2). Lille, 67-76.

Sadr, K., A. Castiglioni and A. Castiglioni,1993. *Interim Report on the Eastern Desert Research Centre's (CeRDO) Archaeological Activities 1989/93,* Varese (unpublished report).

Sadr, K., A. Castiglioni and A. Castiglioni 1994. 'Archaeology in the Nubian Desert', *Sahara* 6, 69-75.

Sadr, K., A. Castiglioni and A. Castiglioni 1995, 'Nubian Desert Archaeology: a Preliminary View', *Archéologie du Nil Moyen* 7, 203-235.

Sadr K, A. Castiglioni and A. Castiglioni 2004. 'The Archaeological Sequence in the Nubian Desert: CeRDO's Explorations 1989-1994', in S. Wenig (ed.), *Neueste Feldforschungen im Sudan und in Eritrea. Akten des Symposiums vom 13. Bis 14. Oktober 1999 in Berlin.* (*Meroitica* 21). Wiesbaden, 191-204.

Salvatori, S. 2012. 'Disclosing Archaeological Complexity of the Khartoum Mesolithic: New Data at the Site and Regional Level'. *African Archaeological Review* 29, 399-472.

Säve-Söderbergh, T. (ed.). 1989. *Middle Nubian Sites.* Scandinavian Joint Expedition 4, 1-2. Partille.

Seidlmayer, S. J. 1991. 'Beispiele nubischer Keramik aus Kontexten des hohen Alten Reiches aus Elephantine', in D. Mendel and U. Claudi (eds), *Ägypten im afro-orientalischen Kontext. Aufsätze Archäologie, Geschichte und Sprache eines unbegrenzten Raumes. Gedenkschrift Peter Behrens.* Köln, 337-350.

Sidebotham, S. E., R. I. Thomas and J. A. Harrell 2010. 'The El-Kab and Nuri-Hamdab/Fourth Cataract Survey. January 2006', in Godlewski and Łatjar (eds), 77-110.

Śliwa, J. 1992. 'Die Siedlung des Mittlelren Reich bei Qasr el-Sagha', *Mitteilungen des Deutschen Archälogischen Instituts Abteilung Kairo* 48, 167-179.

Smith, S. T. 1992. 'Askut, Sudan,' *Bulletin de Liaison du Groupe International d'Etude de la Céramique Egyptienne* 16, 27-34.

Smith, S. T. 1995. *Askut in Nubia. The Economics and Ideology of Egyptian Imperialism in the Second Millennium BC.* London – New York.

Strouhal, E. 1982. 'Hand-made Pottery of the IVth to VIth centuries AD in the Dodecaschoinos', in J. M. Plumley (ed.), *Nubian Studies. Proceedings of the Symposium for Nubian Studies Cambridge 1970.* Warminster, 215-222.

Strouhal, E. 1984. *Wadi Qitna and Kalabsha-South. Late Roman-Early Byzantine Tumuli Cemeteries in Egyptian Nubia, Volume I – Archaeology.* Prague.

Updegraff, R. T. 1988. 'The Blemmyes I. The Rise of the Blemmyes and the Roman Withdrawal from Nubia under Diocletian', in H. Temporini (ed.), *Aufstieg und Niedergang der römischen Welt 2. Principat 10.1. Politische Geschichte (Provinzen und Randvölker: Afrika und Ägypten).* Berlin – New York, 44-106.

Vantini, G. 1975. *Oriental Sources Concerning Nubia.* Heidelberg-Warsaw.

Vila, A. 1987. *Le cimitière kermaïque d'Ukma Ouest.* Paris.

Welsby, D. A. 2001. *Life on the Desert Edge. Seven Thousand Years of Settlement in the Northern Dongola Reach, Sudan.* SARS Publication 7. London.

Welsby, D. A. 2008. 'The Merowe Dam Archaeological Salvage Project', in Godlewski and Łatjar (eds), 33-47.

Welsby Sjöström, I. 2001a. 'The Pottery from the Survey', in Welsby (ed.), 230-348.

Welsby Sjöström, I. 2001b. 'The Pottery from the Kerma Moyen graves at P37', in Welsby (ed.), 349-353.

Welsby Sjöström, I. 2018. 'The ceramic finds at H29', in D. A. Welsby (ed.), *A Kerma Ancien Cemetery in the Northern Dongola Reach. Excavations at Site H29*. SARS Publication 22. London, 71-115.

Wengrow, D. 2006. *The Archaeology of Early Egypt*. Cambridge.

Williams, M. A. J. 2009. 'Late Pleistocene and Holocene environments in the Nile basin', *Global and Planetary Change* 69, 1-15.

Winchell, F. 2013. *The Butana Group Ceramics and their Place in the Neolithic and Post-Neolithic of Northeast Africa*. BAR Int. Ser. 2459, Cambridge Monographs in African Archaeology 83. Oxford.

Wolf, P. 2004. 'The SARS Anglo-German Expedition at the Fourth Cataract of the Nile: the 2003/04 Season', *Sudan & Nubia* 8, 17-26.

Wodzińska, A. 2010. *A Manual of Egyptian Pottery. Volume 3: Second Intermediate Period-Late Period*. Boston.

Appendix 1. Table of concordance for the 'Unnamed' sites.

Name	Latitude	Longitude
U1	21° 02.967' N	32° 26.183' E
U2	21° 39.180' N	32° 24.233' E
U3	21° 14.810' N	32° 33.003' E
U4	21° 45.563' N	32° 16.435' E
U5	21° 40.072' N	32° 29.682' E
U6	21° 34.840' N	32° 30.148' E
U7	21° 45.563' N	32° 16.435' E
U8	21° 17.613' N	32° 32.717' E
U9	21° 14.792' N	32° 30.945' E
U10	21° 27.108' N	32° 42.325' E
U11	21° 44.088' N	32° 17.187' E
U12	20° 54.930' N	34° 13.230' E
U13	21° 17.772' N	32° 32.583' E
U14	20° 59.250' N	34° 02.283' E
U15	21° 33.695' N	32° 44.275' E
U16	21° 04.197' N	33° 44.739' E
U17	21° 16.502' N	32° 30.050' E
U18 Wadi Tonaidba	21° 16.190' N 21° 16.610' N	32° 41.190' E 32° 41.700' E
U19 Wadi Elei (upper)	21° 24.733' N	34° 35.633' E

9. Imported wares in the Sudanese Eastern Desert: finds from the CeRDO Survey 2004

Serena Massa

In February-March 2004 the Centro Ricerche sul Deserto Orientale (Research Centre on the Eastern Desert), directed by Alfredo and Angelo Castiglioni, carried out a new archaeological survey in the Sudanese Eastern Desert. The expedition started from Lake Nubia at Wadi Halfa, following an east-south-east direction to reach Jebel Umm Nabari and the gold-rich Wawat region.[1] During the survey, 67 sites were identified,[2] very distant from one other, between latitudes 19° 23' and 21° 44' North and between longitudes 31° 36' and 34° 59' East (Figures 9.1 and 9.2).

from any facilities. Therefore, the distribution map of the most numerous ceramic class, the late bag-shaped amphorae (Figure 9.25), is to be considered only as indicative of their presence, without quantitative interpretation. It seems anyway that, in general, the number of imported ceramics collected by CeRDO is not very different from the usual percentage of surface sherds dating to the Late Roman Period, between the 5th-7th centuries AD, attested in the Eastern Desert. Numbers of between 50-100 diagnostic fragments are considered normal in the Egyptian section of the desert (Sidebotham *et al.*

Figure 9.1. Satellite image of the study area (Landsat Copernicus, Google Earth 2017).

In addition to the prehistoric material and Eastern Desert Ware recovered by the expedition and presented in this volume by Andrea Manzo, a smaller group of ceramics, curated in the Castiglioni Museum in Varese, is formed of items imported from Late Antique Egypt and the Eastern Mediterranean. These comprise about 150 fragments, amongst which 67 diagnostic sherds have been photographed and, where significant, drawn.

The collection is the result of an unsystematic sampling of the surface sherds discovered along the expedition's itinerary, a methodology determined by understandable logistic factors implicit in a rapid survey over hundreds of kilometres far

2002, 190), like the predominance of amphorae in ceramic assemblages of that area (Tomber 2005, 56; 2018). The Sudanese part of the Eastern Desert, as compared to that in Egypt, is much less well investigated, not only as a result of environmental difficulties, but also because of the relatively limited interest of scholars in that region, far from the Nile and its monumental sites (Manzo 2017, 1). The maps of the Eastern Desert's population give detailed information about settlements and their different functions, water facilities, roads and itineraries connecting the sites with the Nile Valley and the Red Sea ports north of the area here under consideration, but sparse indications of the region south of the Egyptian frontier in the Roman and Byzantine periods (e.g. Barnard 2008, fig. 1-1,1-11; Lassányi 2010, fig. 18.1), with the exception of some mining sites, whose extremely low number is explained by the instability caused by the belligerent activities of the Blemmyes and, later, by the Christian kingdoms of Nobatia and Makuria (Klemm *et al.* 2001, fig. 16; Klemm

---

[1] Castiglioni and Castiglioni 2007.

[2] A preliminary analysis of the ceramics has been carried out by I. Caneva, M. C. Gatto, S. Giuliani and S. Lanna, who give also a functional/chronological sorting of the sites (CeRDO archive, unpublished report). The prehistoric ceramics have been subsequently published by Gatto and Lanna 2010; Gatto 2012.

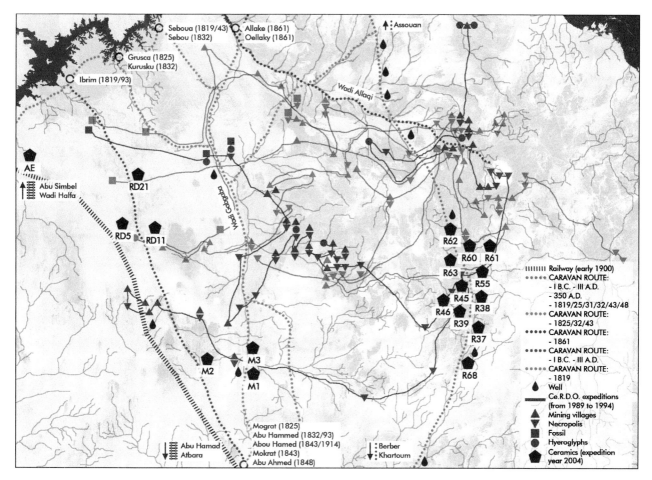

Figure 9.2. GIS elaboration of the study area with the geolocalization of the sites recorded by the CeRDO expeditions, as well as all the sites, oases, wells, wadis and details from ancient geographical maps with information about the trajectory of caravan routes and the location of old towns. From these sources combined, it emerges that the caravan routes followed the course of the wadis to avoid the obstacles presented by mountains along the route and passed near wells and oases that enabled survival in the desert (Ciusani et al. 2017).

and Klemm 2013, 15, figs 6.1, 7.7, 7.10). Regarding the ethnic Blemmyes, however, the considerations expressed by Dijkstra (2012) suggest a multifaceted demographic reality, including a variety of peoples living between the Red Sea and the Nile Valley, in a complex framework of tribal society and with differing relationships with the Roman Empire, not exclusively hostile in nature but rather, especially during the later Empire, involving alliances (Nappo 2018, 117).

The majority of the imported ceramics was recovered from mining sites, some of which have been identified as Egyptian mining settlements with houses formed by circular rooms (Mine 1, Mine 2, Mine 3) (Caneva *et al.* no date, 6-7). The mine sites R-37, 38, 39, 45, 55, 60, 61, 62, 63 and 68 are characterised by rectangular structures, as can be seen on satellite images, exemplified by Figure 9.3. Only at one site was such pottery found by a grave (R46);[3] one was a random find (AE) and a few were found by caves with rock art (RD5, RD11, RD21).[4]

The imported ceramics here considered can be divided into the following classes: amphorae, everyday wares – comprising a few examples of cooking pots and some closed forms, mainly designed to contain liquids – and fine wares. Their

provenance is summarised in the table below, as well as their association with the prehistoric/protohistoric and Eastern Desert Ware groups (Table 9.1).

Methodological approach

The general rarity of material evidence recovered in the study area underlines the importance of the information obtained from the morphological and technological analysis of the ceramics collected by the CeRDO expedition, which have been studied using the standard procedure (Nordström and Bourriau 1993; Ownby 2016; Defernez and Marchand 2016; Massa 2014; 2015).

Close attention has been paid to the application of all the appropriate analytical tools to extract historical information from the material, the main ones concerning the following topics, in addition to the obvious chronological data:

- origin of the material, to define areas of distribution and the relationships that the context of discovery indicates at a local, regional or international level,

- function of the ceramic objects in relation to the social and economic context of the site.

The typological analysis of the ceramic material has been accompanied by the systematic sampling of the different fabrics in which the morphological types occur, illustrated in

---

[3] The identification is recorded on the tags physically attached to the boxes in the Castiglioni Museum in Varese.

[4] The identification of the R-sites as mining settlements is recorded on the tags of the boxes in which the 2004 collection is kept in the Castiglioni Museum.

Figure 9.3: Mine Site R39.

TABLE 9.1. DISTRIBUTION OF THE DIFFERENT CERAMIC CLASSES OF THE CeRDO 2004 EXPEDITION.

Site	Function	Coordinates	Ceramic classes				
			Amphorae	Everyday Ware	Fine Ware	EDW	Prehistoric/ Protohistoric
AE	sporadic	21° 44.285' N 31° 36.025' E	•		•		
M1	mine	20° 09.822' N 33° 19.438' E	•	•			
M2	mine	20° 11.813' N 33° 20.272' E	•				
M3	mine	20° 13.677' N 33° 21.853' E	•	•			
R37	mine	20° 27.242' N 34° 56.823' E	•	•		•	
R38	mine	20° 41.265' N 34° 57.503' E				•	
R39	mine	20° 39.752' N 34° 54.577' E			•	•	
R45	mine	20° 52.063' N 34° 54.003' E	•		•	•	
R46	grave	20° 42.535' N 34° 50.028' E	•			•	•
R55	mine	20° 49.117' N 34° 59.243' E	•			•	
R57	mine	21° 03.765' N 35° 10.755' E	•				
R60	mine	21° 00.057' N 34° 58.245' E	•				•
R61	mine	20° 59.935' N 34° 57.567' E	•	•			•
R62	mine	20° 59.732' N 34° 57.433' E	•	•		•	
R63	mine	20° 59.773' N 34° 56.583' E					
R68	mine	20° 12.438' N 34 °53.022' E	•				•
RD5	rock art	21° 12.707' N 32° 19.957' E					•
RD11	rock art	21° 11.747' N 32° 36.355' E					
RD21	rock art	21° 36.125' N 32° 22.358' E			•		•
R10 12 13 14	mine	19° 23.268' N 34° 12.240' E					•

Figures 9.4 and 9.5. A synthesis of the graphic and photographic information is provided in Figure 9.6.

This documentation, although useful for broadening our knowledge of the material culture of the Sudanese Eastern Desert in Late Antiquity, certainly needs to be expanded with petrographic and chemical analyses, which, until now, have involved mostly prehistoric materials (a.o. Garcea 2006; Klein *et al.* 2004; Dal Sasso *et al.* 2014).

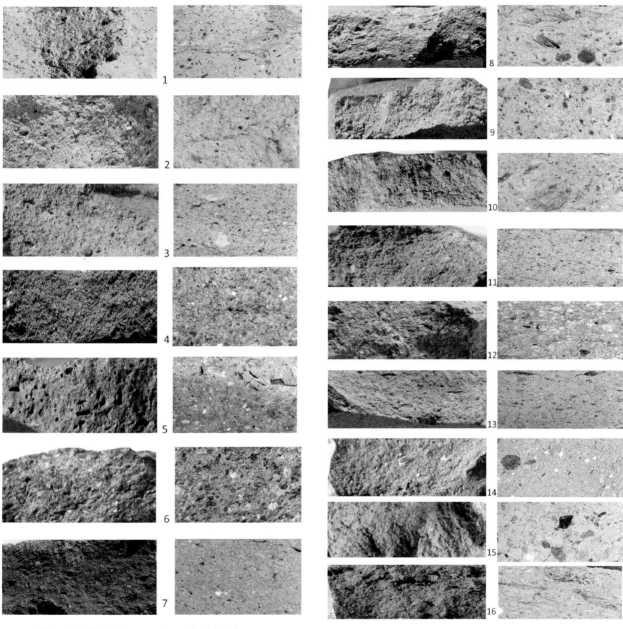

Figure 9.4. Fresh fractures of samples 1-7, left macro,
right digital microscope, 100x.[5]

Figure 9.5. Fresh fractures of samples 8-16, left macro,
right digital microscope, 100x.

The classification of Egyptian ceramics recovered in the Egyptian Eastern Desert relies on the "Vienna System" (Nordström and Bourriau 1993; Bourriau *et al.* 2000; Wodzińska 2010), which, however, classifies raw materials used in pottery manufacture dating not later than the New Kingdom. The fabrics are divided into two large groups, 'Nile silt' and 'marl clays', each with further subdivisions, while a source of kaolin clays is localised mainly at Aswan (Ownby 2012; 2016; Defernez and Marchand 2016 with previous references). Petrographic analyses of Nile clay of more recent date have been conducted on samples from Late-Napatan contexts (Carrano *et al.* 2009) and on Egyptian Red Slip wares from the 5th- 6th century AD North Tombs Settlement at Amarna (Pyke and Ownby 2016), highlighting the potential of the archaeometric investigations to define the relationships between productive

choices and function, but also the challenges to establishing specific provenance for both Nile and Marl clay pottery (Ownby 2016, 468). The problem is evidenced particularly from the existence of Nile silt fabrics apparently lacking the main distinctive elements, plant remains and limestone, documented at the North Tombs Settlement at Amarna on vessels with a cooking function (Pyke and Ownby 2016, 476). It is known that cooking wares in antiquity required advanced technology, exemplified by the Aegean production from the 4th century BC. The finer treatment of the Nile clay could be related to manufacturing advantages, but also to the imitation of imported items from the Eastern Mediterranean (see infra, fabric 9). Imitation is of particular interest not only for its economic or technical aspects, but also for its cultural meaning and social implications. However, a larger series of archaeometric investigations, with samples from well defined contexts in the different producing regions, is needed to address such an issue.

[5] I am grateful to Dr Filippo Airoldi, Laboratorio di Archeologia dell'Università Cattolica di Milano, for the photographic documentation.

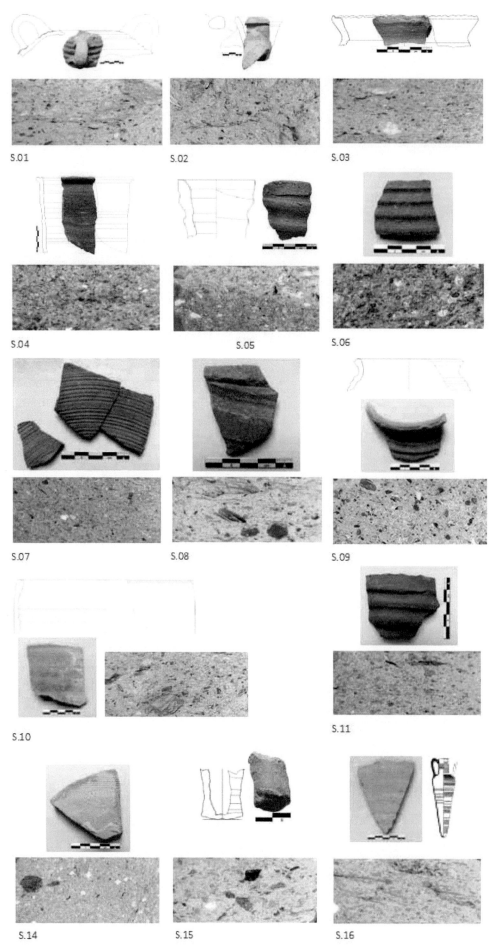

Figure 9.6. The 14 different fabrics and morphological types.

Description of the fabrics

Amphorae

Fabric 11

Sample 11
Very hard fabric
Colour
Reddish brown 5 YR 4/4, grey 5 YR 6/1, light grey 10 YR 7/1
Inclusions
Abundant small brown and grey inclusions of irregular shape and dimensions; sparser and small white

Figure 9.7. Fabric 11, sample 11 – Site R57.

Fabric 11 is attested by a fragment of neck with part of the handle, and by five wall sherds

Their shape can be attributed to the middle Eastern Late Roman Amphora 1 type (Pieri 2005, 69-84). Observing the details of the fragment of neck with handle, large and thick, a closer typological parallel can be made with examples typical of the 6th century AD (Reynolds 2014). The wall fragments, on the basis of their cylindrical shape, seem closer to types LRA 1A transitional or LRA 1B (Pieri 2005, 71, fig. 25). These details are important, as the production of LRA 1 covers a wide span of time, from the second half of the 4th until the 7th century AD, representing the most important and widespread commercial container of the Late Roman – early Byzantine period (Pieri 2005, 69).

The evolution of the body from a pear shape to a cylindrical one, allows these sherds to be dated between the late 5th – early 6th century AD for type LRA 1A transitional, and the 6th– mid 7th century AD for the type LRA 1B.

LRA 1 has a wide distribution in Egypt, a fact that has induced some authors to consider it as a product of that region. However, archaeometric investigations have indicated its origin in the Eastern Mediterranean, particularly Cyprus, Asia Minor, and northern Syria, but also the Black Sea coast. The debate on the Egyptian origin of LRA 1 is complicated by the existence of close imitations probably manufactured at Saqqara (Pieri 2005, 80-81) or in its area, which, however, are characterised by a red *engobe* covering the external surface; other kilns have been discovered at Ouyoun Mousa, on the western side of Sinai Peninsula, near Suez. A further production centre is hypothesised at Aswan, though the diffusion of the type in Egypt is considered quite small and limited to the sites of the Delta and the Nile Valley (Dixneuf 2011, 175-179).

Numerous examples of this amphora type also come from the Egyptian central desert sites (Tomber 1998, 170), from the Egyptian Eastern Desert (Lassányi 2010, 271; Meyer and Heidorn 2014, 72), from the southern Sudanese region of the Red Sea Hills (Magid *et al.* 1995, 169, pl. V,a), and from the Eastern Sudan and Lower Nubia (Manzo 2004, pl. VI, 1-2). As observed by Andrea Manzo, the association of this kind of imported pottery with Eastern Desert Ware indicates an extensive network of contacts between the desert inhabitants, along the tracks connecting Egypt with the Ethiopian plateau (Manzo 2004, 80). The identification of different morphological types of amphorae here analysed can add further evidence on the routes used to transport goods and foodstuffs of Mediterranean provenance. A different distribution, with a preference for maritime routes, is suggested by the scarcity of LRA 1 at Aksum and Adulis, where the bulk of imports is represented by Ayla-Aksum amphorae.

Both wine and oil have been postulated as having formed the contents of LRA 1, and particularly for Egypt also grain, an assumption based on the interpretation of some inscriptions bearing the Egyptian unit of weight used for solid substances. In any event, the thorough examination of literary sources and archaeological evidence discussed by Pieri (2005, 81-85) demonstrates that wine was the main commodity transported in these amphorae, while occasionally the containers could have been reused as storage vessels for different foods.

The fragment of a base from Site R45 (Figure 9.8) can be attributed to the late 6th and 7th centuries on account of its small module, classified by Pieri as LRA 1B and characterised by a beige fabric (Pieri 2005, 71, fig. 25; Reynolds 2014).

Figure 9.8. Late Roman Amphora 1.

Fabric 1

Sample 01
Very hard, finely granular fabric, external surface polished, internal smooth
Colour
Reddish yellow 5 YR 6/6; pink 5 YR 7/4; light red 2.5 YR 6/4
Inclusions
Abundant brown inclusions of different shapes and dimensions; more sparse and larger white

Fabric 1 is attested by late bag-shaped amphorae, which represent the dominant type in the CeRDO collection (Figure 9.25). It is characterised by ring handles on the shoulder and a sagging, globular body. These peculiarities allow us to identify fragments of ribbed walls with handles, either en-

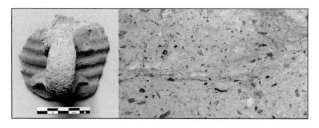

Figure 9.9. Fabric 1, sample 01 – Site M3.

tirely preserved (Site M3, Figure 9.9) or missing, except for the initial portion adhering to the shoulder (Sites AE, RD5, Figure 9.10). The surfaces look well fired to a reddish yellow (5YR6/6) or pink in section (5YR7/49). Observed under the digital stereo microscope, the fresh fracture shows abundant, small inclusions of brown colour and irregular shape, more

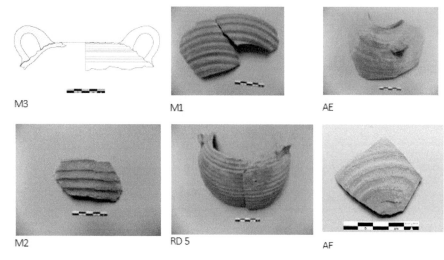

M3 M1 AE

M2 RD 5 AF

Figure 9.10. Late bag-shaped amphorae.

scattered larger white ones and smaller black elements (Figures 9.9 and 9.10).

In the absence of the diagnostic portions of the rim and base, it is not possible to better define the specific variant to which our fragments belong, but it is very probable that they can be assigned to the series typical of the late 5th to 7th centuries, possibly corresponding to the type 3 of the Pieri classification (2005, 119-121, fig. 76). The form is distinguished also by a round base without a foot: this morphology, together with the similarity of the fabric to the example from Site M3 that preserves the handle, allows us also to assign to this type fragments of bases recovered at Sites AE, M1 and M2 (Figure 9.10).

The problem of the origin of this amphora type is complex, as its production centres are very numerous and scattered over a vast geographic area, as are the centres of consumption in both the western and eastern regions of the Late Roman and Early Byzantine world.

Further, other difficulties are posed by the heterogeneity of the clays used for its fabrication. If Judea can be considered the main producing region, products of the monasteries of northern Egypt outside of the Nile Delta are similar to this type, and are considered true copies of the originals but smaller, and characterised by the distinct Nile silt fabric. Production complexes have been identified at Abou Mina, in the Libyan Desert, near Lake Mariout, and at Alexandria.

The phenomenon of imitation of imported Levantine and Aegean amphorae in Egypt seems to date to the beginning of amphora-production in Egypt, in parallel with the introduction of new trade networks starting in the 4th century BC (Defernez and Marchand 2012, 133), and other technology imports from the Aegean world related to the mining process in the Ptolemaic period (Klemm and Klemm 2013, 14).

Thanks to recent archaeological projects carried out in the Delta and on the coast of the Sinai Peninsula, with the aid of archaeometric analyses it has been possible to characterise the Egyptian fabrics locally reproducing the Levantine prototypes at Tell el-Herr in the early Ptolemaic period (Defernez and Marchand 2012). The same fabric is utilized also for the production of different table vessels. Another group of transport amphorae at Tell el-Herr copies Aegean types, with a fabric similar to that used for the Levantine ones. Amphorae produced with these two kinds of fabric, as well as at Tell el-Herr, are also well represented in Egypt, from Alexandria to Coptos and Thebes along the Nile Valley, and also in the Eastern Desert at Berenice and surrounding area.

In the course of the 3rd century BC the morphological assimilation reveals a strong preference for the south-eastern Aegean style, and the Egyptian amphorae inventory imitates the commonest imported containers from Knidos, Rhodes and Chios. The identification of the provenance, in the absence of archaeometric analyses, is complicated further by the export of amphorae produced with Nile silt clay to the Levant (Reynolds 2013, 100). At this level of investigation, the only possible indication derives from the observed absence of plant remains (or their voids left after firing) and micas, abundant in the amphorae of this type produced in Egypt (Dixneuf 2011, 142-153), which together with the morphological details should point to a Levantine origin.

The primary commodity exported in this type of container was wine, produced in Palestine and also in the monasteries of north-western Egypt, but the absence of any trace of pitch on our fragments could suggest a content other than wine, as attested in Rabbinic texts, where beside wine also oil, dry figs and fish sauce are mentioned. It has to be considered, however, that traces of pitching are best preserved under humid conditions, as attested by numerous findings in wreck contexts, while pitch rarely survives on land (Pieri 2005, 125). Further, chemical analyses have identified different contents in pitched examples, for example fish sauce or different treatments due to their reuse, documented also by papyri dating from the Hellenistic to Byzantine periods (Gallimore 2010, 160; Lawall 2011, 25, 130). A number of papyri refer to the supply of grain and fodder to the quarries between the Nile and the Red Sea (Baker 2017).

Fabric 6

Sample 06
Very hard and compact fabric
Colour
Dark grey 5 YR 4/1
Inclusions
Abundant irregular black inclusions; moderate white with angular shape.

Figure 9.11. Fabric 6, sample 06 – Site M3.

Fabric 6 is associated with the series of Late Roman bag-shaped amphora, whose dark reduced grey colour indicates a specific product within the Palestinian bag-shaped amphora group (Hayes 1976, 117; Pieri 2005, 118-119).

It is the reduced-fired amphorae that were manufactured in various centres in the region south of Lake Tiberias and particularly in the city of Beth Shan-Beisan (Scythiopolis); other possible ateliers can be located in the Jordan Valley.

It has a very hard, reduced, dark grey-black fabric and it is typically decorated with white painted loops and horizontal lines. Some variants have a marked ridge separating the shoulder from the upper body, as in the fragment from Site M3.

Largely distributed in the Eastern Mediterranean between the 5th and the 7th century AD, it continued to be produced into the first half of the 8th century AD, during the Ummayad period. Its content was the excellent wine of the Beisan region, very much appreciated for its sweetness and lightness, as we learn from textual references to wine production in the Ummayad period (Pieri 2005, 124, 126).

Fragments from Sites M1 and M3, from two vessels, can be assigned to this type.

Fabric 7

Sample 07
Fine and compact fabric
Colour
Reddish brown 5 YR 4/4, dark reddish brown 2.5 YR 4/6, reddish brown 5 YR 4/4
Inclusions
Sparse sub-angular white and irregular grey; sparse and thin voids.

Fabric 7 is probably related to the Late Roman bag-shaped

Figure 9.12. Fabric 7, sample 07 – Site R62.

amphorae of type 4 (Pieri 2005, 121) on the basis of the characteristics of the clay: very compact and fine with a dark red-brown surface. The fragments come from close to the base, which had to be rounded or have a small 'button', peculiarities which also suggest the attribution to that type, produced in Egypt during the 7th century AD. The production of this amphora in the area of Abu Mina and in the Mareotis region is frequently associated with viticulture and wine processing facilities like presses (Pieri 2005, 126).

However, since the portion of the preserved fragments is very small, one cannot exclude an attribution to a type of cooking pot characterised by a ribbed base, similar to those in use, for example, in the settlement contexts of phase 5 at the site of the Shabaka Treasure at Karnak, dated to the early imperial period (Licitra and David 2016, 95-96, fig. 43 n. 193), and more frequently recurring at Abu Mina in deposits of the 5th-7th century (Engemann 2016, 31-32, taf. 17 Nr. C 58).

Fabric 14

Sample 14
Very hard, compact and fine fabric
Colour
Pink 5 YR 8/4, light brown 5 YR 6/4, Pink 5 YR 8/4
Inclusions
Moderate small white inclusions; sparse round and elongated brown inclusions; occasionally large and sparse voids.

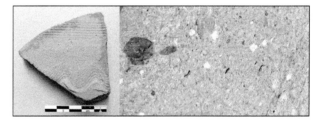

Figure 9.13. Fabric 14, sample 14 – Site R68.

Fabric 14 is probably from amphorae of type LRA 2, C variant of Pieri's classification (Pieri 2005, 88-89). It is characterised by an incised comb decoration with wavy pattern, similar to the example from Saraçhane dated to the 7th - 8th century AD, which shows parallels also in the fabric description: "Clean breaking drab brown to pinkish – red fabric, fired buff or light brownish at surface, with some large lime inclusions (causing eruptions) and occasional flakes of golden mica (biotite)" (Hayes 1992, type 32, 71, fig. 23.13). The type is also present in Cyrenaica and Zeugitana in the 6th - 7th centuries (Riley 1979, 233, fig. 94, n. 380).

The great heterogeneity of capacity as well as of rim shape and the lack of studies on production sites limit the possibility to identify specific production centres. This type of amphora probably originated in the Levant but also, later, in north Africa, southern Italy and Spain (Pieri 2005, 89).

Uncertainties also exist regarding the contents of the LRA 2 amphorae. According to some scholars it was oil, as evident for example in the oil production site of Pefkochori, where the wavy-pattern decoration is attested between the second half of the 6th and the beginning of the 7th centuries (Vasiliou and Tsigarida 2014, 726).

Other examples, like those from the Yassi Ada shipwreck, show traces of pitch, reflecting the transport of wine at the time of the sinking (Pieri 2005, 93).

The incised decoration is documented also on examples of Late Amphora 5/6 produced in the Nile Valley, yet with alluvial fabric apparently different from our fragment (Ballet and Picon 1987, 39-40, fig. 5.2), at Abu Mina (Engemann 2016, 80, taf. 151, F 391).

Fabric 16

Sample 16
Very hard fabric
Colour
Pink 5 YR 7/4, reddish yellow 5 YR 7/5, light reddish brown 5 YR 6/4
Inclusions
Sparse brown rounded inclusions of different dimensions, generally small; some thin elongated voids.

Figure 9.14. Fabric 16, sample 16 – Site R55.

Fabric 16 is tentatively attributed to a fusiform type of amphora, due to the inclination of the surviving wall fragment. The characteristic of the texture, its colour and inclusions cannot be assigned to the Egyptian biconical container known as LRA 7, produced with the typical chocolate brown clay of the Nile Valley.

Possibly the fragment is a portion of a LRA 9/Agorà M334 amphora, distributed in small amounts around the Mediterranean, more frequently in the eastern part, between the 5th and the early 8th century AD. Its origin is thought to be in Syria (Pieri 2005, 137-138) and particularly in northern Palestine, and was probably used to transport wine (Williams 2014).

Another parallel is possible with the Kuzmanov 9 type, dated to the 4th - 5th century AD and quite common, around the Black Sea coast, at Byzantium, Bodrum, Ephesus and in Syria, Lebanon and Egypt. The nature of its contents is unknown but wine has been suggested (Williams 2014).

Everyday wares

Fabric 2

Sample 02
Compact hard fabric, slip on exterior, on the interior covering only the rim
Colour
Reddish brown 2.5 YR 5/4 (slip); light reddish brown 2.5 YR 7/4; light reddish brown 2.5 YR 7/4
Inclusions
Sparse, large inclusions of angular quartz and rounded limestone; abundant small and irregular grey and black elements; sparse voids.

Fabric 2 occurs as a sherd from a one-handled flagon from

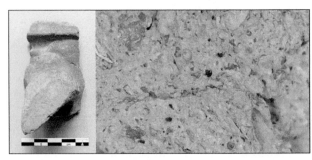

Figure 9.15. Fabric 2, sample 02 – Site AE (drawing scale 1:4).

Site AE, which finds a close parallel in the Early Roman 64 type of the Wodzińska classification, from Mons Claudianus. It is dated to the 2nd century AD or later (Wodzińska 2010, 98).

Fabric 5

Sample 05
Very hard fabric
Colour
Reddish brown 5 YR 5/4, dark grey 5 YR 4/1, reddish brown 5 YR 5/4
Inclusions
Sparse and irregular white inclusions; abundant voids of irregular shape, possibly of vegetal origin.

Figure 9.16. Fabric 5, sample 05 – Site R37 (drawing scale 1:4).

Fabric 05 is attested by a fragment of rim from a closed form with the function of a liquid container. The characteristic ribbing of the neck is similar to that present on jugs documented at Elephantine, in contexts dated to the 4th-5th century AD (Gempeler 1992, 141, Abb. 79, 7-8).

Fabric 10

Sample 10
Porous fabric
Colour
Yellowish red 5 YR 5/6, pink 5 YR 7/6, pink 5 YR 7/6
Inclusions
Abundant small brown inclusions; sparser angular quartz(?).

Fabric 10 is attested by a fragment of rim decorated with fine parallel incisions on the external edge, for which no convincing parallels have been found.

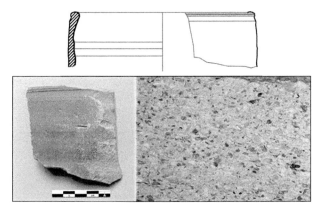

Figure 9.17. Fabric 10, sample 10 – Site M1 (drawing scale 1:4).

Fabric 3

Sample 03
Compact, fine fabric
Colour
Light reddish brown 2.5 YR 6/4, reddish yellow 5 YR 7/6, Light reddish brown 2.5 YR 6/4
Inclusions
Sparse, small and irregular limestone inclusions; sparse and irregular brown.

Figure 9.18. Site R61, Cooking pot, Wodzinska type
Late Roman 39 (drawing scale 1:4).

Fabric 3 occurs on a fragment of vessel similar to the cooking pots with lid-seated rim and applied strip known at Ashmunein (Bailey 1996, 65, fig. 20, n. 40, levels dated to the first half of the 5th century, before the construction of the South Church) and Shenshef and dated to the Late Roman period (type Late Roman 39, Wodzińska 2010, 203; Tomber 1998, 170). This type of cooking pot is also frequent at Elephantine in 5th century deposits (Gempeler 1992, 160, Abb. 93, 1-6).

Fabric 4

Sample 04
Finely granular, very hard fabric
Colour
Dark reddish brown 5 YR 3/2, red 2.5 YR 5/6, red 2.5 YR 5/6
Inclusions
Moderate angular quartz; sparse white and black, irregular inclusions.

Fabric 4 is represented by a ribbed element, which finds a close parallel in pipe items from Abu Mina, dated to the 8th century but manufactured with a different fabric, typical of the ateliers of the town (Engemann 2016, 112, taf. 227 nr. H 286). Other parallels are also possible with *saqiya* pots from the well assemblage excavated at Tell Basta, produced in the 3rd-4th century AD (Mamedow 2013, 410, 417-418), and with canalisation elements like those in use at Tôd during the 4th-9th centuries, which, however, are covered mainly with a

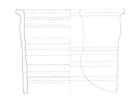

Figure 9.19. Fabric 4, sample 04 – Site M3 (drawing scale 1:4).

white *engobe* (Lecuyot and Pierrat-Bonnefois 2004, 168-169, pl. 7, figs 92-96). It is probable that this pipe element/*saqiya* could be related to the washing system used to process gold, in particular the mechanism for the recycling of water. This hypothesis fits well with the find-context, one of the largest mine settlements of the explored area, the Omar Khabash mine, with its numerous multi-room houses, some built with an accurate mason's technique, consisting of a central core of quartz and sand with two outer bands of granite blocks. Three kinds of Egyptian mine have been recognised in the complex: mines for alluvial gold digging, for superficial quartz veins, and for deep quartz veins, digging by means of galleries and wells (Castiglioni *et al.* 1995, 184, C50; Caneva *et al.* no date, 6-7). The presence of late antique and Islamic pottery, like the proximity of an Islamic cemetery, indicates the continuity of frequentation/exploitation also in later periods.

Fabric 9

Sample 09
Compact, hard fabric
Colour
Reddish brown 5 YR 5/4, pink 5 YR 7/4, reddish yellow 7.5 YR 6/6
Inclusions
Abundant brown and grey inclusions of irregular shape and dimensions; sparser white.

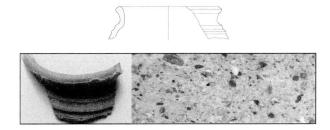

Figure 9.20. Fabric 9, sample 09 – Site M3 (drawing scale 1:4).

Fabric 9 is documented by a fragment of cooking pot which can be closely paralleled by examples from the North Tombs Settlement at Amarna (5th– 6th century AD), very interesting because it introduces a variant of Nile silt fabric distinguished by a refined Nile clay either naturally or intentionally levigated, with no limestone or plant remains added to the paste (Pyke and Ownby 2016, 476, fig. 1.10). Nonetheless, the similarity of our fabric 9 to fabric 1, poses the question of the possible import of other categories of vessel, besides late bag-shaped amphorae, and from the same production workshop. The specialised cooking function of this pot also raises interesting questions about the social context in which it was used.

Ampulla

Sample 15
Finely granular, thin walled fabric
Colour
Light brown 7.5 YR 6/4, pink 5 YR 7/4, light red 2.5 YR 6/4
Inclusions
Abundant and irregular brown inclusions; sparse and large black and white.

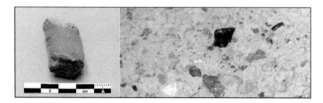

Figure 9.21. Sample 15 – Site M1.

This vessel type was represented by a single sherd from a small container attributable to the fusiform series known as Late Roman *unguentarium*, and similar to the type Hayes 1971, fig. 1. The example from Mine 1 is characterised by a micaceous fabric similar to LR A3 (Hayes 2008, 117), with evident signs of wheel manufacture. The type is widely documented in the whole Eastern Mediterranean between the late 5th- 7th century AD. Considering the uniformity of the fabric, Hayes assumed a single source, probably in Palestine or Jordan, and the possible content of these small flasks as sanctified oil, also on the basis of Christian monograms or inscriptions present on some examples (Hayes 1971, 246). Later studies, with the aid of mineralogical and petrographic analyses, have documented the existence of local production in Turkey, Northern Syria and Cyprus (Lochner *et al.* 2005). The specialised function of this vessel, related to its precious contents, if not of religious origin, certainly consisting of some rare essence, provides a clue on the social context and who might have made use of it, like the rare examples of fine ware presented below.

Fine wares

The category of fine wares is attested only by three examples which, on the basis of fabric, shape and surface treatment, cannot be classified in any of the fine ware productions of the Levant or North Africa. However, they are slipped and manufactured with a fine clay, characteristics which, together with the shape, reveal their function as tableware.

From Site R39 was collected a fragment of rim with carinated wall from a dish (Figure 9.22 dia. 32cm), manufactured with a fine pinkish clay and red slip, similar to an example documented at Ashkelon (Johnson 2008, 20, fig. 57), dated to the 1st - 2nd century AD, and to a vessel from the Ptolemaic deposits of the Temple of Ptah at Karnak, dated between the second half of the 2nd century BC and before the be-

Figure 9.22. Dish – Site R39 (drawing scale 1:4).

ginning of the Roman period, pertinent to the production with calcareous fabric of the Theban region (David 2016, 50-51, fig. 3.1).

The vessel found at site AE (Figure 9.23, dia. 28cm), broken *in situ* into numerous conjoining fragments, is made from a friable and flaky clay of pinkish colour, on the surface of which traces of a red-brown slip are barely visible. It is not classifiable as Terra Sigillata, but as an imitation of it, specifically of the bowl type Hayes 80B/99, produced in African Red Slip Ware, fabric D², and dated to the 5th century AD (Hayes 1972, 154; Carandini and Tortorella 1980, 105; Mackensen 1993, 406). Imitations of form Hayes 99 are known, for example, at Elephantine, where they occur, quite frequently, in deposits dated between the second quarter of the 5th and the 7th century (Gempeler 1992, 96, Abb 39, 12).

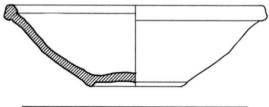

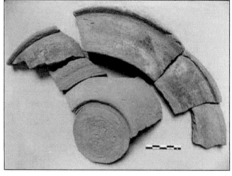

Figure 9.23. Bowl – Site AE (drawing scale 1:4).

From Site RD 21 comes a ledged bowl with ring base and inturned rim, preserved in four conjoining fragments which gives a complete profile (Figure 9.24, dia. 17cm). The fabric is very fine and hard fired, with a red-brown slip. A parallel is possible with examples from Mons Claudianus, which however, have a different shaped wall, rounded and not sharply carinated (Wodzińska 2010, 142, ER 207), dated to the Trajanic period. In general the form repeats well known models, starting from Italian Sigillata (form Dragendorff 24/25), but it is closer to the latest type of flanged bowl Hayes 91D, African Red Slip Ware, dated to the 7th century AD.

Closer parallels for the sharp profile of the wall can be

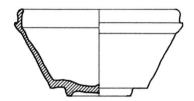

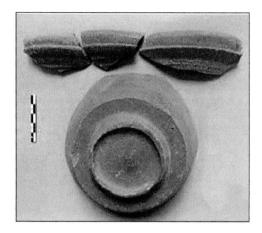

Figure 9.24. Ledge-rimmed bowl – Site RD1 (drawing scale 1:4).

found at Elephantine (Gempeler 1992, 124, Abb. 71 n. 7-8), also considered a late evolution from the Terra Sigillata prototypes and present in deposits dated to the 3rd-4th century.

Concluding remarks

From the vastness of the late ancient Eastern Desert of Sudan, and recovered from its less explored areas, (preserved to our knowledge until a few years ago but today devastated by the new gold rush; De Benetti *et al.* 2014; Brun *et al.* 2018, 2), the material documents presented here offer valuable information on the following aspects:

- *chronology*: together with the Eastern Desert Ware, the Mediterranean amphorae dating from the late 5th to the 7th century AD, common ceramics and fine tableware of the middle and late imperial age, attest to the continuity of activity/frequentation at the mining settlements of the Sudanese Eastern Desert until at least the 7th century AD, a period which is considered to be almost without archaeological evidence. It is generally believed that in Roman times, due to the increasing belligerence of the Blemmyes, there was a decline in mining activity in Nubia, in parallel with the contraction of mining operations in some districts close to roads and water stations already established in the Ptolemaic era in the Egyptian Eastern Desert. In the late ancient and Byzantine periods, gold mining is considered to have been possible only in the vicinity of fortified roads (Klemm and Klemm 2013, 609-616, fig. 7.9);

- *routes by which goods travelled*: the opportunity to identify different types of ribbed amphorae, in addition to the LRA 1, makes it possible to recognize links with better-defined production areas, whose commodities arrived in the Eastern Desert of Sudan more probably via caravan routes connected to the Nile Valley rather than the coast: further south, along the Red Sea, in the port of Adulis there are very few examples of LRA 1 or transport containers different from the Ayla-Aksum type;

- *identity of the consumers*: assumed from the existence of foodstuffs and ceramic types of late Roman custom such as wine and fine tableware. Alongside the presence of local populations, revealed by the decorative tradition of the Eastern Desert Ware, there are "international" cultural traits, which perhaps indicate the presence of people of different origins, or the assimilation by local parties of Mediterranean fashions;

- *social complexity and function of settlements*: the fine tableware ceramics and specialized containers such as the ampulla found

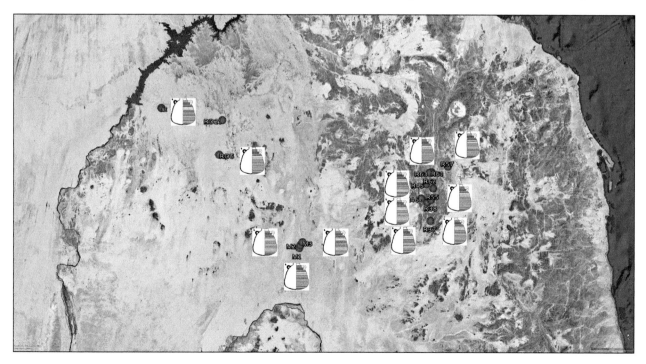

Figure 9.25. Distribution of the late bag-shaped amphorae in the area of study, Sudanese Eastern Desert Sites AE, M1, M2, M3, R45, R46, R57, R60, R62, R63, R68 and RD5.

in mines R39, R45 and M1 and the wine amphorae probably of eastern Mediterranean origin in mines M3, M1, RD5 and R55 (Figures 9.2 and 9.25), may be a further indicator of the social stratification of the communities that in the late ancient and early medieval periods populated the Eastern Desert of Sudan.

As has been noted regarding the Egyptian part of the Eastern Desert, the existence of overseas imported goods, though minor compared to the products from the Nile Valley, probably reflects the presence of high-ranking people in settlements with a function other than a commercial one, relating perhaps to the mining sites or military garrisons (Tomber 2018, 29).

Despite the limits of the documentation here analysed (due, as already mentioned, to the surface provenance and non-systematic collection of the materials), it is nevertheless the case that the collection adds a further useful component to knowledge not only of the Sudanese Eastern Desert, but more generally of the relations between this area, the Nile Valley, the Mediterranean and the Red Sea, highlighting a variegated panorama in which, next to transport containers of probable Mediterranean origin, there are amphorae and tableware of Egyptian production. For these, as yet, in the absence of archaeometric analysis, it is not possible to define a determined atelier among the multiple productive centres of the region, which were active for a long time but are mostly still little known (David 2016, 2).

On this first analysis, the products from the late Roman / Byzantine period of the workshops of Middle Egypt, characterized by strongly micaceous alluvial brown clays (Ballet *et al.* 1991, 134), which would be the closest to the area examined in terms of convenience of supply, are not represented in the CeRDO collection.

Once again, the need for a systematic use of archaeometric analysis has to be underlined, in order to go beyond the level of typological and functional description of ceramic artefacts within generic production areas. It is essential to arrive at a firm determination of the ateliers, whose products can be characterized from a physical-chemical point of view and articulated in chronological phases. This work should be accompanied by similar investigations in the consumer sites, to define the real extent and the relative weight of local productions and imports over time.

Bibliography

Bailey, D. M. 1996. 'The pottery from the South Church at El-Ashmunein', *Cahiers de la céramique égyptienne* 4, 47-112.

Baker, B. 2017. *Shifting Centres of Production: the Amphorae Assemblages at Mons Porphyrites and Bir Umm Fawakir.* Chapel Hill.

Ballet, P., F. Mamhoud, M. Vichy and M. Picon 1991. 'Artisanat de la céramique dans l'Égypte romaine tardive et byzantine. Prospections d'ateliers de potiers de Minia à Assouan', *Cahiers de la céramique égyptienne* 2, 129-144.

Ballet, P. and M. Picon 1987. 'Recherches préliminaires sur les origines de la céramique des Kellia (Égypte). Importations et productions égyptiennes', *Cahiers de la céramique égyptienne* 1, 17-48.

Barnard, H. 2008. *Eastern Desert Ware: Traces of the inhabitants of the Eastern Deserts in Egypt and Sudan during the 4th-6th Centuries CE.* BAR Int. Ser. 1824. Oxford.

Bourriau, J. D., P. T. Nicholson and P. J. Rose 2000. 'Pottery', in P. T. Nicholson and I. Shaw (eds), *Ancient Egyptian Materials and Technology.* Cambridge, 121-147.

Brun, J.-P., T. Faucher, B. Redon and S. Sidebotham 2018. *Le désert oriental d'Égypte durant la période gréco-romaine : bilans archéologiques.* Nouvelle édition [en ligne]. Paris. (généré le 15 avril 2019) : <http://books.openedition.org/cdf/4932>.

Caneva, I., M. C. Gatto, S. Giuliani and S. Ianna. no date. *Ce.R.D.O. Survey 2004 Eastern Desert, Sudan. Preliminary report of the pottery collection.* Unpublished, CeRDO Archive.

Carandini, A. and S. Tortorella 1980. *Ceramica fine romana nel Bacino mediterraneo (medio e tardo Impero).* Enciclopedia dell'arte antica classica e orientale. Atlante delle forme ceramiche, I. Roma.

Carrano, J. L., G. H. Girty and C. J. Carrano 2009. 'Re-examining the Egyptian colonial encounter in Nubia through a compositional, mineralogical, and textural comparison of ceramics', *Journal of Archaeological Science* 36, 785-797.

Castiglioni, A. and A. Castiglioni 2007. 'Les pistes millénaires du désert oriental de la Nubie', *Bulletin de la Société Française d'Égyptologie* 169-170, 17-49.

Castiglioni, A., A. Castiglioni and J. Vercoutter 1995. *L'Eldorado dei Faraoni. Alla scoperta di Berenice Pancrisia.* Novara.

Ciusani, G., N. Russo and B. Casiraghi 2017. *Le miniere d'oro dei faraoni : conservazione, tutela e valorizzazione del sito. Testi di Laurea.* Politecnico di Milan.
https://www.politesi.polimi.it/handle/10589/135752

Dal Sasso, G., L. Maritana, S. Salvatori, C. Mazzoli and G. Artioli 2014. 'Discriminating pottery production by image analysis: a case study of Mesolithic and Neolithic pottery from Al Khiday (Khartoum, Sudan)', *Journal of Archaeological Science* 46, 125-143.

David, R. 2016. 'Céramiques Ptolémaïques de la Région Thébaine. Actes de la Table Ronde de Karnak Les 28 et 29 Septembre 2014', *Cahiers de la céramique égyptienne* 10.

De Benetti, M., M. Grassini and P. Nannini 2014. 'A Berenice sulle orme dei Castiglioni', *Archeologia Viva* 163, 48-53.

Defernez, C. and S. Marchand 2016. 'État actuel de la recherche sur l'industrie amphorique Égyptienne des IVE-IIIE siècles av. J.-C.', in B. Bader, C. M. Knoblauch and E. C. Köhler (eds), *Vienna 2 – Ancient Egyptian Ceramics in the 21st Century: proceedings of the International Conference held at the University of Vienna, 14th-18th of May, 2012.* Orientalia Lovaniensia Analecta 245. Leuven – Paris – Bristol, CT, 127-154.

Dijkstra, J. H. F. 2012. 'Blemmyes, Noubades and the Eastern Desert in Late Antiquity: Reassessing the Written Sources', in H. Barnard and K. Duistermaat (eds), *The History of the Peoples of the Eastern Desert.* Cotsen Institute of Archaeology Monograph 73. Los Angeles, 238-247.

Dixneuf, D. 2011. *Amphores égyptiennes. Production, typologie, contenu et diffusion (IIIe siècle avant J.-C. – IXe siècle après J.-C.).* Études Alexandreines 22. Paris.

Engemann, J. 2016. *Abū Mīnā VI. Die Keramikfunde von 1965 bis 1988.* Deutsches Archäologisches Institut Abteilung Kairo, Archäologische Veröffentlichungen 111. Wiesbaden.

Gallimore, S. 2010. 'Amphora Production in the Roman World. A view from the Papyri', *Bulletin of the American Society of Papyrologists* 47, 155-184.

Garcea, E. A. A. 2006. 'Pottery making processes at Esh Shaheinab, Sudan', in K. Kroeper, M. Chlodnicki and M. Kobusiewicz (eds), *Archaeology of early Northeastern Africa: in memory of Lech Krzyżaniak.* Studies in African Archaeology 9. Poznań, 99-112.

Gatto, M. C. 2012. 'The Holocene Prehistory of the Nubian Desert', in H. Barnard and K. Duistermaat (eds), *The History of the Peoples of the Eastern Desert.* Cotsen Institute of Archaeology Monograph 73. Los Angeles, 42-57.

Gatto, M. C. and S. Lanna 2010. 'Prehistoric human occupation in the Nubian Eastern Desert: an overview', in W. Godlewski and A. Łajtar (eds), Between the Cataracts. Proceedings of the 11th Conference of Nubian Studies 2/1. Warsaw, 319-328.

Gempeler, R. D. 1992. *Elephantine X. Die Keramik römischer bis früharabischer Zeit.* Deutsches Archäologisches Institut Abteilung Kairo, Archäologische Veröffentlichungen 43. Mainz am Rhein.

Hayes, J. W. 1971. 'A new type of early Christian ampulla', *The Annual of the British School at Athens* 66, 243-248.

Hayes, J. W. 1972. *Late Roman Pottery.* London.

Hayes, J. W. 1976. 'Pottery: Stratified Groups and Typology', in J. H. Humphrey (ed.), *Excavations at Carthage 1975 conducted by the University of Michigan.* 1. Michigan, 47-123.

Hayes, J. W. 1992. *Excavations at Saraçhane in Istanbul, 2. The Pottery.* Dumbarton Oaks.

Hayes, J. W. 2008. *The Athenian Agora vol. XXXII. Roman pottery: Fine ware imports.* Princeton, NJ.

Johnson, B. L. 2008. *Ashkelon 2: Imported Pottery of the Roman and Late Roman Periods.* Winona Lake.

Klein, M., F. Jesse, H. U. Kasper and A. Gölden 2004. 'Chemical characterization of ancient pottery from Sudan by x-ray fluorescence spectrometry (xrf), electron microprobe analyses (empa) and inductively coupled plasma mass spectrometry (ICP–MS)', *Archaeometry* 46, 339-356.

Klemm, R. and D. Klemm. 2013. *Gold and Gold Mining in Ancient Egypt and Nubia. Geoarchaeology of the Ancient Gold Mining Sites in the Egyptian and Sudanese Eastern Deserts.* Heidelberg – New York – Dordrecht – London.

Klemm, D., R. Klemm and A. Murr 2001. 'Gold of the Pharaohs – 6000 years of gold mining in Egypt and Nubia', *Journal of African Earth Sciences* 33, 643-659.

Lanno, S. and M. Gatto 2010. 'Prehistoric human occupation in the Nubian Eastern Desert : an overview', in W. Godlewski and A. Łajtar (eds), *Between the Cataracts. Proceedings of the 11th Conference of Nubian Studies, Warsaw University, 27 August – 2 September 2006. Part 2, fasc.1: session papers.* Warsaw, 319-328.

Lassányi, G. 2010. 'Pottery', in U. Luft (ed.), *Bi'r Minayh. Report on the Survey 1998-2004.* Budapest, 271-290.

Lawall, M. L. 2011. 'Socio-Economic Conditions and the Contents of Amphorae', in C. Tzochev, T. Stoyanow and A. Bozkova (eds), *Patabs II. Production and Trade of Amphorae in the Black Sea. Acts of the International Round Table held in Kiten, Nessebar and Sredetz, September 26-30, 2007.* Sofia, 23-33.

Lecuyot, G. and G. Pierrat-Bonnefois 2004. 'Corpus de la céramique de Tôd Fouilles 1980-1983 et 1990', *Cahiers de la céramique égyptienne* 7, 145-210.

Licitra, N. and R. David 2016. 'L'évolution des céramiques ptolémaïques à Karnak d'après la documentation du Trésor de Chabaka', in R. David (ed.), *Céramiques Ptolémaïques de la Région Thébaine. Actes de la Table Ronde de Karnak Les 28 et 29 Septembre 2014. Cahiers de la céramique* égyptienne 10, 77-122.

Lochner, S., R. Sauer and R. Linke 2005. 'Late Roman Unguentaria? - A contribution to early Byzantine wares from the view of Ephesus', in J. M. Gurt Esparraguera, J. Buxeda i Garrigós and M. A. Cau Ontiveros (eds), *LRCW I: late Roman coarse wares, cooking wares and amphorae in the Mediterranean : archaeology and archaeometry.* Oxford, 647-654.

Mackensen, M. 1993. *Die spätantiken Sigillata- und Lampentöpfereien von El Mahrine (Nordtunesien) : Studien zur nordafrikanischen Feinkeramik des 4. bis 7. Jahrhunderts.* Münchner Beiträge zur vor- und Frühgeschichte 50. München.

Magid, A. A., R. H. Pierce and K. Krzywinski 1995. 'Test Excavations in the Southern Red Sea Hills (Sudan): Cultural Linkages to the North', *Archéologie du Nil Moyen* 7, 163-190.

Mamedow, M. 2013. 'Wells and Kilns: Local Ceramic Production and Use at Tell Basta in Roman Times', in B. Bader and M. F. Ownby (eds), *Functional aspects of Egyptian ceramics in their archaeological context: proceedings of a conference held at the McDonald Institute for Archaeological Research, Cambridge, July 24th – July 25th, 2009.* Orientalia Lovaniensia Analecta 217. Leuven, 403-421.

Manzo, A. 2004. 'Late Antique Evidence in Eastern Sudan', *Sudan & Nubia* 8, 75-83.

Manzo, A. 2017. *Eastern Sudan in its Setting: the archaeology of a region far from the Nile Valley.* Cambridge Monographs in African Archaeology 94. Oxford.

Massa, S. 2014. 'The Unglazed Ceramics Productions from the Masjed-i-Jum'a of Isfahan: an Archaeological and Archaeometric Approach', *Newsletter di Archeologia CISA* 5, 320-325.

Massa, S. 2015. 'Manifatture artigianali dell'antica Cossyra. Problemi di organizzazione degli ateliers ceramici, modelli culturali, sfere di influenza', in T. Schäfer, K. Schmidt and M. Osanna (eds), *Cossyra I. Die Ergebnisse der Grabungen auf der Akropolis von Pantelleria/S. Teresa: Der Sakralbereich.* Tübinger Archäologische Forschungen 10, Teil 2. Rahden/Westfalen, 893-904.

Meyer, C. and L. A. Heidorn 2014. 'Pottery', in C. Meyer (ed.), *Bir Umm Fawakhir 3. Excavations 1999-2001.* Oriental Institute Publications 141. Chicago, 33-76.

Nappo, D. 2018. *I porti romani nel Mar Rosso da Augusto al Tardoantico.* Napoli.

Nordström, H.-A. and J. Bourriau 1993. 'Ceramic Technology, Clays and Fabrics', in Do. Arnold and J. Bourriau (eds), *An introduction to Ancient Egyptian Pottery.* Sonderschrift des Deutschen Archäologischen Instituts Abteilung Kairo 17. Mainz am Rhein, 143-190.

Ownby, M. F. 2012. 'The Importance of Imports: Petrographic Analysis of Levantine Pottery Jars in Egypt', *Journal of Ancient Egyptian Interconnections* 43, 23-29.

Ownby, M. F. 2016. 'Petrographic Analysis of Egyptian Ceramic Fabrics in the Vienna System', in B. Bader, C. M. Knoblauch, and E. C. Köhler (eds.), *Vienna 2 – Ancient Egyptian Ceramics in the 21st Century: proceedings of the International Conference held at the University of Vienna, 14th-18th of May, 2012.* Orientalia Lovaniensia Analecta 245. Leuven – Paris – Bristol, CT, 459-470.

Pieri, D. 2005. *Le commerce du vin oriental à l'époque byzantine (Ve-VIIe siècles): Le témoignage des amphores en Gaule.* Bibliothèque Archéologique et Historique 174. Beyrouth.

Pyke, G. and M. F. Ownby 2016. 'A collaborative characterisation of the fabric series at the fifth-sixth century AD North Tombs Settlement at Amarna', in B. Bader, C. M. Knoblauch, and E. C. Köhler (eds), *Vienna 2 – Ancient Egyptian Ceramics in the 21st Century: proceedings of the International Conference held at the University of Vienna, 14th- 18th of May, 2012.* Orientalia Lovaniensia Analecta 245. Leuven – Paris – Bristol, CT, 471-486.

Reynolds, P. 2013. 'Transport amphorae of the First to Seventh Centuries: Early Roman to Byzantine Periods', in W. Aylward (ed.), *Excavations at Zeugma, conducted by Oxford Archaeology, Vol. II.* Los Altos, 93-161.

Reynolds, P. 2014. *Roman Amphorae: a digital resource.* University of Southampton (2014) [data-set]. York: Archaeology Data Service [distributor] https://doi.org/10.5284/1028192.

Riley, J. A. 1979. 'The Coarse Pottery from Berenice', in J. A. Lloyd (ed.), *Excavations at Sidi Khrebish, Benghazi (Berenice), Vol. II.* Supplements to *Libya Antiqua*, V, 91-443.

Sidebotham, S. E., H. Barnard and G. Pyke. 2002. 'Five Enigmatic Late Roman Settlements in the Eastern Desert', *Journal of Egyptian Archaeology* 88, 187-225.

Tomber, R. S. 1998. 'The Pottery', in S. E. Sidebotham and W. Z. Wendrich (eds), *Berenike 1996. Report of the 1996 Excavations at Berenike (Egyptian Red Sea Coast) and the Survey of the Eastern Desert.* Leiden, 163-180.

Tomber, R. 2005. 'Living in the desert: mess kits from Mons Porphyrites, Egypt', in N. Crummy (ed.), *Image, Craft and the Classical World: Essays in honour of Donald Bailey and Catherine Johns.* Monogr. Instrumentum 29. Montagnac, 55-60.

Tomber, R. 2018. 'Carrières, ports et praesidia : approvisionnement et échanges dans le désert Oriental', in J-P Brun, T. Faucher, B. Redon and S. Sidebotham (eds), *Le désert oriental d'Égypte durant la période gréco-romaine : bilans archéologiques.* Collège de France, Paris [en ligne]. Paris : Collège de France, 2018 (généré le 12 avril 2019): http://books.openedition.org/cdf/5179.

Vasiliou, Sp. and E. B. Tsigarida. 2014. 'Late Roman Pottery from recent excavations at Cassandra in Chalcidice', in N. Poulou-Papadimitriou, E. Nodarou and V. Kilikoglou (eds), *LRCW 4. Late Roman Coarse Wares, Cooking Wares and Amphorae in the Mediterranean. Archaeology and Archaeometry. The Mediterranean: a market without frontiers.* BAR Int. Ser. 2616, vol. II. Oxford, 723-736.

Williams, D. F. 2014. *Roman Amphorae: a digital resource.* University of Southampton (2014) [data-set]. York: Archaeology Data Service [distributor] https://doi.org/10.5284/1028192

Wodzińska, A. 2010. *A Manual of Egyptian Pottery. Volume 4: Ptolemaic Period-Modern.* Boston.

10. Preliminary study of the macro-lithic tools collected by CeRDO in the Sudanese Eastern Desert

Francesco Michele Rega

Introduction

The Eastern Desert (Plate 10.1) lies to the east of the Nile Valley in Sudan and Egypt with the Red Sea as its eastern limit. Within it lie the Red Sea Hills, representing one of the major areas of human occupation in the region. Geologically, this arid land is part of the so-called Arabian-Nubian Shield (ANS), which is the eastern portion of the West Sahara Craton and it is very similar to the Sinai Peninsula and especially to the Arabian Peninsula. It is composed of a Precambian basement, rich in metamorphic and igneous rocks, which is characterised by a pre-PanAfrican infrastructure and a PanAfrican superstructure, with tectonic and post-tectonic intrusions (Botros 2002; Johnson and Woldehaimanot 2003; Sidebotham *et al.* 2008; Barnard 2012; Klemm and Klemm 2013). Thanks to this complex geological setting, this area is very rich in stone deposits, particularly exploited in ancient times for different purposes, such as in architecture, statuary, tool production and jewellery. Marbles, sandstone, granite and granodiorite were the most common and their deposits were intensively exploited (Harrell and Storemyr 2009), as also were gneiss (Neumayr *et al.* 1997; Fowler *et al.* 2007; Ali *et al.* 2011), gabbro (Siddal 2013), steatite (Harrell *et al.* 2000; Harrell and Brown 2008) and gemstones, among them amethyst (Shaw and Jameson 1993). Mining activities were particularly intense also for the extraction of metals, like copper and iron, found for example in the mines of the Wadi Abu Gerida area (Abd El-Rahman *et al.* 2013). Gold deposits, which mainly occurred in the Neoproterozoic sequences, were very intensively exploited, thanks to their particular diffusion, a consequence of the numerous episodes of gold mineralization, related to different tectonic-magmatic stages, clearly illustrated by Botros (2002). As regards the different types of gold or gold deposits, the vein type, i.e. the gold inside quartz veins with different directions and dimensions, seems to be the most widespread and was mined intensively (El Bedewi and Kader 1996). The search over millenia for gold deposits led to the creation of different types of settlements, with structures, graves and mining tools, which developed through the centuries (Klemm and Klemm 2013). The recording and study of these mining settlements, as well as of the other settlements and sites to be ascribed to the local inhabitants of the Nubian/Sudanese part of the Eastern Desert, was one of the aims of the explorations conducted by the CeRDO under the direction of Angelo and Alfredo Castiglioni from 1989. Their work made a crucial contribution to our knowledge of this area (Sadr *et al.* 1994; Castiglioni *et al.* 1995; Castiglioni *et al.* 1997; Castiglioni and Castiglioni 2006; Castiglioni *et al.* 2010).

Macro-lithic tools from the Sudanese Eastern Desert

The grinding tools collected by these expeditions are presently kept in the Castiglioni Museum of Varese, and in the Sudan National Museum in Khartoum. During my visits to

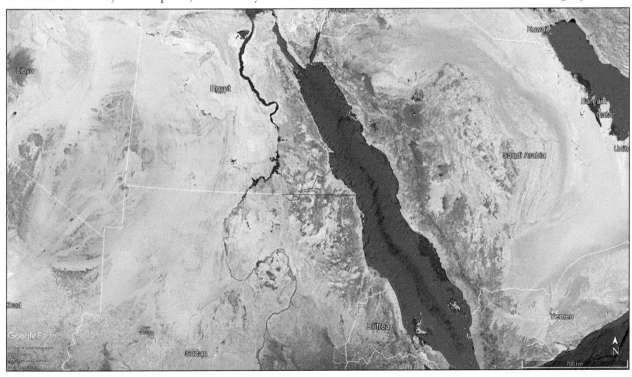

Plate 10.1. Google Earth satellite map, showing the extent of the Egyptian and Sudanese Eastern Desert.

the Castiglioni Museum, I observed, analysed and measured 32 macro-lithic tools, many of which have probably been used for gold working. The same function has been suggested for the materials in the Sudan National Museum, four of which were on display, while one was in storage.[1] They all came from surface collections conducted in different sites of the Eastern Desert (Plate 10.2). The label "macro-lithic tools" has been chosen here following the work of J. L. Adams and other scholars, who consider this term as the best in categorising all the large and heavy lithic tools used for different and specific

tharchides.[3] There, the historian reported the presence of different tools, such as hammers, mortars, grindstones and rotary mills, each one used during specific steps of the process (Eide *et al.* 1996, 657-659; Castiglioni *et al.* 1995, 28-35; Castiglioni *et al.* 2010). Although the description by Agatharchides is related to a specific period (*c.* 3rd-2nd century BC), this is a crucial testimony of the extraction techniques used in this region. Moreover, some of the implements described in the text are very similar to those described here, following a possible typological and functional division.

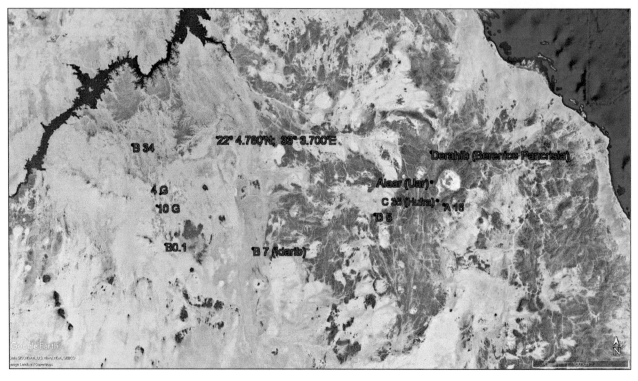

Plate 10.2. Google Earth satellite map, showing the Sudanese-Nubian Eastern Desert sites reported on in the paper.

tasks (Adams *et al.* 2009). This class includes grinding tools, pestles, mortars, hammerstones and other kinds of tools described in this paper, listed partially also following the classification system of K. W. Wright (1992).

All the pieces have been observed by the naked eye, using a magnifying glass, and, in many cases, the traces of use were still visible. Thanks to this observation, it was possible to obtain some insights into the distribution and orientation of the traces, and thus more possible information on the shaping and use of the macro-lithic tools. This was also possible through the observation of the shape of the tools, and sometimes also thanks to comparisons with similar material found elsewhere (see below). The result is a preliminary database recording the dimensions, the materials, the origin and the description of each object.[2]

It should be stressed that the use of these kinds of tools in the process of gold extraction and working is well known thanks to Diodorus Siculus's *Bibliotheca Historica*, which quoted the description of gold mines and gold processing by Aga-

Grinding tools

The first tools are those used for grinding materials. They include both the lower passive stones, divided into grinding slabs and quern (Wright 1992, 61, 63-65), according to the flatness and the concavity of the active surface, and the upper active stones, known as handstones (Wright 1992, 61, 67-69), grinders (Hamon 2008, 1508) and crushers (Hamon 2006, 30-33; 2008). The first tool (N. 1, Plate 10.3) is a sandstone grinding slab characterised by a sub-rectangular shape, with a very flat obverse and less than 40mm thick, found together with other grindstones inside an accumalation at site A16 (Plate 10.4). This site was characterised by a settlement with circular structures, associated with several grindstones, with others reused in the superstructures of the circular tumuli scattered in the area (Castiglioni *et al.* 1995, 178). An oval sandstone grinder (N.2, Plate 10.3) was probably associated with this grindstone, with a length of 143mm, a width of 116mm and a thickness of 60mm.

The second grinding slab (N.3, Plate 10.3) has an irregular oval shape and is flat, with a thickness of 33mm. A grinder (N.4, Plate 10.3) coming from the same area as this grindstone, was round, smaller and used on both sides. These two grinding slabs and the second grinder (N.4) are characterised by

[1] At least two other lower rotary querns are stored in the Sudan National Museum. However, it was not possible to conclusively relate them to the Castiglioni expeditions.

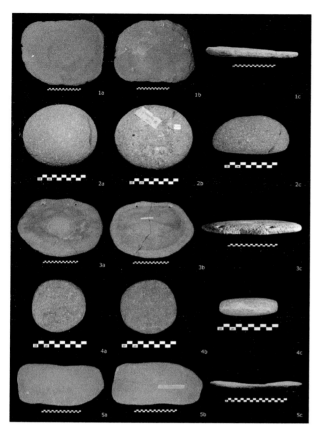

Plate 10.3. Grindstones and grinders.

Plate 10.4. Accumulation of materials in A 16, with the typical oval grinding slabs, also with the double working planes. On the left, a cubic anvil with cupules on the sides. Photograph by A. Castiglioni.

sheens on the working surface, probably the result of the chemical-mechanical reactions due to the rubbing activities between the grinder, the slab and the processed material (tribochemical wear)[4] (Adams 1993a, 62-70; 2002, 31-32; 2014, 133, 136; Bofill *et al.* 2013, 224; Dubreuil and Savage 2013). What materials were processed with these tools is unclear. It is possible that they were not used for gold working, but in a domestic context for food preparation or for grinding softer material, considering the thickness and the shape of the implements, but this hypothesis needs to be confirmed.

As for the dating, the grinding slab from A16 was found among other grinding stones, which may date to the New Kingdom, according to the chronology proposed by Klemm and Klemm; they describe this particular kind of grindstone thus: "consists of a flat slab measuring about 30 × 60 cm, preferably of a hard rock, and a mobile grinding or runner stone" (Klemm and Klemm 2013, 9). Of course, it is not excluded that the tools belong to older or later periods. There are more doubts on the dating of the second grindstone. It was found during the 1993 expedition at the foot of an isolated jebel with rock shelters in site B0.1, characterised by rock engravings (Sadr *et al.* 1994, 10-18, 171). In the area there were scatters of Khartoum Variant pottery sherds and other similar grinding slabs, labelled by the Castiglionis as "palette-shaped grinding stones". However, it is also possible that the tool was transported there from another site. It has two holes in the upper part. They are not perfectly drilled, becoming narrower in the middle, with a resulting outer diameter of 25mm and an inner diameter of 5mm. These holes were probably used for transporting the tool or for hanging it up, after use. If such hypotheses are true, they would confirm the practice of transporting grindstones from one site to another, attested by Klemm and Klemm especially at the site of Alaar (Uar), where there was a mound of rotary discs, made from exotic granites not available at the site (Klemm and Klemm 2013, 392-397, fig. 6.52). Comparison could be made with similar tools found in the Eastern Sahara, characterised by the same holes, interpreted as transport devices, with an identical shape, which date to the "Neolithic period" (Schön and Holter 1990, 370, Tafel 97). Another similar grinding slab was found in the Wadi Shaw, again with holes related to transport and associated with possible plant processing. It has been dated to the 3rd millennium BC, like other examples discovered in this area, where also other kinds of macro-lithic tools have been detected (Jesse 2004, 59, fig. 42; Lange *et al.* 2006, 519-520, 536-538, taf. 8-10, 497-499, taf. 11-13). Moreover, another example with a drilled hole used for suspension, according to the description on the inventory label, is a sandstone saddle quern from Gordon's Tree, exhibited in the Sudan National Museum.[5] The grinding slab in the Castiglioni Museum also has a crack along its middle, probably due to continuous use, which weakened the tool. However, it could also be due to possible post-depositional damage, which occurred after the tool was discarded. Two other grinding tools came from the same site. The first is an irregular sub-rectangular sandstone grindstone (N. 5, Plate 10.3) with longitudinal striations and pits, probably related both to pecking activity, to sharpen the surface, and to pounding actions, which may suggest that the material was first crushed and then ground. The second one is an oval sandstone grinder (N. 6, Plate 10.5) with deep and shallow striations on the flat and rough reverse, probably related to the grindstone.

A quern (N. 7, Plate 10.5) stored in the Castiglioni Museum is very similar to the previously described typical "New Kingdom" tools. It has a slightly concave oval work surface, characterised by a very smooth and polished surface, with clear longitudinal striations. Unfortunately, it was not possible to determine the location from which it was collected. A further tool (N. 8, Plate 10.5) is a sandstone, circular or slightly oval, grinder/crusher, with a rough surface on the obverse, charac-

---

[4] Some sheens could be due to the continuous exposure of the tools to wind and sand activity, which have worn the surface.

[5] Entry N°: 62/11/122

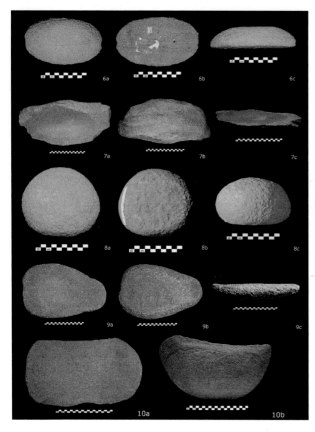

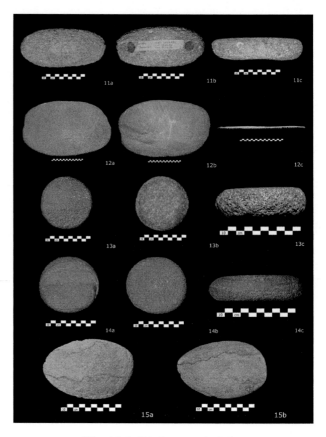

Plate 10.5. Grindstones and grinders.

Plate 10.6. Grindstones and grinders.

terised by clear hammering pits and deep horizontal striations. It cannot be excluded that it was used for gold working. This tool was found near site B 34, where an inscription with the name of Heqanefer, chief of Miam, was recorded (Castiglioni *et al.* 1995, 180-181). Of course, this inscription does not date the tool. However, it suggests a possible period of use of the site, during which the grinder might have been used.

Also, in the Castiglioni Museum there is a conglomerate grinding slab (N. 9, Plate 10.5) approximately 'tear-drop' shaped, with rough areas along the edges and smooth areas with sheens around the central depression, where the tiny pits and striations are concentrated.

A further quern in the Castiglioni Museum (N. 10, Plate 10.5), was found in a site (22° 04.780' N; 33° 03.700' E) near Wadi Gabgaba. It has a very concave working surface with different longitudinal striations and traces of small circular pecking. The base is extremely curved at the edges and slightly flat only in the middle. A grinder with an ellipsoidal shape was found nearby (N. 11, Plate 10.6). Considering the length, which is smaller than the width of the grindstone, it is not impossible that a different type of grinder was related to it, probably long enough to have been used on the whole work surface with two hands, as in the case of many concave querns used for gold processing found in the Eastern Desert (Klemm and Klemm 2013, 12-13, fig. 1.11, 102, 105, fig. 5.50, 153, 155-156, fig. 5.97, 5.98). However, similar grindstones with grinders smaller than the working surface were found in the area of Wadi Abu Gerida, where they were used for copper processing during the Ptolemaic period (Abd El-Rahman *et al.* 2013).

Two grinding slabs in the Castiglioni Museum are very interesting, especially considering their dimensions. The first one (N. 12, Plate 10.6) is 560mm long and 340mm wide. It

has an irregular oval shape and is characterised by tiny pits, striations and sheens. The second one (N. 16, Plate 10.7) has the same traces of use, although it has an ellipsoidal shape, and is 763mm long and 395mm wide. Both querns were found inside a rock shelter at site 4G, in the area of Jebel Duweig (Plate 10.8), and are very similar to those observed at site 10G (Plate 10.9), also related to a rock shelter in the same area. According to the Castiglionis, inside the shelter there was prehistoric material, which may suggest that the two grindstones were particularly ancient. However, it remains possible that they belong to a later occupation, whose chronology is impossible to establish.

Near the first quern, there were three upper active tools, two of which were very similar (N. 13-14, Plate 10.6). Both are possible circular grinders/crushers, with at least two active surfaces, a rough one with pits, and a half smooth, half rough one, with sheens and striations on the smoother part. However, the rough surface of the second tool is particularly irregular. They are very similar to the grinder observed in site 10G. As for the third tool (N. 15, Plate 10.6), it is a possible grinder with an oval shape and a wedge-shaped profile, considering the convexity in the middle of the active surface, dividing the tool into two parts or facets, one smoother than the other, and both with parallel striations. The pattern of the striations is probably the result of a double stroke motion and the different positions of the tool on the quern during use. At first, the pressure was probably exerted on the proximal edge of the tool, keeping the rest of it away from the surface of the quern. Subsequently, moving back the tool, the pressure was exerted on the distal edge, keeping the larger part of the surface against the quern and the proximal edge lifted up. This movement caused a greater pressure on the distal edge,

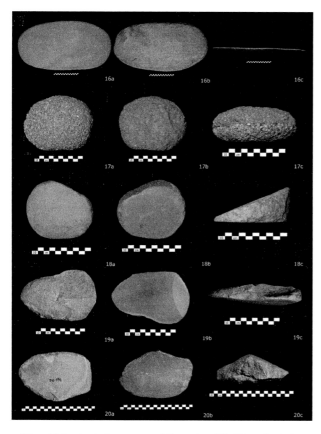

Plate 10.7. A grindstone, a possible crusher (N. 17) and grinders.

Plate 10.8. Rock shelter in 4G (Jebel Duweig).
Photograph by A. Castiglioni

Plate 10.9. Grinding slab and grinders inside a rock shelter
in 10G (Jebel Duweig). Photograph by A. Castiglioni.

which became gradually thinner, as ethnographically observed, e.g. on the grinders used by the Hopi woman (Adams 1993b, 334-336). It should be noted that there is uncertainty regarding the relation of this tool with the first quern.

Two grinders were related to the second quern. The first (N. 17, Plate 10.7) is irregularly rounded, with a rough and irregular surface, with tiny depressions. The second (N. 18, Plate 10.7) is completely different. It has an irregular oval shape, a triangular profile and two active surfaces, both on the flat faces. The first is characterised by multidirectional striations on the whole surface, which has a recess on one edge. The latter has a very smooth and polished surface, with clear striations, tiny pits and sheens, and a wedge near the wider side which forms a smoother and shinier small area, probably

the result of stronger pressure at this point. Considering these evident working traces, it is possible to suggest that this tool was used for processing hard material, probably quartz ore.

Two other grinders (N. 19-20, Plate 10.7) are stored in the Castiglioni Museum. They have a wedge-shaped profile, probably the result of the same double stroke motion described above for the other grinder (N. 15). What differs between the two tools is possibly the way in which the movement was made, as shown by the parallel striations. In the first case (N. 19), the tool was possibly held longitudinally, so the striations are distributed on the long axis, while in the second case (N. 20) the tool was held latitudinally, leaving striations on the short axis. Moreover, it is possible that the first grinder was also used as a core, considering that two or three flakes were probably detached from the lower part of its obverse. However, none of these hypotheses can yet be confirmed. A similar grinder with this triangular cross section is exhibited with the aforementioned grinding slab from Wadi Shaw. It was made in silicified sandstone and came from Djabarona 80/80. The date is unknown (Jesse 2004, 59, fig. 42). However, the area, in particular the site Djabarona 84/13 (3rd-2nd millennium BC), was characterised by different types of grinders and grinding slabs, considered to be possibly connected with food production. Also here a lower tool was characterised by a hole probably used for transporting it (Keding 1997, 195-196).

Two other tools were probably also used as grinders (N. 21-22, Plate 10.10), considering their very flat and polished surfaces, with striations and sheens in the first example (N. 21), and hammering pits concentrated in the middle for the second one (N. 22). In the case of N. 22, it is possible to suggest that it was also used as a small anvil, considering the depression in the middle of one side, caused by possible drilling and pounding actions. However, the depression might have also been used for holding the tool.

The last two possible grinding tools were collected at Alaar (Uar), where the medieval occupation seems to have been particularly intense (Castiglioni *et al.* 1995, 183; Klemm and Klemm 2013, 392-398). The first find (N. 23, Plate 10.10) has a very oblong shape, and a very flat and smooth obverse with striations all over the surface. It is quite possible that this tool was used as a grinder, also considering that it is similar to the Middle Kingdom grinders for cereals, recorded by Har-

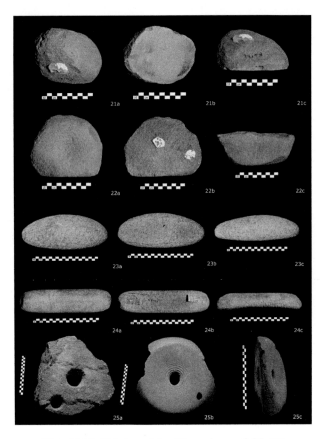

Plate 10.10. Grinders. A possible crusher-anvil (N. 22), a pestle-grinder (N. 24) and a rotary mill.

hole, bigger than the lateral perforation for the handle. The second (N. 26, Plate 10.12) has a circular obverse, with a convex profile and a lateral hole not completely perforated. The reverse is very flat. The third (N. 27, Plate 10.12) has a slightly irregular circular obverse, with a possible lateral perforation, and a circular reverse with a deep concavity in the middle. These examples show at least two different typologies of rotor disc, one with a work surface completely flat, the other with a concavity in the middle, probably corresponding with a convexity in the middle of the lower part. However, all of them have the same traces of use on the work surface and in some cases also on the edges; these are the circular striations caused by the rotary motion, generally thicker and deeper around the centre. As for the lower part (N. 28, Plate 10.12), it has irregular external edges and a circular work surface, with clear striations, especially along the inner sides and around the possible small spindle. According to the Castiglionis, this stationary lower part was found together with the first upper rotor disc here described (N. 25).

Two other lower parts, coming from Derahib in the Wadi Allaqi, are stored in the Sudan National Museum. This is one of the most interesting and important sites in the Eastern Desert, visited during the 1990 fieldwork conducted by CeRDO. It is located on the west bank of Wadi Allaqi and comprises two fortified structures, a settlement with different dwellings on both sides of a central paved road, an Islamic prayer area and a cemetery. This site has been identified by the Castiglionis as *Berenice Pancrisia*, described by Pliny the Elder in his *Naturalis Historia*, which they also consider as the Town of Allaqi, capital of the Rabi'a clan and an important centre

rell in Chephren's Quarry, near Gebel al-Asr, although the tool from Alaar is considerably smaller (Harrell 2012, 8, fig. 5). The other tool (N. 24, Plate 10.10) has an oblong cylindrical shape, possible pounding pits on both edges and a smooth obverse, with striations, pits and sheens, which might indicate its possible use both as a pestle and as a grinder. This tool was found inside a mine and it was broken, probably during use.

Rotary querns

This grinding device largely spread during the Roman and Medieval periods and is well known from many examples found all over the Egyptian and Sudanese Eastern Desert (Plate 10.11) (Castiglioni *et al.* 1995; Klemm and Klemm 1996, 345, 352, fig. 7; Castel *et al.* 1998, 85, photo 4; Klemm and Klemm 2013). It consists of two parts, a fixed lower base and a mobile upper rotating disc, generally with a central axial hole and a lateral one for the handle. As for the three upper discs in the Castiglioni Museum, the first (N. 25, Plate 10.10) has an irregular obverse and a flat work surface on the reverse, slightly concave in the middle, where there is a central

Plate 10.11. Examples of rotary mills. C 38 (top left and right); C 11 (middle left) and Wadi Terfowi (C 14) (middle right); C 33 (bottom left) and Idarib (B 7) (bottom right). Photographs by Alfredo and Angelo Castiglioni.

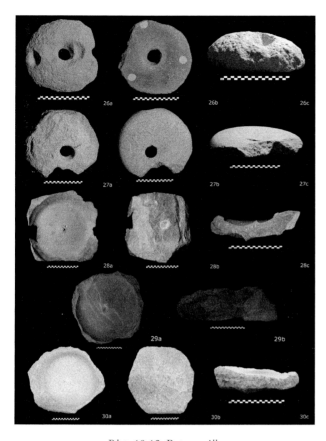

Plate 10.12. Rotary mills.

of the Medieval Beja kingdom, which during the subsequent period became a crucial transit point on the pilgrimage route to Mecca (Sadr *et al.* 1994; Castiglioni *et al.* 1995, 52-71, 180; Castiglioni *et al.* 1997; Castiglioni and Castiglioni 2004; 2006, 128-143). They identified one of the buildings as a church, suggesting that it was an important city even before the arrival of the Arabs. The Klemms, on the contrary, believe that the settlement only developed during the Early Arab period, on the basis of an apparent lack of earlier material (Klemm and Klemm 2013, 439-447). Both tools have the typical rotary traces, although they are significantly different in shape. The first (N. 29, Plate 10.12) is bigger, with a larger work surface, having a shallow convexity in the middle. Moreover, it has a bigger central fill hole, measuring 40 x 25mm, with a depth of *c.* 40mm, while the one in the second example does not exceed 17mm in diameter and *c.* 10mm in depth. It is obvious that this second quern (N. 30, Plate 10.12) had a smaller upper rotor disc with a flatter work surface, probably similar to two of the above described examples in the Castiglioni Museum (N. 25-26), while the one related to the first mill probably had a shallow concavity in the middle, similar to the third described example (N. 27). Indeed, a possible rotary disc with unfinished edges was associated with the second quern, made in the same granite and characterised by three lateral holes (Castiglioni and Castiglioni 2004, 131, fig. 107). However, it was not possible for the author to observe it.

Mortar/anvils

In the Castiglioni Museum, there is also a mortar/anvil (N. 31, Plate 10.13) from site C 35 (Hofra) (Plate 10.14), which could be dated to the New Kingdom or to a later period. This

site was probably occupied also during older periods, but it is mainly characterised by later occupations, as demonstrated by the presence of Romibs, Bedouin tombs and recent burials, one of which belonged to a sheikh (Castiglioni *et al.* 1995, 183; Klemm and Klemm 2013, 399). The tool is 420mm long; its width ranges from 180m to 300mm and is characterised by a depression with evident pounding/hammering pits in the middle. It was also probably related to two tools, an almost rectangular oblong pestle (N. 32, Plate 10.13), with a possible ergonomic manual handle and an almost spherical hammer-stone (N. 33, Plate 10.13).

A further mortar/anvil (N. 34, Plate 10.13) is stored in the

Plate 10.13. Two mortar-anvils (N. 31; 34), a pestle (N. 32), a hammerstone (N. 33) and a hammer (N. 35).

Plate 10.14. Mound of material in Hofra (C 35), with the typical oval grinding slabs and the anvils-mortars. Photograph by A. Castiglioni

Sudan National Museum. It is a block of stone, measuring c. 410 x 440 x 220mm, with three cupules on the upper face, 150, 80 and 35mm in diameter, plus two other depressions, all with a worn surface, possible hammering pits and fractures. Together with this stone block, there were also two hammer stones/hammers, one with a rounded triangular shape (N. 35, Plate 10.13), the other irregular (N. 36, Plate 10.15), both with hammering pits and with three depressions on each of the faces, probably the result of the percussion activity or used for holding the tools.

Stone blocks with circular depressions used for gold

Preliminary remarks

The implements here described show how many different macro-lithic tools could be expected in the archaeological sites of the Sudanese Eastern Desert.

Grinding slabs and querns had distinct shapes, from oval to sub-rectangular, up to one that is oblong, and they were probably used not only for grinding quartz ore, but also for other purposes. The second grinding slab (N. 3) is one of the most interesting, with its slightly oval shape, its double work surface and its two holes in the upper part. Grinders are also of different types. They can be ellipsoidal, oval, oblong or circular in shape and with a single or multiple work surfaces, sometimes also used for crushing. As seen, rotary querns and anvil/mortars can be very varied, the former especially in the shape and curve of the two active surfaces of lower and upper discs.

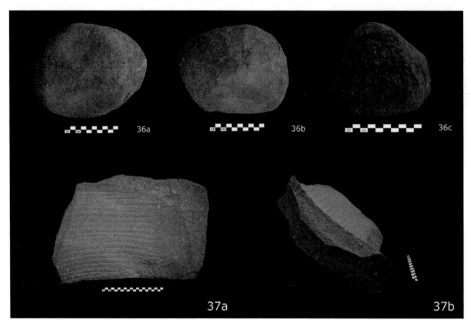

They are mainly made of sandstone and conglomerate, although there are also grinders made of granite (N. 23) and one of siltstone (N. 24). Sandstone was probably used for one of the rotor discs (N. 26), while at least one is made of a metasedimentary rock (N. 25), also used for the oblong pestle (N. 32) associated with the mortar; the mortar itself (N. 31) was made

Plate 10.15. A hammer (N. 36) and a fragment of a possible washing table (N. 37).

working were also reported at El-Urf/Mongul South, one measuring 140 x 160 x 110mm and with a weight of 4.5kg, the other measuring 160 x 160 x 130mm and weighing 5.3kg. They were associated with a trapezoidal grindstone/mortar and rotary mills, with work surfaces similar to those described in this paper (Tawab *et al.* 1990, figs 14-16). Similar associations were found in the Byzantine gold mine of Bir Umm Fawakhir, where there were blocks 150-200mm in diameter with a depression on the top, rotary mills and concave grinding stones about 600-700mm long, the last ones possibly Ptolemaic (Meyer 1995, 222, fig. 16, 223).

Washing table?

In the Castiglioni Museum there is a possible part of a washing table (N. 37, Plate 10.15), measuring 430 x 280 x 106mm. This fragment was found in one of the two washing tables recorded at site D 5 (Plate 10.16), which still had the water recycle system, with a basin and a lateral drain (Castiglioni *et al.* 1995, 185). The upper surface is concave in the middle and has deep grooves, with spaces 10-150mm wide between them, probably used for lowering the speed of the water and holding the gold particles. However, parallel grooves have also been noted on lower grinding slabs, for example those found in the area of Karanis in the Fayum. There, according to Harrell (2012, 8), the grooves were purposely made to enhance the grinding action.

Plate 10.16. Washing table excavated in D 5 during the fifth expedition. Photograph by A. Castiglioni.

from a metamorphic rock, probably ophiolite. Noteworthy is the choice of rock for the lower part of one of the rotary mills (N. 28): it is made from an effusive magmatic rock with a part of intrusive granite. Gneiss was used for the possible fragment of a washing table (N. 37). Unfortunately, it is impossible to determine the provenance of the raw materials, although it is quite possible that most of them were collected locally. However, as already noted, the Klemms observed tools made with exotic materials, which indicates that they were collected elsewhere, and supports the suggestion of the transportation of at least some grinding tools from site to site.

It is difficult to establish a precise chronology for these objects. As has been seen, these lithic implements developed and/or changed over the centuries. Of course, sometimes some comparative points can be proposed. Nevertheless, it should be stressed that the soundness of assumptions related to these proposed comparisons sometimes appears disputable.

In this perspective, a very good example is represented by the so-called "New Kingdom grindstone", represented by the oval grindstone in the Castiglioni Museum (N. 7). Klemm and Klemm have considered this particular kind of quern as a "radically new milling technique", introduced into the Eastern Desert during the New Kingdom and sometimes reused in Kushite times (Klemm *et al.* 2002, 650; Klemm and Klemm 2013). However, C. Meyer has questioned this dating after the study of grindstones found in the site of Hosh el-Guruf, at the Fourth Cataract (Meyer 2010): there some of them have been classified as Type A, large and scooped grindstones made of grey granitoid gneiss, generally *c.* 600mm long, 570mm wide, 350mm high and with a *c.* 190mm deep grinding depression. Actually, no New Kingdom sherds or material were found in association with the grindstones from Hosh el-Guruf, which were generally dated to *Kerma Moyen/Classique* (*c.* 2040-1650 BC), but are also in association with Khartoum Variant and post-Kerma sherds. It should be stressed that a proportion of the sites located in the Fourth Cataract, characterised by the presence of grinding tools, date to the Christian period, although there are also Mesolithic, Early-Late Neolithic and Kerma examples (Welsby 2003; Usai 2003, 106-110). Even though no functional studies have been conducted on these lithic implements, some of them could be related to gold processing, considering their shapes and the deep concavity of the active surface, in one case similar to the Ptolemaic examples (Welsby 2003, pls 5.5-5.11). On the other hand, according to the Klemms, New Kingdom pottery is predominant in the desert mines where this type of grindstone occurs (Klemm *et al.* 2002, 650-651). Moreover, they assume that during the Old and Middle Kingdoms, gold mines were exploited by the local inhabitants of the Eastern Desert and that processing and tailings sites were located near water sources, today hardly recognizable (Klemm and Klemm 2013, 7-8). As a matter of fact, the attribution to the New Kingdom proposed by Klemm and Klemm is based on historical and political considerations, suggesting that, after the conquest of Nubia and during the period of more strict control of the gold mines, there was an increase in the number of exploited gold mines and the Egyptians introduced a new grinding device in the mining sites, previously used in the Nile Valley for domestic purposes, in order to improve the process (Klemm and Klemm 2013, 8-9).

Of course, considering the fact that New Kingdom sites are proportionally much more numerous than the older ones, the possibility that this kind of grindstone dates exclusively to this period could be due to the lack of finds related to the older occupations, but it is not possible to prove this hypothesis. On the other hand, considering the presence of Egyptians, Nubians or local people in the Eastern Desert before the New Kingdom, it is very difficult to imagine that they were not able to adapt domestic grinding devices for gold processing.

Actually, the suggestion by Klemm and Klemm also implies the inability of Egyptians to adapt similar devices for gold working, or to introduce them into the Eastern Desert before the New Kingdom.

Interestingly, grinding implements were also found in older mining contexts, such as the Wadi Dara copper mines. Different grinding workshops were found there, with tables used for grinding scoria. They generally had a concave work surface at ground level, while the rest of the tools were sunk into the ground. Two groups were defined, according to their dimensions. The smaller examples were parallelepiped in shape with a polygonal face, which had a central cupule, similar to the mortars/anvils in the Sudan National Museum and at El-Urf/Mongul South. The larger examples had a square or polygonal shape, with a concave ellipsoidal area on the work surface, not so different from the examples under examination here. The site of Wadi Dara generally dates from the Pre-pharaonic Period to the Old Kingdom (Castel *et al.* 1996). These examples might be a clue to a more complex and ancient technological tradition in Egypt. However, examples of New Kingdom grinding devices were also confirmed in the area of Amara West[6] and in the gold workshops in the area of Saras, especially at sites 11-Q-62 and 11-Q-63, in association with a large number of mortars, grindstones, two-handed hammers and flat rubbing stones. One of the grindstones at 11-Q-62 was raised up on blocks, precious testimony of the introduction of this habit in such a functional context. These workshops, regarded as gold-working sites, were originally dated to the 12th Dynasty (Mills 1973, 204-206, pl. XXXVIII a). However, according to D. N. Edwards these sites are now to be dated to the New Kingdom (pers. comm. 13th May 2017; public conference communication, 12th September 2018). It should also be stressed that querns with oval depressions were indeed found in other working sites, such as 16-O-2, near the hamlet of Jedagur, in association with New Kingdom pottery (Edwards and Mills 2013).

The hypothesis by Klemm and Klemm that this device was only introduced into the Eastern Desert by the Egyptians in New Kingdom times also implies the inability of the Nubians to create grinding tools for gold-ore processing before the Egyptian occupation. The Klemms also suggest that, starting in the Kushite period (700 BC–AD 350), Nubian people reused New Kingdom grindstones, after considering some examples found in the area between Wadi Allaqi, Khor Nubt and the Nile Valley (Klemm and Klemm 2013, 15). But, as the German scholars themselves note, this consideration derives from the lack of detailed archaeological investigations, which would probably clarify the autonomous developments of such a kind of lithic technology in the Sudanese area. Many examples described in this paper could probably demonstrate the existence of different Nubian macro-lithic technologies in the Eastern Desert, used both for gold processing and for other purposes. As we have seen, some of them could also be particularly old, possibly even Neolithic. In any event, this hypothesis could be confirmed only after further fieldwork, hopefully relying on more material and from well dated contexts.

A more systematic study of the grinding stones from the Eastern Desert might also shed further light on another implication of Klemm and Klemm's suggestion, i.e. the lack of grinding tools among desert peoples. After all, two lower and an upper, heavily used, grinding stones were found in site ME03/10/24, located in the area of Wadi Bili, in the Red Sea Hills and dated 4700 BC, thus indicating the presence of grinding devices during the Predynastic period in the Egyptian Eastern Desert (Vermeersch *et al.* 2005; Vermeersch 2012). This hypothesis may also be supported by the grinding slabs described in this paper, in particular the large ones from 4G and 10G, which might suggest the presence of this typology of grinding implements in the Nubian-Sudanese Eastern Desert, in association with rock shelters probably occupied from prehistoric periods. Although their dating is still debatable, similar grindstones were also found at D1, again related to rock shelters. Albeit while inside the rock shelters there was no dating material, Khartoum Horizon style pottery was recovered from the surface around them (Sadr *et al.* 1994, 8-13, 187). If we accept that there was a relationship between the grindstones and the pottery fragments, this would support the hypothesis of the presence of grinding implements in the Nubian-Sudanese part of the Eastern Desert, and possibly among the inhabitants of the region, already in very ancient times.

What we can be certain about for now is that the tradition of making grinding devices is particularly old both in Egypt and Sudan. In fact, grinding tools have been recorded on archaeological sites which date to long before the New Kingdom. Of course, in almost all cases, no specific functional analysis has been made to confirm if these lithic tools were used for food processing or for working other materials. However, they attest to how old the ability of creating such tools is. The earliest examples may date even to Late Paleolithic times and were found in the area of Wadi Kubbaniya, in the Western Desert of Upper Egypt, where some workshops for the manufacture of these lithic implements, used for many purposes and created with different techniques, demonstrating the high level of technology, were recorded (Wendorf *et al.* 1989). The "Sebilian" grindstones from Ezbet el-Sebil, Kom Ombo, also belong more or less to this period and apparently they were used for milling wild cereals, as well as red ochre (Hayes 1965, 59-69). Also in the Western Desert, possible Early-Middle Holocene examples were found in the area of Kharga, where there were some particularly active quarries for grindstone production, in which different kinds of grinding tools were found, including oval lower grinding slabs (Storemyr 2014). Other ancient examples could be those from the quarry area of Aswan West Bank, where there are different grinding stone blocks probably dating from the Upper Palaeolithic, in addition to those dating to the Predynastic and Middle Kingdom (Heldal 2009). Early Neolithic grindstones and other macro-lithic tools were found in the area of Nabta Playa (Wendorf *et al.* 2001) and more to the north in the Farafra Oasis, where, most of the grindstones, apparently used for food processing, were found in the so-called "Hidden Village", dating back to 6000-5000 cal. BC (Lucarini 2014). Grindstones were also found at Merimde Beni-Salame, mostly made of basalt and granite, not the local sandstone, as found elsewhere in the desert area. They generally had an oblong, oval or sub-rectangular shape (Eiwanger 1984; 1988). Two examples from this site are stored in the

Petrie Museum of Egyptian Archaeology,[7] where there are also three others from Fayyum.[8] In the Sudanese Nile Valley, examples of grinding tools date back to at least the Mesolithic, as demonstrated by the examples from Saggai 1 and from the area of Kabbashi (Caneva 1983; Zarattini 1983). These macro-lithic tools are not only a precious testimony of very old tool creation but could also be considered as archetypal for the later Neolithic implements, many of them used in the process of food production. Fragments of "saddle querns" attributed to the Neolithic were found at Kadero, as commonly as small lower grindstones, grinders, palettes and other lithic and stone implements (Krzyżaniak 1978; Haaland 1987; 1992; Jórdeczka 2011). Other examples came from el-Geili, north of Khartoum, which were used for multiple purposes (Caneva 1988), and Um Direiwa and Zakiab, probably associated with wild sorghum cultivation (Haaland 1987; 1992). According to Abdel-Magid, grinding tools were present in Central Sudan in the whole period he examined for his archaeobotanical studies (*c.* 9000 to 1700 BP), stressing the idea that they were probably used for grain or food processing in general. Apparently, their shape changes during the different phases and they become more frequent over time (Abdel-Magid 1989, 144-157). As already noted, tools dated to the "Neolithic period" have been found also in the area of the Eastern Sahara. Some of them have been considered as grinding implements for the processing of wild grasses, at least where the climatic conditions were favourable (Schön and Holter 1990). Many examples have been found inside graves in the cemetery at el-Kadada (Reinold 1982). According to Reinold, some of these graves (zone D) date to 3220 BC (5170 BP), some others (zone A) to 2880-2680 BC (4830-4630 BP), while the occupation level at KDD21 dates to 2840 BC (4790 BP). Likewise, at Kadero some tools have been collected from the graves. In particular, a complete grindstone with pecking traces and a possible palette or grinder came from grave 202, the burial of a child dated around 4400 - 4290±40 BC, derived from the radiocarbon dating of two Aspatharia Sp. samples (Krzyżaniak 2004; Chłodnicki *et al.* 2011).

Perhaps the chronology suggested for the concave quern in the Castiglioni Museum is more certain. According to the Klemms this typology was introduced in Ptolemaic times from the Aegean, together with what was considered a possible circular water device for gold washing, similar to the helicoidally ones used at Démoliaki, in the Laurion area, now reconsidered as possible milling devices themselves (Klemm and Klemm 2013, 155, fig. 5.97, 156, fig. 5.98, 256, fig. 5.199; Conophagos 1980, 250-252, 259-261, fig. 10-30 - 10-36; Papadimitriou 2016). As already seen, some concave grindstones were found by C. Meyer at Bir Umm Fawakhir. Even in this case there was uncertainty on the chronology, although the context, a Byzantine settlement where grindstones were reused in the masonry, could support a possible dating to an earlier period. Other examples of this type were found at Gidami, also in association with upper rubber stones (Fuchs *et al.* 1996, 49, fig. 7). Those are very similar to the ones stored in the British Museum, from the Great Temenos of Naukratis,[9] and in the Petrie Museum of Egyptian Archaeology, from Fayum's

---

[7] Accession number: UC10924 and UC10925
[8] Accession number: UC2957, UC2958 and UC2961
[9] Museum Number: EA27507

108

House 3,[10] all apparently dating to Ptolemaic times. As for our grindstone from Wadi Gabgaba, the associated grinder is completely different, and nothing suggests a more precise dating. However, the already described similarities with the ground stone implements used for copper processing during the Ptolemaic period in the area of Wadi Abu Gerida (Abd El-Rahman *et al.* 2013) might support a possible dating to this period. Nevertheless, the presence of a quern with a deep concave profile among the finds in Kadero could date the introduction or the utilization of such a device in Sudanese contexts to much earlier (Jórdeczka 2011), but more data are needed to confirm such a hypothesis.

Even rotary mills are not exempt from chronological problems. This important innovation is usually considered a marker for identifying Early Arab and Medieval mining sites, but it could have been introduced earlier. In particular, Agatharchides's description could demonstrate the presence of this device even during Ptolemaic times, or at least during the Roman period, considering that the passage was quoted and possibly reworked by Diodorus Siculus. Rotary querns were found at Gidami (Fuchs *et al.* 1996, 35, 48, fig. 6), in the Roman mining site of Wadi Bakariya (Tratsaert 2012), in the mining sites in the area of Wadi Gasus, occupied from the Middle Kingdom to the Roman period, and in the area of Wadi Safaga (Bragantini and Pirelli 2013). Examples of Eastern Desert Roman rotary querns were also found in the vicinity of Gebel Abu Arta and Bir Handosi (Sidebotham and Wendrich 2007) and in the area of Shenshef, where together with a fragment of a saddle quern and different grinders and pounders, there were two types of rotary device. The first labelled "flat rotary quern", with a flat work surface, similar to the examples stored in the Castiglioni Museum, the second labelled "domed rotatory quern", with the lower stone characterised by a domed upper surface (Sidebotham and Wendrich 1998, 438-441). One of these rotary querns was made from vesicular basalt and may have been for grinding cereals; the central hole of the upper disk was filled with the conical rock spindle molded in the middle of the lower stationary part, while the disk itself was rotated with a wooden handle inserted in the lateral hole (Sidebotham and Wendrick 1998, 139; Harrell 2010, 8-9, fig. 7). According to some scholars, this technology, used for grinding cereal, emerged in Western Europe at least during the 5th century BC (Alonso *et al.* 2014), probably slowly replacing saddle querns, which still survived in smaller numbers (Watts 2014, 24). This process has been outlined at the site of Els Vilars, Catalonia (Alonso *et al.* 2011) and also in France, although a bit later (Jaccottey *et al.* 2013) and sometimes, like in the Gallo-Roman mines in the area of Limousine, in clear connection with gold mining activities (Cauuet 1991; 1999). Moreover, some scholars believe that the first rotary equipment was a rudimentary variant of the saddle quern, possibly characterised by an oscillatory motion rather than a complete rotary one (Madureri 1984, 734; Watts 2014, 21). Although some of these rotary mills are clearly different from those found in the Eastern Desert, their occurrence and chronology highlight the possibility that this technology could have been introduced there earlier than usually thought. Such a theory is supported by scholars such as C. Meyer and, in particular, D. Meeks who suggests that the rotary technology, including

the Olynthus-type, Pompeian-type, rotary querns, etc. was introduced into Egypt and then Sudan starting at least from the Hellenistic and Roman periods and that the exploitation of the gold mines increased the spread of such technology, also for other purposes (Meyer 1995; Meeks 1997; Wefers and Mangartz 2014). Some examples were found in the site of Clysma, but the dating to the Greek or Roman period is not certain (Bruyère 1966; Meeks 1997). Very interesting is the quern fragment found inside a tower of the east wall of the fortress of Tell el-Farama (Pelusium), generally dating to the late Imperial era, and bearing an inscription with the name *Lucius Alypios*, attested from the 3rd century BC onwards (Abd El-Maksoud 1992). Of course, the rotary quern may have been especially popular during the Medieval period, when it is well known that such a device was used both for gold and food processing, as it is still widely used today, as demonstrated by the ethnographic evidence from Ernetta, near the ancient site of Amara West.[11]

As for the hammering and pounding tools and the two mortars/anvils, it is quite probable that they were used during the early stages of gold extraction, while quartz veins were hammered and stone blocks were carried outside the mines and smashed into little pieces, in order to be ground by querns and rotary querns (Castiglioni *et al.* 1995). This process starts with the identification of suitable quartz veins and the excavation of pits, shafts or trenches and galleries, using hammers, picks and similar tools, from the New Kingdom also made of metal. As regards the stone implements, the technique used for making galleries also changed during the centuries. The oldest lithic implements were the fist-hammers and the two-handed hammers, probably used together, or alternately, depending on the space inside the mines (Klemm and Klemm 2013, 4-6). These kinds of tools were also used inside other mines or quarries for the extraction of other materials, such as copper, galena, stones, gemstones and so on (Cauuet 1991; Shaw 1996; Castel and Soukiassian 1989; 1992; Harrel and Storemyr 2009; Harrell 2012). Together with them, big handheld pounders and stone tools with wooden handles were used to knock off the corners and the edges of bedrock and to create stone blocks. However, no example of such devices has been observed in either of the museum collections studied. With the introduction of metal tools, lithic implements were often used in combination with them, by sharpening the tips, straightening curvatures, repairing cracks and hitting the base of tools like picks. However, as suggested by Harrell, iron tools inside mines are extremely rare finds, probably because, even when broken, they were taken away, given that iron was a valuable commodity (Harrell *et al.* 2006).

All the examples described above highlight the limits of present knowledge on the grinding devices and show how it is currently difficult to outline the development of the macro-lithic artefacts from the Eastern Desert, including those described in this paper. This remark can also be extended to the traces of use, very evident on one example here described (N. 7), as much as on many Eastern Desert grindstones recorded by the Castiglionis as well as by the Klemms, but absent from other macroscopically examined examples. It is well known that striations are the result of the movement of a harder rock surface across a softer one,

---

breaking bonds between rock particles on both surfaces, which become abrasive agents (Adams 1993a, 62-70; 2002, 33-37; 2014, 132-135). The explanation for the difference in the traces of use may lie in the remarks made by Harrell, who noted that striations on the Hosh el-Guruf grinding devices are shallower than the ones on Eastern Desert examples. It was actually suggested that the grindstones from Hosh el-Guruf were used for working softer auriferous quartz, which naturally disintegrated (Harrell 2010, 78-83). This hypothesis is based on the very similar shape of the macro-lithic tools and of their work surfaces in both areas, suggesting that they were used for the same functions, but that the traces of use characterising them are different. Moreover, it should be stressed that if the hypothesis relating shape and function is correct, the diversity of the shape of the other grinding devices stored in the Castiglioni Museum may be due not only to differing chronology but also to the fact that they were also used for working different materials.

Conclusion

The grinding devices collected by the CeRDO are a precious testimony to the typological variety of macro-lithic tools from the Sudanese Eastern Desert. Some of them could be regarded as specific categories of tools developed locally, while others could demonstrate the adoption in the region of lithic types originating in other areas. As stressed, a great deal can and must be done to improve our knowledge about these materials, as the richness of information on ancient economy and technology which they can provide may already be envisaged from these preliminary interpretative remarks. Of course, it will be necessary to increase comparisons, and in general, the detailed studies of these tools, especially in Sudan. The systematic collection and study of macro-lithic tools from stratigraphic archaeological excavations could certainly provide more rigorous chronological benchmarks in order to clarify the typo-chronological development of macro-lithic tools in the Nubian-Sudanese Eastern Desert, while also improving the classification of those described in this paper. Moreover, it could be very useful to make a more systematic functional analysis, in order to clarify the destination of the tools and make a distinction between those used for gold processing and those used for the production of food or other materials.

Acknowledgments

For all information and data, as well as for their hospitality and kindness, I would like to thank Angelo Castiglioni and Alfredo Castiglioni, with the special hope that this work will honour the memory of Alfredo and his years of inspiring exploration in the Eastern Desert. With them, I would like to thank Dr Marco Castiglioni, for facilitating my documentation of all the material in the Castiglioni Museum. I also wish to thank Dr Serena Massa for her help and Dr Emanuela Barbanti for the geological information. My thanks also go to Prof. Andrea Manzo for giving me the chance to join the Italian Archaeological Expedition to the Eastern Sudan, and for allowing me to spend some days in the Sudan National Museum recording the finds of the CeRDO housed there.

Special thanks are due to Dr Abdelrahman Ali Mohamed, Director of the National Corporation for Antiquities and Museums of the Sudan, and to all the staff of the Corporation and of the Sudan National Museum, for their kindness and support during the days I spent with them. Many thanks go to Dr Donatella Usai, for her precious suggestions and Dr Giulio Lucarini, for his valuable advice and guidance. Any errors in this article remain mine.

Bibliography

Abd El-Maksoud, M. 1992. 'Nouveax anthroponymes pélusiotes', *Societes Urbaines en Egypte et au Soudan. Cahier de recherches de l'Institut de papyrologie et d'égyptologie de Lille* 14, 85-90.

Abd El-Rahman, Y., A. A Surour, A. H. W. El Manawi, M. Rifai, A. Abdel Motelib, W. K. Ali, and A. M. El Dougdoug 2013. 'Ancient Mining and Smelting Activities in the Wadi Abu Gerida Area, Central Eastern Desert, Egypt: Preliminary Results', *Archeometry* 55/6, 1067-1087.

Abdel-Magid, A. 1989. *Plant domestication in the Middle Nile Basin: an archaeoethnobotanical case study*. Cambridge Monographs in African Archaeology 35. BAR Int. Ser. 523. Oxford.

Adams, J. L. 1993a. 'Mechanism of wear on ground stone surfaces', *Pacific Coast Archaeological Society Quarterly* 29/4, 61-74.

Adams, J. L. 1993b. 'Toward understanding the technological development of Manos and Metates', *Kiva* 58/3, 331-334.

Adams, J. L. 2002. *Ground Stone Analysis: A Technological Approach*. Salt Lake City and Tucson.

Adams, J. L. 2014. 'Ground stone use-wear analysis: a review of terminology and experimental methods', *Journal of Archaeological Science* 48, 129-138.

Adams, J. L, J. S. Delgado, L. Dubreuil, C. Hamon, H. Plisson and R. Risch 2009. 'Functional Anlysis of Macro-Lithic artefacts: A focus on working surfaces', in F. Sternke, L. Eigeland and L.-J. Costa (eds), *Non-Flint Raw Material Use in Prehistory. Old prejudices and new directions*. Oxford, 43-63.

Alonso, N., M. Aulinas, M. T. Garcia, F. Martín, G. Prats and S. Vila 2011. 'Manufacturing rotary querns in the 4th century BC fortified settlement of Els Vilars (Arbeca, Catalonia, Spain)', in D. Williams and D. Peacock (eds), *Bread for the people: the archaeology of mills and milling. Proceedings of a colloquium held in the British School at Rome, 4th-7th November 2009*. BAR Int. Ser. 2274. Oxford, 55-65.

Ali, K., A. Andrsen, W. I. Manton, R. J. Stern, S. A. Omar and A. E. Maurice 2011. 'U–Pb zircon dating and Sr–Nd–Hf isotopic evidence to support a juvenile origin of the ~ 634 Ma El Shalul granitic gneiss dome, Arabian–Nubian Shield', *Geological Magazine* 149/5, 783-797.

Alonso, N., F. José Cantero, R. Jornet, D. López, E. Montes, G. Prats and S. Valezuela 2014. 'Milling wheat and barley with rotary querns: the *Ouarten* women (Dahmani, Kef, Tunisia)', in L. Selsing (ed.), *Seen through a millstone*. AmS-Skrifter 24. Stavanger, 11-30.

Barnard, H. 2012. 'Introduction to Part 1: From Adam to Alexander (500,000-2500 Years Ago)', in H. Barnard and K. Duistermaat (eds), *The History of the Peoples of the Eastern Desert*. Cotsen Institute of Archaeology Monograph 73. Los Angeles, 3-31.

Bofill, M., H. Procopiou, R. Vargiolu and H. Zahouani 2013. 'Use-wear analysis of Near Eastern prehistoric Grinding stones', in P. C. Anderson, C. Cheval and A. Durand (eds), *Regards croisés sur les outils liés au travail des végétaux. An interdisciplinary focus on plant-working tools*. Antibes, 219-235.

Botros, N. S. 2002. 'Metallogeny of gold in relation to the evolution of the Nubian Shield in Egypt', *Ore Geology Reviews* 19, 137-164.

Bragantini, I. and R. Pirelli, 2013. 'The Archaeological Mission of "L'Orientale" in the Central-Eastern Desert of Egypt', *Newsletter di Archeologia CISA* 4, 47-156.

Bruyère, B. 1966. *Fouilles de Clysma-Qolzoum (Suez).1930-1932.* Cairo.

Caneva, I. 1983. 'Excavating Saggai 1', in I. Caneva (ed.), *Pottery using gatherers and hunters at Saggai 1 (Sudan): preconditions for food production.* Origini. Preistoria e Protostoria delle Civiltà Antiche 12. Roma, 7-29.

Caneva, I. 1988. *El Geili: The history of a Middle Nile Environment, 7000 B.C.- A.D. 1500.* BAR Int. Ser. 424. Oxford.

Castel, G. and G. Soukiassian 1989. *Gebel el-Zeit I. Les mines de Galén (Egypte, IIe millénaire av. J.-C.).* Fouilles de l'Institut Français d'Archéologie Orientale du Caire 35. Cairo.

Castel, G., B. Mathieu, H. Hélal, T. Abdallah and M. El Hawary 1992. 'Les Mines de Cuivre du Ouadi Dara. Rapport préliminaire sur les travaux de la saison 1991', *Bulletin de l'Institut Français d'Archéologie Orientale* 92, 51-65.

Castel, G., B. Mathieu, G. Pouit, M. El Hawary, G. Shaaban, H. Hellal, T. Abdallah and A. Ossama 1996. 'Wadi Dara Copper Mines', in F. A. Esmael and Z. Hawass (eds), *Proceedings of the First International Conference on Ancient Egyptian Mining & Metallurgy and Conservation of Metallic Artifacts: Cairo, Egypt, 10-12 April 1995.* Cairo, 15-31.

Castel, G., E. C. Köhler, B. Mathieu and G. Pouit 1998. 'Les mines du Ouadi Umm Balad désert Oriental', *Bulletin de l'Institut Français d'Achéologie Orientale* 98, 57-87.

Castiglioni, A. and A. Castiglioni 2004. 'Gold in the Eastern Desert', in D. A. Welsby and J. R. Anderson (eds), *Sudan: ancient treasures: an exhibition of recent discoveries from the Sudan National Museum.* London 122-131.

Castiglioni, A. and A. Castiglioni 2006. *Nubia. Magica terra millenaria.* Firenzei.

Castiglioni, A., A. Castiglioni and J. Vercoutter 1995. *L'Eldorado dei Faraoni. Alla ricerca di Berenice Pancrisia.* Novara.

Castiglioni, A., A. Castiglioni and K. Sadr 1997. 'Sur les traces des Blemmis: Les tombes Bejas au premier millénaire après J.-C. dans les collines de la Mer Rouge', in International Conference for Nubian Studies (eds), *Actes de la VIIIe Conférence internationale des études nubiennes; II-Découvertes archéologiques. Cahier de recherches de l'Institut de papyrologie et d'égyptologie de Lille* 17/2. Lille, 163-167.

Castiglioni, A, A. Castiglioni, and C. Bonnet 2010. 'The gold mines of the Kingdom of Kerma', in W. Godlewski and A. Łajtar (eds), *Between the Cataracts: Proceedings of the 11th Conference for Nubian Studies* 2. Warsaw, 263-270.

Cauuet, B. 1991. 'L'exploitation de l'or en Limousin, des Gaulois aux Gallo-Romains', *Annales du Midi : revue archéologique, historique et philologique de la France méridionale* 103/194, 149-181.

Cauuet, B. 1999. 'L'exploitation de l'or en Gaule à l'Age du Fer', in B. Cauuet (ed.), *L'or dans l'antiquité de la mine à l'objet.* Aquitania, 31-70.

Chłodnicki, M., M. Kobusiewicz and K. Kroeper 2011. *Kadero: The Lech Krzyżaniak Excavations in the Sudan.* Studies in African Archaeology 10. Poznań.

Conophagos, C. E. 1980. *Le Larium antique et la technique grecque de la production de l'argent.* Athènes.

Dubreuil, L. and D. Savage 2013. 'Ground stones: a synthesis of the use-wear approach', *Journal of Archaeological Science* 48, 139-153.

Edwards, D. N. and A. J. Mills 2013. '"Pharaonic" Sites in the Batn el-Hajar – the 'Archaeological Survey of Sudanese Nubia' Revisited', *Sudan & Nubia* 17, 8-17.

Eide, T., T. Hägg, R. H. Pierce and L. Török 1996. *Fontes Historiae Nubiorum. Textual Sources for the History of the Middle Nile Region between the Eight Century BC and the Sixth Century AD. Vol. II: From the Mid-Fifth to the First Century BC.* Bergen.

Eiwanger, J. E. 1984. *Merimde - Benisalame. I: Die Funde der Urschicht.* Archäologische Veröffentlichungen 47. Mainz am Rhein.

Eiwanger, J. E. 1988. *Merimde - Benisalame. II: Die funde der mittleren Merimdekultur.* Archäologische Veröffentlichungen 51. Mainz am Rhein.

El Bedewi, M. A. and K. H. A. Kader 1996. 'A Geological View of the Ancient Egyptian Gold Mines', in F. A. Esmael and Z. Hawass (eds), *Proceedings of the First International Conference on Ancient Egyptian Mining & Metallurgy and Conservation of Metallic Artifacts: Cairo, Egypt, 10-12 April 1995.* Cairo, 55-57.

Fowler, A.-R., H. Khamees and H. Dowidar 2007. 'El Sibai gneissic complex, Central Eastern Desert, Egypt: Folded nappes and syn-kinematic gneissic granitoid sheets – not a core complex', *Journal of African Earth Sciences* 49, 119-135.

Fuchs, G., V. Hašek and A. Poichystal 1996. 'Application of Geophysics in the Research of Ancient Mining in Egypt', in F. A. Esmael and Z. Hawass (eds), *Proceedings of the First International Conference on Ancient Egyptian Mining & Metallurgy and Conservation of Metallic Artifacts: Cairo, Egypt, 10-12 April 1995.* Cairo, 33-53.

Haaland, R. 1987. *Socio-Economic Differentiation in the Neolithic Sudan.* Cambridge Monographs in African Archaeology 20. Oxford.

Haaland, R. 1992. 'Fish, pots, and grain: Early and Mid-Holocene adaptations in the Central Sudan', *African Archaeological Review* 10, 43-64.

Hamon, C. 2006. *Broyage et abrasion au Néolithique ancien. Caractérisation technique et fonctionnelle des outillages en grès du Bassin parisien.* BAR Int. Ser. 1551. Oxford.

Hamon, C. 2008. 'Functional analysis of stone grinding and polishing tools from the earliest Neolithic of north-western Europe', *Journal of Archaeological Science* 35, 1502-1520.

Harrell, J. A. 2010. 'Archaeological Geology of Hosh el-Guruf, Fourth Nile Cataract, Sudan', *Gdańsk Archaeological Museum African Reports* 7, 71-84.

Harrell, J. A. 2012. 'Utilitarian stones', *UCLA Encyclopedia of Egyptology.* [online] (https://escholarship.org/uc/item/77t294df) accessed 29th September 2018.

Harrell, J. A., V. M. Brown and M. S. Masoud 2000. 'An Early Dynastic Quarry for Stone Vessels at Gebel Manzal el-Seyl, Eastern Desert', *Journal of Egyptian Archaeology* 86, 33-42.

Harrell, J. A., S. E. Sidebotham, R. S. Bagnall, S. Marchand, J. E. Gates and J.-L. Rivard 2006. 'The Ptolemaic to Early Roman Amethyst Quarry at Abu Diyeiba in Egypt's Eastern Desert', *Bulletin de l'Institut Français d'Achéologie Orientale* 106, 127-162.

Harrell, J. A. and V. M. Brown 2008. 'Discovery of a Medieval Islamic Industry for Steatite Cooking Vessels in Egypt's Eastern Desert', in Y. M. Rowan and J. R. Ebeling (eds), *New Approaches to Old Stones: Recent Studies of Ground Stone Artifacts.* London-Oakville, 41-65.

Harrell, J. A. and P. Storemyr 2009. 'Ancient Egyptian quarries—an illustrated overview', in N. Abu-Jaber, E. G. Bloxam, P. Degryse and T. Heldal (eds), *Quarry Scapes: ancient stone quarry landscapes in the Eastern Mediterranean.* Geological Survey of Norway, Special Publication 12. Norway, 7-50.

Hayes, W. C. 1965. *Most Ancient Egypt.* Chicago-London.

Heldal, T. 2009. 'Constructing a quarry landscape from empirical data. General perspectives and a case study at the Aswan West Bank, Egypt', in N. Abu-Jaber, E. G. Bloxam, P. Degryse and T.

Heldal (eds), *Quarry Scapes: ancient stone quarry landscapes in the Eastern Mediterranean*. Geological Survey of Norway, Special Publication 12. Norway, 125-153.

Jaccottey, L., N. Alonso, S. Defressigne, C. Hamon, S. Lepareux-Couturier, V. Brisotto, S. Galland-Crety, F. Jodry, J.-P. Lagadec, H. Lepaumier, S. Longepierre, B. Robin and N. Zaour 2013. 'Le passage des meules va-et-vient aux meules rotatives en France', in S. Krausz, A. Colin, K. Gruel, I. Ralston and T. Dechezleprêtre (eds), *L'âge du Fer en Europe : Mélanges offerts à O. Buchsenchutz*. Ausonius, 405-420.

Jesse, F. 2004. 'The Wadi Howar', in D. A. Welsby and J. R. Anderson (eds), *Sudan: ancient treasures: an exhibition of recent discoveries from the Sudan National Museum*. London, 53-60.

Johnson, P. R. and B. Woldehaimanot 2003. 'Development of the Arabian-Nubian Shield: perspectives on accretion and deformation in the northern East African Orogen and the assembly of Gondwana', *Geological Society London, Special Publications* 206. London, 289-325.

Jórdeczka, M. 2011. 'Stone implements', in Chłodnicki *et al.*, 299-323.

Keding, B. 1997. *Djabarona 84/13: Untersuchungen zur Besiedlungsgeschichte des Wadi Howar anhand der Keramik des 3. und 2. Jahrtausends v. Chr.* Africa Praehistorica 9. Köln.

Klemm, D., R. Klemm and A. Murr 2002. 'Gold of the Pharaohs – 6000 years of gold mining in Egypt and Nubia', *African Earth Sciences* 33, 643-659.

Klemm, R. and D. Klemm 1996. 'Evolution of Methods for Prospection, Mining and Processing of Gold in Egypt', in F. A. Esmael and Z. Hawass (eds), *Proceedings of the First International Conference on Ancient Egyptian Mining & Metallurgy and Conservation of Metallic Artifacts: Cairo, Egypt, 10-12 April 1995*. Cairo, 341-354.

Klemm, R. and D. Klemm D. 2013. *Gold and Gold Mining in Ancient Egypt and Nubia*. Berlin-Heidelberg.

Krzyżaniak, L. 1978. 'New Light on Early Food-Production in the Central Sudan', *Journal of African History* 9/2,159-172.

Krzyżaniak, L. 2004. 'Kadero', in D. A. Welsby, and J. R. Anderson (eds), *Sudan: ancient treasures: an exhibition of recent discoveries from the Sudan National Museum*. London, 49-52.

Lange, M., J. Richter and W. Schuck 2006. *Wadi Shaw - Wadi Sahal: Studien zur holozänen Besiedlung der Laqiya-Region (Nordsudan)*. Africa Praehistorica 19. Köln.

Lucarini, G. 2014. 'Large stone tools from the Hidden Valley Village and basin', in B. E. Barich, G. Lucarini, M. A. Hamdan and F. A. Hassan (eds), *From Lake to Sand. The Archaeology of Farafra Oasis, Western Desert, Egypt*. Firenze, 285-299.

Madureri, E. 1984. 'Storia della costruzione dei molini, parte 3', *Tecnica molitoria* 10/84, 733-743.

Meeks D. 1997. 'Les meules rotatives en Égypte. Datation et usages', in D. Meeks and D. Garcia (eds), *Techniques et économie antiques et médiévales : le temps de l'innovation. Colloque international (C.N.R.S.) Aix-en-Provence 21–23 Mai 1996*. Paris, 20-28.

Meyer, C. 1995. 'A Byzantine gold-mining town in the eastern desert of Egypt: Bir Umm Fawakhir, 1992-93', *Journal of Roman Archaeology* 8, 192-224.

Meyer, C. 2010. 'The Kingdom of Kush in the 4th Cataract: Archaeological Salvage of the Oriental Institute Nubian Expedition 2007 Season. Part II. Grinding Stones and Gold Mining at Hosh el-Guruf, Sudan', *Gdańsk Archaeological Museum and Heritage Protection Fund African Reports* 7, 39-52.

Mills, A. J. 1973. 'The Archaeological Survey from Gemai to Dal. Report on the 1965-1966 Season', *Kush* 15, 200-210.

Neumayr, P., A. Mogessie, G. Hoinkes and J. Puhl 1997. 'Geological setting of the Meatiq metamorphic core complex in the Eastern Desert of Egypt based on amphibolite geochemistry', *Journal of African Earth Sciences* 23/3, 331-345.

Oldfather, C. H. 1961. *Diodorus of Sicily, Vol. II. The Loeb Classical Library*. London and Cambridge, Massachusetts.

Papadimitriou, G. D. 2016. 'The so-called 'helicoidal' ore washeries of Laurion: their actual function as circular mills in the process of beneficiation of silver and lead contained in old litharge stocks', in E. Photos-Jones, Y. Bassiakos, E. Filippaki, A. Hein, I. Karatasios, V. Kilikoglou and E. Kouloumpi (eds.), *Proceedings of the 6th Symposium of the Hellenic Society for Archaeometry*. BAR Int. Ser. 2780. Oxford, 113-118.

Reinold, J. 1982. *Le site préhistorique d'El-Kadada (Soudan central). Volume I-II-III*. Thèse de doctorat de troisième cycle. Université de Lille III.

Sadr, K., A. Castiglioni, A. Castiglioni and G. Negro 1994. *Interim report of the Eastern Desert research centre's (CeRDO) archeological activities 1989/93*. Varese.

Schön, W. and U. Holter 1990. 'Grinding implements from the Neolithic and recent times in desert areas in Egypt and Sudan', *Beitrage zur allgemeinen und vergleichenden Archäologie* 9-10, 359-379.

Shaw C. T. 1996. 'New Kingdom Mining Technology with reference to Wadi Arabah', in F. A. Esmael and Z. Hawass (eds), *Proceedings of the First International Conference on Ancient Egyptian Mining & Metallurgy and Conservation of Metallic Artifacts: Cairo, Egypt, 10-12 April 1995*. Cairo, 1-14.

Shaw, I. and R. Jameson 1993. 'Amethyst Mining in the Eastern Desert: A Preliminary Survey at Wadi el-Hudi', *Journal of Egyptian Archaeology* 79, 81-97.

Siddal, R. 2013. 'Geology in the British Museum: the monumental stones of the Eastern Desert', *Museum Geology* 1, 1-16.

Sidebotham, S. E. and W. Z. Wendrich 1998. *Berenike '96: Report of the 1996 excavations at Berenike (Egyptian Red Sea coast) and the Survey of the Eastern Desert*. Leiden.

Sidebotham, S.E. and W. Z. Wendrich 2007. *Berenike 1999/2000: report on the excavations at Berenike, including excavations in Wadi Kalalat and Siket, and the survey of the Mons Smaragdus region*. Cotsen Institute of Archaeology Monograph 56. Los Angeles.

Sidebotham, S. E., M. Hence and H. M. Nouwens 2008. *The Red Land. The Illustrated Archaeology of Egypt's Eastern Desert*. Cairo-New York.

Storemyr, P. 2014. 'A prehistoric grinding stone quarry in the Egyptian Sahara', in L. Selsing (ed.), *Seen through a millstone*. AmS-Skrifter 24. Stavanger, 67-82.

Tratsaert, B. J. M. 2012. 'Roman Gold Mining in the Eastern Desert: The Mining Settlement in Wadi Bakariya', in H. Barnard and K. Duistermaat (eds), *The History of the Peoples of the Eastern Desert*. Cotsen Institute of Archaeology Monograph 73. Los Angeles, 245-255.

Tawab, M. A., G. Castel, G. Pouit and P. Ballet 1990. 'Archéo-géologie des anciennes mines de cuivre et d'or des régions El-Urf / Mongul-Sud et Dara-Ouest', *Bulletin de l'Institut Français d'Archéologie Orientale* 90, 359-364.

Usai, D. 2003. 'The Lithic Industries', in D. A. Welsby (ed.), *Survey above the Fourth Nile Cataract*. Sudan Archaeological Research Society Publication 10. London, 79-110.

Vermeersch, P. M. 2012. 'Contributions to the Prehistory of the Eastern Desert in Egypt', in H. Bernard and K. Duistermaat (eds), *The History of the Peoples of Eastern Desert*. Cotsen Institute of Archaeology Monograph 73. Los Angeles, 25-34.

Vermeersch, P. M., V. Van Peer, V. Rots and R. Paulussen 2005. 'A Survey of the Bili Cave and its Surroundings in the Red Sea Mountains, El Gouna, Egypt', *Journal of African Archaeology* 3/2, 267-276.

Watts, S. R. 2014. *The Life and Death of Querns. The deposition and use-contexts of querns in South-Western England from the Neolithic to the Iron Age.* Southampton.

Wefers, S. and F. Mangartz 2014. 'Millstones of Aswan red granite found on the island of Elephantine, Egypt', in L. Selsing (ed.), *Seen through a millstone.* AmS-Skrifter 24. Stavanger, 83-96.

Welsby, D. A. 2003. *Survey above the Fourth Nile Cataract.* Sudan Archaeological Research Society Publication 10. London.

Wendorf, F. and R. Schild 1989. *The Prehistory of Wadi Kubbaniya Volume 3. Late Paleolithic Archaeology.* Dallas.

Wendorf, F. and R. Schild 2001. *Holocene Settlement of the Egyptian Sahara. Volume 1. The Archaeology of Nabta Playa.* New York.

Wright, K. W. 1992. 'A Classification System for Ground Stone Tools from the Prehistoric Levant', *Paléorient* 18/2, 53-81.

Zarattini, A. 1983. 'Ground stone implements from Saggai 1', in I. Caneva (ed.), *Pottery using gatherers and hunters at Saggai 1 (Sudan): preconditions for food production.* Origini. Preistoria e Protostoria delle Civiltà Antiche 12. Roma, 234-242.

Websites

http://www.blog.amarawest.britishmuseum.org/
http://www.britishmuseum.org/
http://www.ucl.ac.uk/museums

Appendix A

TABLE 10.1. LIST OF MACRO-LITHIC TOOLS CITED IN THE TEXT, WITH THE RELEVANT GENERAL INFORMATION.

	TYPE	MATE-RIAL	DIMENSION	SHAPE	PROFILE	OBVERSE	REVERSE	SIDES	WEIGHT	COMMENTS	PROVE-NANCE	DATING
1	Grinding slab	Sandstone	L: c. 480mm W: c. 375mm Th: 340-370mm L depression: 210mm W depression: 145mm Depth depression: 180mm	Subrectan-gular	Irregularly flat	Oval working plan, with possible pecking pits, shallow striations & little sheens	Probably shaped for making a flat base	Possible shaping pecking marks	9.9kg	Associated with a grinder (N° 2)	A 16 21° 34.640' N 32° 15.630' E	New Kingdom?
2	Grinder	Sandstone	L: 143mm W: 116mm Th: c. 60mm	Oval	Plano-convex	Crack at one edge	Rough surface, slightly smooth in the middle, with scattered pecking pits, possible striations at the edges & a crack along one side	Possible pounding marks	1.8kg	Associated with a grindstone (N° 1)	A 16 21° 34.640' N 32° 15.630' E	New Kingdom?
3	Grinding slab	Sandstone	L: 475mm W: 319mm Th: 33mm L depression: 165mm W depression: 110mm Depth depression: 17mm Outer ø holes: 25mm Inner ø holes: 5mm L depression (reverse): 100mm W depression (reverse): 80mm Depth depression (reverse): 8mm	Irregularly oval	Irregularly flat	Oval working plan, with pits, shallow striations & evident sheens	Very rough surface, smoother in the middle. Sheens around a central depression	Possible shaping marks	6.5kg	Two drilled holes in the upper part of the tools. The tool is crossed by a crack in the middle. Piece together. Associated with a grinder (N° 4).	B0.1 21° 8.380' N 32° 33.310' E	Neolithic period?

TABLE 10.1. LIST OF MACRO-LITHIC TOOLS CITED IN THE TEXT, WITH THE RELEVANT GENERAL INFORMATION (CONT).

	TYPE	MATE-RIAL	DIMENSION	SHAPE	PROFILE	OBVERSE	REVERSE	SIDES	WEIGHT	COMMENTS	PROVE-NANCE	DATING
4	Grinder		ø: 100 mm Th: 30mm	Circular	Rounded flat	Quite smooth surface, with multidirectional striations, sheens and scattered tiny pits	Smooth and worn surface, with multidirectional striations, sheens & scattered tiny pits	Rough surface, with worn areas & possible pits	0.5kg	Associated with a grindstone (N° 3)	B0.1 21° 8.380' N 32° 33.310' E	Neolithic period?
5	Grinding slab	Sandstone	L: 432mm W: c. 200mm Th: 35mm L (depression): c. 165mm W (depression): c. 150mm Depth (depression): 19mm	Irregularly subrectangular	Flat and curved	Very smooth surface. Striations on the curved part, depression in the middle, with pits & longitudinal striations of different dimensions and depth	Curved sides. Flat in the middle, probably shaped for making a flat base	Irregular	4.1kg		B0.1 21° 8.380' N 32° 33.310' E	Neolithic period?
6	Grinder	Sandstone	L: 167mm W: 96mm Th: 42mm	Oval	Plano-convex	Rough surface, especially in the middle	Rough surface characterised by shallow & deep longitudinal striations	Natural rock surface	0.9kg		B0.1 21° 8.380' N 32° 33.310' E	Neolithic period?
7	Quern	Sandstone	L: 480mm W (max.): 225mm W (min.): 103mm Th (max.) : 135mm Th (min.): 59mm L depression: 380mm W depression: 210mm Depth depression: 20mm	Irregular	Irregular	Oval working plan characterised by very smooth and polished surface, with evident longitudinal striations	Probably partially shaped for making a flat base	Irregular	14.6kg		?	New Kingdom?
8	Grinder/ Crusher	Sandstone	L: 122mm W: 139mm Th: 81mm	Slightly oval	Plano-convex	Rough surface in the middle, smoother at the edges, with hammering pits	Quite rough surface characterised by hammering pits & deep horizontal striations	Possible pecking and hammering pits	1.9kg		Near B 34	New Kingdom?

TABLE 10.1. LIST OF MACRO-LITHIC TOOLS CITED IN THE TEXT, WITH THE RELEVANT GENERAL INFORMATION (CONT).

	TYPE	MATE-RIAL	DIMENSION	SHAPE	PROFILE	OBVERSE	REVERSE	SIDES	WEIGHT	COMMENTS	PROVE-NANCE	DATING
9	Grinding slab	Conglomerate	L: 410mm W (max.): 260mm W (min.): 86mm Th. (max.): 84mm Th (min.): 40mm L (depression): 135mm W (depression): 115mm Depth (depression): 15mm	Tear drop shape	Irregularly flat	Rough area, especially at the edges, smooth areas with sheens especially around the depression in the middle, characterised by evident pits & striations	Rough surface partially shaped for making a flat base	Probably shaped	8.9kg		16 G 21° 28.583' N 32° 28.133' E	?
10	Quern	Sandstone	L: 473mm W: 260mm H.: 130mm	Ellipsoidal	Concave-convex	Working plan on the whole surface, characterised by a smooth surface, with oval & circular pecking pits & parallel longtitudinal striations	Particularly curved sides. Slightly flat in the middle, probably shaped for making a flat base	Probably shaped	24.7kg		Wadi Gabgaba 22° 4.780' N 33° 3.700' E	?
11	Grinder	Conglomerate	L: 190mm W: 850mm Th: 440mm	Ellipsoidal	Plano-convex	Rough surface characterised by tiny pits at the edges & possible scattered multidirectional striations. Depression in the middle	Rough surface characterised by tiny pits and holes at the edges & scattered multidirectional striations. Depression in the middle	Natural rock surface	1kg		Wadi Gabgaba 22° 4.780' N 33° 3.700' E	?

TABLE 10.1. LIST OF MACRO-LITHIC TOOLS CITED IN THE TEXT, WITH THE RELEVANT GENERAL INFORMATION (CONT).

	TYPE	MATERIAL	DIMENSION	SHAPE	PROFILE	OBVERSE	REVERSE	SIDES	WEIGHT	COMMENTS	PROVENANCE	DATING
12	Grinding slab	Conglomerate	L: 560mm W: 340mm Th: 26mm L. (depression): c. 190mm W (depression): c. 140mm Depth (depression): 14mm	Oval	Flat	Rough surface, smoother in upper part and at one edge. Slightly decentralized depression characterised by longitudinal striations & small polish sheens. Pits & little striations on the whole obverse	Very rough surface probably shaped for making a flat base	Probably shaped		In the same area of three grinders/pestles (N° 28-30)	4G 21° 34.823' N 32° 30.182' E	?
13	Grinder/ Crusher	Coarse rock	ø: 112mm Th: 35mm	Circular	Flat	Very rough surface, with tiny hammering pits & scattered	Two halves, one very smooth & polished, with small sheens & striations, one very rough as the edges	Rough. Natural rock surface	0.8kg	In the same area of the grindstone (N° 27) & two grinders/ pestles (N° 29 & 30).	4G 21° 34.823' N 32° 30.182' E	?
14	Grinder/ Crusher	Coarse rock	ø: 117mm Th: 25-30mm	Circular	Flat in upper part, slightly oblique in the lower one	Rough surface, with tiny hammering pits	Two halves, one rough & irregular, one smooth, especially in the middle, with small sheens	Polished & smoothed areas on the sides	0.7kg	In the same area of the grindstone (N° 27) & two grinders/ pestles (N° 28 & 30).	4G 21° 34.823' N 32° 30.182' E	?
15	Grinder	Sandstone	L. (max.): 96mm L. (min.): 22mm W: 149mm Th (max.): 42mm Th (min.): c. 8mm	Oval	Biconvex (wedge-shaped)	Rough surface, with possible hammering pits at the edges	Two halves, one very smooth and worn, one rougher, both with shallow parallel striations		0.6kg	Possible double stroke motion. In the same area of the grindstone (N° 27) & two grinders/ pestles (N° 28 & 29).	4G 21° 34.823' N 32° 30.182' E	?

TABLE 10.1. LIST OF MACRO-LITHIC TOOLS CITED IN THE TEXT, WITH THE RELEVANT GENERAL INFORMATION (CONT).

	TYPE	MATE-RIAL	DIMENSION	SHAPE	PROFILE	OBVERSE	REVERSE	SIDES	WEIGHT	COMMENTS	PROVE-NANCE	DATING
16	Grinding slab	Conglom-erate	L: 763mm W: 395mm Th: 41mm L (depression): c. 210mm W (depression): c. 145mm Depth (depression): c. 18mm	Ellipsoidal	Flat	Rough surface, especially at the edges. Slightly decentralized depression characterised by a smooth surface	Rough surface probably shaped for making a flat base	Probably shaped	20.9kg	In the same area of a grinder/pounder (N° 32) & a grinder (N° 33)	4G 21° 34.823' N 32° 30.182' E	?
17	Grinder/ Crusher	Conglom-erate	L: 136mm W: 107mm Th: 54 mm	Oval	Irregularly flat	Very rough surface	Irregular rough but levelled surface, with small smooth areas & different depressions, one in the middle	Divided in two halves, one rough, one smoother & levelled	1.3kg	In the same area of a grindstone (N° 31) & a grinder (N° 33).	4G 21° 34.823' N 32° 30.182' E	?
18	Grinder		L: 113 mm W: 95 mm Th (max.): 34mm Th (min.): c. 3mm	Irregularly oval	Irregularly triangular	Multidirectional striations on the whole smooth surface, which has a recess at one edge	Very smooth & polished surface, with evident striations, tiny pits & sheens & a convexity near the wider side, which form a smoother & shinier little area	Rough sides	0.5kg	Double working plan. In the same area of a grindstone (N° 31) & a grinder/pounder (N° 32).	4G 21° 34.823' N 32° 30.182' E	?

TABLE 10.1. LIST OF MACRO-LITHIC TOOLS CITED IN THE TEXT, WITH THE RELEVANT GENERAL INFORMATION (CONT).

	TYPE	MATE-RIAL	DIMENSION	SHAPE	PROFILE	OBVERSE	REVERSE	SIDES	WEIGHT	COMMENTS	PROVE-NANCE	DATING
19	Grinder		L: 153mm W (max.): 100mm W (min.): 59mm Th (max.): 33mm Th (min.): 2mm	Irregular drop shape	Irregular wedge-shape	Rough surface, with cracks. Two or three flakes were probably detached from the lower part	Very smooth surface characterised by evident parallel longitudinal striations on the whole working plan. Wedge near the rounded edge, which form a little oval area with evident striations too	Irregular, with possible flaking or detachment.	0.6kg	Possible long use	?	?
20	Grinder	Siltstone	L: c. 200mm W (max.): 126mm W (min.): 37mm Th (max.): 44mm Th (min.): 3mm	Irregular drop shape	Flat – wedge shaped	Quite smooth surface, with shallow horizontal parallel striations. Rough surface at the edges	Very smooth & polished surface, with evident parallel transversal striations, perpendicular to the wedge in the middle	Quite irregular	1.5kg	Irregular edges. Possible double stroke motion.	?	?
21	Grinder		L: c. 130mm W: 95mm Th (max.): 70mm Th (min.): 26mm	Oval	Plano - convex	Very convex at one edge, characterised by a rough surface with possible hammering pits & cracks	Very smooth surface, characterised by shallow longitudinal & oblique striations & sheens, concentrated in particular at the edges.	Striations on the edges. Possible shaping marks & hammering pits.	1.4kg			

TABLE 10.1. LIST OF MACRO-LITHIC TOOLS CITED IN THE TEXT, WITH THE RELEVANT GENERAL INFORMATION (CONT).

	TYPE	MATERIAL	DIMENSION	SHAPE	PROFILE	OBVERSE	REVERSE	SIDES	WEIGHT	COMMENTS	PROVENANCE	DATING
22	Crusher/Anvil	Siltstone	L: 153mm W: 118mm Th: 63mm L. (base): 125mm W. (base): c. 55mm ø (depression): 28mm Depth. (depression): 8mm	Irregularly polygonal	Irregularly trapezoidal	Quite smooth surface, with irregular edges. Depression in the middle with tiny pits, probably the result of chopping and drilling actions (working plan/handle). Straight edge in the lower part	Very rough and irregular surface	Hammering pits along the sides. Flat base characterised by a quite smooth surface, with striations & hammering pits especially in the middle	1.5kg		?	?
23	Grinder	Granite	L: 245mm W: 98mm Th: c. 75mm	Ellipsoidal	Plano-convex	Rough surface, with two small lateral depressions	Smooth surface characterised by little shallow scattered transversal & oblique striations	Probably shaped	2.5kg	Tiny pits on both tips. Possible multi-purpose tool.	C 37 (Alaar) 21° 41.967' N 35° 8.650' E	Medieval Period?
24	Pestle/Grinder		L: 265mm W: 65mm Th: 49mm	Oblong cylindrical	Plano-convex	Smooth surface characterised by pits at the two ends. Crack at ¾ of length	Smooth surface, characterised by pecking pits, horizontal striations & sheens. Crack at ¾ of length	Pounding pits on the two tips. Possible shaped sides	1.6kg	Possible multipurpose tool. Found in the mines. Piece together	C 37 (Alaar) 21° 41.967' N 35° 8.650' E	Medieval Period?
25	Rotary quern (upper part)	Metasedimentary rock	ø: 255mm Th: c. 9mm ø (central hole): 40mm ø (lateral hole): 20mm	Irregular	Irregularly flat	Rough surface, characterised by fractures, cracks & two circular holes	Smooth surface, with evident circular striations, deeper in the middle, & two circular holes	Circular striations along the sides. Wedge border.	11.4kg	Associated with a lower part (N° 13)	B 7 (Idarib) 21° 6.630' N 33° 24.930' E	Roman/Medieval Period

TABLE 10.1. LIST OF MACRO-LITHIC TOOLS CITED IN THE TEXT, WITH THE RELEVANT GENERAL INFORMATION (CONT).

	TYPE	MATERIAL	DIMENSION	SHAPE	PROFILE	OBVERSE	REVERSE	SIDES	WEIGHT	COMMENTS	PROVENANCE	DATING
26	Rotary quern (upper part)	Sandstone	ø: c. 260mm Th: 76mm ø (central hole): 65mm ø (lateral hole): 56mm Depth (lateral hole): 48mm W. lateral recess: 35mm	Irregularly circular	Plano-convex	Rough surface with shaping marks. Central hole with a depression in the upper part. Hole not perforated on one side, recess on the other	Smooth surface characterised by shallow circular striations	Shaping marks along the sides		Working marks around the central hole & on the depression. The lateral recess originally may have been a second hole for the handle	Near C 37 (Alaar)	Roman/Medieval Period
27	Rotary quern (upper part)	Granite?	ø: c. 360mm Th. max: 134mm Th. min: 54mm ø (central hole): 57mm W. lateral hole: 27mm (as preserved)	Irregularly circular	Irregular	Rough surface, characterised by cracks & fractures, especially at one side & by a central hole	Concave, with a smooth surface, characterised by shallow circular striations & a central hole	Circular striations along the sides. Wedge border			Near C 37 (Alaar)	Roman/Medieval Period
28	Rotary quern (lower part)	Effusive magmatic rock with an intrusive granite part	L. max: 410 mm W. max: c. 480mm H. max: c. 110mm H. min: c. 5mm inner ø: 330mm inner depth: c. 60mm ø (hole): 10mm Depth. (hole): c. 5mm ø spindle: 260mm h spindle: 11mm	Irregular	Irregular	Circular working plan, characterised by a smooth surface, with evident circular striations, a possible central little spindle & a little hole near it	Probably shaped for making a flat base. Circular depression in the middle	Irregular, with fractures	16.7kg	Associated with an upper part (N° 10)	B 7 (Idarib) 21° 6.630' N 33° 24.930' E	Roman/Medieval Period
29	Rotary quern (lower part)		L. (max): c. 500mm H. (max): c. 210mm H. (min): 116mm inner ø: 440mm inner depth (max): c. 50mm inner depth (min): c. 3mm L. (hole): 40mm W. (hole): 250mm depth (hole): c. 4mm	Irregular	Irregular	Circular working plan characterised by a smooth surface with evident circular striations & shallow cracks	Probably shaped for making a flat base	Irregular. Probably shaped			Derahib (Berenice Pancrisia) 21° 57.167' N 35° 8.333' E	Roman/Medieval Period

TABLE 10.1. LIST OF MACRO-LITHIC TOOLS CITED IN THE TEXT, WITH THE RELEVANT GENERAL INFORMATION (CONT.).

	TYPE	MATE-RIAL	DIMENSION	SHAPE	PROFILE	OBVERSE	REVERSE	SIDES	WEIGHT	COMMENTS	PROVE-NANCE	DATING
30	Rotary quern (lower part)	Granite	L.: c. 500mm (as preserved) W.: c. 470mm (as preserved) inner ø: 320mm inner depth. (max): c. 75mm inner depth (min): c. 45mm H. max: c. 153mm H. min: c. 110mm ø hole: 17mm depth hole: c. 10mm	Irregular	Irregular. Flat in the lower part	Circular working plan, characterised by a quite smooth surface, with evident circular striations & scattered pits of different dimensions	Probably shaped for making a flat base	Rough. Probably shaped			Derahib (Berenice Pancrisia) 21° 57.167' N 35° 8.333' E	Roman/ Medieval Period
31	Mortar/ Anvil	Metamorphic rock (Ophiolite?)	L.: 420mm W. (max): c. 300mm W. (min): c. 180mm H. (max): 200mm H. (min): c. 130mm Outer ø depression: c. 160mm Inner ø depression: c. 90mm Depth depression: 60mm	Irregularly rectangular	Irregular	Slightly concave. Characterised by cracks, fractures & a depression in the middle, with pounding & hammering pits	Probably partially shaped for making a flat base	Irregular. Natural rock surface	38.4kg	Associated with two pestles (N° 7 & 8)	C 35 21° 31.850' N 35° 11.733 'E	New Kingdom?
32	Pestle	Metasedimentary rock	L.: 190mm W.: 70mm Th.: 66mm	Irregular rectangular	Plano-convex	Quite smooth surface with cracks	Quite smooth surface with fractures on the left edge	Shaped & smooth sides	3.8kg	Probably shaped to obtain an ergonomic handle. Associated with a mortar/anvil (N° 6) & a pestle (N° 8)	C 35 21° 31.850' N 35° 11.733 'E	New Kingdom?

TABLE 10.1. LIST OF MACRO-LITHIC TOOLS CITED IN THE TEXT, WITH THE RELEVANT GENERAL INFORMATION (CONT).

	TYPE	MATE-RIAL	DIMENSION	SHAPE	PROFILE	OBVERSE	REVERSE	SIDES	WEIGHT	COMMENTS	PROVE-NANCE	DATING
33	Hammerstone	Granite	ø: 890mm Th: 75mm	Almost spherical	Almost spherical	Rough surface with pounding & hammering pits on the edges	Rough surface with pounding & hammering pits on the edges	Rough surface with pounding & hammering pits	0.7kg	Multiple working plans. Associated with a mortar/anvil (N° 6) & a pestle (N°7)	C 35 21° 31.850' N 35° 11.733 'E	New Kingdom?
34	Mortar/Anvil		L: 410mm W: 440mm H.: 220mm ø (right cupule): 50mm Depth (right depression): 35mm ø (middle cupule): 150mm Depth (middle depression): 70mm ø (upper cupule): 80mm Depth (upper depression): 40mm	Irregular	Irregular	Quite smooth surface, with cracks and working marks. Three cupules & two depressions characterised by a smooth surface & evident hammering pits	Probably shaped for making a flat base	Probably shaped		Associated with two pounders/hammers (N° 17 and 18)	Derahib?	Medieval Period?
35	Hammer		L: 150mm W: 165mm Th (max): c. 160mm Th (min): 100mm ø (depressions): 50mm	Rounded triangular	Irregularly triangular	Rough surface. Depression in the middle	Very rough surface, with abrasions & depression in the middle	Fractures and hammering pits		Multiple working plan. Possible ergonomic handle. Associated with a mortar/anvil (N° 16) & a pounder/hammer (N° 18)	Derahib?	Medieval Period?

TABLE 10.1. LIST OF MACRO-LITHIC TOOLS CITED IN THE TEXT, WITH THE RELEVANT GENERAL INFORMATION (CONT).

	TYPE	MATE-RIAL	DIMENSION	SHAPE	PROFILE	OBVERSE	REVERSE	SIDES	WEIGHT	COMMENTS	PROVE-NANCE	DATING
36	Hammer		L: 140mm W: 125mm Th. (max): 125mm Th. (min): 70mm ø (depressions): 30-50mm	Irregular	Irregular	Divided by a convexity near the middle in two areas with central depressions characterised by smooth surfaces. Hammering pits along at the edges	Divided by a convexity near the middle in two areas, one with a central depression characterised by a smooth surface	Fractures and hammering pits		Multiple working plan. Possible ergonomic handle. Associated with a mortar/anvil (N° 16) & a pounder/hammer (N° 17)	Derahib?	Medieval Period?
37	Washing table fragment?	Gneiss	L: 280mm (as preserved) W: 430mm (as preserved) Th: 106mm W (between the grooves): 10-15mm	Irregular	Concave	Slightly rough surface characterised by shallow striations on the side & deep grooves	Flat in the middle, curved at the edges. Rough surface	Natural rock surface	21.1kg		D 5 21° 24.733' N 34° 35.633' E	Medieval Period?

124

Part II

The SARS
Korosko Road Project
(2013)

11. The Korosko Road as a major cross-desert route: a brief overview

Derek A. Welsby

The 18th and 19th century evidence

The Korosko Road was one of the most important desert routes connecting Egypt and Sudan. Leaving the Nile along the Wadi Korosko it ran approximately due south crossing the watershed via the Bab Korosko or Bab es-Silik (Plates 11.1 and 11.2) heading for the Wadi Murat where there was an abundant source of water reached by digging shallow wells. From there it rejoined the Nile in the vicinity of Abu Hamed. It was not, however, the only route available between Egypt and Sudan through the Eastern Desert. Another left the Nile at Deroueh (Daraou) a little downstream of Aswan (Figure 11.1). Although this route was longer there were apparently frequent sources of good water along it. It was this route which was used in the 1770s by James Bruce and in the early 19th century by Burckhardt (1819, 163ff.; Hoskins 1835, 19). Bruce's journey took him direct from Berber to Aswan via the 10 wells at Shikrib and other wells

Plate 11.1. Looking south towards the Bab es-Silik.

Plate 11.2. The desert midway between Bab es-Silik and Wadi Murat looking north.

at Tarfawi, to the east of the Korosko Road (Bruce 1805 VI, 455ff.). He noted that the desert nomads had had a good reputation for honesty and their profitable work depended upon it in the days when there were many caravans making the journey. In Bruce's day, however, trade had fallen off, there were fewer professional guides and they were less trustworthy (in Reid 1968, 254).

Burckhardt describes this eastern route thus as well as a more westerly route – The Korosko Road:

> "The road, which we had travelled is the only one that leads from Berber to Egypt, and is the general route of the Shendy and Sennaar caravans. There is a more western route from Berber to Seboua, a village on the Nile in the Berbera country, not far from Derr, the inhabitants of which actively

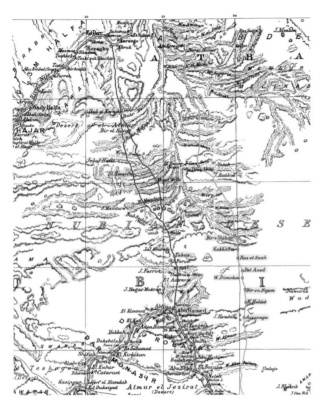

*Figure 11.1. The Korosko Road and the more
easterly route along the Wadi Gabgaba.*

engage in the slave trade. On that road the traveller finds only a single well,[1] which is situated
midway, four long days distant from Berber, and
as many from Seboua. It is called el Morrat (ألمرة),
and is very copious, but the water is ill-tasted. A
great inconvenience on that road is that neither
trees nor shrubs are anywhere found, whence
the camels are much distressed for food, and
passengers are obliged to carry wood with them
to dress their meals, and to warm themselves in
winter. The journey from Daraou to Berber had
taken us twenty-two days."

(Burckhardt 1819, 208).

Although the caravan which Burckhardt joined spent 22
days on the journey he notes that "Messengers on dromedar-
ies have often gone in eight days from Daraou to Berber."

In 1821, at the time of the invasion of Sudan by the army
of Mohammed Ali Pasha, Ismail Pasha granted to Sheikh
Khailfa of the Ababda the right to charge 10% duty on goods
passing through the desert north of Abu Hamed in return for
protection against the Bisharin and on provision of guides and
camels. This arrangement broke down in 1828 when Abbas
el-Jundi, governor of Berber, killed the sheikh seeking to
reduce what he considered an excessive duty.

A substantial military force passed along the road leaving
Korosko on 1st January. This comprised Egyptian reinforce-
ments for the governor of Sudan, Ali Khurshid Pasha's pro-
jected invasion of Abysinia, the 8th Regiment, along with 900

cavalry and two field guns. This was followed in the reverse
direction in February-March 1839 by the Egyptian viceroy
Mohamed Ali who was escorted along the Korosko Road
back to Egypt by Sheikh Baraka's nephew Hassan Khalifa
(Udal 1998, 284, 306).

It may have been a result of Mohammed Ali Pasha's
first hand experience of the Korosko Road that in 1845
d'Arnault, who worked as a civil engineer for the Egyptian
government, was charged with creating a military road
across the desert and to this end he was based at Korosko
with a large detachment of soldiers. He endeavoured to
provide water from artesian wells but failed. Instead, apparently at the urging of the Viceroy, he created a number
of cisterns against his better judgment as the extreme rarity
of rain in the region rendered them useless (Romer 1846,
186-8 quoted in Malek 1984; see also Žába 1974, 118-9).

In the same year as the Viceroy traversed the Korosko
Road Suleiman Agha, who had come to escort Abbas'
family, following his death, back to Egypt, was ambushed
by Sheikh Baraka of the Ababda, Khalifa's successor, and
killed near Murat Wells in revenge for Khalifa's death. This
caused a temporary closure of the road until Baraka was
killed and replaced as sheikh by Suliman Abu Nimr (Udal
1998, 305-6).

In a journal written around 1840 by an unknown hand it is
recorded that up until the conquest of Sudan by Mohammed
Ali Pasha traders from Egypt travelling south congregated
at Daraw on an appointed day to be led by the chief of the
Ababda Sheikh Khalifa on the 18 day journey to Shendi
(trans. in Santi and Hill 1980, 75).

Hassan Khalifa, Mohammed Ali Pasha's guide, was by
about April 1841 the Ababda sheikh in charge of the Korosko
Road and forced to reside in Berber under the eye of the
government (Udal 1998, 306).

The crossing of the desert still held many dangers
throughout the 19th century.[2] Hoskins travelled along the
Korosko Road without undue incident in February 1833
reaching Abu Hamed in eight days, although he did come
across innumerable dead camels and seven people who appeared to have died not long before from lack of water and
fatigue (Hoskins 1835, 18ff). In 1837 Russegger apparently
had an uneventful journey merely noting:

> "I followed the Nile as far as Korosko, but then
> left it and went through the great desert that
> ran between this stream and the Red Sea, to El
> Mucheireff, the capital of the Berber country,
> where I embarked again on the Nile ...."
>
> (Russegger 1841, 29).

> "When Lepsius travelled to Sudan in 1840 [sic.]
> he took eight days from Korosko to Abu Hamed,
> though he had every appliance for safe and rapid
> travelling across the desert."
>
> (Ward 1905, 19).

While at Murat in January 1844 Lepsius noted that coming from the north the road at that point split into an eastern
and western route, both with the same ultimate destination
(Lepsius 1853, 140). On 2nd September 1857 the trader
Adolfo Antognoli wrote to his mother from Abu Hamed

---

[1] Only a few years later English notes that there were five wells along
the route, two of which however, as he clarifies, were rock pools - *gulat*
(1822, 214 fn.).

[2] The references to those who traveled along the Korosko Road which
follows are by no means exhaustive.

having just survived a harrowing journey "I have suffered the torments of the dammed ..." through what he terms the 'Atmur Desert. He recounts how he nearly lost his life in sandstorms, how three camels died on the road and seven more had to be relieved of their 18 cases of merchandise which were left in the desert but that "... my health and my courage were never better; had they not been I would have been food for the hyenas." (trans. in Santi and Hill 1980, 194, see also 196). He returned by the same route in August 1862 happening across seven Arab camelmen two days along the 'road' who had died of thirst. His own water becoming putrid in the water skins he was forced to drink from the wells at Murat which he describe as foul (trans. in Santi and Hill 1980, 205).

It is not clear, at least to the writer, what was the reason for the establishment of the post at the southern end of the Bab es-Silik as evidenced by the inscriptions at site KRP19 (see Welsby, this volume, 152-155) which was manned certainly from October 1852 to October 1853. There is no mention of such a post in the detailed account of the desert crossing by Cardinal Massaia in the summer of 1851 (trans. in Toniolo and Hill 1974, 304ff.) nor in the brief account of the same journey made by John Petherick who left Korosko on 16th February 1853 (Petherick 1861, 107). Perhaps these travellers passed through the Bab el-Korosko 9km to the west (Figure 11.2). The American Bayard Taylor traversed the road in late December 1851. He also does not mention the post but does record an informal toll point in this area of the route, a story also recounted earlier by Burckhardt. It appears that the guides had a tradition here to build mock graves and then obliquely threaten the travellers in their care that if a small sum of money were not paid to them the graves would be for them (Taylor 1856, 178).

In 1859 the Korosko Road was closed by orders of the Viceroy, perhaps an attempt to hide the movement of slaves along the road from Sudan to Egypt from European eyes at a time when the slave trade was under increasing scrutiny (Udal 1998, 456).

It was the route taken by Samuel Baker in 1862:

"........ we started across the Nubian desert, thus cutting off the western bend of the Nile, and in seven days' forced camel march we again reached the river at Abou Hamed. The journey through

that desert is most fatiguing, as the march averages fifteen hours a day through a wilderness of scorching sand and glowing basalt rocks. The simoom was in full force at that season (May), and the thermometer, placed in the shade by the water skins, stood at 114 degrees Fahrenheit"

(Baker 1866, Vol. 1, 3).

The intrepid explorers Speake and Grant passed along the Korosko Road from south to north, an eight day journey, on their return from Central Africa in 1863. Grant describes it thus:

"Of all the journeys I have made in Africa— Abyssinia included—and in India, from the Kyber Pass to Calcutta and Bombay, this from Abu Hamed to Korosko is the very worst, from its barrenness, its heat, and from the fatigue and discomfort it necessitates"

(Grant 1884, 326).

From the map published by Grant to illustrate his account it is clear that he passed through the Bab el-Korosko rather than the Bab es-Silik (Figure 11.3) and this is also the line of the route depicted on the 19th century map (Figure 11.1).

In the 1870s Licurgo Santoni, who was Director of Posts in Upper Egypt and Nubia, noted that the postal service relied heavily on the Ababda on account of their prowess at crossing the deserts, and it was men of this tribe that carried the post along the Korosko Road, a regular service which was established in 1873 (trans. in Santi and Hill 1980, 225ff).

For most travellers during the winter the route could be traversed at some leisure in 15 or 16 days but in the summer, on account of the heat, it was essential to make the crossing in eight days, four days to the wells at Murat and another four to the Nile. Should the journey be prolonged, disaster would ensue as the camels were at that season only able to go without water for four days. The postman, however, travelling alone, could make much faster progress completing the journey in five days. A safety net was in operation, at least for the postman, and should he fail to arrive in Korosko or Abu Hamed on the expected day someone was at once sent to meet him (trans. in Santi and Hill 1980, 226).

Early in 1881 the Dutch traveller Juan Maria Schuver crossed south from Korosko making the journey entirely on foot. He deviated from the usual route which passed the wells in Wadi Murat, instead travelling further to the west along a little used path via Teniba where good quality water was to be had, in what he describes as "an almost underground pool, so much overshadowed with rocks, which hide it from the rays of a tropical sun." (James et al. 1996, 6). According to the editors of his work this reservoir was generally kept secret from travellers by the local Arabs and, although the British during the 1884-5 campaign were aware of the pool's existence, its exact location remained unknown (James et al. 1996, 5, fn. 1).[3]

Charles Gordon, making haste to reach Khartoum, left Korosko on 2nd February 1884 and arrived at Abu Hamed on 7th February apparently after an uneventful trip (Gordon 1888, 375-6). The Korosko Road was to be used for

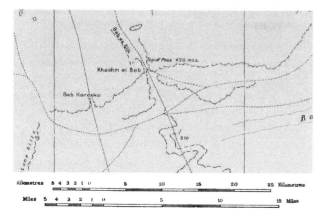

Figure 11.2. Map of the watershed along the Korosko Road with the Bab es-Silik and the Bab Korosko (after Sudan Survey Department 1:250,000 map sheet NF-36-J - Murrat).

---

[3] It does not appear in the Index Gazetteer of place names produced by the Sudan Government in 1931 (Sudan Survey Department 1932).

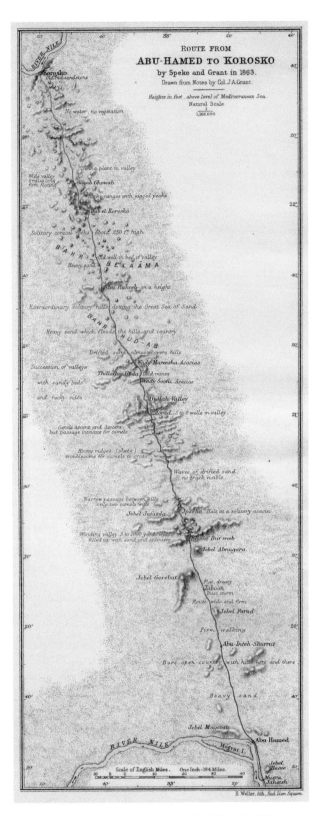

ROUTE FROM
ABU-HAMED TO KOROSKO
by Speke and Grant in 1863.
Drawn from Notes by Col. J.A.Grant.

*Figure 11.3. The route taken between Abu Hamed and Korosko
by Speke and Grant in 1863 (Grant 1884).*

control of the 'road' a fort was built at Murat Wells in 1893 to defend the wells and to deny any enemy force access to them, the only reliable source of water on the route. It was connected to Korosko by telegraph (Knight 1897, 59). The garrison was regularly replaced and the march of a detachment of troops from the Egyptian 15th Battalion to Murat fort in 1896 is described by Knight. The troops made the journey on foot, 120 miles at the hottest time of the year, in 65 hours (Knight 1897, 55ff.).

Even at the very end of the 19th century the route could prove fatal. "It is hard to believe that not so many years ago an entire caravan from Korosko perished in a sandstorm in attempting to cross it" (Ward 1905, 19), killed according to Gleichen after being caught in one of the 'waves of super-heated air' which are an occasional feature of the climate in the region, in 1897 (Gleichen 1905, 87). Taylor had noted in the middle of that century that although there were piles of stones forming *alamat* at frequent intervals along the route they were not necessary for navigation as the route could be easily located by following the bones and carcasses of dead animals (Taylor 1856, 176).

The important role that the Korosko Road played in communications between Egypt and Sudan came to an abrupt end with the construction of the railway. In 1896 railway construction began at Korosko with the intention of the line following the Korosko Road initially as far as Murat Wells, but was soon abandoned in favour of a line from Wadi Halfa to Abu Hamed (Welsby 2011, 11). That railway was begun on 1st January 1897 and reached Abu Hamed on 31st October of that year (Gleichen 1905, 213). As early as 1905 Gleichen could write:

> "The one main road through this country, that from Korosko to Abu Hamed via Murrat, which used to be the artery through which the commerce of the Sudan flowed to Egypt, has fallen into disuse since the construction of the railway, and there are now no other tracks except those made by the Nomad Arabs."
>
> (Gleichen 1905, 88).

Antiquities along the Korosko Road

Some of the early travellers were on the lookout for evidence of ancient activity. At the well of Shigre along the eastern route, on 18th March 1814, Burckhardt wrote:

> "I searched about the well for some traces of ancient works, in the supposition that the place was as well known and frequented in the time when the trade of Meroe flourished as it is at present. But I could find nothing, although the situation is well suited to the construction of a fortress"
>
> (Burckhardt 1819, Vol. 2, 196).

Hoskins had more success when camped at Murat Wells he noted:

> "On one of the rocks of the valley of the spring are some hieroglyphics. I distinguished the name of the god Horus, and the hawk, the emblem of that divinity."
>
> (Hoskins 1835, 24).

transporting supplies to the River Column in 1885 had it reached Abu Hamed and continued its march towards Berber. Contact with the Bisharin and Ababda along the desert route had already been made by Captain Kitchener and their support had guaranteed that the Dervish army could not continue its advance north along the Korosko Road (Arthur 1920, 66-68; Gleichen 1905, 248). To further strengthen

He further mentions the presence of gold mining installations some of which were considered to be relatively recent.

Linant de Bellefonds's journey along the Korosko Road was, unlike most travellers, not simply a way of getting from A to B but part of a regional survey for minerals in the Eastern Desert. He thus deviated off the usual route to traverse Jebel Rafit to the north of Wadi Murat recording evidence for gold mining activities – he illustrated a gold washing table. While at Murat he noted rock art of long-horned cattle and horses and the hieroglyphs (Linant de Bellefonds 1868, 150-151). Similar rock art had been noted at Murat by English in the early 1820s (1822, 218).

In 1844 Lepsius while at Murat:

Plate 11.3. Rock formation between the Nile at Buhen and the Wadi Murat.

"inspected some hagr mektub (stones with inscriptions) for which we enquire everywhere, viz. some rocks in the neighbourhood, on which, in somewhat modern times, a number of horses, camels, and other creatures have been roughly scratched ..."

(Lepsius 1853, 140).

Early travellers crossing the Eastern Desert

Perhaps the earliest person known to have used one of the Eastern Desert routes was the missionary, Bishop Longinus, in AD 580 on his way south from Nobadia to Alodia.[4] Owing to problems with the Kingdom of Makuria that territory had to be avoided and the desert route rather than that along the Nile had to be used. Longinus, along with some of his companions, 'in the company of some people who know the desert' became ill on the journey and 17 camels died because of the heat (John of Ephesus in Vantini 1975, 17).

Egyptians during the New Kingdom were certainly present along the 'road' but their purpose in using it was presumably to access the gold mining areas rather than seeking to travel from Egypt down to the Abu Hamed reach of the Nile and beyond. As noted elsewhere in this volume some of the individuals were associated with Buhen and will only have joined the Korosko Road in its middle section (Plate 11.3). There is little to recommend the idea of a crossing of the Eastern Desert by the armies of Thutmose I and III on their way to the Hagr el-Merwa at Kurgus (Davies 2017, 94; and this volume, 213).[5]

There is no evidence for an Egyptian presence on the

'road' to the south of Murat Wells and, while the Korosko Road, has been claimed to be the single most important reason for the eclipse of Napata by Meroe, there is no evidence whatsoever for its use by the Kushites nor for it becoming by the Meroitic period "the main link between the Central Sudan and the Mediterranean world" (Adams 1977, 304).[6] Literary sources make no mention of these routes apart from that between Meroe and Napata.

In this context it is interesting to recall the probable route of Harkhuf who travelled into what is now Sudan in the 6th Dynasty (c. 2200 BC). He appears to have travelled on one of his journeys through the Western Desert oasis (Valbelle 2014, 104). What may have been a similar route was chosen by the first western traveller into Sudan the details of whose journey we know. When Poncet made his visit to Sennar in 1692 he followed the Darb el-Arbain from Asyut to Selima Oasis before joining the Nile at Moshi a little downstream of Argo. This was also the route taken by du Roule in 1704 (Budge 1907 I, 2-3, 9-10).

Bibliography

Adams, W. Y. 1977. *Nubia: Corridor to Africa*. London – Princeton.

Anderson, J. R. 2006. 'Bread moulds and 'throne halls': recent discoveries in the Amun Temple precinct at Dangeil', *Sudan & Nubia* 10, 95-101.

Anderson, J. R. and S. M. Ahmed 2002. 'Recent Excavations at Dangeil, Nile State', in T. A. Bács (ed.), *A Tribute to Excellence. Studies Offered in Honor of Ernö Gaál, Ulrich Luft, László Török*. Studia Aegyptiaca. Budapest, 45-52.

Anderson, J. R. and Salah Mohamed Ahmed 2014. 'Early Kushite

---

[4] The assertion made by Griffith (1937, 118) that the Meroitic envoy who visited Philae during the reign of the Roman emperor Trebonianus Gallus used the Korosko Road appears to be based on an inaccurate translation of the envoy's graffito, Philae 416 (see Pope 2014, 578).

[5] For the possible use of the Korosko Road, or at least a part of it, by the Egyptian Viceroy Setau under Ramesses II, see Davies 2017, 97.

[6] There is now increasing evidence for a Kushite presence in the area which coincided with the southern end of the eastern of the cross-desert routes, that via the Wadi Gabgaba, at Dangeil (see amongst others Anderson 2006; Anderson and Ahmed 2002; Anderson and Salah Mohamed Ahmed 2014) and Berber (see Mahmoud Suliman Bashir 2010; 2013; 2014; 2016; Mahmoud Suliman Bashir and David 2015). The reason for the locations of these sites, whether for purely local reasons, associated with gold exploitation in the Eastern Desert, or associated with cross-desert routes, to the north, east or west, is unknown.

Royal Statues at Dangeil, Sudan', in Anderson and Welsby (eds), 613-619.

Anderson, J. R. and D. A. Welsby (eds) 2014. *The Fourth Cataract and Beyond. Proceedings of the 12th International Conference for Nubian Studies*. British Museum Publications on Egypt and Sudan 1. Leuven – Paris – Walpole, MA.

Arthur, G. 1920. *Life of Lord Kitchener*. 3 vols. London.

Baker, S. W. 1866. *The Albert N'Yanza Great Basin of the Nile; and Exploration of the Nile Sources*. London.

Bruce, J. 1805. *Travels between the years 1765 and 1773 through Part of Africa, Syria, Egypt and Arabia into Abyssinia To Discover the Sources of the Nile*. 2nd ed. Edinburgh.

Budge, E. A. W. 1907. *The Egyptian Sudan*. London.

Burckhardt, J. L. 1819. *Travels In Nubia*. London.

Davies, W. V. 2017. 'Nubia in the New Kingdom: The Egyptians at Kurgus', in N. Spencer, A. Stevens and M. Binder (eds), *Nubia in the New Kingdom. Lived Experience, Pharaonic Control and Indigenous Traditions*. British Museum Publications on Egypt and Sudan, 3 Leuven – Paris – Walpole, MA, 65-106.

English, G. B. 1822. *A Narrative of the Expedition to Dongola and Sennaar*. London.

Gleichen, A. E. W. 1905. *The Anglo-Egyptian Sudan: a Compendium Prepared by Officers of the Sudan Government*, Vols I-II. London.

Gordon, C. G. 1888. *Letters of General C. G. Gordon to his Sister M. A. Gordon*. London and New York.

Grant, J. 1884. 'Route March, with Camels, from Berber to Korosko in 1863', *Proceedings of the Royal Geographic Society* 6/6, 326-335.

Griffith, F. L. 1937. *Catalogue of the Demotic Graffiti of the Dodecaschoenos II*. Oxford.

Hoskins, G. A. 1835. *Travels in Ethiopia above the Second Cataract of The Nile, Exhibiting the State of that Country, and its Various Inhabitants under the Dominion of Mohammed Ali; and Illustrating the Antiquities, Arts and History of the Ancient Kingdom of Meroe*. London.

James, W., G. Baumann and D. H. Johnson (eds) 1996. *Juan Maria Schuver's Travels in North East Africa 1880-1883*. London.

Knight, E. F. 1897. *Letters from the Sudan: Reprinted from "The Times" of April to October, 1896*. London, New York.

Lepsius, C. R. 1853. *Discoveries in Egypt and Ethiopia and the Peninsula of Sinai in the Years 1842-1845*. London.

Linant de Bellefonds, L. M. A. 1868. *L'Etbaye. Pays habité par les Arabes Bicharieh, Géographie, Ethnologie, Mines d'or.* reprinted in *Voyage aux Mines d'or du Pharaon*. Paris 2002.

Mahmoud Suleiman Bashir 2010. 'A Recently Discovered Meroitic Cemetery at Berber, River Nile State, Sudan. Preliminary Report', *Sudan & Nubia* 14, 69-74.

Mahmoud Suliman Bashir 2013. 'A Third Season of Rescue Excavations in the Meroitic Cemetery at Berber, October 2012: Preliminary Report', *Sudan & Nubia* 17, 90-100.

Mahmoud Suliman Bashir 2014. 'The Archaeological Material from the Meroitic Cemetery at Berber', in Anderson and Welsby (eds), 805-808.

Mahmoud Suliman Bashir 2016. 'Excavations in the Meroitic Cemetery at Berber, Seasons 2015 and 2016', *Sudan & Nubia* 20, 57-61.

Mahmoud Suliman Bashir and R. David 2015. 'The Meroitic Cemetery at Berber. Recent Fieldwork and Discussion on Internal Chronology', *Sudan & Nubia* 19, 97-105.

Malek, J. 1984. 'The Date of the Water-Cisterns Discovered along the Desert Crossing from Korosko to Abu Hamed in 1963', *Gottinger Miszellen* 83, 47-50.

Petherick, J. 1861. *Egypt, the Sudan and Central Africa with explorations from Khartoum on the White Nile to the regions of the equator*. Edinburgh and London.

Pope, J. W. 2014. 'Meroitic Diplomacy and the Festival of Entry', in Anderson and Welsby (eds), 577-582.

Reid, J. M. 1968. *Traveller Extraordinary. The Life of James Bruce of Kinnaird*. London.

Romer, I. F. 1846. *A Pilgrimage to the Temples and Tombs of Egypt, Nubia and Palestine*. London.

Russegger, J. R. 1841. *Reisen in Europa, Asien und Afrika*. Stuttgart.

Santi, P. and R. Hill (eds). 1980. *The Europeans in the Sudan 1834-1878*. Oxford.

Sudan Survey Department 1932. *Index Gazetteer of the Anglo-Egyptian Sudan showing Place Names*. London.

Taylor, B. 1856. *A Journey to Central Africa; or, Life and landscapes from Egypt to the Negro kingdoms of the White Nile*. New York.

Toniolo, E. and R. Hill (eds) 1974. *The Opening of the Nile Basin*. London.

Udal, J. O. 1998. *The Nile in Darkness: conquest and exploration 1504 - 1862 AD*. Norwich.

Valbelle, D. 2014. 'International Relations between Kerma and Egypt', in Anderson and Welsby (eds), 103-109.

Vantini, G. 1975. *Oriental Sources Concerning Nubia*. Heidelberg, Warsaw.

Ward, J. 1905. *Our Sudan, its Pyramids and Progress*. London.

Welsby, D. A. 2011. *Sudan's First Railway, The Gordon Relief Expedition and The Dongola Campaign*. Sudan Archaeological Research Society Publication No. 19. London.

Žába, Z. 1974. *The Rock Inscriptions of Lower Nubia. Czechoslovak Concession*. Czechoslovak Institute of Egyptology in Prague and in Cairo Publications Vol. 1, Prague.

12. Gazetteer of sites

Derek A. Welsby

The Korosko Road survey described in this report sought principally to visit a number of sites with Egyptian inscriptions which had been recorded by the expeditions of CeRDO in the Eastern Desert of Sudan (Figure 12.1, Plates 15.1 and 15.2). The recording of additional archaeological sites was secondary to this core aim. The survey is thus not in any way systematic but the results are deemed worthy of publication.

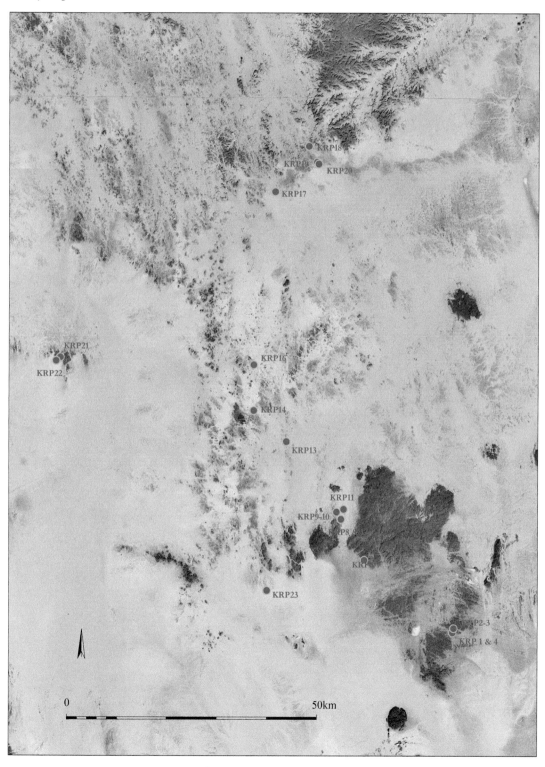

Figure 12.1. Sites recorded along the Korosko Road and on the route west towards the Second Cataract (Google Earth satellite image April 2018).

Figure 12.2. Sites in the Wadi Murat (scale 1:10,000) (Google Earth satellite image April 2018).

Site code: KRP1   **Co-ordinates**: 21° 04.103' N 32° 55.088' E   **Name**: Murat Wells
Site type: Military installations   **Period**: 1893-
Location: Set on the southern side of the Wadi Murat immediately to the west of the side wadi leading towards Abu Hamed. The three forts are set on the hilltops enjoying extensive views along the wadis and over the surrounding countryside (Figure 12.2, Plate 12.1). Below and immediately to the west of forts (1) and (2) the mouth of the embayment is blocked by a wall and the protected area is occupied by buildings. There are also buildings (5) below Fort (3). The forts were constructed late in 1893 for the protection of the wells by Captain Machell and are described in some detail by Edward Fredrick Knight, correspondent for *The Times* (Knight 1897, 47-50, 64ff., map between pgs 42 & 43). Forts (1) and (2) were each provided with seven-pounder brass guns.

Description: Three forts, which dominate the Wadi Murat to the north where wells were dug, are much destroyed. Forts (1) and (2) are on the top of a long narrow and steep-sided ridge overlooking the continuation of the Korosko Road to the south towards the Nile at Abu Hamed. Fort (3) crowns a higher hill 475m to the north west. A little below Fort (3) on its west side is a single rectangular room and a sentry post allowing observation of the wadi and slopes to the south. All the installations are linked by cleared paths following where possible the contours of the hill. Beyond the col at the head of the embayment extending down into the steep slope into a wadi is the rubbish dump (6), a large number of tin cans with some glass bottles and ceramic sherds. The embayment immediately to the west of the ridge occupied by Forts (1) and (2) is cut off from the wadi to the north by a casemated wall and covered with buildings. Rooms A-H were all a part of the casemated wall with C and D flanking the main gate 2.6m wide through it. Within the 'enclosure' was an area of stones perhaps where the animals were corralled.

Plate 12.1. KRP1 – Forts (1) and (2) looking south across the wadi.

Plate 12.2. KRP1 – Fort (1).

Plate 12.3. KRP1 – Fort (2).

Feature	Type	Description
(1)	Fort	Along the narrow crest of a steep sided ridge, small rectangular rooms, poorly preserved with walls of stone, the core and the face bonded in an orange mud mortar, mud mortar rendered. path terraced into the slope gives access to the fort (Plate 12.2).
(2)	Fort	As (1). One wall has two narrow slit windows or loopholes (Plate 12.3).
(3)	Fort	Rectangular with stone walls bonded in a mud mortar (Plate 12.4). Original form uncertain.
(4)	Camp	Buildings are scattered on the slopes of the embayment up to the col (Plate 12.5). Overall dimensions *c.* 115 x 65m. Gateway through the N casemated wall
A	Casemated wall	Rectangular room and detached wall at west end of 'blocking wall'.
B	Casemated wall	Long rectangular room, E end well preserved to height of about 3m. Two small openings visible in N wall, at different heights.
C	Casemated wall	Rectangular room, much destroyed (Plate 12.6)
D	Casemated wall	6.15 x 4.7m. Doorway 710mm wide. Windows with timber lintels, 2 windows in N wall, 3 small rectangular openings in S wall (Plate 12.6). Internal walls mud plastered.
E	Casemated wall	
F	Casemated wall	
G	Casemated wall	
H	Casemated wall	At E end of casemated wall.

Feature	Type	Description
I J	Building	Part of a two-roomed building aligned with Building K/L (Plate 12.7)
K L	Building	Part of a two-roomed building aligned with Building I/J (Plate 12.7)
M	Building	Rectangular and poorly preserved, doorway in S wall
N	Building	Doorway in E wall. Loophole 250 x 250mm, stone lintels
O	Building	5.3 x 4.3m. Doorway 910mm wide in E wall, 2 windows in N wall with wooden lintels, window 380 x 630mm, 2 very small 'windows' in S wall. Mud plaster with graffiti internally (Plate 12.9; Castiglioni *et al.* 1995, 116)
P	Building	5.45 x 5.45m. Doorway 1.08m wide in E wall. 2 windows in N wall, 1 window in S and E walls (Plates 12.8 & 12.9). *Mastaba* against W wall.
Q	Building	Use of mud bricks
R	Building	Doorway in E wall
S	Building	3 windows 350mm wide x 610mm high
T	Building	3 roomed structure. S room, W wall with stone socle, then of mud brick – 2 courses stretchers, 1 course shinners, 1 course headers, 1 course stretchers, 1 course rowlocks, 1 course stretchers, 1 course rowlocks, 1 course stretchers, 1 course headers, 1 course stretchers, 1 course stone. E and S walls lower part stone, upper part mud brick, in S wall crowned with more stone.
U	Building	
V	Building	Doorway in S wall
W	Building	Doorway in E wall
X	Building	
Y	Building	Doorway in E wall
Z	Building	Stone door lintel *in situ*, in S wall (Plate 12.10)

Plate 12.4. KRP1 – Fort (3).

Plate 12.5. KRP1 – Installations in the embayment with the wall blocking off the entrance to the camp in the foreground.

Plate 12.6. KRP1 – camp gate, Buildings C-D.

Plate 12.7. KRP1 – camp, Buildings L-I.

Plate 12.8. KRP1 – camp, Building P.

Plate 12.9. KRP1 – camp, Buildings O and P.

Plate 12.10. KRP1 – camp, Building Z.

*Plate 12.11. KRP1 –
Looking east north east
from Fort (3) with
buildings (5) in the
middle distance.*

Feature	Type	Description
(5)	Settlement	A concentration of 9 rectangular stone structures (Plate 12.11) on a terrace high above the floor of the Wadi Murat and immediately below Fort (3)
(6)	Rubbish dump	

Finds:

A small number of finds were noted in the camp but a greater concentration came from the rubbish dump. Additional finds were noted along the wadi to the south west of the rubbish dump and at the base of the slope to the east of Forts (1) and (2). Cans and glassware along with part of the barbed wire entanglements came from the vicinity of Fort (3).

Pottery – 4 sherds from a bowl, white glazed with horizontal blue bands, the main register infilled with a floral motif in black. Rim and wall of a blue and white 'China' cup (Plate 12.12).

Metal – 2-strand barbed wire - according to Knight each fort was surrounded by wire entanglements.

Rectangular tins with rounded corners, one stamped on base PRODUITS IMPORTES (cf. Welsby 2011, 123, no. 241), another with an illegible inscription, one long and narrow (Plate 12.13).

Petrol can with oval wire handle. Stamped on top 125º and MADE IN RUSSIA (Plate 12.15). For similar tins see Welsby 2011, 116ff, nos 205-212.

Cartridge case (Plate 12.14) stamped on the base G.K, the mark of the manufacturer George Kynoch of Birmingham, UK (cf. Welsby 2011, 108, nos 147, 148, 150).

Glass – tall bottle neck with flange, as Welsby 2011, 103, no. 105 but flange of D-shaped profile.

Bibliography: Castiglioni *et al.* 1995, 115f, 177 - site A2; Knight 1897, 64ff.

Plate 12.12. KRP1 – glazed ceramic bowl from the rubbish dump.

Plate 12.13. KRP1 – tin cans from the rubbish dump.

Plate 12.14. KRP1 – cartridge case.

Plate 12.15. KRP1 – petrol can.

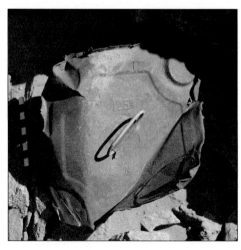

Site code: KRP2   **Co-ordinates**: 21º 04.509' N, 32º 55.380' E   **Name**: Wadi Murat

Site type: Inscriptions, rock art   **Period**: New Kingdom, ?-

Location: On the right bank of the Wadi Murat at a point where it runs south to north. Here low cliffs rise from the wadi giving way to the steep rocky slopes above. Several substantial trees now mask the rock face in places.

Description: Several discrete rock faces over a distance of a few hundred metres with abundant rock art as well as New Kingdom rock inscriptions (Plates 12.16-12.23). A small amount of the rock art and one inscription are on boulders and outcrops high above the wadi floor. There is also some rock art on boulders and outcrops on the other side of the wadi at this point.

Plate 12.16. KRP2 – the rock art and inscriptions are on the cliffs close to the wadi floor in the centre of the image.

Plate 12.19. KRP2 – rock art.

Plate 12.17. KRP2 – rock art.

Plate 12.20. KRP2 – rock art.

Plate 12.18. KRP2 – rock art.

Plate 12.21. KRP2 – rock art.

137

Plate 12.22. KRP2 – recording the Egyptian inscriptions.

Among the rock art are the following:
    Innumerable long-horned cattle
    Simple crosses
    Anthropomorphs
    Horse with man holding its reins
    Warriors with small circular shields

Plate 12.23. KRP2 – Egyptian inscription.

Finds: No artefacts were noted.
Bibliography: Castiglioni *et al.* 1995, 177 - site A2; Davies, this volume, 208-210.

Site code: KRP3   **Co-ordinates**: 21° 4.423' N, 32° 55.287' E   **Name**: Wadi Murat
Site type: cemetery   **Period**: Islamic
Location: Close to the left bank of the wadi immediately downstream of a small isolated rock on a gentle slope up from the wadi's sand-filled bed. It lies 625m north east of the Anglo-Egyptian fort.
Description: In excess of 10 tomb monuments, some graves marked by an upright slab, others a low oval to sub-rectangular mound delimited by a line of stones (Plate 12.24). Possibly the cemetery mentioned by Knight where the Egyptian troops killed in November 1893 fighting a Dervish band were buried (1897, 70).
Finds: No artefacts were noted.

Plate 12.24. KRP3 – general view across the cemetery.

Site code: KRP4   **Co-ordinates**: 21° 4.094' N, 32° 55.181 E
Name: Wadi Murat
Site type: Rock art   **Period**: ?
Location: On the steep slope and at the base of the north-south ridge crowned by the remains of Forts (1) and (2) adjacent to the route turning south off the Wadi Murat towards Abu Hamed.
Description: Several boulders have fine representations of long-horned cattle, some with herdsmen (Plates 12.25-12.28).

Plate 12.25. KRP4 – rock art on the slope of the hill crowned by KRP1, forts 1 and 2.

Plate 12.26. KRP4 – long-horned cattle and herdsman.

Plate 12.28. KRP4 – long-horned cattle and herdsman.

Plate 12.27. KRP4 – long-horned cattle.

Plate 12.29. KRP4 – Huntley and Palmer's biscuit tin lid.

Finds:
   Metal – lid of a square biscuit tin stamped in an oval HUNTLEY & PALMER BISCUITS with READING & LONDON
      ENGLAND within (Plate 12.29).

Site code: KRP5   **Co-ordinates**: 21° 11.663' N, 32° 44.769' E   **Name**: Umm Gereifat/Wadi Tonaidba
Site type: Cave, inscriptions, rock art   **Period**: New Kingdom, ?
Location: On the east side of a vast sandy plain lies an oval rounded sandstone hill (Figure 12.3, Plate 12.30) flanked to the
south, north and east by hills of granite boulders and outcropping bedrock. Running down a gulley from the east is a khor which

139

Figure 12.3. KRP5-7 (scale 1:10,000 (Google Earth satellite image, April 2018).

cuts straight through the sandstone hill and debouches into the plain to the west joining the Wadi Tonaidba.

The cave (Plates 12.31 and 12.32) is along the line of a fissure in the bedrock infilled with a conglomerate of hard rounded boulders set into a much softer matrix. This material can be seen forming the roof of the cave. It is this weak material that has allowed the water to pierce the hill. The floor of the cave slopes down gradually from the east for a distance of 19m where it is choked by large boulders forming a vertical step down of *c.* 3.4m. From there to the west entrance is 42m. The eastern mouth of the cave is 5.3m wide and 5.1m high, the western 3.2m wide and 7.54m high.

Description: The New Kingdom inscriptions lie just inside the western mouth of the cave (Plate 12.33)as does a small representation of a 'pharaonic' boat (Plate 12.34). A little beyond this point to the west and on the south side of the *khor* a vertical rock face bears the representations of a number of long-horned cattle much obscured by modern graffiti (Plate 12.35). In the eastern mouth of the cave on its north side is a large isolated boulder bearing a representation of a single cow facing east, i.e. away from the cave. The cattle by the western mouth likewise face away from the cave.

Finds: No artefacts were noted.

Bibliography: Castiglioni and Castiglioni 2006, 171; Davies, this volume, 185, 187-188

Plate 12.30. KRP5-7. KRP7 occupied the summit of the hill pierced by the cave at KRP5. KRP6 sits on the plain immediately to the south.

Plate 12.31. KRP5 – the mouth of the cave on the south-western side of the hill.

Plate 12.32. KRP5 – the mouth of the cave on the north-eastern side of the hill.

*Plate 12.34. KRP5 – rock art immediately inside
the south-western mouth of the cave.*

*Plate 12.33. KRP5 – recording a rock inscription in the mouth
of the cave with the plain to the south west beyond.*

*Plate 12.35. KRP5 – rock art immediately outside
the south-western mouth of the cave.*

Site code: KRP6   **Co-ordinates**: 21° 11.581' N, 32° 44.818' E   **Name**: Umm Gereifat/Wadi Tonaidba
Site type: Occupation scatter   **Period**: Mesolithic, Neolithic
Dimensions: *c.* 150 x 100m
Location: At the eastern edge of the vast plain and immediately to the south of the hill pierced by the cave, site KRG5. The surface is covered by a sparse scatter of stones from the hillside and is cut/delimited by the meandering bed of a *khor* to the south.
Description: Scattered on the surface are pottery sherds, grinding stones, lithics and debitage. There are also two concentrations of stone (Plates 12.36-12.38).
(1) an oval feature with its long axis oriented south east to north west (L: 1.8m; W:1.5m; H: 260mm).
(2) similar to (1) but shape indistinct.

*Plate 12.36. KRP6 – general view with the two stone
concentrations visible in the foreground.*

Plate 12.37. KRP6 – the stone spread and occupation scatter.

Plate 12.38. KRP6 – concentration of stones.

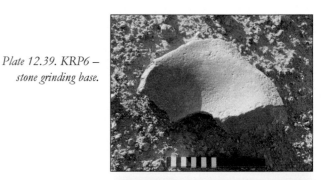

Plate 12.39. KRP6 – stone grinding base.

Plate 12.40. KRP6 – fragment of a grooved stone, front and back views.

Finds:
  Pottery – 13 sherds from the surface scatter.
  Stone objects – half of a grinding base; stone with small rounded grooves on both sides (Plates 12.39 and 12.40)

Site code: KRP7   **Co-ordinates**: 21° 11.663' N, 32° 44.769' E   **Name**: Umm Gereifat/Wadi Tonaidba
Site type: Occupation scatter   **Period**: Neolithic
Location: Occupying the gently rounded summit of the sandstone hill cut by the cave. It enjoys extensive views across the plain to the west. The surface is strewn with gravel and small stones with the bedrock visible in places. There are a few concentrations of larger stones.
Description: A scatter of pottery. Towards the north end of the site is a very ephemeral feature describing an area *c.* 3.5m in diameter. In places there is a single line of stones but these may be natural.
Finds:
  Pottery – Five sherds from the surface scatter.

Site code: KRP8   **Co-ordinates**: 21° 16.201' N, 32° 41.959' E   **Name**: Umm Gereifat/Wadi Tonaidba
Site type: Inscriptions, rock art, occupation scatters, etc.   **Period**: New Kingdom, ?
Location: A very approximately oval sandstone hill has vertical cliff faces around most of its perimeter up to about 4m in height (Plate 12.41). The hilltop consists of extensive flat terraces at different levels. The hill is isolated in the plain with the main wadi to the east and a tributary wadi and the mountain massif to the west.
Description: The rock art and inscriptions are on the eastern side of the hill on the vertical cliffs. The pottery scatters are on the gravel and stoney gentle slopes at the base of the cliffs mainly along the east and south-east sides of the hill but one was noted on the north side and another to the west. None are directly associated with the inscriptions and rock art. On the summit are at least two *alamat*, a few circular features – some associated with pottery sherds – and at least one poor quality representation of a cow on the bedrock pavement.

Feature no.	Type	Dimensions	Description
(1)	Pot scatter		Low concentration of sherds
(2)	Pot scatter		
(3)	Pot scatter		
(4)	Pot scatter		N side of hill
(5)	Pot scatter		Low concentration of sherds in a rock shelter, W side of hill
(6)	Structure, pot scatter	Ext. 1.52 x 1.5m	A ring of small to medium-sized stones (largest 310 x 230 x 180mm), much disturbed (Plate 12.42). Many sherds from a single vessel found scattered in and around the structure and extending a few metres to the N and NE. It sits on the flat summit of the *jebel*.
(7)	Pot scatter		12m to the S of (6), on the summit and over a wide area down the slope
(8)	Structure	2.25 x 1.6m	Oval area delimited by 1 row of stones 460 x 400mm to 360 x 260mm (Plate 12.43)
(9)	Structure	2.1 x 1.93m	Oval area delimited by stones between 600 x 300m and 380 x 290mm, W side largely missing (Plate 12.43).
	Rock art		Long-horned cattle, 'trophy' (Plates 12.44-12.48).
	Inscriptions		(Plate 12.45)

142

Plate 12.41. KRP8 – general view of the hill from the south with the cliff face on which the rock art and inscriptions are carved.

Plate 12.42. KRP8(6) – stone structure associated with pottery sherds.

Plate 12.43. KRP8(8) and (9).

Plate 12.44. KRP8 – rock art with long-horned cattle and 'trophy'.

Plate 12.45. KRP8 – Egyptian inscriptions and rock art; long-horned cattle.

Plate 12.46. KRP8 rock art; long-horned cattle with infilled bodies.

Finds:
Pottery – (1) 5 sherds; (2) 1 sherd; (3) 1 sherd; (4) 1 sherd; (5) 2 sherds; (6) 1 sherd; (7) 1 sherd; (8) 3 sherds; (9) 2 sherds.
Bibliography: Castiglioni *et al.* 1995, 118; Davies, this volume, 188-193

Site code: KRP9 **Co-ordinates**: 21° 16.610' N, 32° 41.700' E **Name**: Wadi Tonaidba
Site type: Inscriptions, rock art **Period**: New Kingdom, ?
Location: On the western side of a wide sandy plain 9km to the north north west of KRP8. The rock art and inscriptions occupy the walls of a rock shelter/cave and the cliffs on the south side of the flat-topped *jebel* (Plate 12.49). Further rock art is found on the cliff faces around the sides of the embayment to the north and north east while pot scatters were found below the inscriptions. On the hilltop is an isolated tumulus set on bedrock; also three stone structures (7) and grinding hollows on the bedrock pavement.

Plate 12.47. KRP8 – rock art; long-horned cattle.

Plate 12.48. KRP8 – rock art; a row of long-horned cattle processing left, with infilled bodies.

Plate 12.49. KRP9 – view looking north towards the cliff face and rock shelter containing the Egyptian inscriptions.

Plate 12.50. KRP9(7).

Plate 12.51. KRP9(7).

Description:

Feature no.	Type	Description
(1)	Pot scatter	Low concentration of sherds immediately in front of the inscriptions
(2)	Pot scatter	1 sherd
(3)	Rock art	Few pieces below an overhang, 1 cow quite recent – no patination, few other cows and a fine 'pharaonic' boat
(4)	occupation scatter	Stone features, pottery and 1 stone tool (Plate 14.2)
(5)	inscriptions	
(6)	Rock art	Long-horned cattle, billy goats? and giraffe by inscription
(7)	Structures	3 of MDASP type CS07* (Plates 12.50 and 12.51).

* For the Merowe Dam Archaeological Salvage Project type series of monuments see
https://nubianstudiessociety.files.wordpress.com/2014/02/mdasp_ts_12-2012.pdf

Finds:
Lithics – Denticulated tool (Plate 14.2).
Pottery – (1) Marl D amphora sherd, Kerma(?) sherd: (2) Marl D amphora sherd.
Bibliography: Castiglioni and Castiglioni 2007, 32-3, figs 17-18; Davies, this volume, 193-195.

Site code: KRP10   **Co-ordinates**: 21° 16.690' N, 32° 41.794' E   **Name**: Wadi Tonaidba
Site type: Rock art   **Period**: ?
Location: An embayment with sheer rock walls much obscured by a large sand dune (Plate 12.52).
Description: Some rock art, mainly cattle but one anthropomorph wearing a tall headdress holding a bow (Plates 12.53-12.55) are visible above the dune and extending along the face against which the dune rests.
Finds: No artefacts noted.

Plate 12.52. KRP10 – view looking north east towards the cliff face (centre) and rock shelter containing the rock art.

Plate 12.53. KRP10 – rock art; long-horned cattle with infilled bodies or in outline moving right. Between two of the cattle is an anthropomorph.

Plate 12.54. KRP10 – rock art; long-horned cattle with infilled bodies moving right and two in outline moving left and a sub-circular motif. Possible anthropomorph on the left of the panel.

Plate 12.55. KRP10 – rock art; long-horned cattle and a sub-circular motif.

Site code: KRP11   **Co-ordinates**: 21° 17.088' N, 32° 42.373' E   **Name**: -
Site type: Rock art   **Period**: ?
Location: An isolated *jebel* to the north north east of KRP9 in the middle of a sand and gravel strewn plain over 4km wide.
Description: Rock art on a single vertical rock face half way up the *jebel's* steep western slope (Plate 12.56). Several small long-horned cattle, all infilled with pecking apart from one with the hind quarters blank. They fall into two groups, the northern of three animals much more carefully rendered that the southern group again of three animals.
Finds: No artefacts were noted.

Plate 12.56. KRP11 – rock art; long-horned cattle.

Site code: KRP12   **Co-ordinates**: (1) 21° 15.992' N, 32° 41.990' E   **Name**: Wadi Tonaidba
Site type: Cemetery, campsite   **Period**:
Location: On the gentle gravel strewn slope between the sand-filled wadi and the low sandstone *jebel* 350m to the south of site KRP8 (Plate 12.57).

Plate 12.57. KRP12 – general view.

Plate 12.58. KRP12(1) – recording the tumulus.

Plate 12.59. KRP12(2) – the tumulus.

Plate 12.60. KRP12(4) – the stone structure after clearing away windblown sand.

146

Description: A range of features are visible within a sparse occupation scatter with some pot sherds, lithics and a grinding base. These include three tumuli, a concentration of stones and, to the south east of the tumuli along the edge of the wadi, a line of stones (MDASP type LN01a) 10s of metres in length. There are also features of types CS08, CS09, SS02 and SS10.

Feature no.	Type	Dimensions	Description
(1)	Tumulus	5.5 x 5.4m H: 600mm	Constructed of large stones forming a revetment infilled with smaller stones (Plate 12.58).
(2)	Tumulus	3.07 x 3.05m H:570mm	Similar to (1) (Plate 12.59).
(3)	Tumulus	3.3 x 2.6m H: 230mm	A pile of small stones
(4)	Structure	1.7 x 1.6m	Large stones forming a cylindrical structure 400 x 350mm in size internally (Plate 12.60). The wind-blown sand fill was excavated to a depth of 350mm at which point work was halted. When found the cylinder was sealed by a flat roughly triangular slab 630 x 510mm in size by 180mm thick

Finds:
Pottery – (4) 1 sherd.

Site code: KRP13   **Co-ordinates**: 21° 24.140' N, 32° 35.666' E[1]   **Name**: -
Site type: Rock shelter, rock art, inscription   **Period**: New Kingdom, ?,
Location: An isolated but prominent rocky *jebel* with a substantial rock shelter on its southern side partly masked by massive slabs of rock fallen from the hillside (Plates 12.61 and 12.62).
Description: The rock art was on the fallen slabs near the shelter, the inscription was within the shelter on its western wall.
Finds:
Pottery – 3 sherds.
Bibliography: Davies, this volume, 195

Plate 12.61. KRP13 – general view looking north.

Plate 12.62. KRP13 – recording the Egyptian inscription within the rock shelter.

Site code: KRP14   **Co-ordinates**: not available   **Name**: -
Site type: Rock art, inscription   **Period**: Kerma: pre-New Kingdom
Location: An isolated *jebel*, one of several in the vicinity on a stoney plateau in which sand filled wadis are incised draining to the south (Plate 12.63).
Description: The rock art and inscriptions are on a large boulder set at the entrance to a small rock shelter a little way up the eastern slope. The boulder is partly under the overhang of the shelter. This is not a prominent location and the most impressive rock art and the inscription are on the side of the boulder facing into the shelter and are thus invisible from anyone passing by. The boulder has a number of small and crudely incised representations of cattle on the top and sides and an anthropomorph (Plate 12.64). The inner face bears a very fine hieroglyphic inscription which has been superimposed over complex designs. These

Plate 12.63. KRP14 – general view. The rock art and inscriptions are on a loose boulder near the base of the jebel *just to the left of the people.*

Plate 12.64. KRP14 – rock art on the top of the boulder. The inscription is on its left-hand side.

Plate 12.65. KRP14 – grinding base.

consist of single lines of closely spaced dots and carefully incised curvilinear grooves the overall scheme of which is unclear.
Finds:

Stone – at the foot of the *jebel* on its south side was a thin oval grinding base broken into five fragments with some pieces missing (Plate 12.65). It was approximately 400mm long and 200mm wide.

Bibliography: Castiglioni and Castiglioni 2006, 170, 176-7; Davies, this volume, 195-198

Site code: KRP16   **Co-ordinates**: 21° 32.087' N, 32° 32.006' E[2]   **Name**: -
Site type: Occupation scatter   **Period**: ?
Location: At the base of a small *jebel* on the flat wadi floor.
Description: A dense scatter of pottery.
Finds:

Pottery – 13 sherds.

Site code: KRP17   **Co-ordinates**: 21° 50.233' N, 32° 34.368' E   **Name**: -
Site type: Rock shelter, inscriptions, camp   **Period**: Anglo-Egyptian
Location: A small isolated rock towards the northern end of a vast sandy plain adjacent to the route leading north towards the Bab Korosko.
Description: Two deep rock shelters penetrate the rock accessed at ground level (Plate 12.66). On the walls within are many graffiti in Arabic (Plate 12.67) among them a record of military personnel and a vet here in the early 1950s. When visited by the CeRDO team the body of an old lorry lay abandoned close by.

---

[2] Location approximate.

Plate 12.66. KRP17 – rock outcrop with rock shelters.

Plate 12.67. KRP17 – rock shelter with graffiti.

Plate 12.68. KRP17 – petrol can.

The area has been much disturbed by the presence of a recent gold miners' camp.

Finds:

Metal – a 'tinny' (Plate 12.68) marked on the top with the following:

THE SHELL COMPANY LIMITED
"SHELL" BENZINE
HIGHLY INFLAMMABLE
4 IMPERIAL GALLONS

Bibliography: Castiglioni and Castiglioni 2006, 26

Site code: KRP18   **Co-ordinates**: (1) 21° 54.866' N, 32° 38.368' E   **Name**: Khashm el-Bab
(2) 21° 54.810' N, 32° 38.496' E
(3) 21° 54.802' N, 32° 38.498' E
(4) 21° 54.791' N, 32° 38.501' E
(5) 21° 55.193' N, 32° 38.071' E
(6) 21° 54.869' N, 32° 38.372' E
(7) 21° 54.417' N, 32° 38.344' E
(8) 21° 54.849' N, 32° 38.382' E

Site type: Inscriptions, rock art, pot scatters, rock shelters   **Period**: Palaeolithic, New Kingdom, Christian, Islamic

Location: The Khashm el-Bab is the entrance to a low pass, the Bab es-Silik (Plate 12.69), attaining a maximum elevation of 430m running slightly west of north through an extensive range of hills 9km south of the Egyptian-Sudanese border.

Description: This route has been extensively used in the past as is evident from the deeply incised camel tracks leading up to it from the south. As the pass begins to narrow a low rocky spur juts out from the hills to the east (Plate 12.70). On the vertical face of this (6) are inscriptions and rock art. There are many ephemeral features in the area, small cairns and wind-breaks as well as pot sherds some concentrations of which were logged as separate features. Although there are suitable rock faces and boulders, particularly on the west side of the pass, rock art was very rare – cows by the Pharaonic inscriptions and a single cow in a rock shelter a little to the south of (5) (Figure 12.4).

Figure 12.4. KRP18, scale 1:10,000 (Google Earth satellite image, April 2018).

Feature no.	Type	Description
(1)	Pot scatter	A few sherds immediately in front of (6) and in the adjacent *khor*
(2)	Pot scatter	Concentration of sherds between two small sandstone outcrops
(3)	Pot scatter	A rock shelter in the southern outcrop, 3 sherds from within it
(4)	Pot scatter, tent bases?	Concentration of sherds about 10m to the south of the southern outcrop. Close by some penannular rings of stones (Plate 12.71) – tent bases?

Plate 12.69. KRP18 – looking north from the Khashm el-Bab to the Bab es-Silik. (8) is in the sandy khor *in the foreground, (1) and (6) are on the rock outcrop on the right.*

Plate 12.70. KRP18 – looking south from the Khashm el-Bab. (1) and (6) are on the rock outcrop on the left.

Plate 12.71. KRP18(4) – tent base?

Plate 12.72. KRP18(5) – rock shelter with occupation scatter on the slope below it.

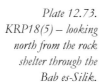

Plate 12.73. KRP18(5) – looking north from the rock shelter through the Bab es-Silik.

Feature no.	Type	Description
(5)	Rock shelter, pot scatter	On the west side of the pass a rock shelter perhaps 10m above the wadi floor (Plates 12.72 and 12.73). A few sherds of pot in the shelter and an extensive scatter down the slope on to the wadi floor.
(6)	Inscriptions, rock art	
(7)	Rock shelter, pot	Small rock shelter with several sherds from 1 pot
(8)	Hand-axe	On the bank of a small *khor* (Plates 12.69 and 14.1)

Finds:

Pottery – (1) sherds from 3(?) vessels; (2) 80+ sherds; (3) glazed sherds; (4) 37+ glazed sherds; (5) 10+ sherds; (6) 3 glazed sherds; (7) 4+ sherds.

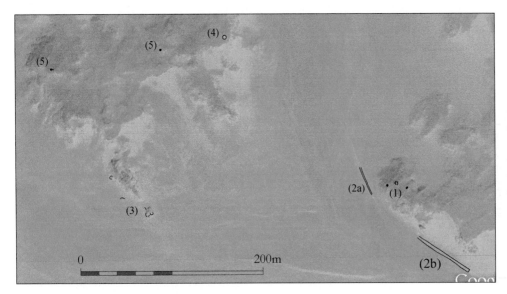

*Figure 12.5.
KRP19, scale
1:4,000 (Google
Earth satellite
image, April
2018).*

Stone – (8) lanceolate hand-axe, see Usai, this volume, 184.
Bibliography: Castiglioni *et al.* 1995, 113, 180 - site B33; Davies, this volume, 198-206

Site code: KRP19   **Co-ordinates**: (3) 21° 53.297' N, 32° 39.069' E   **Name**: Khashm el-Bab
Site type: *Alamat*, huts, linear features, inscriptions   **Period**: Turkiya, ?,
Location: Towards the mouth of the wadi leading up to the Khashm el-Bab from the vast sandy plain to the south.
Description: The *alamat*, of which there are many on both sides of the wadi, guide the way northwards towards the pass and at a confluence indicate which of the two large wadis should be followed. (1) and (2) are on the east side of the wadi (Plate 12.74), (3) is 250m to the west at the confluence while (4) is on the hilltop on the west side of the wadi leading to Khashm el-Bab 245m to the north west of (1) (Figure 12.5).

Feature no.	Type	Description
(1)	*Alamat*, structures	A - rough column made of thin stone slabs approximately 600mm high B - a circular structure about 3m in diameter with well-built stone walls nearly 1m high open to the south. Three orthostats are set into the wall top. There are five long buttresses spaced equally around the walls of rougher construction than the primary structure (Plate 12.75). C - a small oval structure standing to a height of about 1m.
(2)	Linear features	A – two parallel lines of stone blocks (Plate 12.77) a little over 1m apart set on the wadi floor slightly curving around the base of the hill occupied by (1). It is approximately 35m in length and is open ended. In places the sides of the feature are a minimum of three courses of stone slabs while elsewhere single large slabs are set on edge (cf. Castiglioni and Castiglioni, this volume, pl. 4.62). B – similar to (2a) but separated from it by *c.* 64m (Plate 12.76). The sides, nearly 2m apart, are formed of slabs or single large stones. In some parts there is also an internal line of stones parallel with the sides. It is closed off at the south end (Plate 12.78) and is about 37m in length.
(3)	Huts, inscriptions	A number of features are built around three large boulders; two hut circles abut them to the south, another to the north (Figure 12.6, Plates 12.79-12.81). The largest boulder has inscriptions a-f carved on its flat top and sloping flanks. A large and complete storage jar is set in the fissure where the three boulders meet (Plate 12.83). On the bedrock pavement immediately to the south were the depressions of a *mancala*. In the wadi bed a little to the north west is a semi-circular windbreak associated with a storage jar and another abuts the steep rocky slope of the *jebel*.
(4)	Structure	A semicircle of stone walling survives on the north side (Plate 12.82) while a slight gravel ridge suggests the rest of the circular structure about 3m in diameter with part of an internal partition. Inscription (g) lay immediately to the east of the structure.
(5)	*Alamat*	On the *jebel* a little north of (3) are three *alamat*, two close together, one isolated. The isolated example standing about 1m high has its lower half built of black sandstones, its upper half of white sandstones (Plate 12.85). Of the other two each about 1m high, one is a rough column of black sandstones with an upright slab on top, the other is a large orthostat with smaller stones packed around its base to support it (Plate 12.84).

Inscriptions – these were read, transcribed and translated by our Arabic epigrapher Mahmoud Suliman Bashir. Inscriptions (a) to (f) were on the large boulder at (3), (g) was on a white sandstone slab at (4), broken into several pieces and not complete.

Plate 12.74. KRP19(1) and (2) – general view from (3). (1) is on the top of the hill, (2) in the wadi *at its base.*

Plate 12.75. KRP19(1) – general view looking north into the Khashm el-Bab.

Plate 12.76. KRP19(2b) – general view looking south east.

Plate 12.77. KRP19(2a) – detail of construction.

Plate 12.78. KRP19(2b) – the squared off south-eastern end of the stone alignments.

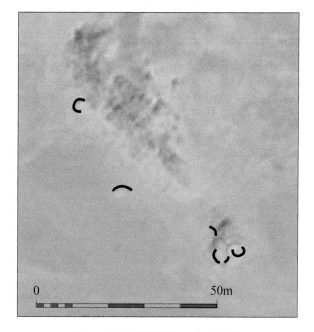

0   50m

Figure 12.6. KRP19(3), scale 1:1,000 (Google Earth satellite image April 2018).

Plate 12.79. KRP19(3) – the prominent structure on the skyline to the left of the outcrop is (4).

Plate 12.80. KRP19(3) – room constructed of stone abutting the rock outcrop.

Plate 12.81. KRP19(3) – the inscriptions are carved into the top and sloping upper part of the face of the outcrop.

Plate 12.82. KRP19(4).

Plate 12.83. KRP19(3) – complete pottery vessel set amongst the rocks of the outcrop.

Plate 12.84. KRP19(5) – alamat.

Plate 12.85. KRP19(5) – alam.

(a) We stayed[3]   نزلنا

here   ها هنا

Then we travelled again   ثم إرتحلنا

Life is like that   هكذا الدنيا

Staying and travelling   نزول و إرتحال

(b) Seleim Salim Haj Ahmed,   سليم سالم حاج احمد

Curator of Khashm el-Bab Station   أمين محطة خشم الباب

in 14-1-1269   فى ١٤.١. سنة ١٢٦٩

until 1270[4] G   لغاية سنة ١٢٧٠

(c) Ibrahim   إبراهيم

Effendi   أفندى

Abdul el-Kheir   أبو الخير

(d) Seleim Salim   سليم سالم

There is no God but Allah   لا اله الا الله

Mohammed Rasoul Allah   محمد رسول الله

(e) Ibrahim   إبراهيم

(f) Ibrahim Effendi   إبراهيم أفندى

(g) [Seleim] Salim [Haj Ahmed]   [......] سالم [......]

Curator of Station [Khashm]   أمين محطة

el-Bab 1269   الباب سنة ١٢٦٩

G   ج

[................]   ....

---

[3] Stayed / camped / arrived

[4] AH 1269 = beginning 15th October AD 1852

AH 1270 = beginning 4th October AD 1853

Finds:
Pottery – (3) *zir* and glazed sherds.

Site code: KRP20   **Co-ordinates**: 21° 53.136' N, 32° 39.468' E   **Name**: Khashm el-Bab
Site type: Rock art   **Period**: ?
Location: On the east side of the wadi down from the Khashm el-Bab just before it debouches into the plain to the south. A massive boulder is detached from the cliff face and the rock art is inscribed on the bedrock and on the adjacent boulder face (Plates 12.86 and 12.87).

Plate 12.86. KRP20 looking north towards the Khashm el-Bab – the site by the rock face on the right.

Plate 12.87. KRP20 - the rock art is on the left side and back of the large boulder and on the rock wall beyond it.

Plate 12.88. KRP20 rock art on the rear face of the isolated boulder – giraffe and an infilled long-horned cow.

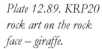

Plate 12.90. KRP20 rock art on the rear face of the isolated boulder – detail of a giraffe.

Plate 12.89. KRP20 rock art on the rock face – giraffe.

Description: Representations of several attenuated giraffe with very long thin legs and neck and an oval body infilled with peck marks. Also a small long-horned cow (Plates 12.88-12.90).

Finds: No artefacts were noted.

Site code: KRP21   **Co-ordinates**: 21° 32.535' N, 32° 8.751' E   **Name**: -

Site type: Rock art   **Period**: ?

Location: Carved on a vertical face of a fine sandstone stratum on the lower slopes of an isolated *jebel* (Figure 12.7, Plate 12.91).

Description: A single finely carved long-necked quadruped with a tail curving up over its back and long upright ears projecting from its small head (Plate 12.92).

Finds: No artefacts were noted.

Site code: KRP22   **Co-ordinates**: 21° 32.873' N, 32° 9.262' E   **Name**: Jebel Nasb Enat

Site type: Rock art, inscriptions   **Period**: New Kingdom, Kushite (Meroitic), ?

Location: On the vertical cliff faces of a prominent *jebel* at the western end of a wide *wadi* where it debouches into the vast plain (Figure 12.7). The inscriptions are on the cliff rising from ground level as is much of the rock art. More rock art is on the cliff faces above, each rising from a narrow terrace.

Description: Two New Kingdom inscriptions and many rock art motifs including

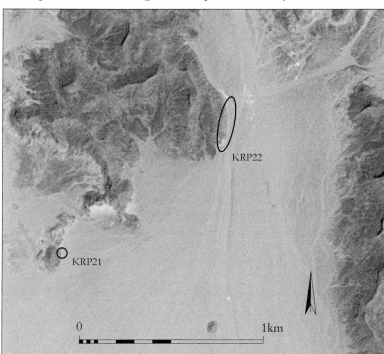

Figure 12.7. KRP21 and KRP22, scale 1:20,000 (Google Earth satellite image, April 2018).

Plate 12.91. KRP21.

Plate 12.92. KRP21 – animal motif.

Plate 12.93. KRP22 – giraffe grazing on a palm tree.

Boats of 'pharaonic' type
Long-horned cattle
Giraffe grazing the top of a palm tree (Plate 12.93) – a well-known motif from the Meroitic period[3]

___

[3] For discussions of this motif only known from a later Kushite context see Kleinitz 2008a; 2008b. For examples of the motif on pottery see Woolley and

Quadruped identical to that at site KRP21
Birds

Finds: No artefacts were noted.

Bibliography: Castiglioni and Castiglioni 2007, 19-20 - site E; Davies, this volume, 206-207

Site code: KRP23   **Co-ordinates**: (2) 21° 8.688' N, 32° 33.507' E   **Name**: Nasb Atiliya
(3) 21° 8. 666' N, 32° 33.483' E
(4) 21° 8.659' N, 32° 33.453' E
(5) 21° 8.625' N, 32° 33.437' E
(6) 21° 8.691' N, 32° 33.311' E
(7) 21° 8.800' N, 32° 33.410' E

Site type: Rock art, inscriptions, symbols,   **Period**: Neolithic, New Kingdom, Medieval, ?
rock shelters, occupation scatters

Location: An isolated very prominent *jebel* attaining an elevation of 719m, with almost vertical cliff faces on all sides (Figure 12.8, Plate 12.94). There are large numbers of rock shelters, many of those easily accessible towards the base of the mountain, contain rock art and other evidence of human activity. The Egyptian inscription is found in one of these.

Description:

Feature no.	Type	Description
(1)	Rock shelter	A very long frieze of animals following a good but narrow stratum of rock around the shelter into the cave. There was also rock art on other rock surfaces; one horizontal slab has carved sandals (Plates 12.95-12.98).
(2)	Rock shelter	Small cave with a large 'glyph' (Plates 12.99 and 12.100).
(3)	Rock shelter	Rubbing base in the centre and a slab laid on the floor with a representation of a camel suckling its young (Plate 12.101).
(4)	Rock shelter	Sherds of Neolithic pottery within, plus carved on the walls a large 'glyph', animals and some painted decoration (Plates 12.102-12.105). Much of the rock art on the bedrock pavement at the entrance to the shelter is fine incised work. Motifs include a hunter with bow and arrow and his dog and beak-headed anthropomorphs. For a similar form at site 332 near Naga Abidis on the Nile see Vahala and Cervicek 1999, Taf. 84. 'Beak'-headed anthropomorphs are known elsewhere in the Sahara as for example at Jabbaren in the Tassili-n-Ajjer where the figures have a distinctively Egyptian character (Lhote 1960, I). In Libya the 'beak' effect is actually a stylized horse's head (Le Quellec 1987, 83).
(5)	Occupation scatter	Extends from the base of the *jebel* over the stoney terrace (Plate 12.106). Very rich in pottery.
(6)	Large rock shelter	On the west face of the *jebel* (Plate 12.107). Rock art includes a Christian cross, grooves, animals including ostrich (Plates 12.108-12.112).
(7)	Cave	Contains rock art of animals, symbols, 'glyphs', and one New Kingdom inscription (Plates 12.113-12.116). For not dissimilar glyphs/symbols, see Hellström 1970 Corpus X51; Verner 1974, cat. no. 853 from Korosko East. At el-Kab in Laqiya, to the west of Dongola, the wavy lines and the double pointed 'glyphs' are combined, the former set within the latter (Plate 12.117) (Kröpelin and Kuper 2007, 224).
(8)	Rock shelter	Three large 'glyphs'/symbols plus some other rock art. Located just above (4).
(9)	Pot scatter	On east side of *jebel*
(10)	Pot scatter	On east side of *jebel*

Randall-Maciver 1910, pls 41 - 8183, 43 - 8293, 61-8213; Rose 1998, 165, fig. 6.21; Edwards 2014, 58. According to Kleinitz "Rather than designating giraffes (apparently grazing from trees) as motifs drawn from the natural environment, this evidence indicates that they may have been a popular motif relating to the magico-religious sphere of the Meroitic world, and that they were appropriate to be placed in various object, built and landscape contexts." (2014, 102). See also Hofmann and Tomandl 1987, 108ff.. For examples in the Nile Valley see Hellström 1970, site 160 – pl. 54.5; site 380 d2 – pl. 102.1.

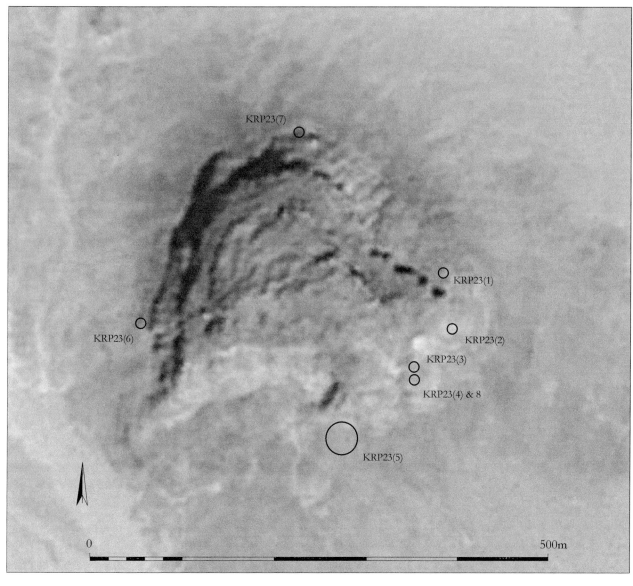

Figure 12.8. KRP23, scale 1:4,000 (Google Earth satellite image, April 2018).

*Plate 12.94.
KRP23,
Nasb Atiliya from
the north east.*

Plate 12.95. KRP23(1) – the rock art is on the smooth rock wall to the right of the rock shelter entrance.

Plate 12.96. KRP23(1) – detail of the long horned-cattle facing right and left. One appears to have been modified, the head being crowned with a long neck and bird's head with prominent curving beak.

Plate 12.97. KRP23(1) – frieze of animals.

Plate 12.98. KRP23(1) – long-horned cattle and billy goat.

Plate 12.99. KRP23(2) – the cave entrance.

Plate 12.100. KRP23(2) – glyphs within the cave.

Plate 12.101. KRP23(3) - camel carved on a loose block.

Plate 12.102. KRP23(4) – rock art carved on the bedrock pavement.

Plate 12.103. KRP23(4) – anthropomorphs holding palm fronds, and quadrupeds.

Plate 12.104. KRP23(4) – a hunter armed with a bow and arrow stalking a quadruped.

Plate 12.105. KRP23(4) – anthropomorphs rendered in red paint.

Plate 12.106. KRP23(5) – general view over the area of the Neolithic occupation scatter.

Plate 12.107. KRP23(6) – the rock shelter.

Plate 12.108. KRP23(6) – long-horned striped cattle.

Plate 12.109. KRP23(6) – quadrupeds.

161

Plate 12.110. KRP23(6) – birds.

Plate 12.111. KRP23(6) – Medieval Christian cross.

Plate 12.112. KRP23(6) – long-horned cow carved over what appears to be a geometric motif.

Plate 12.114. KRP23(7) – general view of the rock shelter.

Plate 12.113. KRP23(7) – glyphs.

Plate 12.115. KRP23(7) – glyphs.

Plate 12.116 KRP23(7) – long-horned cattle, other quadrupeds and glyphs.

Plate 12.117. El-Kab – one of the symbols in the rock shelter adjacent to the post-medieval fort.

Finds:
Pottery: (4) 4 sherds; (5) many sherds; (6) 11 sherds; (7) 7 sherds; (9) 2 sherds; (10) 2 sherds.
Bibliography: Castiglioni and Castiglioni 2007, 19-20, - site L; Davies, this volume, 207

Bibliography

Castiglioni, A. and A. Castiglioni 2006. *Nubia. Magica Terra Millenaria*. Luglio.

Castiglioni, A. and A. Castiglioni 2007. 'Les pistes millénaires du désert oriental de Nubie', *Bulletin de la Société Française d'Égyptologie* 169-170, 17-49.

Castiglioni, A., A. Castiglioni and J. Vercoutter 1995. *L'Eldorado dei Faraoni. Alla scoperta di Berenice Pancrisia*. Novara.

Edwards, D. N. 2014. 'Early Meroitic Pottery and the creation of an early imperial culture?', in A. Lohwasser and P. Wolf (eds), *Ein Forscherleben zwischen den Welten Zum 80. Geburtstag von Steffen Wenig*. Der antike Sudan. Mitteilungen der Sudan-archäologischen Gesellschaft zu Berlin e.V. Berlin, 51-63.

Hellström, P. 1970. *The Rock Drawings*. The Scandanavian Joint Expedition to Sudanese Nubia Publications 1. Copenhagen.

Hofmann, I. and H. Tomandl 1987. *Die Bedeutung des Tieres in der meroitischen Kultur*. Beiträge zur Sudanforschung Beiheft 2. Vienna.

Kleinitz, C. 2008a. 'Neue Arbeiten zu den Sekundärbildern der Großen Anlage von Muswwarat es Sufra', *Der Antike Sudan. Mitteilungen der Sudanarchäologischen Gesellschaft zu Berlin* 19, 27-38.

Kleinitz, C. 2008b. 'Rock Art on Us Island: A window into past life-worlds at the Fourth Nile Cataract', in B. Gratien (ed.), *Actes de la 4ᵉ Conférence Internationale sur l'Archéologie de la 4ᵉ Cataracte du Nil*. Cahiers de Recherches de l'Institut de Papyrologie et d'Egyptologie de Lille Supplément 7. Lille, 85-107.

Kleinitz, C. 2014. 'The graffiti of Musawwarat es-Sufra: current research on historic inscriptions, images and markings at the Great Enclosure', *Sudan & Nubia* 18, 93-103.

Knight, E. F. 1897. *Letters from the Sudan: Reprinted from "The Times" of April to October, 1896*. London, New York.

Kröpelin, S. and R. Kuper 2007. 'More Corridors to Africa', in B. Gratien (ed.), *Mélanges offerts à Francis Geus*. Cahiers de Recherches de l'Institut de Papyrologie et d'Égyptologie de Lille. Lille, 219-229.

Le Quellec, J.-L. 1987. *L'art rupestre du Fezzan septentrional (Libye)*. BAR Int. Ser. 365. Oxford.

Lhote, H. 1960. *The Search for the Tassili Frescoes. The story of the prehistoric rock-paintings of the Sahara*. London.

Rose, P. J. 1998. 'The Pottery. Part 1: The Meroitic Pottery', in D. N. Edwards, *Gabati. A Meroitic, Post-Meroitic and Medieval Cemetery in Central Sudan Volume 1*. Sudan Archaeological Research Society Publications No. 3. London, 142-177.

Váhala, F. and P. Cervicek 1999. *Katalog der Felsbilder aus der Tschechoslowakischen Konzession in Nubien*. Prague.

Verner, M. 1974. *Some Nubian Petroglyphs*. Acta Universitatis Carolinae, Philologia Monographia XLV 73. Prague.

Welsby, D. A. 2011. *Sudan's First Railway, The Gordon Relief Expedition and The Dongola Campaign*. Sudan Archaeological Research Society Publication No. 19. London.

Woolley, C. L. and D. Randall-Maciver 1910. *Karanog: The Romano-Nubian Cemetery*. Philadelphia.

13. The Korosko Road Project: Final Report on the Pottery

Philippe Ruffieux and Mahmoud Suliman Bashir

1. Introduction

A systematic pottery survey was conducted alongside the epigraphic and archaeological prospections of the SARS 2013 Korosko Road Project. The aim of this survey was to identify the presence of cultural groups at the different locations visited by the KRP team.

As one of the main concerns of the project was to find and study epigraphic evidence left by pharaonic expeditions on their way to the strategic Nubian gold mining areas, a special effort was made to find pottery contemporary with these hieroglyphic inscriptions. In this respect, a preliminary report was published in 2014, presenting the interesting find of an 18th Dynasty amphora in its archaeological context.[1] But, of course, this was only a limited part of the pottery survey results. More pottery was found on many of the prospected sites.

It is the purpose of this final report to offer a wider picture of the material traces left by travellers or dwellers in this desert crossed by the ancient Korosko Road.

2. Method of the pottery survey

The method applied to the pottery survey was to record every potsherd – or group of potsherds if identifiable as belonging to a single vessel – that could be found in the prospected areas. Pottery remains can be very scarce in such remote areas; it was necessary, therefore, to record not only the usual diagnostic sherds (rims, bases, handles or decorated sherds), but everything that might yield information regarding the passage of travellers or the presence of settlers. When only body sherds are available, they may be diagnostic to some extent, but in many cases it is very difficult to identify them culturally with any certainty. This is partly due to their surfaces often being eroded by aeolian sand.

A recording form for the pottery was used on every site, taking into consideration the area within the site, typology, morphology, fabric, and surface properties of the finds, as well as any other information of interest.[2] As there was no excavation in the project, all the material recorded in the course of this survey originates from the surface. Once recorded, the sherd – or group of sherds – was photographed and then replaced in its original position. It was normally not drawn, except for a few specific cases where we decided to collect all the finds of a site.[3]

In the following account, we will present the pottery site by site and focus on elements that bear any diagnostic characteristics.

3. Description of the pottery finds from the Korosko Road

3.1. Sites KRP6 and KRP7

These two sites are in the immediate vicinity of site KRP5, a cave running through a hill on the south-western side of Jebel Umm Nabari. KRP6 lies in the plain to the south of the cave, whereas KRP7 is above it on the top of the hill.

3.1.1. KRP6

Four rim sherds and nine body sherds were recorded on this site. Their main characteristic is the presence of very recognizable impressed decoration on their outer surface. Similar pottery has been observed in the recent past at several sites of the Eastern Desert, and particularly in the surroundings of Jebel Umm Nabari,[4] where it is generally associated with lithic tools and fragments of ostrich eggshells. Such sites may be the remains of seasonal camps for Early Holocene population groups (Lanna and Gatto 2010, 323).

The pottery of this period found in the Western and Eastern Deserts of Egypt and Sudan is mainly classified according to the type of decoration, through a common descriptive system[5] that will be employed for the following presentation. All the sherds show a light brown or pale red surface and mineral tempered fabric. The decorations are well preserved, although a few pieces are quite eroded.

Four rim sherds (nos 06-00-01–04, Plates 13.1-13.4) are decorated with different variations of "alternately pivoting stamp, double-grained line motif", type A7 (Lanna and Gatto 2010, 327 and 325, fig. 8). No. 06-00-02 shows one horizontal motif close to the rim, whereas 06-00-01 has three. Apparently more elaborate, the two larger sherds nos 06-00-03–04 are decorated with multiple double rows of the same motif. In lower Nubia, a similar decoration type is observed, for example, in the Khartoum Variant assemblages from Faras (site 18A) or Abka (site 428).[6] It is also known from the Kerma region, in contexts of the Kerma Mesolithic.[7]

Body sherd no. 06-00-05 (Plate 13.5) was ornamented using the alternately pivoting stamp, return technique, type A12, well attested in Kerma, at site 45 (Busharia) and dated to the Kerma Mesolithic I (8300-7800 BC) (Honegger 2014, 23, pl. 1; Gatto 2013, 8-9 and 7, fig. 3.2.). No. 06-00-06 (Plate 13.6) is not very well preserved but still exhibits a motif obtained through a simple impression technique.[8] The two pieces, nos

---

[1] Ruffieux and Suliman Bashir 2014; on the inscriptions, see Davies 2014 and this volume.

[2] The recording sheet we used is based on a model provided by Isabella Welsby Sjöström, to whom we are very grateful.

[3] The collected material is now stored in Jebel Barkal Museum.

[4] These sites were discovered by the CeRDO survey project in 2004 and 2005; see Lanna and Gatto 2010.

[5] See, for example, Gatto 2002, 65-66 and 67, fig. 5.1; Gatto 2013, 6.

[6] See Nordström 1972, pl. 60, no. 5 (Faras site 18A), pl. 123 nos 8-9 (Abka site 428). Concerning the Khartoum Variant, see also Gatto 2006.

[7] Honegger 2014, 23, pl. 1; Jakob and Honegger 2017, 45, fig. 35; Gatto 2013, 9-10 and 7, fig. 3.3-4, 3.8.

[8] See, for example, Gatto 2002, 69, fig. 5.3m-n (type S1).

06-00-07 and 06-00-11 (Plates 13.7 and 13.8), are decorated with the rocker packed dotted zigzag pattern, type R1. Already seen in the Eastern Desert (Lanna and Gatto 2010, 327 and 325, fig. 8), it is also present in Kerma from the Kerma Mesolithic I, notably on sites 45 and 84 (Gatto 2013, 8-9) and in the Khartoum Variant of the Second Cataract, in Abka (site 428), where it is described as "parallel dotted-line impressions" made with a rocker-stamp (Nordström 1972, 213 and pl. 122 nos 16-19). No. 06-00-12 (Plate 13.9) probably bears an eroded specimen of the same type of decoration.

Two sherds, nos 06-00-08 and 06-00-09 (Plates 13.10 and 13.11), are adorned with a herring-bone pattern, an alternately pivoting stamp technique of type A1, observed in the Eastern Desert, the Second Cataract area (Abka, site 428, Khartoum Variant), the Western Desert (Nabta Playa) as well as in Kerma (Wadi el-Arab, phases II-V).[9] No. 06-00-10 (Plate 13.12) was treated according to the alternately pivoting stamp return technique (types A9-A10), known from the Eastern Desert and the Second Cataract region.[10] The last type of decoration observed on KRP6 (no. 06-00-13, Plate 13.13) is the Nubian dotted wavy line pattern of type R5, seen in the Eastern Desert, the Second Cataract area, the Western Desert and the Kerma region.[11]

3.1.2. KRP7

Only five pieces of pottery were recorded at KRP7. Nos 07-00-01–02 and 04 (Plates 13.14-13.16) are decorated with the rocker packed dotted zigzag pattern (R1) also present on KRP6.[12] The other two sherds show decorations which do not appear on KRP6; no. 07-00-03 (Plate 13.17), for example, seems to bear a kind of rocker stamp impression, whereas no. 07-00-05 (Plate 13.18) is impressed with alternately pivoting stamp double-grained line motifs divided in the middle by a dotted line. Quite similar patterns – although their middle line appears to be continuous, not dotted – were observed in the Khartoum Variant of Second Cataract SJE concession, site 428 (Nordström 1972, 213 and pl. 122, no. 1, pl. 123, nos 8, 10).

The material from these two sites presents obvious similarities with that found on the nearby sites visited by the CeRDO mission, which were considered to be associated with the Khartoum Variant and the Kerma Mesolithic and dated to the second half of the 7th and 6th millennium BC (Lanna and Gatto 2010, 327). This period coincides with a humid climatic phase that witnesses the establishment of populations, notably in the Kerma area, on the margins of the alluvial plain, in locations which were to become too arid for a sustainable life around 5300 BC (Honegger 2014, 20-21).

3.2. Site KRP8

This site is an elongated north to south sandstone hill located to the north west of Jebel Umm Nabari. On its eastern flank

were found rock-drawings of cattle as well as hieroglyphic inscriptions of the New Kingdom. Pottery sherds of various periods were recovered from nine different areas on the perimeter of the hill and on its summit.

3.2.1. KRP8 area 1

Area 1 is situated at the south-eastern foot of the hill. Five pieces of pottery were found on its surface. No. 08-01-01 (Plate 13.19) is a fragment of wheel-made pot in a greenish beige fabric identified as a MARL A3 of the Vienna System.[13] It belonged to a large container, presumably a jar imported from Egypt. Due to the absence of a recognizable shape, any precise dating other than Middle to New Kingdom would be risky.

Three sherds, nos 08-01-02–04 (Plates 13.20-13.22), may originate from a single vessel or from several vessels of a similar type. Their very dense salmon-pink fabric and the strongly wheel-ridged surface of no. 08-01-03 suggest that they once belonged to an amphora of a type described further in relation to site KRP18.[14]

The last piece in this area is no. 08-01-05 (Plate 13.23), a very rough hand-made vessel with a mineral-tempered fabric containing a high amount of mica. It may have been a kind of cooking pot.

3.2.2. KRP8 areas 2, 3 and 4

Very close to each other, areas 2 and 3 are located down the hill, on its north-eastern side, not far away from, and to the north of, a group of hieroglyphic inscriptions. One sherd was found in each area; both are hand-made.

No. 08-02-06 (Plate 13.24) is a thick body sherd made in a black organic-tempered fabric. The outer surface is red brown, slightly polished, and part of it is black. Although one might think of a Middle Nubian black topped red polished vessel, the thickness of the wall and the general aspect might also suggest a much later date than the 2nd millennium BC.

On the other hand, no. 08-03-07 (Plate 13.25) is a Middle Nubian cooking pot with incised decoration. The wall thickness corresponds to this type of vessel as well as the fabric, which is quite fine, mixed tempered (mineral/organic) but with more abundant mineral components. Incised triangles and geometric motifs are well known particularly on Kerma and C-Group vessels.[15]

A single potsherd, no. 08-04-08 (Plate 13.26), was found in area 4, lying on the northern side of the hill. It is made of a fine black fabric tempered with fine to medium sand and fine white rock particles. With its polished, though slightly eroded, surface, red outside and black inside, it belongs to the Kerma culture.[16] Unfortunately, the absence of morphological detail does not allow a more precise determination.

3.2.3. KRP8 area 5

Two fragments of pottery were found to the south west of the hill, area 5. No. 08-05-10 (Plate 13.27) has a fine mineral-tempered fabric with abundant fine to medium sand and

[9] Lanna and Gatto 2010, 327 and 325, fig. 8; Nordström 1972, 213 and pl. 123 no. 15; Gatto 2002, 69, fig. 5.3l; Honegger 2014, 23, pl 1; Jakob and Honegger 2017, 45, fig. 35.

[10] Lanna and Gatto 2010, 327 and 325, fig. 8; Nordström 1972, pl. 123 no. 5.

[11] Lanna and Gatto 2010, 326-327 and 325, fig. 8; Nordström 1972, pl. 123, no. 25; Gatto 2002, 69, fig. 5.3d; Honegger 2014, 23, pl. 1.

[12] See, for example, Gatto 2002, 69, fig. 5.3m-n (type S1); Lanna and Gatto 2010, 327 and 325, fig. 8; Gatto 2013, 8-9.

[13] This fabric finds its origin in Upper Egypt and was in use during the Middle and New Kingdoms, see Nordström and Bourriau 1993, 177.

[14] See below, § 3.6.1., KRP18, nos 18-05-17–18.

[15] See, for example, Gratien 2000.

[16] See Reisner 1923; Gratien 1978; Dunham 1982; Privati 1999.

Plate 13.1. No. 06-00-01,
site KRP6.

Plate 13.2. No. 06-00-02, site KRP6.

Plate 13.3. No. 06-00-03, site KRP6.

Plate 13.4. No. 06-00-04, site KRP6.

Plate 13.5. No. 06-00-05, site KRP6.

Plate 13.6. No. 06-00-06,
site KRP6.

Plate 13.7. No. 06-00-07, site KRP6.

Plate 13.8. No. 06-00-11,
site KRP6.

Plate 13.9. No. 06-00-12,
site KRP6.

Plate 13.10. No. 06-00-08,
site KRP6.

Plate 13.11. No. 06-00-09, site KRP6.

Plate 13.13. No. 06-00-13, site KRP6.

Plate 13.12. No. 06-00-10,
site KRP6.

*Plate 13.14. No. 07-00-01,
site KRP7.*

*Plate 13.15. No. 07-00-02,
site KRP7.*

Plate 13.16. No. 07-00-04, site KRP7.

*Plate 13.17. No. 07-00-
03, site KRP7.*

Plate 13.18. No. 07-00-05, site KRP7.

*Plate 13.19. No. 08-01-01,
site KRP8.*

*Plate 13.20. No. 08-01-02,
site KRP8.*

*Plate 13.21. No. 08-01-03,
site KRP8.*

Plate 13.23. No. 08-01-05, site KRP8.

*Plate 13.22.
No. 08-01-04,
site KRP8.*

*Plate 13.24.
No. 08-02-06,
site KRP8.*

*Plate 13.25. No. 08-03-07,
site KRP8.*

Plate 13.26. No. 08-04-08, site KRP8.

167

white rock particles. The surface is black inside, red outside, and was originally polished. It may be identified as a Kerma container, or at least as a Middle Nubian red polished pot.

The other piece found in this location, no. 08-05-09 (Plate 13.28), is the rim of a hand-made neckless jar or pot made in a brown fabric including a mineral temper. The surface is brown inside and black outside with traces of prominent burnishing. The technical properties as well as the surface treatment corresponds well with the description of common Islamic pottery found in Sudanese Nubia and dated from the 14th to the 18th centuries AD (Phillips 2004).

3.2.4. KRP8 areas 6 and 7

Area 6 is located on top of the sandstone hill and centred on the remains of a small, poorly preserved, circular stone structure (Plate 13.29). A scatter of potsherds was discovered all around this structure, extending to the west down the steep sides of the hill, in area 7.

A total of 73 sherds was collected in both areas and appeared to originate from a single vessel, which could be partly reconstructed (nos 08-06-11 and 08-07-12, Plate 13.30, Figure 13.1). The vessel was made of a fabric belonging to the MARL D family, a very dense fabric showing a dark greyish

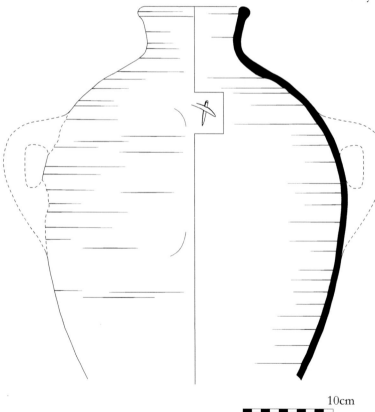

10cm

Figure 13.1. Profile of amphora no. 08-06-11/08-07-12 (scale 1:4).

brown section, a greenish beige outer surface and containing an abundant limestone temper (Nordström and Bourriau 1993, 181-182). It was mainly employed, during the New Kingdom, to produce amphorae in the Memphite region of Northern Egypt (Bourriau 2004, 85-88; Aston 2004, 185-187).

The profile is representative of Early 18th Dynasty amphorae, down to the reigns of Thutmose III and Amenhotep

II.[17] Unfortunately, the handles were not preserved, but it was possible to see the attachment point of one. Just beside it, one can see an incised mark in the form of two strokes crossing each other, applied before firing.

In 2004, the Italian CeRDO expedition found a complete amphora of a similar type deposited on the rocky ground and partly covered with stones (Castiglioni, this volume, 48-9, pl. 5.4). Since then it has been housed in the storerooms of the Sudan National Museum in Khartoum under the inventory number SNM 31405. Thanks to the kindness of our Sudanese colleagues, it was possible to retrieve and study it (Plate 13.31). It seems to be made in the same fabric and, despite the erosion of the surface, one can still see traces of burnishing, a usual treatment for such vessels. Another feature is the presence of an incised mark like the one on KRP8's amphora, partly covered by the upper attachment of one of the handles. Made before the handles were applied, it may have served as a marker to position them correctly.[18] It should be noted that the two handles are not opposite each other as should be expected but are slightly offset to one side of the pot.

Other fragments of amphorae were recovered on the Korosko Road, notably at site KRP9, close to a rock shelter bearing hieroglyphic inscriptions. Large pieces were also found by the CeRDO expedition in front of the so-called "rock shelter of Heqanefer", a short distance north of the Egyptian border.[19] At site KRP12, a circular stone structure covered with a stone slab was discovered (Plate 13.32). After excavation, it was found to be empty, but it appears nonetheless very similar to the one from KRP8. Thus, in the case of each of these New Kingdom sites, we are probably dealing, with some sort of water reserve, "hidden" or stored in a secure cache, and meant to be used by travellers crossing the desert on the road linking the Nile Valley to the gold mining areas.

In the Western Desert of Egypt, the Abu Ballas trail, leading from Dakhla Oasis to the Gilf Kebir plateau, some 400km to the south west, was equipped from the Old Kingdom with a network of "filling stations" set at regular intervals along the road. These filling stations were provided with tens if not hundreds of jars and later amphorae filled with water for the supply of men and donkeys (Förster 2013; Hendrickx *et al.* 2013). The scale is, of course, very different from what we observed on the Korosko Road, where each of the discovered cache only housed a single amphora. The amount of available water would, therefore, be very limited in comparison. On the other hand, although this kind of vessel was originally intended for the transport and storage of wine, another issue could be the time during which the water would last inside the

---

[17] Hope 1989, 93-94 (category 1a); fig. 1, 1-5; Aston 2004, 187-191 (type B1), fig. 6.

[18] Although incised marks can be variously interpreted (see, for example, Gallorini 2009), in this case the meaning seems quite secure.

[19] Castiglioni *et al.* 1995, 118-122; this volume, 33; cf. Manzo, this volume, 75.

Plate 13.27. No. 08-05-10, site KRP8.

Plate 13.28. No. 08-05-09, site KRP8.

Plate 13.30.
No. 08-06-11
and 08-07-12,
site KRP8.

Plate 13.29. Remains of the circular stone structure on KRP8 area 6.

Plate 13.32. Stone structure on KRP12, before clearing.

Plate 13.31. Amphora from the CeRDO survey, Sudan National Museum no. 31405.

amphora, especially in such extreme weather conditions as in the desert. These difficulties may, however, have been partly alleviated by the presence of multiple caches along the route.

3.2.5. KRP8 areas 8 and 9

These two areas were on top of the hill, south of area 6. In area 8, four sherds belonged to a single vessel, no. 08-08-13. Being represented only by weathered body sherds, it proves difficult to identify. It is made of a mineral-tempered fabric and seems to be hand-made and red polished outside (Plate 13.33). No. 08-08-14 is also a group of three sherds from one pot (Plate 13.34). Although the fragments have suffered from the weather conditions, one can still see the grooves due to the throwing on the wheel. The fabric is quite coarse and mineral tempered. Sherd no. 08-08-15 (Plate 13.35) is made of a fine fabric with mineral inclusions. The outer surface is red and very smooth, once probably polished, while the inside is black and also smooth. It matches well with a red-polished Kerma pot.

In area 9, another group recorded as one vessel is no. 08-09-16 (Plate 13.36). It is comprised of 20 fragments including a rim, all quite damaged by the weather. The vessel – a cooking pot or a large bowl – was hand-made and manufactured in a fabric with mineral temper. The outer surface was burnished and the rim sherd exhibits fine incisions (or impressions) on the lip (Plate 13.37), a kind of decoration well attested in assemblages dated to the *Kerma Ancien*.[20] Neolithic contexts also provide that kind of lip decoration, but in a thicker form.[21] The last piece in this area, no.

Plate 13.33. No. 08-08-13, site KRP8.

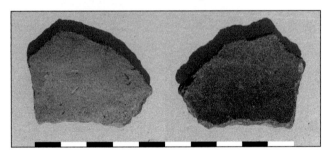

Plate 13.35. No. 08-08-15, site KRP8.

Plate 13.37. No. 08-09-16, site KRP8, detail view of the decorated rim.

Plate 13.38. No. 08-09-17, site KRP8.

08-09-17 (Plate 13.38), is poorly preserved; it is again made of a mineral fabric, and one can see on its surface the remains of a dotted impressed decoration.

3.3. Site KRP9

Site KRP9 is a rock shelter situated not far north of KRP8. There are hieroglyphic inscriptions in the interior. Three body sherds from two distinct areas close to the cave were recorded.

3.3.1. KRP9 area 1

No. 09-01-01 (Plate 13.39) belongs to a wheelmade vessel with a greyish-brown MARL D fabric. The outer surface is covered with a greenish-beige burnished slip, typical of

New Kingdom amphorae (Aston 2004, 185). No. 09-01-02 (Plate 13.40) is hand-made in a rather fine mineral-tempered fabric. The inner surface is black and very smooth while the outer surface is red but quite eroded. It looks like the product of a Middle Nubian cultural group, possibly Kerma.

Plate 13.34. No. 08-08-14, site KRP8.

Plate 13.36. No. 08-09-16, site KRP8.

3.3.2. KRP9 area 2

Sherd no. 09-02-03 is identical with no. 1 and comes from the same amphora.

3.4. Site KRP13

This site is located on the way from KRP8 and KRP9 to the north west, towards KRP14 (where an important inscription was discovered by the CeRDO mission). KRP13 is a cave carved into a small sandstone massif. A short hieroglyphic inscription, was found inside it, on the northern side. Around the sandstone massif, three potsherds were observed.

Sherd no. 13-00-01 (Plate 13.41) is quite eroded, but still recognizable. The fabric is fine, with a mineral temper. It is hand-made and decorated on the outside with what seems to be the "rocker packed dotted zigzag pattern" (type R1),

[20] See, for instance, Gratien 1986, 108, fig. 105a; 109, fig. 106g; Privati 2004, 178 and 181, fig. 138.2.

[21] For example, Salvatori and Usai 2004, 36, fig. 4; Honegger 2004, 42, fig. 4 "type 10".

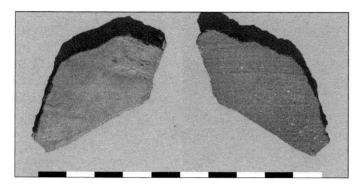

Plate 13.39. No. 09-01-01, site KRP9.

Plate 13.40. No. 09-01-02,
site KRP9.

found on sites KRP6 and KRP7 described above.[22] No. 13-00-02 (Plate 13.42) is a large body sherd made in a fabric with mineral inclusions. The inside is red and smoothed but the outside has been damaged by erosion, so it is not possible to determine the manufacturing technology. Hand-made in a mineral tempered fabric, no. 13-00-03 (Plate 13.43) has a

are both decorated with incisions on the rim and on the body. No. 16-00-02 (Plate 13.45) has short oblique crossing lines on the rim and oblique multiple lines below, probably in the form of a reversed triangle, and a repair hole. A similar decoration can be observed on No. 16-00-03 (Plate 13.46), except that the short lines on the rim do not cross each other but are parallel.

Plate 13.41. No. 13-00-01,
site KRP13.

Plate 13.42. No. 13-00-02,
site KRP13.

Plate 13.43. No. 13-00-03,
site KRP13.

smooth black inner surface and a red decorated exterior. The decoration shows multiple parallel dotted-line impressions made with ropes. Similar types are recorded in the Khartoum Variant assemblages of the SJE concession (Nordström 1972, 213 and pl. 123.7).

3.5. Site KRP16

KRP16 is a rock shelter located in a hill to the north of KRP14. In front of this shelter were found a dozen potsherds, exclusively hand-made, some of which are difficult to identify.

Sherd no. 16-00-01 (Plate 13.44) has a greyish-brown outer surface, black and smooth inside, and is pierced by a repair hole. It bears incised decoration outside, of three parallel lines apparently intersected by at least two other lines, at a quite narrow angle. This pattern may correspond to a type of decoration well represented in the Pan-Grave repertoire.[23]

Nos 16-00-02 and 03 belong to cooking pots and have brown outer surfaces and grey to black inner surfaces. They

These patterns on the rim and the triangles are frequent in the Kerma pottery, particularly in the *Kerma Moyen*.[24]

Three other hand-made body sherds may also be of Kerma origin: no. 16-00-05 (Plate 13.47) is red outside and black smoothed inside, whereas no. 16-00-07 (Plate 13.48) is brown outside, decorated with two incised lines, and black inside. No. 16-00-08 (Plate 13.49), another hand-made rim, is quite eroded but the reddish-brown outer surface still exhibits fine superimposed chevron impressions, a pattern which appears on *Kerma Ancien* and C-Group cooking pots (Gratien 2000, 115 and fig. 1b-d).

Two body sherds with a beige to reddish-brown surface, nos 16-00-06 and 09 (Plates 13.50 and 13.51), are similar to pieces found at KRP6: the decoration shows "alternately pivoting stamp, double-grained line motif", characteristic of the Khartoum Variant and Kerma Mesolithic.[25]

Finally, five pieces, nos 16-00-04 and 16-00-10 to 13 (Plate 13.52), all body sherds, do not allow of any reliable identification.

[22] See above site KRP6, § 3.1.1. nos 06-00-07 and 11; site KRP7, § 3.1.2. nos 07-00-01, 02 and 04.

[23] Säve-Söderbergh 1989, 54 and pl. 31.4, type PIb4, 47/121:1; Ayers and Moeller 2012, 108-111 and fig. 4, 6.

[24] See, for example, Gratien 1978, 240-241; 2000, 115 and fig. 2c; Privati 1978, pl. IV.7; 1999, 58, fig. 9.3 and 9.6; 47-48 and 64, fig. 15.1; 46 and 58, fig. 9.10; 63, fig. 14.3-4.

[25] See above § 3.1.1. nos 06-00-03 and 04, n. 6-7.

Plate 13.44. No. 16-00-01, site KRP16.

Plate 13.45. No. 16-00-02, site KRP16.

Plate 13.46. No. 16-00-03, site KRP16.

Plate 13.47. No. 16-00-05, site KRP16.

Plate 13.48. No. 16-00-07, site KRP16.

Plate 13.49. No. 16-00-08, site KRP16.

Plate 13.50. No. 16-00-06, site KRP16.

Plate 13.51. No. 16-00-09, site KRP16.

3.6. Site KRP18

Known as "Khashm el-Bab", site KRP18 is the northernmost location reached during the survey. It is close to the Egyptian border and is situated at the junction of different desert trails. A large rock surface bears several inscriptions left by Egyptian officials. Seven areas have provided us with surface pottery of different periods, but similar types of vessel were often found in more than one area. Area 1 was just in front of the inscribed rock, while areas 2 to 6 were located to the south, around another sandstone rock, and area 7 was a rock shelter further to the north of area 1. Sherds apparently originating from a single pot or from different pots of the same kind, from one area, were often regrouped for practical reasons under a single inventory number.

3.6.1. KRP18 areas 1, 2 and 5

Three sherds found in area 5, possibly belonging to the same

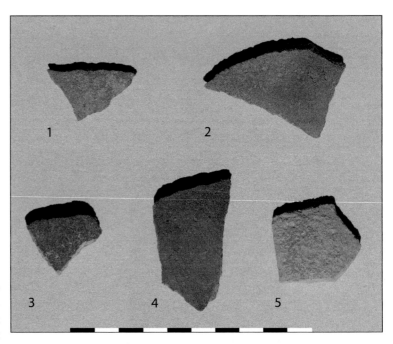

Plate 13.52. Nos 16-00-04 and 10-13, site KRP16.

vessel (no. 18-05-08), are incised with deep parallel lines (Plate 13.53). The surface is black inside and brown to red outside, while the coarse alluvial organic-tempered fabric appears black in section. Such a type of decoration is typical of Pan-Grave cooking pots.[26] Two other undecorated pieces (no. 18-05-09) are probably also of Middle Nubian cultural origin (Plate 13.54). The identity of fragments no. 18-05-10 and no. 18-05-16 (Plates 13.55 and 13.56) is more problematic although a Middle Nubian origin cannot be ruled out.

[26] Gratien 2000, 119 and fig. 13b, 12b; Ayers and Moeller 2012, 109 and fig. 6 (2659 N3).

They share a similar coarse alluvial fabric tempered with fine to medium white rock particles, the section is black and the surface dark red.

A huge number of fragments from areas 1, 2 and 5 (nos 18-05-17, 18-05-18, 18-05-19, 18-01-03 and 18-02-05), amongst which were found rims, handles and body sherds, are all made in a hard and dense pink fabric with a fine mineral temper. The outer surface is covered with a brownish-red slip and all body sherds show a pronounced ribbing (Plates 13.57-13.59). The presence of handles and their position close to the rim, as seen on fragments no. 18-05-17, ensure their identification as amphorae. A precise determination of the types is uncertain considering the degree of fragmentation. Nonetheless, these amphorae might have been imported from Egypt but might also be Nubian products and would range in date from the 6th-7th centuries AD down to the 12th century AD; maybe even later.[27]

A few unidentified sherds were found in area 1. These include three fragments of a possible bottle neck (no. 18-01-01), made in a fine pink fabric and decorated with some sort of "fishbone" impressions (Plate 13.60). Seven body fragments (no. 18-01-02) have a black to greyish-beige fabric tempered with coarse white mineral temper (Plate 13.61). These probably belong to a cooking pot of unknown date. A more interesting find from this area is a fragment of porcelain bowl (no. 18-01-04, Plate 13.62). It is equipped with a ring base and made of a white paste. An underglaze dark blue motif is seen on the exterior. It consists of a horizontal line painted at the junction of the body and base. It underlines a floral or vegetal motif. It is tempting, despite the fragmentary state of the piece, to consider a Chinese origin. This vessel would have made its way to here via Egypt, which had been connected to China by sea trade since the 13th century (Stern 2012, 145).

3.6.2. KRP18 area 4

Several very interesting sherds were found in area 4, possibly related to the remains of two small stone structures of rectangular shape built against the rock. The material is comprised mainly of rims and body sherds of at least four bowls made in a soft fine mineral-tempered white to beige fabric, and all covered with glaze.[28] Three bowls have a black painted decoration under a transparent turquoise glaze (nos 18-04-07a, b and c), while a fourth is bichrome painted (cobalt-blue and black) under a transparent colourless glaze (no. 18-04-07d). A few other fragments apparently belonging to the same vessels were also present in areas 3 and 6.

The outer surface of the three turquoise-glazed vessels consists of one horizontal line close to the rim and probably one or two lines in the lower part, close to the base. These lines are linked by vertical irregular patterns resembling petals or leaves. The inner surface of each vessel is different. Bowl no. 18-04-07a is adorned with a horizontal stylized rope motif

or double "guilloche" painted between two double lines just below the rim (Plates 13.63 and 13.64). No. 18-04-07b has a simpler decoration of vegetal inspiration (Plates 13.65 and 13.66), while no. 18-04-07c is more elaborate and bears a mix of geometric and vegetal designs (Plates 13.67 and 13.68). It is the only bowl whose lower part is partly preserved even if erosion has destroyed the (ring?) base, the inside has survived thanks to the glazing. It has a large centred spot from which four double lines radiate symmetrically. A few fragments prove that the base surface was left unglazed.

The colourless glazed bowl no. 18-04-07d (Plate 13.69) is a bichrome version of no. 18-04-07a. The same patterns are painted in black (lines) and blue (stylized rope and "petals").

Both the soft paste and the surface treatment of these pots match the characteristics of the "Raqqa Ware" made in Syria during the first half of the 13th century.[29] The designs however seem to be less carefully executed than most of the available comparisons of proven Syrian origin. Therefore, one cannot rule out the possibility that these specimens may have been manufactured in Egypt, where a production of Raqqa Ware style pottery is very likely.[30] Raqqa Ware pottery has previously been recorded in Sudan, in the Fourth Nile cataract region.[31]

3.6.3. KRP18 area 7

Another interesting piece was discovered in area 7 (no. 18-07-12). Its rim and part of the upper body are missing, but the general shape can still be identified with some confidence, notably thanks to the nature of the base: it is flat, quite narrow compared to the width of the body, string cut and carelessly finished (Plates 13.70 and 13.71). It probably belongs to a wheel-made Egyptian "beer jar" of small size (Figure 13.2), made in a rather fine alluvial fabric containing organic and mineral inclusions in moderate concentration. Similar "miniature" beer jars are attested at Elephantine (Upper Egypt) and dated to between c. 750 and 600 BC (25th to mid-26th Dynasty) (Aston 1999, 170 and pl. 50, nos 1577-1585).

Figure 13.2. Profile of miniature beer jar no. 18-07-12 (scale 1:4).

5cm

Finally, four body sherds from area 7 were recorded as three containers. All of them come from hand-made pottery with rather thick walls, coarse fabric and a roughly polished or burnished surface. They remain unidentified so far.

3.7. Site KRP19

Not far to the south of the inscriptions at KRP18, site KRP19, the station of "Khashm el-Bab", was surveyed. Egyptian keepers used to live here in the 19th century, and the remains of a small stone house are still partly preserved. One of these men left an inscription engraved in Arabic on a large flat horizontal

---

[27] Although it is always difficult to compare fabrics on the basis of publications alone, see, for example, Egloff 1977, 112 and pl. 57.4 (type 164); Adams 1986 I, 107 and fig. 89.8 (type Z8); 1986 II, 553 (ware U8) and 549, fig. 309; Adams 2018, 307 (ware U8); see also the production from Old Dongola, Pluskota 2005, 231, fig. 8B.

[28] We are much indebted to Isabella Welsby Sjöström, who was able to identify the number of pots, although any reconstruction attempt was made very difficult by the fact that the paste was extremely eroded whereas the glazing was much better preserved.

[29] See, for example, Tonghini 1998, 46-51, "Fritware 2" and wares Y and AH. See also Tonghini 1995, 253-255; Jenkins-Madina 2006.

[30] Tonghini 1998, 50; 1995, 255; Avissar and Stern 2005, 26.

[31] Fuller 2004, 8, col. pl. VI; Ali Mohammed 2014, 206 and pl. 9.

Plate 13.54.
No. 18-05-09,
site KRP18.

Plate 13.53.
No. 18-05-08,
site KRP18.

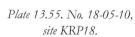

Plate 13.55. No. 18-05-10,
site KRP18.

Plate 13.56. No. 18-05-
16, site KRP18.

Plate 13.57. No. 18-05-17, site KRP18.

Plate 13.59. No. 18-02-05, site KRP18.

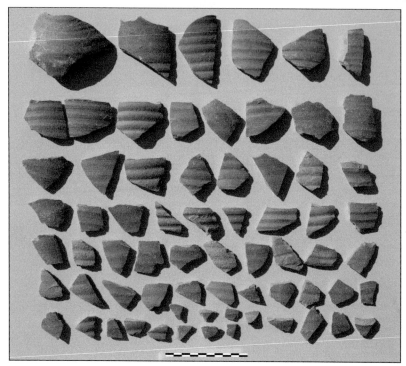

Plate 13.60. No. 18-01-01, site KRP18.

Plate 13.58. No. 18-05-18, site KRP18.

174

Plate 13.62. No. 18-01-04, site KRP18.

Plate 13.61. No. 18-01-02, site KRP18.

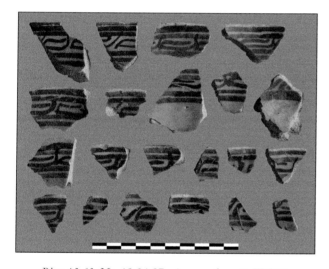

Plate 13.63. No. 18-04-07a, inner surface, site KRP18.

Plate 13.64. No. 18-04-07a, outer surface, site KRP18.

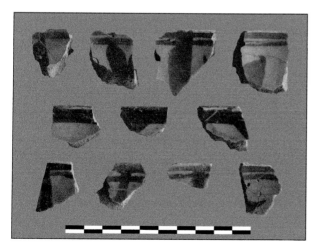

Plate 13.65. No. 18-04-07b, inner surface, site KRP18.

Plate 13.66. No. 18-04-07b, outer surface, site KRP18.

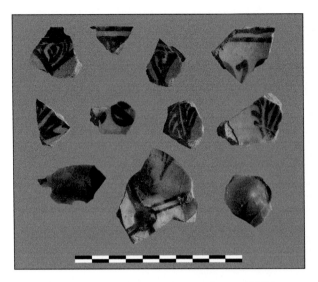

Plate 13.67. No. 18-04-07c, inner surface, site KRP18.

Plate 13.68. No. 18-04-07c, outer surface, site KRP18.

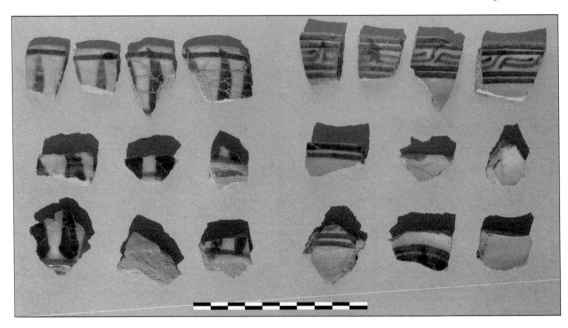

Plate 13.69. No. 18-04-07d, site KRP18.

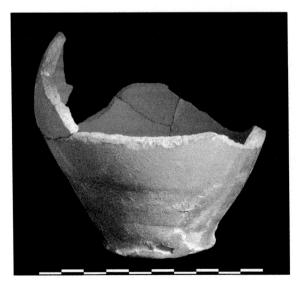

Plate 13.70. No. 18-07-12, site KRP18.

Plate 13.71. No. 18-07-12, detail view of the string-cut base, site KRP18.

rock near to the house. A water jar, or *zir*, was found standing in the middle of the ruined walls (no. 19-03-01). It is a large hand-made neckless container with an oval body, rounded base and a wide aperture finishing in a rolled-out rim (Plate 13.72). A thick finger impressed moulding encircles the body horizontally at about 10cm below the rim. Another moulding (barely visible on the photograph), about 10cm in length, descends vertically from there. The water jars in use in the present day show no significant evolution; they are very similar to this one.

Five other fragmentary containers of the same type were discovered all around the remains of the keeper's house (nos 19-03-02–05 and 10). The rims are simple and vertical, and the decorations show variations in the number of horizontal mouldings as well as in the position of the short vertical one (Plates 13.73-13.75). The base of no. 19-03-04, almost flat, is also different from the complete vessel no. 19-03-01 (Plate 13.76).

Fragments of wheelmade vessels made of fine mineral-tempered pink or pinkish beige fabrics were also observed on this site (nos 19-03-06–09). Nine sherds may belong to two different pots. They are covered with yellow to brown and green lustrous coatings but are in a very fragmentary and eroded condition (Plates 13.77 and 13.78). One body sherd with a pinkish coating outside and one rim were recorded (Plates 13.79 and 13.80). These wheelmade pots may be contemporary with the *zirs*.

Plate 13.74.
No. 19-03-05,
site KRP19.

Plate 13.75.
No. 19-03-10,
site KRP19.

Plate 13.72.
No. 19-03-01,
site KRP19.

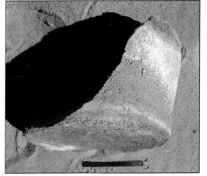

Plate 13.76.
No. 19-03-04,
site KRP19.

Plate 13.73.
No. 19-03-02,
site KRP19.

Plate 13.77.
No. 19-03-06,
site KRP19.

177

*Plate 13.79.
No. 19-03-07,
site KRP19.*

Plate 13.78. No. 19-03-08, site KRP19.

3.8. Site KRP23

About 20km west of the Umm Nabari massif and 44km to the north of railway station 6 is a sandstone hill (KRP23) on whose side were found inscriptions of a 'Priest Herunefer'.[32] The whole perimeter of the hill, measuring a little more than 1km, was surveyed and pottery fragments recorded. A few lithic tools were also observed. The pottery was found in six different locations. Areas 4, 5, 6 and 7 were on the south-eastern, south-western, north-western and north-eastern sides of the hill respectively, area 9 was about 100m away to the north and area 10 about 200m to the north east.

3.8.1. KRP23 area 4

Four body sherds of hand-made pots are recorded from area 4. No. 23-04-12 (Plate 13.81) is made in mixed tempered fabric and has a polished surface, red outside and black inside, and may well belong to the Kerma culture. Nos 23-04-13 and 15 (Plates 13.82 and 13.83) both have smooth brownish surfaces, but the latter is decorated with crossing incised lines, a type of ornament identified as both Pan-Grave and Kerma in the Eastern Desert and at the fortress of Mirgissa.[33] The last piece in this area, no. 23-04-14 (Plate 13.84), is black polished inside and brown to dark-brown outside with patterns of parallel incised lines covering large portions if not the whole surface, in a style well known in the Pan-Grave repertoire.[34]

3.8.2. KRP23 area 5

Six body sherds from this area, located in front of a large natural shelter on the hillside, were recorded under no. 23-05-16a–f. The fabrics are fine with mineral temper and range from beige to pinkish beige or light brown. Nos 23-05-16a–e (Plate 13.85, A–E) are impressed with variations of the rocker packed dotted zigzag pattern, type R1, present in the material from sites KRP6 and KRP7.[35] No. 23-05-16f (Plate 13.85, F) is

Plate 13.80. No. 19-03-09, site KRP19.

decorated with the alternately pivoting stamp return technique (types A9 and A10), also recorded in KRP6 (See above, site KRP6 and n. 10). Stone tools were observed on the surface along with the fragments of pottery (Plates 13.86-13.88).

3.8.3. KRP23 area 6

Eleven conjoining fragments of a hand-made pot (23-06-17, Plate 13.89) were found scattered on area 6, on the north-western slope close to the bottom of the hill. The fabric is dark, nearly black and has a mixed temper. The dark brown to black surface is horizontally burnished on both sides and the upper half of the outside is adorned with deeply incised oblique lines, starting just below the slightly thickened rim. The burnishing traces are large and obvious, especially inside. The surface treatment, the position of the decoration and the decoration itself are all characteristic of a Pan-Grave cooking pot, although variations are frequent.[36]

3.8.4. KRP23 area 7

This area located in the immediate vicinity of the inscriptions of Herunefer yielded seven body sherds. Nothing much can be said about four of them, nos 23-07-03–05 and 07, except that they belonged to undecorated hand-made pots.

No. 23-07-06 is hand-made in a mixed tempered fabric, the outer surface is olive green, burnished and decorated with very lightly incised oblique crossing lines, while the inside is light brown and smoothed with a comb (Plate 13.90). Although the surface colour is quite unusual, it might well be Middle Nubian, if not Kerma.

The rim sherd of a cooking pot (no. 23-07-09) is made in a reddish-brown mineral-tempered fabric and decorated with an inverted radial triangle beneath a horizontal line. This decoration is not incised but seems to be impressed possibly with a roulette or with another rather sharp tool (Plate 13.91). A

---

[32] The site and inscriptions were first discovered by the CeRDO mission (site L).

[33] See Manzo 2012, 80 and fig. 17d-e; Gratien 2007, 155 and fig. 2g.

[34] See, for example, Säve-Söderbergh 1989, 54 and pl. 20, 31.3 (type PI b4, no. 193/3:1); Gratien 2000, 119 and fig. 13b; Manzo 2012, 80 and fig. 17b.

[35] See above, sites KRP6 and KRP7, § 3.1.1., 3.1.2.

[36] Giuliani 2006, 651-653 and 657; Bietak 1968, 120 and pl. 16 (P8α, P9); Gratien 2000, 119 and fig. 13b; Säve-Söderbergh 1989, pl. 37.7; Manzo 2012, 80 and fig. 17c; Ayers and Moeller 2012, 109 and 110, fig. 6 (ED 2659.N.3).

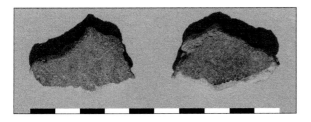

Plate 13.81. No. 23-04-12, site KRP23.

Plate 13.82. No. 23-04-13, site KRP23.

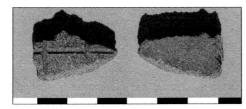

Plate 13.83. No. 23-04-15, site KRP23.

Plate 13.84. No. 23-04-14, site KRP23.

Plate 13.85. No. 23-05-16A-F, site KRP23.

Plate 13.86. Lithic tool from site KRP23 area 5.

Plate 13.87. Lithic tool from site KRP23 area 5.

Plate 13.88. Lithic tool from site KRP23 area 5.

Plate 13.89. No. 23-06-17, site KRP23.

Plate 13.90. No. 23-07-06, site KRP23.

Plate 13.91. No. 23-07-09, site KRP23.

repair hole has been left unfinished. Inverted triangles are very common in the C-Group and *Kerma Moyen* repertoire,[37] most of them are incised, but specimens impressed with a roulette are also recorded (Privati 1978, 134 and 132, pl. IV.2, IV.8).

Body sherd no. 23-07-08 belonged to a wheelmade vessel (Plate 13.92). The fabric is alluvial and close to the common NILE B2 of Egyptian tradition.[38] The outer surface is covered with a thick, vertically burnished red slip. Considering the thickness of the slip, we should consider a dating later than the New Kingdom. Red slipped, vertically burnished wheel-made pots are frequent in Napatan assemblages, as one can see, for example, in Qustul (Egypt), Missiminia or Kerma.[39]

3.8.5. KRP23 area 9

Two hand-made body sherds were recorded in this area (nos

23-09-01–02). They both share a similar greyish brown fabric, with a mineral temper and a pink surface bearing a rocker packed dotted zigzag pattern decoration (type R1), as seen at sites KRP6 and KRP7 (Plates 13.93 and 13.94).[40]

3.8.6. KRP23 area 10

The first piece found in area 10 is a hand-made body sherd (no. 23-10-10), whose fabric is a pinkish-beige colour, containing a mineral temper. The surface is pinkish and decorated with horizontal rope impressions (Plate 13.95), as seen notably in Khartoum Variant assemblages of Lower Nubia (Abka, site 428).[41]

The second piece is a hand-made reddish-brown body sherd (no. 23-10-11). Remains of an incised decoration can be observed on its outer surface. It consists of lines drawn in presumably horizontal and oblique orientations and possibly of Middle Nubian culture, although the colour of the fabric would be quite unusual in that case (Plate 13.96).

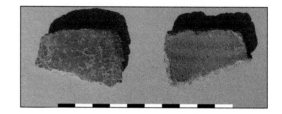

Plate 13.92. No. 23-07-08, site KRP23.

Plate 13.93. No. 23-09-01, site KRP23.

Plate 13.94. No. 23-09-02, site KRP23.

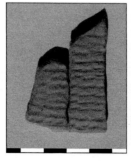

Plate 13.95. No. 23-10-10, site KRP23.

Plate 13.96. No. 23-10-11, site KRP23.

---

[37] Gratien 2000, 116 and fig. 4a; Privati 1999, 46, 58, fig. 9.10, 59, fig. 10.9.
[38] See Nordström and Bourriau 1993, 171-173.
[39] Williams 1990, 71, fig. 22b; Vila 1980, 157 and 156, fig. 167 (type II-1A); Ruffieux 2007, 226 and 235, pl. 3.25.

[40] See above, § 3.1.1., 3.1.2., nos 06-00-07 and 07-00-01.
[41] See, for example, Nordström 1972, 213 and pl. 123 no. 7.

4. Conclusions

With all its limitations, a pottery survey such as this one provides an interesting overview of the nature and identity of the human presence in the prospected area, in this case the Korosko Road, and more largely the Eastern Desert.

A clear distinction is apparent in the nature of the sites. On the one hand, the concentrations of potsherds dating to the Early Holocene period reveal the presence of camp sites, probably seasonal, of Mesolithic and Early Neolithic human groups populating these areas in times when the whole region supported sustainable living conditions, that is before the second half of the 6th millennium BC. Two sites in our survey are particularly representative of this, sites KRP6 and KRP7, but other traces were found, notably at KRP13 and KRP23, and we shall also mention a few sherds from a location 8km to the west of Jebel Umm Fitfit, an ancient mining station that we visited on the way from Kerma to the Jebel Umm Nabari massif.[42] The material scatters are always located close to the hills or on top of them, but this observation may be a consequence of the main objective of the survey: the location and study of pharaonic inscriptions, which are likely to be found on the sides of hills where much of our effort was concentrated.

On the other hand, the rest of the pottery finds, dating from the second half of the 3rd millennium BC down to the 19th century AD, for the most part bear witnesses to traffic passing through this arid environment, in conditions all the more hostile since the 6th millennium climate shift. Particularly well represented are the 3rd to 2nd millennium BC Middle Nubian ceramics from the Kerma and Pan-Grave cultures.

Although the condition of the sherds often proved challenging with regard to any precise identification of the pottery, the Kerma culture seems to have been present from the *Kerma Ancien* period, though the *Kerma Moyen* is more frequently observed. As for the *Kerma Classique*, while none of the very typical vessels of this period has been recorded, its pottery can be very similar to that of the *Kerma Moyen* (especially the cooking pots) and we can probably assume that it was present as well, if not clearly distinguished. Kerma sherds were found at sites KRP8, KRP9, KRP16 and KRP23, all located around the Jebel Umm Nabari massif (one should also mention a single sherd of probable Kerma origin recorded between Kerma and Jebel Umm Fitfit). These finds tend to show that the Kerma people reached this important gold mining area from the *Kerma Ancien* onwards (and likewise the easternmost areas of "Oshib" and "Onib", closer to the Red Sea)[43] and that gold must have been their primary motivation.

It is also worth noting that Pan-Grave elements were observed at sites KRP16, KRP18 and KRP23, so representing a northwards extension on the Korosko Road (KRP18 is located close to the Egyptian border). This significant fact as well as the Kerma presence, already revealed by the CeRDO mission, was recently discussed by A. Manzo.[44] In this respect, it is surprising that we do not seem to have found any material related to Eastern Sudanese groups, nor to the later Eastern Desert Ware of the 1st millennium AD,[45] though a contributory factor here might be that relevant sherds had already been collected by the CeRDO mission.

It may be for this same reason that only two sites, KRP8 and KRP9, yielded New Kingdom pottery fragments, whereas hieroglyphic inscriptions are relatively numerous through the desert along the Korosko Road and associated routes. The recorded sherds belong to amphorae and the case of KRP8 areas 6 and 7 is very representative of the archaeological context in which Egyptian presence shows up, as can be seen, similarly, through the CeRDO finds discussed above (See § 3.2.4). Indeed, access to the gold mining region of Umm Nabari appears to have been well organized by the pharaonic administration, with supply stations for the caravans probably located at regular intervals. The dating of the KRP8 amphora (no. 08-07-12) and its counterpart from the CeRDO (SNM No. 31405) suggests that this system was already operating during the first half of the 18th Dynasty, so probably not long after the military campaign of Thutmose I in the Nile Valley.

The post-New Kingdom periods are not equally represented amongst the material evidence from the survey. Twenty-fifth Dynasty and Napatan pottery for instance is very scarce. Only one pot has been identified with confidence, at KRP18 area 7 (no. 18-07-12), but surprisingly none of the very recognizable amphorae of the period was recorded. Fragments of Late Antique or maybe later containers are, however, present, for example at KRP18 (nos 18-05-17 and 18). The same site provides evidence for a long-lasting frequentation of this desert road, well-illustrated by the 13th century Ayyubid glazed bowls (no. 18-04-07a, b, c and d) and a little further to the south the remains of the Khashm el-Bab station (KRP19) revealing the Egyptian interest in controlling access through the Eastern Desert during the 19th century.

Notwithstanding these very clear testimonies, many sherds remain unidentified and would certainly, if they could tell us their story, fill the gaps in our knowledge of the human presence along the Korosko Road.

Acknowledgements

We would like to express our sincere gratitude to our Sudanese colleagues of the Sudan National Museum in Khartoum, for their kind help in our work at the Museum storerooms, to Isabella Welsby Sjöström, who gave us very useful comments and information on the material, to Pierre Meyrat for proofreading our English and finally to Vivian Davies and Derek Welsby for their comments on the text.

Bibliography

Adams, W. Y. 1986. *Ceramic Industries of Medieval Nubia. Parts I and II.* Memoirs of the UNESCO Archaeological Survey of Sudanese Nubia 1. Lexington.

Adams, W. Y. 2018. 'The Aswan Wares in Nubia, AD 1-1500', in R. David (ed.), *Céramiques égyptiennes au Soudan ancien.* Cahiers de la Céramique Égyptienne 11, 303-328.

---

[42] The Umm Fitfit station was surveyed years ago by the CeRDO mission; see Castiglioni *et al.* 1995, 110; Castiglioni and Castiglioni 2007, 35; Klemm and Klemm 2013, 549, 6.7.6. It has been almost completely destroyed by the recent gold mining activity.

[43] Castiglioni and Castiglioni 2007, 44-50; Manzo 2012, 82; this volume, 80.

[44] Manzo 2012, 79-82; this volume, 79-80.

---

[45] See, for example, Manzo 2004; Barnard 2002; 2018; Barnard and Magid 2006.

Ali Mohammed, A. 2014. 'The Islamic Period in the Fourth Cataract', in Anderson and Welsby (eds), 201-208.

Anderson, J. R. and D. A. Welsby (eds) 2014. *The Fourth Cataract and Beyond. Proceedings of the 12th International Conference for Nubian Studies.* British Museum Publications on Egypt and Sudan 1. Leuven – Paris – Walpole (MA).

Aston, D. A. 1999. *Elephantine XIX: Pottery from the Late New Kingdom to the Early Ptolemaic Period.* Archäologische Veröffentlichungen 95. Mainz am Rhein.

Aston, D. A. 2004. 'Amphorae in New Kingdom Egypt', *Ägypten und Levante* 14, 175-213.

Avissar, M. and E. J. Stern 2005. *Pottery of the Crusader, Ayyubid, and Mamluk Periods in Israel.* Israel Antiquities Authority Reports 26. Jerusalem.

Ayers, N. and N. Moeller 2012. 'Nubian Pottery Traditions during the 2nd Millennium BC at Tell Edfu', in I. Forstner-Müller and P. Rose (eds), *Nubian Pottery from Egyptian Cultural Contexts of the Middle and Early New Kingdom. Proceedings of a Workshop held at the Austrian Archaeological Institute at Cairo, 1-12 December 2010.* Ergänzungsheft zu den Jahresheften des Österreichischen Archäologischen Institutes in Wien 13. Vienna, 103-115.

Barnard, H. 2002. 'Eastern Desert Ware, a first introduction', *Sudan & Nubia* 6, 53-57.

Barnard, H. 2018. 'Eastern Desert Ware', in R. David (ed.), *Céramiques égyptiennes au Soudan ancien.* Cahiers de la Céramique Égyptienne 11, 279-302.

Barnard, H. and A. A. Magid 2006. 'Eastern Desert Ware from Tabot (Sudan). More Links to the North', *Archéologie du Nil Moyen* 10, 15-34.

Bietak, M. 1968. *Studien zur Chronologie der Nubischen C-Gruppe. Ein Beitrag zur Frühgeschichte Unternubiens zwischen 2200 und 1550 vor Chr.* Österreichische Akademie de Wissenschaften Denkschriften 97. Vienna.

Bourriau, J. D. 2004. 'Chapter 5: The Beginnings of Amphora Production in Egypt', in J. D. Bourriau and J. Phillips (eds), *Invention and Innovation. The Social Context of Technological Change 2: Egypt, the Aegean and the Near East, 1650-1150 BC. Proceedings of a conference held at the McDonald Institute for Archaeological Research, Cambridge, 4-6 September 2002.* Oxford, 78-95.

Castiglioni, A. and A. Castiglioni 2007. 'Les pistes millénaires du désert oriental de Nubie', *Bulletin de la Société française d'égyptologie,* 169-170, 17-50.

Castiglioni, A., A. Castiglioni and J. Vercoutter 1995. *L'Eldorado dei Faraoni. Alla scoperta di Berenice Pancrisia.* Novara.

Davies, W. V. 2014. 'The Korosko Road Project: Recording Egyptian inscriptions in the Eastern Desert and elsewhere', *Sudan & Nubia* 18, 30-44.

Dunham, D. 1982. *Excavations at Kerma. Part VI.* Boston.

Egloff, M. 1977. *Kellia: La Poterie Copte. Quatre Siècles d'Artisanat et d'Échanges en Basse-Égypte, Tome 1.* Recherches Suisses d'Archéologie Copte 3. Geneva.

Förster, F. 2013. 'Beyond Dakhla: The Abu Ballas Trail in the Libyan Desert (SW Egypt)', in F. Förster and H. Riemer (eds), *Desert Road Archaeology in Ancient Egypt and Beyond.* Africa Praehistorica 27. Köln, 297-337.

Fuller, D. Q 2004. 'The Central Amri to Kirbekan Survey. A Preliminary Report on Excavations and Survey 2003-04', *Sudan & Nubia* 8, 4-10.

Gallorini, C. 2009. 'Incised marks on pottery and other objects from Kahun', in B. J. J. Haring and O. E. Kaper (eds), *Pictograms or Pseudo Script? Non-textual Identity Marks in Practical Use in Ancient Egypt and Elsewhere. Proceedings of a Conference in Leiden, 19-20 December 2006.* Leiden, 107-142.

Gatto, M. C. 2002. 'Early Neolithic Pottery of the Nabta-Kiseiba Area: Stylistic Attributes and Regional Relationships', in K. Nelson and Associates, *Holocene Settlement of the Egyptian Sahara. Volume 2: The Pottery of Nabta Playa.* New York, Boston, Dordrecht, London and Moscow, 65-78.

Gatto, M. C. 2006. 'The Khartoum Variant Pottery in Context: Rethinking the Early and Middle Holocene Nubian Sequence', *Archéologie du Nil Moyen* 10, 57-72.

Gatto, M. C. 2013. 'Preliminary Report on the Most Ancient Pottery from the Kerma Region', in M. Honegger and collab., *Archaeological excavations at Kerma (Sudan). Kerma, Documents de la mission archéologique Suisse au Soudan* 5. Neuchâtel, 4-10.

Giuliani, S. 2006. 'Defining Pan-Grave Pottery', in K. Kroeper, M. Chłodnicki and M. Kobusiewicz (eds), *Archaeology of Early Northeastern Africa. In Memory of Lech Krzyżaniak.* Studies in African Archaeology 9. Poznań, 647-658.

Gratien, B. 1978. *Les cultures Kerma. Essai de classification.* Lille.

Gratien, B. 1986. *Saï I. La nécropole Kerma.* Mission archéologique française au Soudan. Paris.

Gratien, B. 2000. 'Les pots de cuisson nubiens et les bols décorés de la première moitié du IIe millénaire avant J.-C. Problèmes d'identification'. *Cahiers de la Céramique Egyptienne* 6, 113-128.

Gratien, B. 2007. 'Au sujet des Nubiens au Moyen Empire et à la Deuxième Période Intermédiaire dans les forteresses égyptiennes de la deuxième cataracte', in B. Gratien (ed.), *Mélanges offerts à Francis Geus.* Cahiers de Recherches de l'Institut de Papyrologie et d'Égyptologie de Lille 26, 151-161.

Hendrickx, S., F. Förster and M. Eyckerman 2013. 'The Pharaonic pottery of the Abu Ballas Trail: 'Filling stations' along a desert highway in southwestern Egypt', in F. Förster and H. Riemer (eds), *Desert Road Archaeology in Ancient Egypt and Beyond.* Africa Praehistorica 27. Köln, 339-379.

Honegger, M. 2004. 'The Pre-Kerma: a cultural group from Upper Nubia prior to the Kerma civilisation', *Sudan & Nubia* 8, 38-46.

Honegger, M. 2014. 'Recent Advances in our Understanding of Prehistory in Northern Sudan', in Anderson and Welsby (eds), 19-30.

Hope, C. A. 1989. 'Amphorae of the New Kingdom', in C. A. Hope, *Pottery of the Egyptian New Kingdom. Three Studies.* Victoria College Archaeology Research Unit Occasional Paper 2. Burwood, 87-110.

Jakob, B. and M. Honegger 2017. 'From the Mesolithic to the Beginning of the Neolithic in Upper Nubia: The Sequence of Wadi el-Arab (8300-5400 BC Cal)', in M. Honegger (ed.), *Archaeological excavations at Kerma (Sudan). Kerma, Documents de la mission archéologique Suisse au Soudan 7.* Neuchâtel, 42-48.

Jenkins-Madina, M. 2006. *Raqqa Revisited. Ceramics of Ayyubid Syria.* New York.

Klemm, R. and D. Klemm 2013. *Gold and Gold Mining in Ancient Egypt and Nubia: Geoarchaeology of the Ancient Gold Mining Sites in the Egyptian and Sudanese Eastern Deserts.* Heidelberg; New York; Dordrecht; London.

Lanna S. and M. C. Gatto 2010. 'Prehistoric Human Occupation in the Nubian Eastern Desert: An Overview', in W. Godlewski and A. Łajtar (eds), *Between the Cataracts. Proceedings of the 11th Conference of Nubian Studies Warsaw University, 27 August-2 September 2006. Part 2, Fascicle 2.* PAM Supplement Series 2.2/1. Warsaw, 319-328.

Manzo, A. 2004. 'Late Antique Evidence in Eastern Sudan', *Sudan & Nubia* 8, 75-83.

Manzo, A. 2012. 'From the sea to the deserts and back: New research in Eastern Sudan', *British Museum Studies in Ancient Egypt and Sudan* 18, 75-106.

Nordström, H.-Å. 1972. *Neolithic and A-Group Sites.* The Scandinavian Joint Expedition to Sudanese Nubia 3. Lund.

Nordström, H.-Å. and J. D. Bourriau 1993. 'Ceramic Technology: Clays and Fabrics', in D. Arnold and J. D. Bourriau (eds), *An Introduction to Ancient Egyptian Pottery*, Fascicule 2. Deutsches Archäologisches Institut Abteilung Kairo Sonderschrift 17. Mainz am Rhein, 143-190.

Phillips, J. 2004. 'Islamic pottery in the Middle Nile', *Azania: Archaeological Research in Africa* 39, 58-68.

Pluskota, K. 2005. 'Amphorae of Old Dongola: Evolution of Local Products (Exploration of Kiln R1 F)', *Gdańsk Archaeological Museum African Reports* 3, 227-232.

Privati, B. 1978. 'La poterie de la ville de Kerma. Premières observations', *Genava* n.s. 26, 128-134.

Privati, B. 1999. 'La céramique de la nécropole orientale de Kerma (Soudan): essai de classification', *Cahiers de Recherches de l'Institut de Papyrologie et d'Égyptologie de Lille* 20, 41-69.

Privati, B. 2004. 'Contribution à l'étude du quartier religieux. Le matériel céramique', in C. Bonnet *et al.*, *Le temple principal de la ville de Kerma et son quartier religieux.* Paris, 162-189.

Reisner, G. A. 1923. *Excavations at Kerma. Part IV–V.* Harvard African Studies VI. Cambridge, MS.

Ruffieux, P. 2007. 'Ensembles céramiques napatéens découverts durant les campagnes 2005-2006 et 2006-2007 à Doukki Gel (Kerma)', *Genava* n.s. 55, 223-239.

Ruffieux, P. and Mahmoud Suliman Bashir 2014. 'Preliminary report on some New Kingdom amphorae from the Korosko Road', *Sudan & Nubia* 18, 44-46.

Salvatori, S. and D. Usai 2004. 'Cemetery R12 and a possible periodisation of the Nubian Neolithic', *Sudan & Nubia* 8, 33-37.

Säve-Söderbergh, T. (ed.) 1989. *Middle Nubian Sites.* The Scandinavian Joint Expedition to Sudanese Nubia 4. Partille.

Stern, E. J. 2012. '*Akko I. The 1991–1998 Excavations. The Crusader-Period Pottery.* Israel Antiquities Authority Reports 51/1. Jerusalem.

Tonghini, C. 1995. 'The fine wares of Ayyubid Syria', in E. J. Grube (ed.), *Cobalt and Lustre: The first centuries of Islamic pottery.* The Nasser D. Khalili Collection of Islamic Art IX. London, 249-282.

Tonghini, C. 1998. *Qal'at Ja'bar Pottery. A study of a Syrian fortified site of the late 11th-14th centuries.* New York.

Vila, A. 1980. *La prospection archéologique de la Vallée du Nil, au sud de la cataracte de Dal (Nubie Soudanaise) 12. La nécropole de Missiminia.* Paris.

Williams, B. B. 1990. *Twenty-Fifth Dynasty and Napatan Remains at Qustul: Cemeteries W and V.* The University of Chicago Oriental Institute Nubian Expedition VII. Chicago.

14. The hand-axe and denticulated tool

Donatella Usai

Lanceolate hand-axes like that found at site KRP18(8) (Plate 14.1) are common to Middle Pleistocene/Early to Middle Palaeolithic sites in the Nile Valley. The first known assemblage that produced similar artefacts is Khor Abu Anga, discovered by Arkell (1949) in the area of Omdurman, close to Khartoum; during the Nubian Salvage Campaign other sites of the same phase were found at Arkin District, notably Arkin 8 (Chmielewski 1968). The material recovered at these sites come from surface context but a dating at the Middle Pleistocene/Middle Palaeolithic period has been recently substantiated by the excavation at Sai island, slightly upstream from the Second Cataract (Van Peer 2004; (Van Peer, *et al.* 2003; 2004). Here hand-axes have been found in a Late Acheulean/Sangoan inter-stratified context dating *c.* 180 Ka.

Plate 14.2. KRP9(4) – denticulated tool.

emergence of modern human behaviour at site 8-B-11, Sai Island, Sudan', *Journal of Human Evolution* 45, 187-193.

Van Peer, P., V. Rots and J. M. Vroomans 2004. 'A story of colourful diggers and grinders: the Sangoan and Lupemban at site 8-B-11, Sai Island, Northern Sudan', *Before Farming* 3, 1-28.

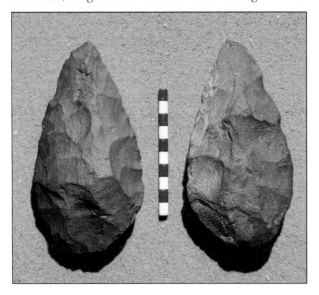

Plate 14.1. KRP18(8) – hand-axe.

To a later period may be possibly attributed the denticulated tool from KRP9(4) (Plate 14.2) made on a multiplatform core blade-like blank. Denticulated tools start to appear common in association with core technologies, especially with Levallois, in Middle Palaeolithic (Guichard and Guichard 1968).

Bibliography

Arkell, A. J. 1949. *The Old Stone Age in the Anglo-Egyptian Sudan*. Sudan Antiquities Service, Occasional Papers. Khartoum.

Chmielewski, W. 1968. 'Early and Middle Palaeolithic sites near Arkin, Sudan', in F. Wendorf (ed.), *The Prehistory of Nubia*. Dallas, 110-147.

Guichard, J. and G. Guichard 1968. 'Contributions to The Study of The Early And Middle Palaeolithic of Nubia', in Wendorf (ed.), *The Prehistory of Nubia*. Dallas, 148-193.

Van Peer, P. 2004. 'Did Middle Stone Age Moderns of Sub-Saharan Africa descent trigger an Upper Palaeolithic revolution in the Lower Nile valley?', *Anthropologie* XLII/3, 241-251.

Van Peer, P., R. Fullagar, S. Stokes, R. M. Bailey, J. Moeyersons, F. Steenhoudt, A. Geerts, T. Vanderbeken, M. De Dapper and F. Geus 2003. 'The Early to Middle Stone Age transition and the

15. Securing the Gold of Wawat: pharaonic inscriptions in the Sudanese-Nubian Eastern Desert

W. Vivian Davies

This paper gives an account of the Egyptian rock-inscriptions in the Sudanese-Nubian Eastern Desert – in the gold-bearing region of Umm Nabari, and along the 'Korosko Road' and related tracks – located by expeditions of the Centro Ricerche sul Deserto Orientale (CeRDO) from 1989 to 2006 (Plate 15.1, sites B, E, F, G, H, I, L and M)[1] and further documented by the Sudan Archaeological Research Society's 'Korosko Road Project' (KRP) in 2013.[2] Drawing substantially on (and replicating in part) the initial KRP report,[3] I provide here, where appropriate and possible, a fuller treatment and include additional illustrations.[4] The route followed (starting and ending at Abu Hamed) and sites visited (marked KRP; see also Welsby, this volume) are recorded in Plate 15.2.[5] Almost all the inscriptions in this regional corpus appear to relate to the pharaonic gold-mining industry of the New Kingdom.[6]

KRP5. Wadi Tonaidba/Umm Gereifat, cave (Plate 15.3; CeRDO site I; Castiglioni and Castiglioni 2003, 47, n.1, 48, pls 1-2, colour pl. xxx; 2006a, 404, figs 5-6; 2006b, 171; 2007, 32-34, figs 20-22; Roccati 2007, 58; Davies 2014, 31-2, fig. 1, pls 3-5; Castiglioni and Castiglioni, this volume, 25, pls 4.9 and 4.10; Welsby, this volume, 139ff).

This tunnel-like cave, measuring about 62m in total length, runs downwards, approximately east-west, straight through a sandstone hill, with its western and eastern mouths measuring 7.54m and 5.3m in height respectively. There are two hieroglyphic inscriptions, both referring to the same individual, possibly done on separate visits. They are incised into the walls, roughly opposite each other but at different heights, just inside the western entrance.

1) The longer and more complete inscription is located on the right (south) wall about half a metre above the bedrock floor of the cave (Plate 15.4; Figure 15.1, upper). It consists of a single horizontal line of hieroglyphs reading, and tapering in size, right to left, 'Chief of Tehkhet Paits(y)' (*Wr n Tḥḫt P3its(y)*). Associated, to the left, is a standing male figure (now damaged), the only such figure in our corpus, almost certainly representing Paitsy. Facing right (west) towards the cave-entrance, he is shown wearing a short wig and long skirt, his arms raised in worship, evidently with reference to the sun (Plates 15.4 and 15.5).[7]

2) The second inscription is located on the opposite wall about 2.5m above the floor (Plates 15.6 and 15.7; Figure 15.1, lower). It is arranged in two horizontal lines reading right to left, the beginnings of which are eroded. It reads, '[Chief] of Tehkhet, P[aits]y.'[8]

Dating to the early 18th Dynasty (temp. Thutmose III/Hatshepsut), these two inscriptions, together with the figure, represent the earliest known attestations of a pharaonic official in this gold-mining area.

Comment

The chief of Tehkhet Paitsy, who had two names, 'Djehutyhotep called Paitsy' (the first name Egyptian, the second

---

[1] Castiglioni and Castiglioni 2006b, 178-179; 2007, 18, fig. 1; Castiglioni *et al.* 2010, 269, fig. 19. The sites marked A and C on the map are located on the Egyptian side of the modern Egypt-Sudan border. Site A, near to the Wadi Hamid, contains the inscription of the Nubian chief, Hekanefer, for which see Castiglioni and Castiglioni, this volume, 33-34, pl. 4.37, and below, with Plate 15.9. Site C, Bir Ungat, contains an Old Kingdom inscription (6th Dynasty), for which see Castiglioni and Castiglioni, this volume, 38, pl. 4.54 (Damiano-Appia 1999, 535-537, 542, fig. 3; file-card no. 13; Andrassy 2002, 13-14; Castiglioni and Castiglioni 2006a, 409, fig. 28; 2006b, 180-181; Roccati 2007, 54-56, fig. 2; Auenmüller 2019b, 402), and an unpublished inscription of a 'scribe Amenhotep' (PM vii, 318; Schweinfurth 1903, 278; Damiano-Appia 1999, 536; Klemm and Klemm 2013, 337). Omitted from the map is the site of a fourth inscription (Castiglioni and Castiglioni, this volume, 31-32, pl. 4.31), in the Wadi Nesari, a tributary of the Wadi Allaki, which dates to the New Kingdom; see below, Plate 15.61). Note also that the copy of another rock-inscription, apparently of an 'Amenemhat', from Jebel Ungat, is included in Damiano-Appia 1999, 537-538, 542, fig. 3, file-card no. 14, but appears to be otherwise undocumented.

[2] The work was carried out over a three week period in November-December, 2013, with the permission and co-operation of the National Corporation for Antiquities and Museums of Sudan (NCAM), and with site-information kindly supplied by Alfredo and Angelo Castiglioni. The team consisted of Vivian Davies (Director, epigrapher), Mahmoud Suliman Bashir (archaeologist, NCAM representative), Philippe Ruffieux (ceramic specialist), Bert Verrept (epigrapher), Derek Welsby (archaeologist) and Mohamed Ibrahim (cook). I was able briefly to revisit a number of the sites, while en route across the desert as part of a separate expedition in December 2018 (see Cooper and Vanhulle 2019, 3). For the preliminary record of a previously unnoted pharaonic rock-drawing made during this more recent visit, with the assistance of Pierre Meyrat, see below KRP2, with Plate 15.57, Figure 15.25 (in general, rock-drawings recorded as part of the KRP project are noted by Derek Welsby, this volume). In order to protect the inscriptions, specific GPS co-ordinates are not provided in this report.

[3] Davies 2014. For a recent useful summary of the distribution and location of pharaonic rock-inscriptions in Nubia including some of the KRP material, see Auenmüller 2019b, 401-407, fig. 4; 2019c, 194-196, fig. 12.1.

[4] The copies of the inscriptions have been inked by Will Schenck. The photographs are those of the writer unless otherwise stated. The maps, Plates 15.2 and 15.60, are the work of Derek Welsby. I am grateful to Ken Griffin (Swansea), Dietrich Raue and Kerstin Seidel (Leipzig), Wouter Claes (Brussels) and Martina Ullmann (Munich) for bibliographic and archival information, Rob Demarée (Leiden) for advice on dating, Renée Friedman (Oxford) for technical assistance, and Julien Cooper (Yale) for helpful discussion.

[5] Cf. Cooper and Vanhulle 2019, 3, map 1.

[6] On ancient gold-production sites and gold mining (largely 'wadi-workings') in Nubia/Sudan, see now Klemm and Klemm 2013, viii, 9-11, 341-598, fig. 6.1, especially 543-556 (Group 6.7, the region of many of the KRPsites), 606-611, figs 7.3, 7.4; Klemm and Klemm 2017; Spencer *et al.* 2017, 30-33; Klemm and Klemm 2018, 59-62; Klemm *et al.* 2019, 24, fig. 3, 26, fig. 4, 32-33; Edwards and Mills 2020, 398-407. On the overall organization of the industry and of Eastern Desert expeditions, see Hikade 2001, 57-63, with fig. 5, 68-71, 80-85; Müller 2013, 39-42, 55-56, 75-79.

[7] Further to the left, not connected to the Paitsy material, is an earlier representation of a boat; see Welsby, this volume, pl. 12.34.

[8] In addition to the final y of the name, the tip of the front wing of the *p3*-bird is preserved. On the name, see Zibelius-Chen 2011, 114; for the full writing, see Griffith 1929, 99, pl. xxix, 2; Säve-Söderbergh and Troy 1991, 195-6, fig. 49, C1.

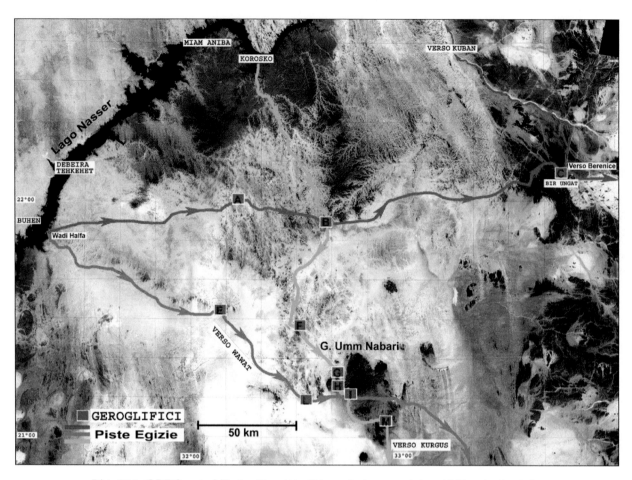

Plate 15.1. CeRDO map of Eastern Desert identifying ancient routes and sites with Egyptian inscriptions (courtesy Alfredo and Angelo Castiglioni).

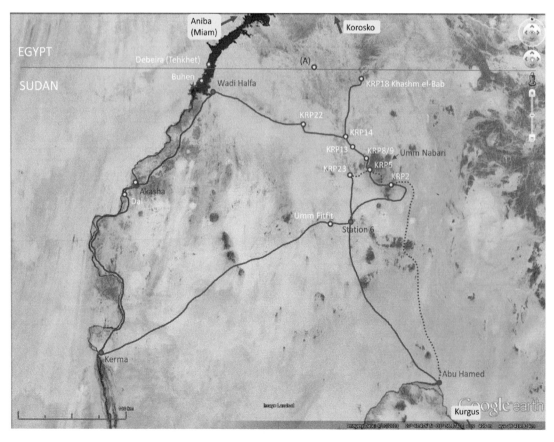

Plate 15.2. Korosko Road Project (KRP) map, showing route followed and sites documented.

Plate 15.3. KRP5, Wadi Tonaidba, cave, entrance from west.

Plate 15.4. KRP5, south side, inscription of Paitsy with figure to the left.

Plate 15.6. KRP5, north side, Bert Verrept recording inscription.

Plate 15.5. KRP5, south side, figure of Paitsy.

Plate 15.7. KRP5, north side, inscription of Paitsy.

0   10cm

0   10cm

Figure 15.1. KRP5, inscriptions of Chief of Tehkhet Paitsy.

native), is well known from his tomb at Debeira/Serra (ancient Tehkhet) and other monuments. Belonging to a family of indigenous chiefs (preceded as chief by his father and succeeded by his brother) with relatives/forebears in Aswan, he governed his region as part of the colonial administration of the early 18th Dynasty.[9] Several of his other inscriptions associate him closely with Queen Hatshepsut. The presence of his name, title, and image at Umm Nabari, marking his authority and reach, suggests that his duties included oversight of the gold-mining area. He is one of three 'Chiefs', no doubt with similar briefs, attested as travelling in the Nubian Eastern Desert.[10] The second, also of the 18th Dynasty, is the well-known 'Chief of Miam (Aniba), Hekanefer', who served Tutankhamun's viceroy, Huy. His title and name occur at CeRDO site A (Plates 15.1 and 15.2) incised in large hieroglyphs into the rear wall of a rock-shelter (Plates 15.8 and 15.9),[11] in front of which were found fragments of con-

temporary amphorae (Plate 15.10).[12] The third is the 'Chief of Miam, Mer', a successor of Hekanefer, known from the Khashm el-Bab (KRP18, no. 21, below).

KRP8. Wadi Tonaidba/Umm Gereifat, rock face (Plate 15.11; CeRDO site H; Castiglioni and Castiglioni 2003, 48-49, pls 3-7; 2006a, 405-406, figs 8, 10-13; 2006b, 174-5; 2007, 28-30, 33, figs. 12-15, 19; Davies 2014, 32-4, figs 2-4, pls 6-10; Castiglioni and Castiglioni, this volume, 24, pl. 4.7; Welsby, this volume, 142-3).

Incised into the eastern face of a long, low sandstone hill, which bears a huge number of rock-drawings, mostly of cattle, there are two major sets of inscription (nos 1-2, below), a little roughly done, both featuring the Ramesside official Hornakht, each set possibly representing a separate visit. A third set (3) is contemporary and related. A fourth (4) is unrelated and earlier in date.

1) The northernmost set (Plate 15.12) consists of two horizontal lines of large hieroglyphs, some cursive, reading from right to left, '(1) General, Deputy of the troop, (2) Mayor Hornakht' (*imy-r mšꜥ idn(w)* [13] *n pdt ḥꜣty-ꜥ Ḥr-nḫt*) (Plate 15.13; Figure 15.2). To its upper left is another similar inscription (Plate 15.14, Figure 15.3), reading, 'General, Deputy of the troop' (*idn(w) pdt*), clearly referring to the same individual.

2) Some distance to the south (Plate 15.15), Hornakht's name and titles feature in a long horizontal line, in the same style, here with an important filiation and place of origin (Plates 15.16 and 15.17; Figure 15.4, upper), 'Mayor

[9] On attestations and various aspects of the 'princes of Tehkhet', including Djehutyhotep-Paitsy, his father and mother, Ruiu and Runa, his brother Amenemhat, and other relatives, see PM vii, 128; Smith 1976, 208-209; Säve-Söderbergh and Troy 1991, 190-211; Trigger 1996, 807; Davies 2004b; Edwards 2004, 108; Davies 2005, 54, with n. 68; Edel *et al.* 2008, 924-925, 927-928, 937, Abb. 9, Taf. LXI, scene 17-18; Zibelius-Chen 2007, 403; Török 2009, 265-270, 272; Zibelius-Chen 2011, 170-171, 174; Morkot 2013, 945-947; Müller 2013, 51-54, 244-246, nos 1-4; Näser 2013, 148; Zibelius-Chen 2013, 144-145, Abb. 9; Arpagaus 2015, 475-477; Smith 2015, 768, pl. VII, fig. 2; Doyen and Gabolde 2017, 152; Spencer *et al.* 2017, 42; Williams 2017, 311-312; 2018, 100, 104; Cooper 2018a, 676; Spence 2019, 545-546, 553-556. Note that Ruiu is not be confused with his contemporary namesake, the 'Deputy of the Viceroy', Ruiu, from Aniba (tomb S 66); see now Zibelius-Chen 2011, 170; Müller 2013, 198, no. 3; Näser 2017, 566-571, figs 7-9, 11.

[10] On a suggested Medja-ancestry for such chiefs, see Trigger 1996, 807; cf. Zibelius-Chen 2007, 403-404; 2011, 170-171; Cooper 2018a, 676.

[11] Castiglioni and Castiglioni 1994, 20; Castiglioni *et al.* 1995, 26, 112, map (Itinerario C), 118-122, 180-181, B 34; Sadr *et al.*, 1995, 225, pl. 3, b; Damiano-Appia 1999, 513-517, 540, fig. 1, WH-1; Castiglioni and Castiglioni 2006a, 409, fig. 27; 2007, 37-8, fig. 26; Cooper and Vanhulle 2019, 3, Map 1, and 5; Castiglioni and Castiglioni, this volume, 33-4, pl. 4.37; further, on Hekanefer, see Simpson 1963; Zibelius 1972, 37, V E b 40; Trigger 1996, 803-807; Edwards 2004, 108; Fitzenreiter 2004, 176-7; Mahfouz 2005, 69-70; Zibelius-Chen 2007, 403; Török 2009, 271-2; Zibelius-Chen 2011, 170-171;

Darnell 2013, 828-829; Brown and Darnell 2013, 133-135; Morkot 2013, 946-950; Müller 2013, 51-54, 246-247, 2.5.4, no. 7; Zibelius-Chen 2013, 144-145, Abb. 8; Budka 2015, 75; Kawai 2015, 318, no. 10; Smith 2015; Spence 2019, 553, 562; Raue 2019b, 581; on his attestations in the Egyptian Eastern Desert, in the Wadi Barramiya and elsewhere, see now Brown 2017, 187-191.

[12] Castiglioni *et al.* 1995, 118-119, top right; Castiglioni *et al.* 1999, 501-502; Damiano-Appia 1999, 514; Castiglioni and Castiglioni, this volume, 33, pl. 4.36; cf. Manzo, this volume, 75; Ruffieux and Bashir, this volume, 168.

[13] For the unusual sign functioning as the determinative (?) of *idn(w)*, cf. the same title in set no. 2, top line (see n. 14).

Plate 15.9. CeRDO site A, inscription of Hekanefer, with Alfredo Castiglioni (courtesy CeRDO).

Plate 15.8. CeRDO site A, cave of Hekanefer (courtesy CeRDO).

Plate 15.12. KRP8, 1, north, rock-drawings and inscriptions.

Plate 15.13. KRP8, 1, north, titles and name of Hornakht.

Plate 15.10. CeRDO site A, ceramic remains, with Alfredo Castiglioni (courtesy CeRDO).

Plate 15.11. KRP8, Wadi Tonaidba, long hill, eastern side.

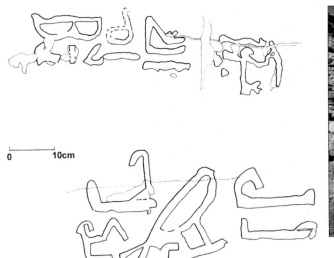

Plate 15.15. KRP8, 2, south, rock-drawings and inscriptions.

Figure 15.2. KRP8, 1, north, titles and name of Hornakht.

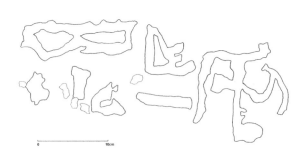

Figure 15.3. KRP8, 1, north, titles of Hornakht.

Plate 15.14. KRP8, 1, north, titles of Hornakht.

Plate 15.16. KRP8, 2, south, two inscriptions, upper with titles and name of Hornakht and filiation, lower incomplete.

190

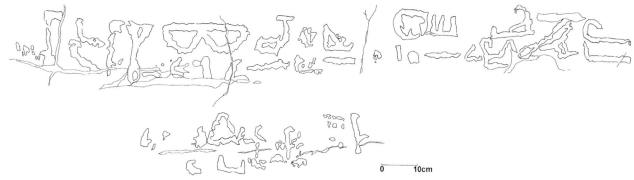

Figure 15.4. KRP8, 2, south, two inscriptions, upper including Hornakht titles and filiation.

Plate 15.17. KRP8, 2, detail, end of upper inscription, toponym, 'Miam'.

Plate 15.18. KRP8, 2, to right of main inscription, title, 'Deputy'.

Hornakht, son of Penniut, Deputy of the troop (*idnw*[14] *n pḏt*), of Miam (Aniba)'.[15] At the same level to the right, his title, *idn(w)*, 'Deputy', is inscribed below a natural recess in the cliff-face (Plate 15.18).[16] The reading of a second shorter horizontal line, placed on an uneven, febrile surface underneath the main inscription (Plate 15.19, Figure 15.4, lower), remains to be established. It is eroded and incomplete with clarity further diminished by the presence of 'interference' in the form of accidental tool-marks, not easily distinguishable in such a context from genuine components. Probably written here were a name and title(s). Among the signs on the centre-left, the title *idn(w)*, 'Deputy', may be identifiable again (sign F21 with D40 underneath, possibly followed to the left by the remnants of *pḏt*), in which case (not unexpectedly) the line will have borne reference (as in set 3 below) to an associate of Hornakht.[17]

3) A few metres to the left is another group in three horizontal lines (Plate 15.20; Figure 15.5), probably recording members of Hornakht's entourage (though perhaps done on a separate visit) including apparently his son, '(1) Scribe Mery, son of Mer, (2) Scribe Meri[…](3) Retainer Haty, son of the Deputy[18] of the troop'.

Comment

The 'General, Deputy of the troop of Miam, Mayor, Hornakht' is surely the same man as the 'Scribe of commands of the army, Scribe of the treasury, Reckoner of gold of the lord of the two lands in Ta-Sety, Mayor of Miam, Deputy of Wawat, Hornakht, justified, son of Mayor Penniut [of] Miam', known from a rock-inscription at Abu Simbel, as well as from funerary objects at Aniba (including shabtis from tomb SA 35), a representation in the Ibrim shrine of Setau (viceroy of Ramesses II, Years 38-63), and possibly a rock-inscription from Arminna East.[19] His father, Penniut, had been 'Scribe of the treasury, Reckoner of gold of lord of the two lands' and 'Mayor of Miam' before him,[20] while a son, Mery, follow-

[14] A fuller writing of *idnw* here (signs F21 + N35 + W24 + G43 or D40), ending with the same determinative (?; the sign yet to be confidently identified) as in the previous set (for various attested writings of the title, see Al-Ayedi 2006, 183ff.). Coincidentally, another curious sign appears to determine the rare verb *idn* (*Urk.* iv, 57, 13; Faulkner 1962, 35; Hannig 2006, 131; cf. Dziobek 1992, 49, 53, n. 178).

[15] For the writing of Miam here, cf. the rock-inscription, Jacquet-Gordon 1981, 228-9, fig. 2, pl. 88c. On writings of the toponym in general, see Zibelius 1972, 120-122; cf. Leitz 2002, III, 643-644; El-Sayed 2011, 202, L 179; and below, KRP18, nos 7 and 21.

[16] The pecked motif immediately to the left is not related.

[17] The first sign of the inscription looks like *i* (M17), perhaps the beginning of a title, like *iˁw* (?), 'washer (of gold)' (Al-Ayedi 2006, 2, no. 5), or, alternatively, the beginning of a name (*Imn* [?]...).

[18] In the context the reading *idn(w)* seems assured; the surface here is poor and the sign (F21) misaligned.

[19] KRI III, 118, III.7; KRITA III, 81; DRITANC III, 105-106; Simpson 1963, 32, pl. 14, f; Caminos 1968, 48, no. 10, pl. 15; Peden 2001, 114-115, n. 342; Raedler 2003, 159, fig. 13, 161, 163, fig. 15; Mahfouz 2005, 71-72, 77; Gnirs 2013, 683, n. 184; Müller 2013, 48, 202, 2.5.1, no. 17; Auenmüller 2013, 927, BMAniba-05; Cooper 2020, 133, n. 121.

[20] KRI III, 125, III, 24; KRITA III, 85; DRITANC III, 113; Mahfouz 2005, 70-72; Müller 2013, 207, 2.5.2, no. 4; Auenmüller 2013, 927, BMAniba-04. On the administration of Nubian towns and central role of the 'mayor', see Müller 2013, 46-49; Auenmüller 2013, 652-775; 2018, 254-256; Budka 2015, 70, 74-75; cf. Zibelius-Chen 2013, 144; Spencer *et al.* 2017, 29. Our Hornakht appears to be one of only two mayors known to have been elevated to the senior post of 'Deputy of Wawat', the other being the later Penniut (temp.

```
0          10cm
```

ing broadly in his father's footsteps, is identified as 'Scribe of the treasury, General of the lord of the two lands in Ta-Sety, Deputy of Wawat', and 'Chief of the treasury of the lord of the two lands in Nubia', under Amenmesses/Sety II.[21]

Another son, 'Retainer (*šmsw*) Haty', appears to be attested here for the first time; he is to be added (with KRP18, nos 9,

---

Ramesses VI), also from Aniba (Müller 2013, 46, 48, 77-78, 319-320, An. 2.7. no. 4; Auenmüller 2013, 928, BMAniba-06).

[21] KRI IV, 207, III.1; KRITA IV, 149-150; DRITANC IV, 188; KRI IV,

282-5, III.1; KRITA IV, 202-205; DRITANC IV, 246-248; KRI VII, 247, III.1; KRITA VII, 170; Žába 1974, 146-7, no. 123; Gnirs 2013, 683, n. 183; Müller 2013, 202, 2.5.1, no. 18 (without recognizing the filiation).

14, 19 and 22, below) to the list of known desert 'retainers' and 'chief retainers' (military aides well represented at the gold mines of Wadi Allaki),[22] who are thought to have operated in such contexts as escorts and liaison officers.[23] Hornakht's titles here, 'General' and 'Deputy of the troop',[24] are consistent with his known career trajectory, the steps in his advancement to 'Deputy of Wawat', showing, as also in the case of Mery, the close connection (even a degree of integration) between Military and Treasury portfolios, with the presence of his troop at Umm Nabari no doubt related to the need for protection of the workforce and secure transit of the gold.[25]

4) Represented below and to the right of the main Hornakht group (2) is a large, pecked figure of a falcon, its lower legs partially superimposed on the head of an earlier cattle-drawing (Plates 15.15 and 15.21). Associated, to the right, is a short semi-hieratic inscription, pecked, like the falcon, into a difficult surface and occupying a cramped space, some of the signs a little incomplete and malformed owing to slippage of the tool (Plate 15.21, Figure 15.6). I suggest the following reading (from right to left): *Ḥr nb St(y) sš Tiy* + name-determinative, 'Horus lord of Nubia,[26] Scribe Tiy', the inscription thus identifying the falcon-figure and its creator, which gives good sense.

Comment

Prominent rock-representations of the god Horus (dating mostly to the New Kingdom) are relatively widespread in mining-related contexts in the Nubian and Egyptian Eastern Deserts, many associated with private inscriptions asserting agency, either explicitly ('made by…'; see KRP2 below) or by juxtaposition as here.[27]

Note that a 'Scribe Tiy' is known from the site of Tombos, the unusual name written in exactly the same way.[28] A member of the colonial administration, he was the owner of a pyramid-tomb in the site's elite cemetery, containing objects inscribed with his name and titles (he was a *wab*-priest as well as a scribe).[29] Datable to the mid-late 18th Dynasty, this Tiy was a near-contemporary of the well-known Siamun, owner of the site's largest tomb, whose title was 'Scribe reckoner of the gold of Kush',[30] an indication of the administration's central priority.[31] It is not impossible that the 'Scribe Tiy' of Tombos and the 'Scribe Tiy' of our gold-mining region were one and the same person.

KRP9. Cave, Wadi Tonaidba/Umm Gereifat (Plate 15.22; CeRDO site G; Castiglioni and Castiglioni 2003, 50, pls 8-9; 2006a, 406-407, figs 15-16; 2006b, 179; 2007, 30, 32-3, figs 17-18; Davies 2014, 34, figs 5-6, pl. 11; Welsby, this volume, 143-145.

Three sets of incised inscription (1-3), each a single, horizontal line, done in different hands, are located near to the entrance on the northern side of the cave, a metre and a half (or thereabouts) above ground-level (which is uneven), together with animal-drawings, including notably a row of giraffe-figures.[32]

1. The outermost, in a practised, semi-cursive, hand: 'Mayor Mesu' (Plate 15.23, Figure 15.7).
2. A little further inside, in large hieroglyphs, slightly cursive: 'High Priest Nebnetjeru' (Plate 15.24, right, Figure 15.8).[33]
3. To the left, above the row of giraffe-figures, small hieroglyphs, slightly cursive, at least one section superimposed on the neck of a giraffe-figure, the whole now eroded and partly illegible: 'Scribe of the district (*sš spȝt*)[34] Amen[…] (?), … (?)' (Plates 15.24 and 15.25).

Comment

Given that Aniba (Miam) appears to have been the primary source of the region's travelling officials, the 'Mayor Mesu' (no. 1) is very probably the 'Mayor of Miam Mes(u)' attested in a visitor inscription at the temple of Ellesiya,[35] possibly of

[22] Piotrovsky 1983, 82 (Index).

[23] Černý 1947, 57; Chevereau 1994, 92-3, 94-96 ('Cadres de la Garde'); Hikade 2001, 70; and Müller 2013, 42-43, 188-190: '*Die Mehrzahl der Belege sind Felsinschriften entlang des Nils zwischen den Niederlassungen und auf den Karawanenwegen, wie im Wadi Allaqi. So stellten sie die Verbindung zwischen Residenz und den Bergwerken…*'; see further on the 'military connotations of the *šmsw* and *ḥry šmsw* titles', Klotz and Brown 2016, 295. On the comparable roles and versatility of earlier *šmsw*, serving in Lower Nubian fortresses during the Middle Kingdom/late Middle Kingdom, see Vogel 2004, 104-105; Liszka and Kraemer 2016, 191-193; Gratien 2019, 158-163.

[24] The title *idnw n pdt/idnw pdt* is uncommon; see Chevereau 1994, 89-90, 11161; cf. Pamminger 2003, 33 (p. 90).

[25] See Müller 2013, 40, 56; DRITANC, III, 246: 'Mery would have been responsible for the transhipment of gold accruing from the mines of the eastern desert of Lower Nubia back to the Nile valley'. In the context of such protection, note the letter from the High-Priest of Amenre, Ramessesnakht (temp. Ramesses IX), to a 'troop' of Nubians of the land of Ikyt (Wadi Allaki; see Zibelius-Chen 1994, 412-416; 2011, 101; Cooper 2018a, 671, fig. 1, 672; 2020, 130-136) acknowledging their success in protecting gold-washing teams against Bedouin enemies from the Red Sea coast and ordering that the work-force be escorted back with the gold to Egypt (Helck 1967, 140-144, 148-150; KRI VI, 519-521, Doc. C; KRITA VI, 385-386; Zibelius-Chen 1988, 157; Wente 1990, 38-39, no. 38; Zibelius-Chen 1994, 413; Hikade 2001, 59-60; Morris 2005, 786; Zibelius-Chen 2007, 405; 2011, 101; Müller 2013, 77).

[26] For reasons of space, an abbreviated writing of the more usual *nb Tȝ-Sty*, 'lord of the Land of Nubia'; for the latter epithet, Leitz 2002, III, 772-3; cf. El-Sayed 2011, 13, 254, L 309; Zibelius-Chen 2014, 268; Gabolde 2018, 99-100; Ullmann 2019, 511; for a similar, contemporary abbreviation (*Tȝ* omitted), cf. Reineke 2017, 271-272, Askut 7, column 2; also the partial precedent, *Ḥr Sty*, 'Horus of Nubia', from Wadi el-Hudi (Middle Kingdom), Leitz 2002, V, 291.

[27] Cf. Černý 1947, 57, pls x, 2-3, xi, 2-3; Piotrovsky 1983, 45-48, 50, 55, 57, 58-59, 61-63; Gasse and Rondot 2007, 385 (Index); Rothe *et al.*, 2008, 26, 176, 252, 269, 336; Espinel 2012, 98-102; Brown and Darnell 2013, 135, nn 83-84; Brown 2017, 189-191; cf. an interesting scene of Horus-worship, in

a rock-stela at the Dal Cataract, of a form more typical of a desert context, the owner probably known also from the Wadi Allaki (Davies 2018, 53, no. 3, fig. 11, pl. 13). The earliest inscriptional reference to the god Horus in our corpus is that of the pre-New Kingdom KRP14 (see below).

[28] For the name in general, see *PN* i, 378, 4, both male and female, mostly the latter, to which add, from Aniba, Steindorff 1937, 164-5 (S 23), no. 19, and 234-5 (SA 34), no. 4.

[29] Smith and Buzon 2017, 618, fig. 3, 620-622, 624, fig. 11, b; Smith 2018, 74-5, fig. 5, 80-81, pl. 12; Smith and Buzon 2018, 207, 211, fig. 6.

[30] Smith and Buzon 2017, 616-617, fig. 1, 620, fig. 6; Smith 2018, 73-4, fig. 4; Smith and Buzon 2018, 207-208, fig. 2, and 222; Spencer 2019b, 113.

[31] Cf. Müller 2013, 87.

[32] The figures are eroded but shown as if progressing one after the other. On the iconography and symbolism of the giraffe in rock-art and other media in Egypt and Nubia, see Cannuyer 2010, 39-194; Kleinitz 2013, 346, 349-350, fig. 5; for its role in the painted scenes/ royal funerary iconography of the *Kerma Classique* period at Kerma, see Bonnet 2000, 76, 79-83, figs 58-61, 98-99, fig. 70; Chaix 2000, 165, fig. 118; cf. Doyen and Gabolde 2017, 154.

[33] Reading *ḥm-ntr tp(y)*, '*Il sacerdote di primo rango*' (Roccati in Castiglioni and Castiglioni 2006b, 179), the *tp*-sign (D1) simplified in form, as it is in the title of the same man in KRP18, no. 24; cf., perhaps, López 1966, 18, no. 9, 20, no. 13, pls vi and ix, 1 (photos a little unclear).

[34] For the form of the *spȝt*-sign (Aa8) here, cf. Piotrovsky 1983, 50, 90, 149, no. 59.

[35] PM vii, 91; Borla 2010, 90, a5, 103, 233, pl. 21, a.5; Müller 2013, 206,

Plate 15.21. KRP8, 4, south, Horus-figure with inscription of Tiy.

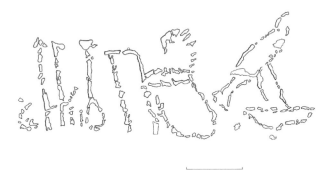

Figure 15.6. KRP8, 4, south, inscription of Tiy.

Plate 15.22. KRP9, Wadi Tonaidba, cave.

Plate 15.23. KRP9, 1, inscription of Mayor Mesu.

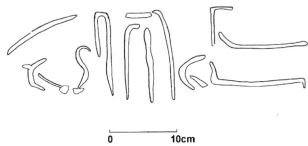

Figure 15.7. KRP9, 1, Mayor Mesu.

Plate 15.24. KRP9, 2-3, interior inscriptions, including (bottom right) High Priest Nebnetjeru.

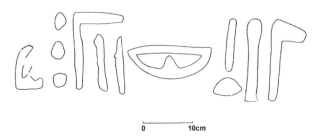

Figure 15.8. KRP9, 2, High Priest Nebnetjeru.

the 18th dynasty, sometime after the reign of Thutmose III (the temple was built at the very end of the latter's reign).[36] Aniba might also have been the 'district' of our 'Scribe of the district' (no. 3, name and date uncertain; cf. KRP18, no. 20).[37]

The 'High Priest Nebnetjeru' (no. 2), seemingly the only 'High Priest' ($ḥm-nṯr tp(y)$) so far attested in the Nubian min-

ing regions,[38] is known also from KRP18, nos 3 and 24. If, as seems likely, he is the same man as the well-known 'Scribe

2.5.2, 1, and 412, 28.6; Auenmüller 2013, 926, BMAniba-02, a and b.

[36] Davies and Welsby Sjöström 2016, 18, with n. 5. The inscription, now incomplete, is located on the ingress (right wall) to the temple-doorway. Note the observation of Dewachter 1971, 91, n. 6, that private inscriptions might not have been permitted inside the temple proper before the Ramesside period.

[37] For the title with the toponym, see 'Scribe of the district, Djehutymose, of Miam', dating to the 18th Dynasty, from the Wadi Barramyia in the Egyptian Eastern Desert (Rothe *et al.* 2008, 117, BR07; Brown 2017, 191-193, fig. 9).

[38] No 'High Priest' is certainly attested among the many priests (twentynine in all, mostly $ḥm-nṯr$) recorded at the Wadi Allaki; see Piotrovsky 1983, 82-83 (Index). On the role of temple-personnel (often numerous) in such expeditions, see Hikade 2001, 43: '*Ihre Funktion ist nicht sicher zu bestimmen. Neben ihren priesterlichen Aufgaben dürften zie z.T. dem Versorgungsapparat der Expedition angehört haben*'.

Plate 15.25. KRP9, 3, inscription of Scribe of the district, name uncertain.

Plate 15.26. KRP13, cave, from west (Photograph: Derek Welsby).

Nebnetjeru' (see below, KRP18, 10-12),[39] he is possibly to be connected to Kuban, though an affiliation with Aniba is not out of the question. Dated to the Ramesside Period (reign of Ramesses II), he would have been a near-contemporary of Hornakht of Aniba, known to have travelled the same Wadi Tonaidba route (KRP8, nos 1-2). He is one of two priests in our corpus, the other, also Ramesside, being a priest (*ḥm-nṯr*) from Buhen (see KRP2, 22-23, below), the third major temple of Lower Nubia (the others, at Aniba and Kuban) with proprietorial interests in the gold-working industry. As a High Priest, Nebnetjeru would have been a senior member of his desert expedition, perhaps even its leader,[40] a role for which his previous experience as a much travelled regional scribe (again assuming the equivalence) would have stood him in good stead.

KRP13. Cave (Plate 15.26; site not recorded by CeRDO; Davies 2014, 34-5, fig. 7; Welsby, this volume, 147).
Located on the cave's left wall, not far above the floor, is a short, line of semi-cursive hieroglyphs (Plate 15.27, Figure 15.9), reading from right to left: 'Scribe Nyny'. Almost certainly datable to the New Kingdom, this scribe, or at least his name in this form,[41] is not otherwise attested in the region.[42]

KRP14. Cave (Plate 15.28; CeRDO site F; Castiglioni and Castiglioni 2006b, 170, 176-177; 2007, 21, fig. 4; Roccati 2007, 57-58; Davies 2014, 35-36, figs 8-9, pl. 12; Cooper 2018b, 143-144, 148-9, 157, fig. 3, pl. 3; Auenmüller 2019b, 396; Cooper and Vanhulle 2019, 3, map 1, and 5; Castiglioni and Castiglioni, this volume, 23-24, pl. 4.5; Welsby, this volume, 147-148).
A boulder at the left of the cave-entrance (Plate 15.29), which is covered with rock-drawings of animals, largely cattle, and other indigenous decoration, bears a prominent hieroglyphic inscription, by far the finest in the Eastern Desert corpus (Plate 15.30, Figure 15.10). Done in sunk relief, partly superimposed on an earlier motif, it consists of large, skilfully

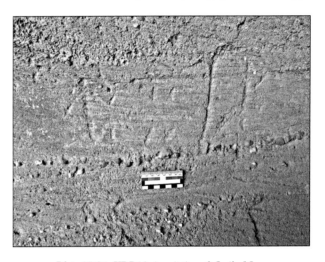

Plate 15.27. KRP13, inscription of Scribe Nyny.

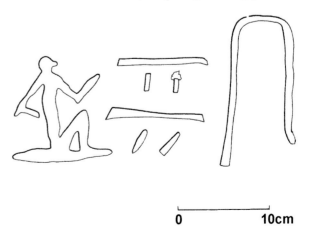

Figure 15.9. KRP13, Scribe Nyny.

[39] Cf. also 'Priest (*ḥm-nṯr*) of Thoth, god's father, mayor, Nebnetjeru' from Abu Simbel, rock-stela no. 26 (PM vii, 119; Weigall 1907, pl. lxviii, 3; KRI III, 121, n. 1a; Müller 2013, 211, 2.5.2, no. 26; Altenmüller 2013, 936, BMNubien-04), an inscription never properly published and therefore difficult to evaluate.

[40] Cf. the several High Priests (of various deities) of the New Kingdom, mostly Ramesside, charged with leading expeditions to the Wadi Hammamat in the Egyptian Eastern Desert; see Hikade 2001, 36-46 (with Diagrams 2 and 3), 196, no. 98, 199-201, no. 113, 201, no. 114, 205-209, no. 120, 210, no. 122.

[41] Cf. PN i, 181, no. 16, 205, no. 19 etc.

[42] Cf. perhaps the scribe with the name 'Nana' at Sahabu in the Batn el-Hajar (Hintze and Reineke 1989, 168, no. 551, pl. 233; Müller 2013, 275, no. 41, 452, 42.31).

Plate 15.28. KRP14, *cave entrance, from south.*

Plate 15.29. KRP14, *interior, boulder with inscriptions.*

carved hieroglyphs, including a lion and a falcon (Horus). Arranged in three lines, carefully disposed so as to accommodate a deep irregular fault in the surface, the inscription, almost certainly that of a Kushite (Kerma) king, reads from right to left and from bottom to top: *'Trh* (or *Trrh*), lion,[43] beloved of Horus, Lord of desert lands'. To its left, there are several smaller signs and motifs, quite crudely incised, including two Horus-figures, one surmounting the hieroglyphs *ḥ* (O4) and *nb* (V30),[44] possibly marks of homage to the deity by later visitors.

Comment

The clearly indigenous name, *Trh/Trrh*, may be compatible

with that of the 'ruler of Kush *Triȝh/Tri-ȝhi*'[45] included as an enemy of Egypt in the execration texts from Mirgissa (Figure 15.11),[46] long assessed to be dated to around the mid-12th Dynasty,[47] more recently argued to be of the later Middle Kingdom.[48]

The work of an accomplished artist in the service of Kush, the inscription recalls in style, quality and content that on the well-known Egyptian border stela of the Middle Kingdom from the desert east of Argin in Lower Nubia,[49] the kind of monument to which it might have served as a territorial counterpoint. An 'expression of kingship concordant with Egyptian norms',[50] including the appropriation of 'Horus, Lord of desert lands',[51] it represents an assertion of status consistent with the impressive growth through the *Kerma Moyen* period in the power and reach of the King-

[43] The striding lion, an icon of Kushite kingship and embodiment of the king (as in Egypt), may have served here as a determinative of the name (Davies 2014, 35, n. 17, with earlier literature; Manzo 2014, 1149; 2016, 24-25, fig. 14; Cooper 2018b, 148, with n. 27, fig. 3, pl. 3; Gabolde 2018, 97-98).

[44] Both perhaps reproduced randomly from the well-known epithet *nb Bḥn*, 'Lord of Buhen' (cf. KRP22, no. 1).

[45] Davies 2014, 35-36; Cooper 2018a, 674; 2018b, 144, with n. 2; cf. Ilin-Tomich 2016, 9; Rilly 2017, 71-72.

[46] Koenig 1990, 103, A1, 104, b, 118-119, line 1, 120-121, line 1, 124-125, line 1; El-Sayed 2011, 294-295, L 400.

[47] Koenig 1990, 102; cf. Ritner 1993, 140, n. 620, 153, n. 695; Ryholt 2010, 253-254, Table 70.

[48] The Mirgissa corpus is closely related to two other sets of execration texts, originally from Thebes and Saqqara respectively (on the Levantine content of the latter two, see now Streit 2017; for a new project on the Saqqara set, in Brussels, see Van der Perre 2017). All three sets record the names of Nubian royal family members, representing a lineage which, according to a reassessment by Williams (2013, 73, n. 71; cf. Williams 2018, 101), should be dated 'from the end of the Twelfth into the Thirteenth Dynasties' (see also now Cooper 2018b, 159-161, who admits of remaining uncertainties).

[49] Khartoum, SNM 14221; Wildung 1997; Berengeur 2003; Vogel 2004, 77, n. 70; Roccati 2007, 57-58, fig. 4; Vogel 2011, 323-324; Knoblauch 2012, 90, fig. 2, and 93. The figural iconography of the Argin stela is very similar to that on military stamp-sealings known from a number of Middle Kingdom fortress-sites (Wegner 1995, 144-148, figs 9-10) and on broadly contemporary stelae, possibly border-markers, from Buhen and elsewhere (Knoblauch 2012; cf. Manzo 2016, 21-23; Cooper 2018b, 157; Williams 2018, 102).

[50] Cooper 2018b, 143, 148.

[51] Cf. the deity's presence on the Argin border stela cited above (n. 49; cf. Davies 2014, 35, n. 19; Cooper 2018b, 148, n. 26), as well as, further afield, on late Middle Kingdom/Second Intermediate Period royal stelae from the galena mining-site at Gebel el-Zeit (Régen and Soukassian 2008, 15-16, 18-20, 19, 52, 56-57, nos 3 and 5; cf. Leitz 2002, III, 710-711).

Plate 15.30. KRP14, inscription with indigenous name and dedication to Horus.

Figure 15.10. KRP14, inscription of Trḫ/Trrḫ.

0   10cm

197

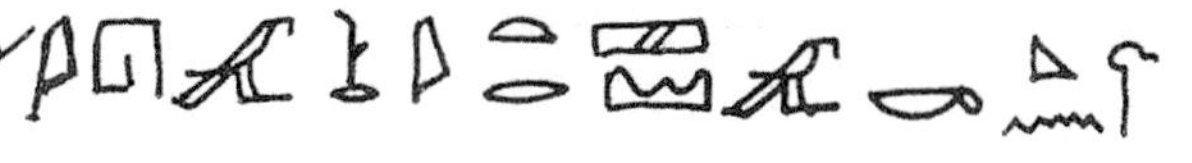

Figure 15.11. Ruler of Kush Teri-ahi, from execration text (after Koenig 1990).

dom of Kush.[52] Strategically located,[53] it might well have been intended to mark – during this period of contested borders[54] – the Kingdom's authority over the desert gold-bearing region, a state of affairs confirmed by the lack of *in situ* evidence (inscriptional or otherwise) for the presence in the area of Egyptian military or mining personnel before the New Kingdom (KRP5).[55]

KRP18. Khashm el-Bab, rock-face (Plate 15.31; CeRDO site B; Castiglioni and Castiglioni 1994, 20; Castiglioni *et al.* 1995, 112-114; Sadr *et al.* 1995, 224-225; Damiano-Appia 1999, 522-534, 541, fig. 2; Andrassy 2002, 10-13; Castiglioni and Castiglioni 2006a, 409, fig. 25; Castiglioni and Castiglioni 2006b, 172; 2007, 26-28, fig. 11; Roccati 2007, 58; Castiglioni *et al.* 2010, 267-8, fig. 18; Davies 2014, 36-37, figs 10-11, pls 13-15; Cooper and Vanhulle 2019, 3, Map 1, and 5; Castiglioni and Castiglioni, this volume, 22-23, pls 4.3-4.4; Welsby, this volume, 149-151).

This prominent sandstone outcrop, with a distinctive overhang, has the greatest single concentration of Egyptian inscriptions in the Sudanese Eastern Desert, reflecting its location at the entrance to a pass (Khashm el-Bab, 'Lock of the Door') where various desert routes come together.[56] The main decorated area, at the south (right) end of the west side (Plate 15.32 and 15.33), measures about 1.4m in height and 2.9m in width. It bears twenty-three recognisable inscriptions or remains thereof, comprising names and titles (see list below, nos 1-23, of which one, no. 15, is vestigial), some animal drawings, and a number of random incisions and motifs of indeterminate meaning. It once extended further to the left but the surface here is now lost. What we see today is thus only a proportion of what was originally present here. A single inscription (no. 24) occurs, above head-height, at the far left (north) end of the rock-face, where there are also earlier animal drawings.

Some of the inscriptions are written in hieroglyphs, one or two a little clumsily done; others are rendered in a form of hieratic or semi-hieratic script.[57] Most are arranged in horizontal lines, the majority incised or pecked into the natural surface of the rock, an exception being the group of three, nos 6-8, where the surface was carefully lowered and smoothed in advance (possibly removing existing decoration in the process), the resultant simulation of a papyrus-document serving to emphasise scribal credentials. The members of this group form a coherent unit, as do nos 21-23, and almost certainly nos 13-14, the personnel, travelling together, listed in order of status.

The name and title of certain individuals occur more than once (nos. 3 and 24; 10-12; and perhaps 4 and 6), each possibly marking a separate visit, while a number can probably be linked to other sources (see comment, below). Some of the inscriptions may have been abbreviated, most likely, for example, where the title 'Scribe' alone was written (nos 4, 6, 10-12), perhaps for the fuller 'Scribe reckoner of gold'[58] or similarly appropriate scribal office, while in two cases (nos 2 and 18), for reasons unknown, only the name was recorded.[59] All of the inscriptions are New Kingdom in date, except for nos 16-17, which are of questionable antiquity.

South end of rock-face

Right, from top (Plates 15.33-15.35):
1. 'Man of reckoning (*s n ḥsb*) Pashed' (Plate 15.34, Figure 15.12)
2. 'Ramose'[60] (Plate 15.35, upper)
3. 'High Priest (*ḥm-nṯr tp(y)*) Nebnetjeru'[61] (Plate 15.35, lower).

---

[52] See Török 2009, 87, on the 'spectacular unfolding of the power of Kerma' as a major determinant in the building by the Egyptians of the 12th Dynasty chain of Nubian fortresses; and Vogel 2004, 150; 2009, 174; 2013, 80, on Egypt's goal 'to build a staggered defensive system against the rulers of Kerma'; cf. also Zibelius-Chen 2014, 277; Valbelle 2015, 476; 2018, 445-446. For a recent overview of the fortresses and issues attached, see Knoblauch 2019. As is well known, Kush's military reach was to culminate in the *Kerma Classique* period with at least one hostile incursion into Egypt proper (as reported in the inscription of Sobeknakht II, Elkab, 16th Dynasty), with Kush leading an army of peoples drawn from the Middle Nile valley and the Eastern Desert (a proportion of the Egyptian objects buried in the royal tumuli at Kerma and elsewhere in Nubia possibly representing 'trophies' from such raids); see Davies 2003a, 2003b; 2004a; 2005, 49-50; 2010, 223, n. 2; cf. Edwards 2004, 95; El-Sayed 2004, 361, n. 62; Zibelius-Chen 2007, 399-400; 2011, 9; 2014, 271, 293-294; Gnirs 2009, 103; Raedler 2009, 328, 341; Vogel 2009, 181, n. 73; Török 2009, 109-110; Franke 2010, 297-298; Thill 2011-12, 284; Valbelle 2012, 450, 464; 2014, 106-107; Näser 2013, 140-141, n. 41; Shirley 2013, 558, 565, 570; Williams 2013, 61, 66-67, 71, n. 29; Ilin-Tomich 2014, 160, n. 93, 164, 166; 2016, 8, 11; Manzo 2014, 1150; 2016, 17; 2017, 110; this volume, 80; Liszka 2015, 59, nn 128, 144; Cooper 2018b, 144, 149, n. 29, 161; Gabolde 2018, 91; Moeller and Forstner-Müller 2018, 11; Müller 2018, 201, 213; Polz 2018, 229, n. 52, 231; Conner 2019, 294; Raue 2019b, 572). Note also in the same vein the cartouche 'of a Kerman ruler adopting formal elements of royal Egyptian titulary' present on a sealing from Elephantine of the late Second Intermediate Period/early 18th Dynasty (von Pilgrim 2015, 225; cf. Fitzenreiter 2012; Cooper 2018b, 144, 147-149, 157; Polz 2018, 230; Raue 2019a, 314; 2019b, 572).

[53] See Cooper and Vanhulle 2019, 5, emphasizing the significance of 'the location of this inscription… right on the junction of where the north-south 'Korosko Road' met with the east-west route leading from the Second Cataract'; cf. Knoblauch 2019, 370, n. 13. The tentative suggestion that the KRP14 name might alternatively be that of a later Kushite ruler, perhaps a descendant of the Execration Text king, dating to the *Kerma Classique* period (Davies 2014, 35-36), is speculative, though remains a possibility (Rilly 2017, 71-72; Cooper 2018b, 144; Williams 2018, 101). However, the location of the inscription clearly better fits the earlier political/territorial situation than the later.

[54] Cf. Vogel 2011; Knoblauch 2012, 90-93.

[55] For archaeological/ceramic evidence indicating consistent Kerma/Kushite presence in these desert gold-bearing areas, from the Kerma Ancien period onwards, see Bonnet 2007; Castiglioni *et al.* 2010; Manzo 2012, 81-82; Bonnet 2014, 82; Manzo, this volume, 80; Ruffieux and Bashir, this volume, 181.

[56] Cf. Cooper and Vanhulle 2019, 3, Map 1, and 5.

[57] Dated by Dr Rob Demarée (pers. comm.) on palaeographic grounds to the late 18th or early 19th Dynasty.

[58] Cf. Brown 2017, 184-5, with Table 1.

[59] Cf. Lazaridis 2017, 329-330; Auenmüller 2019b, 397; 2019c, 195, with n. 58; Žába 1974, 261-262.

[60] The single incised line underneath (cf. also no. 9) serves perhaps as a mark of separation and to 'maximise the effect' (Lazaridis 2015, 50, n. 30, 60, fig. 9); cf. examples at the Wadi Allaki (Piotrovsky 1983, 61, 174, no. 160, 63, 177, no. 171).

[61] The inscription was deliberately pecked out in antiquity but traces of the original are clearly visible.

Plate 15.31. KRP18, Khashm el-Bab, from the south.

Plate 15.32. KRP18, decorated face, from the west (Photograph: Bert Verrept).

Plate 15.33. KRP18, main decorated area.

Plate 15.34. KRP18, no. 1, Man of counting Pashed.

Figure 15.12. KRP18, no. 1, Man of counting Pashed.

Plate 15.35. KRP18, nos 2 and 3, Ramose (upper) and [High Priest Nebnetjeru], effaced (lower).

Centre, from top (Plates 15.33, 15.36-15.42):

4. 'Scribe Amenaa (*sš ꜣImn-ꜥꜣ*)'[62] (Plate 15.36, Figure 15.13).

5. 'Scribe reckoner of gold (*sš ḥsb nbw*) Djehutyhotep' (Plate 15.37, top right, Figure 15.14).

6. 'Scribe Amenaa, son of Paser' (Plate 15.37, centre, Figure 15.15).

7. 'Man of reckoning P(a)-en-Mia(m),[63] (son of) Panakht' (Plate 15.37, centre, Figure 15.15).

Plate 15.36. KRP18, no. 4, Scribe Amenaa.

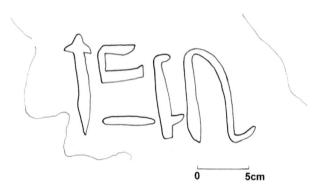

Figure 15.13. KRP18, no. 4, Scribe Amenaa.

8. 'Man of reckoning Kheper,[64] son of Ankhty' (Plate 15.37, centre, Figure 15.15).

9. 'Chief retainer' (*ḥry šmsw*), Huy'[65] (Plate 15.38, upper, Figure 15.16).

10. 'Scribe Nebnetjeru' (Plate 15.38, lower, Figure 15.17).

11. 'Scribe Nebnetjeru' (Plate 15.39, centre, Figure 15.18).

12. 'Scribe Nebnetjeru'[66] (Plate 15.40).

13. 'Scribe reckoner of gold Meryure' (Plate 15.41, upper, Figure 19).

14. 'Retainer[67] Amenneb' (Plate 15.41, lower, Figure 15.19).

15. Part of a circular hieroglyph; first sign of an inscription otherwise lost (Plate 15.41, Figure 15.19, lower left).

---

[62] The name's second element is written with a single vertical sign, O29, for reasons of space; cf. the fuller writing (perhaps referring to the same man), no. 6, below, and *PN* i, 26, no. 26.

[63] The name, lit. 'The (man) of Miam (Aniba)', here surely a true 'Herkunftsname' is otherwise attested for a scribe of the Viceroy Merymose on a stela of uncertain provenance (BM EA 860; Hall 1925, 7, pl. 12; *PN* i, 108, 5; Dewachter 1978, i, 103-5, Doc. 91; Ragazzoli 2017, 213, fig. 15; Auenmüller 2013, 286-287). For writing of the toponym without final *m*, see also no. 21 below; cf. Zibelius 1972, 120-121; Leitz 2002, III, 643-644; Gasse and Rondot 2007, 184, 507, SEH 304, line 2; El-Sayed 2011, 202, L 179; Brown 2017, 192, figs 9-10.

[64] For the name, possibly an abbreviation, cf. Piotrovsky 1983, 99 (Index).

[65] The only *ḥry šmsw* in our corpus though there are several *šmsw* (nos 14, 19, 22), to which add KRP8, no. 3 (see n. 23). The usual 'book-roll' determinative (Y1) of the first part of the name *Ḥwy* (*PN* i, 233, 18) is here highly abbreviated, with only the detached seal of the roll represented (cf. its form in no. 6). For the line underneath, cf. no. 2 above.

[66] In this case, the inscription, done in the same style as nos 10-11, has been clumsily squeezed into the triangular space between two diverging cracks resulting in some malformation, redundancy, and displacement of the signs, though the intended reading is clear.

[67] See nn. 23 and 65.

200

Plate 15.37. KRP18, no. 5, Scribe Djehutyhotep (upper), nos 6-8, Scribe Amenaa and two others (lower).

0   5cm

Figure 15.14. KRP18, no. 5, Scribe reckoner of gold Djehutyhotep.

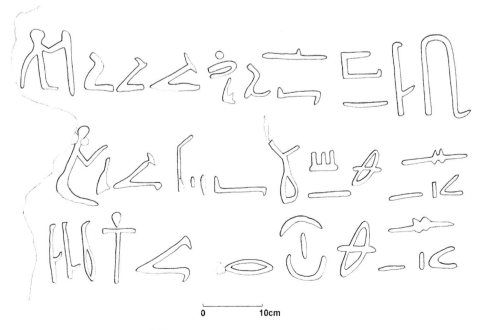

Figure 15.15. KRP18, nos 6-8, Scribe Amenaa, and Men of counting Penmiam and Kheper.

0   10cm

201

Plate 15.38. KRP18, nos 9-10. Chief retainer Huy (upper),
Scribe Nebnetjeru (lower).

Plate 15.39. KRP18, no. 11, Scribe Nebnetjeru.

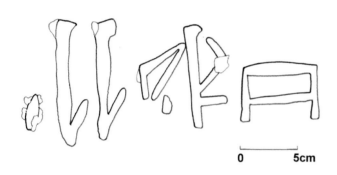

Figure 15.16. KRP18, no. 9, Chief retainer Huy.

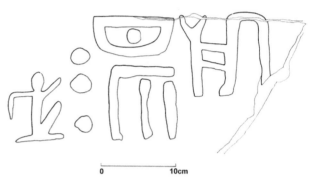

Figure 15.18. KRP18, no. 11, Scribe Nebnetjeru.

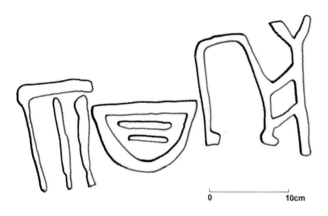

Figure 15.17. KRP18, no. 10, Scribe Nebnetjeru.

16. 'Mayor, Scribe Desnefer' (Plate 15.42, upper).
17. 'Mayor, Scribe Desnefer' (Plate 15.42, lower).
Left, right to left, top to bottom (Plate 15.43, Figure 15.20):
18. 'May' (*Mȝy*)[68] (?)
19. 'Retainer[69] Nakh(t)'[70]

_____

[68] Taking the first hieroglyph as a writing of the *mȝ*-sign (U2); for the
name, possibly *Mȝi*, 'Lion', see *PN* i, 144, 1, with 144, 2-14; cf. Rothe *et al.*
2008, 228, SL09; Brown and Darnell 2013, 127, with n. 17; on the name's
extended variants, see now Lakomy 2016, 65-66, with n. 84, to which add
Davies, 2017b, 61, fig. 1, with n. 16.

[69] See nn. 23 and 65.

[70] Cf. *PN* i, 209, 16.

Plate 15.40. KRP18, no. 12, Scribe Nebnetjeru.

Plate 15.41. KRP18, nos 13-15, Scribe reckoner of gold Meryure (upper), Retainer Amenneb and one vestigial (lower).

Figure 15.19. KRP18, nos 13-15, Scribe reckoner of gold Meryure and others.

```
0                    10cm
```

Plate 15.42. KRP18, nos 16-17, Mayor, Scribe Des (upper and lower).

20. 'Scribe of the dist[rict] (*sš sp3t*) [title damaged, name lost]'[71]

21. 'Chief of Mia(m)[72] Mer'
22. 'Retainer[73] Mer'
23. 'Man of reckoning Panehsy, son of Paser'
North end of rock face
24. 'High Priest Nebnetjeru'[74] (Plate 15.44, Figure 15.21).

Comment

The 'Scribe reckoner of gold Djehutyhotep' (no. 5) is quite feasibly the well-known 'Scribe Djehutyhotep', who was also 'Scribe, mayor, overseer of the priests of Khnum, Anuket and Satet', the son of 'Scribe of the town'/ 'Scribe reckoner of Wawat Sen-Djehuty', and brother of 'Overseer of the treasury Smakhasut', a prominent family of gold-industry/ treasury officials based at Elephantine, well attested in rock-inscriptions from Nubia and the Aswan region,[75] dating to the

---

[71] For the title, that of a Treasury official (Müller 2013, 56-57, 252-255), see also KRP9, no. 3, the 'district' here in question probably that of 'Miam'; note the nearby inscription of the 'Chief of Miam' (no. 21) and the name 'P(a)-en-Mia(m)' (no. 7), Miam being the only toponym attested at the Khashm el-Bab (for the title in full, from the Egyptian Eastern Desert, see n. 37 above). The title (again without toponym) is well attested at the Wadi Allaki (Piotrovsky 1983, 81, Index), where the 'district' referred to is possibly that of Kuban (cf. Černý, 1947, 57); for numerous examples associated with

the 'district of Elephantine' (*3bw*), see Müller 2013, 254-255, nos 38-41, to which add Gasse and Rondot 2007, SEH nos 398, 415, 416, 462, 463, 464.

[72] Cf. no. 7 above, with n. 63.

[73] See nn 23 and 65, the 'retainer' in this unit of three (nos 21-23) probably acting as the Chief's 'aide' (right-hand man); cf. the *šmsw* Huy, 'aide' to Viceroy Amenemipet, attested at Jebel Dosha and Buhen (Davies 2017, 62-63, n. 28, pl. 7).

[74] Part of the title is missing owing to natural loss of surface.

[75] De Morgan *et al.* 1894, 128, nos 11 and 15; Hintze and Reineke 1989, i, 37, no. 62, 39, no. 68, 40, no. 73, 174, no. 569, ii, pls 32, 34, and 243; Gasse and Rondot 2007, 189-190, SEH 311-312, pl. 510; Davies 2018, 52-53, fig. 10, pls 10-12; cf. Müller 2013, 253, 2.6.1, nos 12, 30, 33, and 43, 271, 2.7.6, no. 7; Auenmüller 2013, 735 and 922, BMElephantine-01.

Plate 15.43. KRP18, nos 18-23, Chief of Miam Mer and others; surface to the left lost.

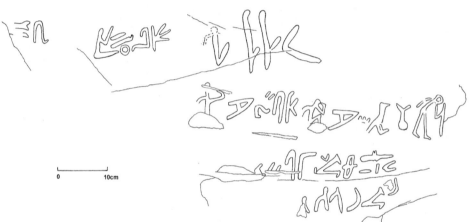

Figure 15.20. KRP18, nos 18-23, Chief of Miam Mer and others.

Plate 15.44. KRP18, no. 24, High Priest Nebnetjeru.

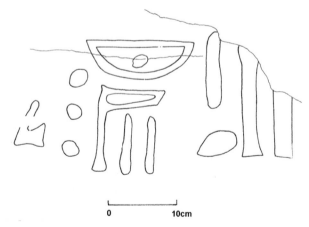

Figure 15.21. KRP18, no. 24, High Priest Nebnetjeru.

18th Dynasty;[76] he is also almost certainly to be recognized in the rock-inscription 'Mayor of Elephantine, Scribe reckoner of gold Djehutyhotep' at Abrak in the Egyptian south-eastern desert.[77] Possibly contemporary is no. 13, 'Scribe reckoner of

[76] The rock-inscriptions of Djehutyhotep and his brother at Abu Sir (Hintze and Reineke 1989, i, 37, no. 62, 39, no. 68, 40, no. 73, ii, pls 32 and 34) are distinctively similar in arrangement, orthography and type of content not only to each other but to the nearby inscription of the Scribe Amenhotep, which is dated to Year 16 of Thutmose III (Hintze and Reineke 1989, i, 38, no. 64, ii, pl. 30). If this link is valid, it follows that they were contemporaries

of our other Djehutyhotep, the 'Chief of Tehkhet' of KRP5.

[77] De Bruyn 1956; cf. Andrassy, 2002, 10, n. 12; Müller 2013, 253, 2.6.1, no. 33; Auenmüller 2013, 922, BMElephantine-01. For the location of Abrak and the route of a mooted desert road between it and Aswan, see Sidebotham

gold Meryure', perhaps the same man as 'scribe Meryre, son of scribe Simut' attested in the Wadi Allaqi,[78] the two sets of inscription, both hieroglyphic, done in a similar, somewhat unpractised style, with quite distinctive *i*-signs (M17), observable also in our no. 14, the inscription of 'Retainer Amenneb'.[79] In any case, these and related data amply support the view that 'of all the officials dealing with gold, he [scribe reckoner of gold] is the one most often reported on the desert roads…'.[80] Note, in particular, the data relating to the 'Scribe reckoner of gold Siamun' (temp. Amenhotep III), whose corpus of twelve inscriptions reveals that his 'primary duties within the Egyptian Eastern Desert consisted of circulating through the gold mines east of Edfu "inspecting the mines of the desert".'[81]

The 'Chief of Miam Mer' (no. 21) is to be added to the list of chiefs of the Aniba/Toshka region, of which three others, all 18th Dynasty, are known.[82] These are Amenhotep,[83] Rahotep,[84] and Hekanefer (see under KRP5 above, with Plate 15.9), of whom Mer, datable to the late 18th/early 19th Dynasty,[85] might have been the successor. The third member (no. 23) of Mer's entourage has the title *s n ḥsb*, lit. 'man of (or 'for') reckoning', as do two of the personnel in the unit led by the scribe Amenaa (nos 6-8) and one other in the standalone inscription (no. 1) on the right, all three sets done in the same style and probably contemporary (to which add, on palaeographic grounds, nos 18-20). Taken at face value and given the context, it seems likely that the latter title's reference is to a supportive gold-counting function, operating at an administrative level below that of the scribe.[86] To date, it appears to be attested only at the Khashm el-Bab.

The 'Scribe Nebnetjeru', attested here three times (nos. 10-12), is probably the ubiquitous 'Scribe Nebnetjeru' often identified as 'of Kuban (Bak)'[87] or 'son of Hori of Kuban', known from numerous rock-inscriptions in the Wadi Allaki and in several Lower Nubian sites (Kalabsha, Hindaw, Mediq and Tonqala),[88] as well as from a fragmentary temple-

stela at Aniba.[89] He is datable by association to the reign of Ramesses II (in one case probably to Year 40).[90] His scribal duties, integrating separate but related functions, appear to have served both practical and ritual purposes. He is once, at Mediq, identified as a 'Scribe of the granary' (*sš šnwt*),[91] a position, it is suggested, involving the 'responsibility… to maintain the supply-chain (from the granary) to the gold miners',[92] which would explain the necessity for his multiple desert journeys. In one of the Wadi Allaki inscriptions, he has the title 'Scribe of the temple (*sš ḥwt-nṯr*)',[93] no doubt with reference to the temple of 'Horus Lord of Kuban',[94] his home-town deity (note that one of the Wadi's finest rock-drawings, an adoration-scene showing a male figure kneeling before Horus, was 'made by Scribe Nebnetjeru, son of Hori, for his lord').[95] In the stela from the temple of Aniba, he is identified as 'Scribe of every temple' (*sš ḥwt-nṯr nb*),[96] suggesting an elevation in status and a wider regional remit. On the basis of the Khashm el-Bab attestations ('Scribe Nebnetjeru', KRP18, nos 10-12), he is quite possibly to be equated, in turn, with 'High Priest (*ḥm-nṯr tp(y)*) Nebnetjeru', whose name and title occur twice at KRP18 (nos 3 and 24),[97] and once, further

et al. 2008, 345-346, fig. 15.1, 352-353; Auenmüller 2019a, 40, fig. 1, and 55. It is suggested that Elephantine probably housed at this period a branch of the Egyptian Treasury with responsibility, under the direction of the mayor, for the Nubian province (Müller 2013, 255; Zibelius-Chen 2013, 142-143).

[78] Piotrovsky 1983, 63, 177, no. 171; Hikade 2001, 243, 260, no. 269.

[79] For the name in this form, in the inscription of a scribe at Tangur, see Hintze and Reineke 1989, 171, no. 555, 175, no. 576, pls 236 and 246; Müller 2013, 272, 2.7.6, no. 15.

[80] Vercoutter 1959, 146-147; cf. Müller 2013, 55-57, 79, 255; Klotz and Brown 2016, 284; Spencer 2019, 113.

[81] Brown 2017, 184-6, Table 1, fig. 4.

[82] Davies 2014, 37; Spencer *et al.* 2017, 42.

[83] Minault-Gout 2011-2012, 190, no. 2, 196-198.

[84] Simpson 1963, 25, fig. 20, 26-27; Zibelius 1972, 37, V E b 30; Trigger 1996, 804; Zibelius-Chen 2007, 403; 2011, 170; Müller 2013, 53, 246, 2.5.4, no. 6. Note that Rahotep is also attested in a rock-inscription in the Wadi Barramiya in Egypt; see Davies 2014, 37, n. 28; Brown 2017, 191-192, fig. 10.

[85] Here on palaeographic grounds, see n. 57 above.

[86] For an alternative possibility, that there might be a connection between *s n ḥsb* and the term *ḥsb(w)*, 'counted man', 'enlistee' (*Wb.* 3, 168, 1; Hannig 2006, 604), a project-worker often recruited from local sources and assigned to mining and other expeditions, see Davies 2014, 37, n. 29; for a possible Wadi Allaki example, see Piotrovsky 1983, 57, no. 122.

[87] For the toponym, Černý 1947, 57; Zibelius 1972, 111-112; Hein 1991, 12-14; Giddy 1998, 35-37; Ullmann 2009, 249; Klemm and Klemm 2013, 294.

[88] Wadi Allaki: Černý 1947, 53-57, nos. 11, 20, 21, 28, pls 9 (2-3), 10 (2); Piotrovsky 1983, 45, nos. 2 and 7; 47, no. 22; 49, nos. 47 and 52; 53, no. 101; 54, 161, no. 104 (the latter very close in style to the Khashm el-Bab examples); 56, no. 116, and 60, no. 155. Other sites: Weigall 1907, 76 (Kalabsha)

and 113 (Tonqala); Roeder 1911, 182-3, pl. 118, d (Hindaw); Firth 1910-11, pl. 12, c and e (Mediq); cf. Žába 1974, 221; KRI III, 121, III.12; KRITA III, 82-83; DRITANC III, 108-109; Peden 2001, 117, n. 363; Hikade 2001, 239-240, 259, nos. 228-231; Espinel 2012, 101, fig. 7.7; Müller 2013, 265, 2.6.4, no. 12; Köpp-Junk 2015, 238; Auenmüller 2019b, 406-407, with fig. 4. Another Lower Nubian official with the same name, though different title and no clear connection to our scribe, is 'Retainer (*šmsw*) Nebnetjeru' from Toshka East/Gebel Agg (PM vii, 94; Černý 1947, 57; Simpson 1963, 41, fig. 33, pl. xx, c; KRI III, 121, n. 1a; Müller 2013, 189, 2.4. 1, no. 14); cf. also 'Priest (*ḥm-nṯr*) of Thoth, god's father, mayor, Nebnetjeru' from Abu Simbel (see n. 39 above).

[89] PM vii, 81; Steindorff 1937, 27, no. 57, pl. 13, no. 55; Žába 1974, 221; KRI III, 121, n. 1a; Müller 2013, 217, 2.5.3 a 30; 421, 30. 64.

[90] Černý 1947, 55, nos 27-28, pl. ix, 3; Piotrovsky 1983, 53, 160, nos 100-101; Hikade 2001, 239, nos 227-228; DRITANC III, 109.

[91] Firth 1910-11, pl. 12, c, upper line; KRI III, 121, III.12, 2; KRITA III, 83; DRITANC III, 108-109; Müller 2013, 224, 2.5.3 C 10. The inscription is closely associated with that of the contemporary 'Overseer of the granary (also 'Scribe of the granary'), Horemheb, son of Nakhtmin, of Kuban' (Firth 1910-11, pl. 12, c, lower line; KRI III, 124, III. 20; KRITA III, 84; DRITANC III, 111; Müller 2013, 265, 2.6.4, no. 8).

[92] DRITANC III, 108-109.

[93] Piotrovsky 1983, 60, 171, no. 155. The inscription is located directly above the rock-stela of the 'Overseer of the granary, Deputy of Wawat, Horhotep…' (Piotrovsky 1983, 60, 170, no. 154; Hikade 2001, 70, 260, no. 264; Müller 2013, 64, 201, 2.5.1, no. 16, 263, 2.6.4, no. 2).

[94] On the temple and deity, see Kormysheva 1996, 141-142; Leitz 2002, III, 619-620; Török 2009, 222, 234, 261; Ullmann 2009, 249, with n. 14; Kormysheva 2013, 154; Müller 2013, 89, 223-224, 2.5.3 C, no. 4, relating to the 'First lector-priest of Horus Lord of Kuban Khnummose' (see now Gasse and Rondot 2007, 185, 508, SEH 305; and cf. 'Priest Khnummose of Horus Lord of Kuban', perhaps the same person [Piotrovsky 1983, 72, no. 72; also 73, no. 96]); Kuckertz and Lohwasser 2016, 25-26, fig. 4; Ullmann 2019, 511, 521, 528.

[95] Černý 1947, 54, no. 11, pl. X, 2; Piotrovsky 1983, 45, 140, no. 7; Espinel 2012, 100, fig. 7.6; DRITANC III, 108-9. Though the Horus-figure in question is unidentified, there is little doubt that it represents Horus of Kuban. In the one case in the Wadi Allaki where a falcon-figure is specifically identified, with the accompanying inscription still intact, the falcon is named 'Horus Lord of Bak' (Piotrovsky 1983, 59, 169, no. 153, to which add, very probably, 59, 167, no. 151; cf. Espinel 2012, 100, fig. 7.6). For the frequency and overwhelming prevalence of the deity's mentions in the inscriptional corpus, see Piotrovsky 1983, 84 (Index).

[96] See n. 89 above.

[97] The effacement of one of the examples (no. 3) is noteworthy, as a targeted *damnatio memoriae* of this kind is relatively rare in such contexts (cf.

south, in the Wadi Tonaidba cave (KRP9),[98] the priestly title perhaps representing another, later career-progression. The inscriptions in each case are very close in style. If the scribe and priest are the same individual, it seems feasible, given the former's strong links with Kuban, that the high-priesthood in question was that of 'Horus, Lord of Kuban' (see above), though clearly there are other options, not least, in view of the temple-stela, an affiliation with Aniba.

Partly superimposed on two of the Scribe Nebnetjeru's inscriptions are the horizontal lines nos 16-17, differently sized, but identical in content, both purporting to read 'Mayor, Scribe Desnefer'. They are deeply cut and crudely done with an incongruous final sign representing a standing man, the man in in the second, lower line shown as if holding the preceding *nfr*-sign, its form patently misunderstood. Perhaps copied in part from a group of hieroglyphs at Khor el-Mediq, which includes an inscription of a 'Scribe Des',[99] nos 16-17 should be treated with caution, as they may well be relatively modern.[100]

KRP22 Jebel Nasb Enat, Rock face (Plate 15.45; CeRDO site E; Castiglioni and Castiglioni 2007, 19-20, fig. 3; Roccati 2007, 58; Davies 2014, 37-38, pls 17-18; Cooper and Vanhulle 2019, 3, Map 1, and 7); Castiglioni and Castiglioni, this volume, 49, pl. 5.6; Welsby, this volume, 157-158.

Incised into the southern cliff-face of a long sandstone hill, densely covered by rock-drawings, there are two horizontal lines of hieroglyphs located several metres apart, well above head-height (Plate 15.46), both referring to 'Herunefer'

(*H<rw>-nfr*),[101] possibly the products of separate visits.

1. On the right (the easternmost), an abbreviated offering-formula: '(Gift that) the king gives and Horus Lord of Buhen,[102] (for) priest (*ḥm-nṯr*) Herunefer' (Plate 15.47, Figure 15.22).

Plate 15.46. KRP22, recording inscription no. 1 (Photograph: Bert Verrept).

2. On the left (Plate 15.48, Figure 15.23), a title, name and filiation: 'Priest (*ḥm-nṯr*) Herunefer, son of [pri]est (*ḥm-nṯr*) [Ho]remheb'.[103] An animal drawing (a quadruped of some kind) has been partly superimposed on the father's name and title with consequent loss to parts of some of the signs but the reading is clear on *in-situ* inspection.

Plate 15.45. KRP22, rock face.

Lazaridis 2019, 596-7). The second example (no. 24) was probably the result of a subsequent visit; it is located on a different section of the rock, to the left of the main face, much higher up and well out of easy reach.

[98] See n 33 above.

[99] López 1966, 20, no. 12, pl. viii, 2 (centre); Müller 2013, 279, Tab. 2.7.6, no. 80, 411, 27.25.

[100] For an account of modern travellers and inscriptions/graffiti along the 'Korosko Road' (the section in modern Egypt), including the rendering of a name in 'hieroglyphs' dated to 1845, see Žába 1974, 118-119, figs 179-180; Malek 1984, 47, 49-50.

[101] Cf. *PN*, i, 228, 229, no. 2, 231, no. 4.

[102] For the epithet, Leitz 2002, III, 621; Ullmann 2019, 512, 521. For the toponym *Bhn* written, as here, without the final *n*, see Zibelius 1972, 109; Smith 1976, 88, 90, VII-VIII; El-Sayed 2011, 191, L 57; Brown and Darnell 2013, 131, n. 44, fig. 2; Davies 2017b, 63-64, n. 31, figs 2-3, pl. 9; Cooper 2018b, 153. This inscription represents the sole example of an offering-formula, albeit abbreviated, in this desert corpus (cf. Auenmüller, 2009b, 398; 2019c, 196), here emphasising the author's close relationship with, and dependence on, his home deity.

[103] Part of the tail of the Horus-sign survives.

Plate 15.47. KRP22, no. 1, inscription of Herunefer invoking Horus Lord of Buhen.

Figure 15.22. KRP22, no. 1, Priest Herunefer, invocation to Horus Lord of Buhen.

Plate 15.48. KRP22, no. 2, inscription of Herunefer with filiation.

Figure 15.23. KRP22, no. 2, Priest Herunefer with filiation.

KRP23. Jebel Nasb Atiliya, Cave, at base of prominent sandstone hill (Plate 15.49; CeRDO Site L; Davies 2014, 37-8, pl. 16; Cooper and Vanhulle 2019, 3, map 1; Castiglioni and Castiglioni this volume, 49, pl. 5.14; Welsby this volume, 158-163). In the interior, to the right of the cave's entrance, about 1

metre above the floor, is a single, roughly pecked, horizontal line of hieroglyphs (Plates 15.50 and 15.51) reading, right to left, 'Priest (ḥm-nṯr) Herunefer'.[104]

Plate 15.49. KRP23, cave, from north.

Plate 15.50. KRP23, interior, rock-drawings and inscription.

Plate 15.51. KRP23, inscription of Priest Herunefer.

---

[104] The two incised 'signs' to the left are not part of the inscription but probably relate to the motif above.

KRP2. Wadi Murrat/Murrat Wells, rock faces (Plate 15.52; CeRDO site M; Castiglioni *et al.* 1995, 117-8; Damiano-Appia 1999, 518-519,540, fig. 1, BM-A/1, BM-A/2, BM-B, BM-C; Andrassy 2002, 8-9; Castiglioni and Castiglioni 2006a, 407-408, figs 19-20; 2007, 22-3, fig. 6; Espinel 2012,101-102, figs 7.7 and 7.8; Klemm and Klemm 2013, 544 (6.7.3); Davies 2014, 37-39, figs 12-13, pls 19-21; Castiglioni and Castiglioni, this volume, 32-33, pl. 4.35; Welsby, this volume, 136-138).

There are two decorated areas, possibly the result of multiple visits, including hieroglyphic inscriptions and figures, pecked into the surfaces of the low sandstone hill bordering the right (east) side of the wadi. These are currently the southernmost known inscriptions in this gold-mining region.

1. The first and foremost is located on a protruding rockface, in a wooded area, at the base of the hill (Plate 15.53), where water, evidently here regarded as a gift of the god Horus, is readily accessible, just below the wadi-surface (Plates 15.54 and 15.55).[105]

Plate 15.53. KRP2, wooded area with inscribed rock faces.

Plate 15.52. KRP2, Wadi Murrat.

At the top of the rock-face (Plate 15.56, Figure 15.24) is a figure of Horus, in the form of a falcon, sun-disc on his head, standing before an altar surmounted by a lotus flower, parts of it now eroded. A column of hieroglyphs behind the figure to the left reads, 'Made by Priest Herunefer' (*ir.n ḥm-nṯr Ḥrw-nfr*).[106] Below, is a smaller, slightly disjointed inscription, arranged horizontally, reading 'Priest of Horus Herunefer' (cf. no. 2 below).

On the side of the same rock, adjacent to the inscriptions, and probably contemporary, are two further figures of Horus (Plate 15.57, Figure 15.25). One, on the right, partly

---

[105] The images, taken during a short visit in December 2018, show the results of the recent digging for water by gold-miners, who had also cut down most of the trees and damaged the hill-side, a scene of some devastation in what had previously been a relatively pristine setting.

[106] For such signatures, see comment on KRP8, no. 4, with n. 27.

Plate 15.54. KRP2, recent excavation of wadi floor by gold miners.

*Plate 15.55. KRP2, water revealed not far
beneath the wadi surface.*

anthropomorphic, is shown standing facing outwards,
sun-disc with uraeus above his head, holding a sceptre
(probably a *was*-scepter) in the front hand and a summar-
ily shaped *ankh* in the rear.[107] Before it, on a very rough
surface, is a second figure, partly eroded, in the form of
a falcon, again facing outwards, its head surmounted by
a disc or crown (the intended form now unclear).[108] The
figure is positioned so as to appear to stand on the back
of an earlier, indigenous cattle-drawing (the animal
shown with characteristic long horns), a significant
icon in its own right,[109] here partly appropriated by
the later icon.[110]

2. Located on a prominent boulder near to the top
of the same hill (Plates 15.58 and 15.59) is a horizontal
line of relatively large hieroglyphs, evidently designed
to catch the eye from the wadi below, reading 'Priest
of Horus Herunefer'.[111]

Comment

The three sets of inscription located at widely separated stations (KRP22, 23, 2) evidently mark stopping
points on the route taken by Herunefer (probably there
and back and perhaps on more than one occasion)
from Buhen, his home town, to Murrat Wells deep
in the gold-bearing region (Plates 15.2 and 15.60), a
journey of at least 170km.[112] The final station, a major

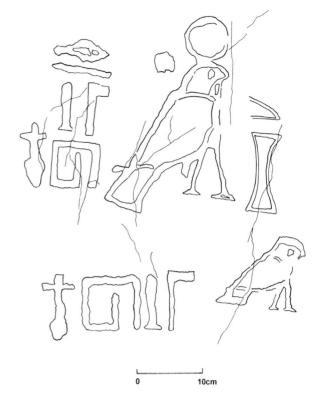

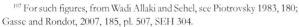

Figure 15.24. KRP2, no. 1, Priest Herunefer, figure of Horus.

*Plate 15.56. KRP2, no. 1, inscriptions of Priest Herunefer
with Horus-figure.*

source of water,[113] was also a place of special ritual import

---

[107] For such figures, from Wadi Allaki and Sehel, see Piotrovsky 1983, 180;
Gasse and Rondot, 2007, 185, pl. 507, SEH 304.

[108] Cf., for example, Piotrovsky 1983, 45, 50, 55, 62, 63 and 180. The copy
(Figure 15.25) should be regarded as provisional.

[109] The surrounding rock-faces are replete with such drawings, as they are
in other nodes, representing a symbolic 'world of cattle' for the pastoralist
communities of the region (Kleinitz 2013, 347-350; on the special importance
of bovines to Nubian ritual life, see Raue 2019a, 321; as evidenced in Kerma
royal funerary iconography and ritual, see Bonnet 2000, 76, 78, fig. 57, 85,
figs 63-64, 88, 91-93, figs 66-67, 96, 171-174, fig. 125-128; Chaix 2000, 171-
175, fig. 128; Bonnet 2014, 87-88; cf. Doyen and Gabolde 2017, 154-155).

[110] Cf. the Horus-figure, KRP8, no. 4, pl. 15.21.

[111] Unusually, the two components of the title (*ḥm nṯr*) are not transposed.

[112] Castiglioni and Castiglioni 2007, 57; cf. Cooper and Vanhulle 2019, 3,
Map 1, 4-5; Auenmüller 2019b, 406. The journey, if direct, might have taken
perhaps six days or so by donkey-caravan, assuming an average daily travel
rate of a loaded pack donkey of around 25-30km (Hendrickx, *et al.* 2013,
365-6; Köpp 2013, 109-110, 127; Köpp-Junk *et al.* 2017, 292-296). On the
use and suitability of the donkey for desert travel, see Förster *et al.* 2013.

[113] Cf. Cooper and Vanhullen 2019, 4-5; Cooper 2020, 129-130. Such a
resource does not appear to have been readily available for contemporaries
working in the Wadi Allaki, hence the attempts there at deep well-digging
(see the Ramesses II Kuban stela, PM vii, 83; KRI II, 355,1-360,6; KRITA
II, 161-163; KRITANC II, 214-216; Piotrovsky 1983, 66, no. 197, 129, and
178; Hein 1991, 13, 91; Zibelius-Chen 1994; Hikade 2001, 70; Köpp 2013,
127; Müller 2013, 41; Klemm and Klemm 2013, 294-295, 301, fig. 5.243, and
611; Cooper 2020, 132). The latter work was undertaken during a period recently characterized as one of 'significant hydrological and geomorphological
change in the Nile Valley', with generally lower Niles and increasing aridity
(Woodward *et al.* 2017, 239-240, 253-254), adverse climatic conditions held
to be at least partly responsible for what appears to have been diminishing
gold-production through the Ramesside period (cf. Vercoutter 1959, 135-137;

Plate 15.57. KRP2, no. 1, figures of Horus and native cattle-drawing.

to 'Horus, Lord of Buhen', and by another rock-inscription from Tōmas, done in his distinctive style, which reads, 'Priest Herunefer of Buhen'.[114] The name and title of his father, 'Priest Horemheb', recorded in KRP22, no. 2, is important new information. The latter is very likely the same man as the 'Second Priest of Horus, Lord of [Buhen], Horemheb', the member of a well-known family of temple-priests from Buhen with roots in the gold-working industry.[115] This Horemheb was the second son of the 'Overseer of craftsmen, overseer of the priests of all the gods, Mernodjem' (an associate of the viceroy Setau),[116] and grandson of the 'Chief goldworker (*ḥry nbyw*) Khnummose'.[117] His elder brother, another Herunefer, was 'High Priest of Horus of Buhen', 'God's scribe' and 'Mayor'.[118]

Within its domain, this well-placed Buhen

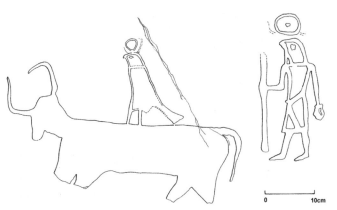

Figure 15.25. KRP2, no. 1, Horus-figures with earlier drawing.

Plate 15.59. KRP2, no. 2, inscription of Herunefer.

family is broadly comparable to the contemporary Aniba family of Hornakht (KRP8), and indeed to the earlier Djehutyhotep family based at Elephantine (KRP18, no. 5), displaying similar in-house advancement and monopoly of senior roles, across official spheres and through the generations, with the

Plate 15.58. KRP2, no. 2, boulder with inscription of Priest Herunefer.

for travellers, as signalled by Herunefer's rock 'shrine' with tableaux featuring figures of Horus, no doubt in acknowledgement of the god's benevolence, as well as by the huge quantities of native rock-drawings, already noted, on the wadi sides.

Herunefer's close connection with the temple and town of Buhen is indicated by the invocation in KPR22, no. 1,

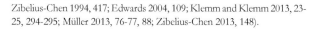

Zibelius-Chen 1994, 417; Edwards 2004, 109; Klemm and Klemm 2013, 23-25, 294-295; Müller 2013, 76-77, 88; Zibelius-Chen 2013, 148).

[114] Leclant, 1963, 21-22, pl. vi, fig. 11; 1965, 9, fig. 1; cf. Espinel 2012, 101; Auenmüller 2019b, 406. The inscription is placed directly underneath, and aligned with, an inscription of the viceroy Setau (KRI III, 101-102, 51, no. 44; KRITA III, 70; DRITANC 88-89; Raedler 2003, 142, no. 62, 155; Müller 2013, 409, 27.2).

[115] The family dominates the surviving record of the priesthood at Buhen; see Smith 1976, 203-205. On the hierarchy among the priests and other staff in the Nubian temples, including the roles accorded to well-connected females (wives, daughters, etc), see Müller 2013, 49-51, 55, 64; cf. Auenmüller 2018, 255-256.

[116] Cf. Raedler 2003, 158, 163, fig. 15.

[117] Smith 1976, 136-7, no. 1713, pls xxxiv, 4, lxxvi, 4; 145, no. 1737, pls xxxix, 1 and lxxvii, 5; 203-204, and 216; Bierbrier 1982, 23-4, pls 54-55; KRI III, 94-95, no. 26; 132-135, no. 84, III.33; KRITA III, 65, 89-91; DRITANC III, 82, 120-123; Müller 2013, 50, 185, 2.3.2, no. 32, 221, 2.5.3 B, nos 2-3, 236-237, 2.5.3 H, no. 1, 440, 38.73, 441, 38.74 and 38.80.

[118] Smith 1976, 203, 216; Bierbrier 1982, 23-4, pls 54-55, stela, second register, and bottom section, last line; KRI III, 132, no. 84, III. 33, 133, 4-5, 134, 2-3 and 14, 135, 2; DRITANC III, 121-122; Müller 2013, 221, 2.5.3 B, no. 2; Auenmüller 2013, 929, BMBuhen-03; also perhaps the same individual in the rock-inscription, 'Made by Priest, Mayor, Herunefer', at Abd el-Qadir, not far south of Buhen (where the inscription below it, done in a different style, is surely not connected); see Hintze and Reineke 1989, 34-35, no. 57, pl. 27; Müller 2013, 211, 2.5.2, no. 25; Auenmüller 2013, 936-937, BMNubien-06. For the relatively uncommon title 'God's scribe', see Al-Ayedi 2006, 558, nos 1862-63; Lazaridis 2015, 48, n. 21, 58, fig. 7; 2017, 331, n. 17, fig. 8.

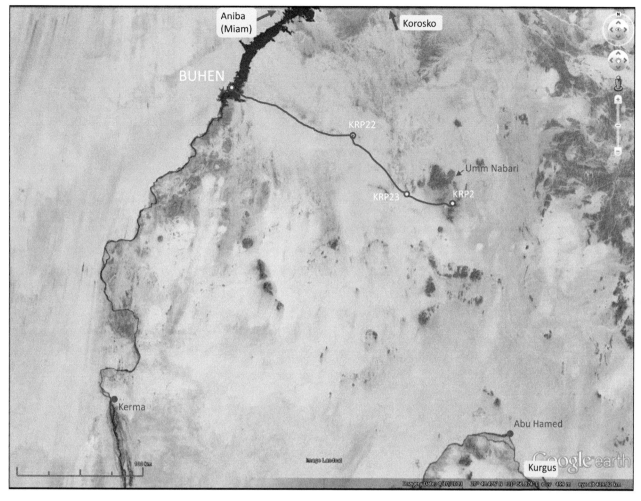

Plate 15.60. Map with possible route of Herunefer's journey(s).

business of gold-procurement remaining a core priority.[119]

CeRDO, Wadi Nesari (WN), rock-face (Plate 15.61; not included in the CeRDO map, Plate 15.1; Castiglioni *et al.* 1995, 70, top left; Castiglioni and Castiglioni 2003, 51; Castiglioni and Castiglioni 2006a, 409-410, fig. 29; 2007, 42, 44, fig. 33; Castiglioni and Castiglioni, this volume, 31-32, pl. 4.31).[120]

Located in the Wadi Nesari (near to the source of the Wadi Allaki),[121] this is the easternmost of the inscriptions in the CeRDO corpus, previously published without comment on its meaning. I include it here to complete the available record. It consists of a short horizontal line of hieroglyphs, reading right to left, representing a title and personal name, 'Deputy

Plate 15.61. Wadi Nesari, inscription of Bakenamun, with Alfredo Castiglioni (courtesy CeRDO).

Bakenamun' (*idn(w) B3k-n-'Imn*), an official otherwise not certainly attested, dating to the New Kingdom (possibly Ramesside).[122]

---

[119] Cf. Müller 2013, 55, 67: '*Die Angestellten des Schatzhauses gehörten zu der in Nubien ansässigen Beamtenschicht*', and '*Beamtenfamilien, die die wichtigsten Posten in der Provinzverwaltung innehatten und die Ämter vom Vater auf den Sohn vererbten*', citing the case, among others, of the serial occupation of Treasury-offices at Aniba by members of the family of the later Mayor and Deputy Penniut (temp. Ramesses VI; see n. 20 above). For a much earlier precedent, cf. the situation following the withdrawal of the Egyptian state from Nubia during the 13th Dynasty: 'Many colonists...for example, at Buhen, Aniba and Kuban, thrived, presumably by contracting to act as intermediaries between the Egyptian Nile Valley and Kush, and as bases for resource extraction, but now increasingly for their own benefit. At Buhen, important positions in the hierarchy were monopolised by a small circle of families over a number of generations ...' (Knoblauch 2019, 382).

[120] See above, n. 1.

[121] For the location, see Castiglioni and Castiglioni 2006a, 409, fig. 26, right; Auenmüller 2019b, 403, fig. 4.

[122] Cf. 'Deputy of the army (*idnw n mš'*), Bakenamun' (temp. Sety II; P. Anast. V, 23, 7; Gardiner 1937, 69, 14; Gnirs 1966, 152; Pamminger 2003, 29, 3.08.bis). Note that the name of a Ramesside military official 'Bakenamun'

Summary

Though problems remain, progress continues to be made in understanding these desert inscriptions and their context. Over forty individual inscriptions (some in association with figural components) have been documented to date, most of them writing the title and name of an official, a number wholly in hieroglyphs, the majority in various forms of mixed, semi-cursive script.[123] They are located in 11 different stations, all convenient stopping points along well-trodden tracks,[124] each a special node in the landscape long patronised by indigenous peoples, often already imbued with ritual or symbolic significance.[125] Over half the stations (KRP5, 9, 13, 14, 23, also CeRDO A) are caves or rock shelters of obvious potential benefit to travellers; the others (KRP2, 8, 18, 22, also CeRDO WN) offer natural camping spots (one of them near to a well, KRP2), protected by adjacent hills from the elements. All have nearby rock-surfaces suitable (to varying degrees) for decorating.[126] With regard to risk, it is increasingly clear that such travellers, no doubt proceeding in groups by donkey-caravan, were assisted, certainly during the 18th Dynasty, by an organized support system similar in principle, if on a smaller scale, to that of the Western Desert Abu Ballas trail,[127] involving the provision along the routes to the mines of 'filling stations', in the form of amphorae for storing water (there is ceramic evidence from KRP8, 9, and elsewhere, including CeRDO A, Plate 15.10).[128]

Complementing the data from related prosopographical sources, especially the Wadi Allaki, the corpus (save for KRP14) comprises a valuable if limited *in-situ* record of personnel, typically senior and middle range officials,[129] some shown as organized into hierarchical units (KRP18), involved in the administration, provisioning and protection of the Eastern Desert gold-working industry. The epigraphic distribution testifies to their considerable mobility and reach, also perhaps to some career-progression and versatility over time, with a proportion attested more than once, and from more than one source, both within the mining regions and outside (KRP5; 8; 9; 18; 2, 22-23);[130] in terms of the wider social and political context, several are also identifiable as members of, or connected to, important families with long-term vested interests in the industry and nepotistic control of much of the administrative apparatus (KRP5; 8; 18; 2, 22-23). Within the territory, the personnel 'signatures' effectively mark their zones of responsibility or their routes thereto[131] (their goal here, for the most part, the mines of the Umm Nabari massif and its surrounds, Plates 15.1 and 15.2),[132] while also, as at KRP18 (a point of major convergence), commemorating their presence and status as members through time of a kindred community. The range of core officials and functions mirrors broadly that of the Wadi Allaki corpus – scribes (by far the largest component), retainers, deputies, mayors, priests[133] – but in addition includes, among the senior field-personnel, three indigenous 'Chiefs' (KRP5; 18; CeRDO A), a 'General' in direct command of a regional troop (KRP8), and a 'High Priest' (KRP9; 18); at a lower level, it includes functionaries with a title 'man of reckoning' or similar, as yet known only from KRP18. Although all the officials have Egyptian names, it is probable that, like the 'chiefs', some among them (perhaps the majority) were ethnic Nubians/north-east Africans or of mixed heritage.[134]

Associated toponyms and other, inferred data indicate that the expeditions were despatched from important riverine centres in Lower Nubia (Wawat), namely Buhen (KRP2, 22-23), Debeira/Serra (KRP5), and especially Aniba (KRP8; 9;

---

from Buhen (listed as such in Chevereau 1994, 83, 11130), is actually to be read 'Bakenseth' (Pamminger 1997, 17; cf. Caminos 1974, 44, pl. 56, 2; Gnirs 1996, 186; Müller 2013, 164, no. 12), the same man also now attested at Dokki Gel (Bonnet and Valbelle 2018, 176, fig. 151, 180, 301, Inv. 140).

[123] So-called 'lapidary hieratic', a script 'marrying the relative speed of hieratic with the formality of hieroglyphs ... ideally suited to the requirements of expeditions in desert regions' (Darnell 2013, 808; cf. Žába 1974, 259-64).

[124] See Cooper and Vanhulle 2019, 'the presence of a phase of prehistoric rock art in many of the same nodes where one finds pharaonic inscriptions suggests that the later pharaonic tracks tapped into an indigenous network of sites and routes in the desert'; cf. Seidlmayer 2013, 209, emphasising the importance of the study of rock-inscriptions as a form of 'landscape archaeology in its full sense'; Auenmüller 2019b, 393, 406.

[125] On the Egyptian appropriation/transformation of similar focal places, see Piotrovsky 1967, 134, describing the well-spaced Wadi Allaki stations: 'grottos and rock salients', with 'rock carvings dating from various periods' and 'concentrations of inscriptions'; more generally, Edwards 2006, 58-59; Thum 2016, 75-76; Brown 2017, 170-171; Davies 2017a, 94, n. 81; 2018, 50-51; Auenmüller 2019b, 402, 404, 405-407; 2019c, 192-193, 205-206; Davies 2019, 42-43. On the widespread indigenous use of landscape features, shelters and caves as natural 'shrines', see Williams 2006.

[126] On the different techniques, broadly pecking or incising, see the summary in Auenmüller 2019b, 401; for their influence on palaeography, Žába 1974, 259-264. No trace of paint now survives within our corpus, but would surely have been present in at least some of the cases, whether for drafting or enhancing 'visual impact' (Seidlmayer 2013, 208); cf. the rock-stela at the Dal Cataract, with remains of drafting lines and internal decoration in paint (Davies 2018, 53, no. 3, fig. 11, pl. 13), the pigment's survival, albeit partial, owed to its location within a natural recess.

[127] Förster 2007; 2013; Hendrickx et al. 2013; Köpp-Junk 2015, 312-313; Köpp-Junk et al. 2017, 282; 284-285, fig. 8, 2, 292-296; cf. Darnell 2013, 820-822.

[128] See Ruffieux and Bashir 2014, 44-46; this volume, 165, 168-170, 181, KRP8, KRP9; Castiglioni and Castiglioni, this volume, 33, 48-49, pls 4.36 and 5.4; Cooper and Vanhullen 2019, 4. Add to the CeDRO and KRP material 'a deposit of what I think to be New Kingdom pots in the middle of the desert between Number 2 and Number 3 stations on the railway line from Wadi Halfa to Abu Hamed. This could be an indication of how the Egyptians managed to cross the desert: with small stores of water jars from

place to place where the expeditions could stop and refill their water skins and water their pack animals' (Vercoutter 1966, 154, n. 101; cf. Berg 1987, 8, n. 11, whose objections have been overtaken by the more recent data).

[129] On the typical exclusion of lower ranks of the work-force, including the actual labourers, from such records, see Müller 2013, 78; more generally, Köpp 2013, 120; Köpp-Junk et al. 2017, 279-280; Davies 2017a, 86, n. 56; note here Spencer et al. 2017, 32-3, on 'how little is known of the social context of mineral extraction in Nubia'.

[130] Cf. Espinel 2012, 101, with fig. 7.7; Auenmüller 2019b, 406-407.

[131] See Brown 2017, 184-187, on 'the use of rock inscriptions to delineate a professional jurisdiction'; cf. Auenmüller 2019b, 406-407.

[132] Cf. Castiglioni and Castiglioni 2003, 50- 51, fig. 2, col. pls 28-29; Cooper and Vanhulle 3-4, map 1.

[133] See the index of titles, Piotrovsky 1983, 81-83. On the enormous professional range and numbers of participants recorded for Egyptian desert expeditions generally, see the summary, Köpp 2013, 120-1.

[134] See Müller 2013, 51: '*Die Zahl der Nubier, die die Provinzverwaltung beschäftigte, war wohl grösser als aus den Texten zu schliessen ist*'; cf. Budka 2015, 70, 75-76, 80; Smith 2015, 773; Spencer 2019a, 446-447; Raue 2019b, 581. In terms of mixed heritage, note the new scientific and funerary evidence for intermarriage between the local and colonial communities at New Kingdom Tombos (Smith and Buzon 2017, 624-626; Spencer et al. 2017, 45; Smith 2018, 72; cf. Minault-Gout and Thill 2012, 415-417).

18),[135] the region's administrative headquarters.[136] There are one or two tentative links also to Kuban (KRP9; KRP18), though the latter was, of course, largely a source for the Wadi Allaki mines.[137] With one possible exception (KRP8, no. 4), there is no reference in the current corpus to any official from a town or temple in Upper Nubia (Kush proper), which is consistent with the view that the mining region of Umm Nabari was predominantly a source of the 'gold of Wawat', as opposed to the 'gold of Kush'.[138] The latter is believed to have been largely sourced from mines close to the river in Upper Nubia, extending from around Duweishat in the north of the Batn el-Hajar upstream to near the Third Cataract,[139] the operations probably overseen by officials based at the major 'temple-towns' along this reach.[140]

Almost all our rock-inscriptions are of the New Kingdom, on the basis of the surviving datable examples from the period of the co-regency of Hatshepsut/Thutmose III (KRP5; also probably KRP18, no. 5) through the later 18th/early 19th Dynasties (CeRDO A; KRP18, no. 21), to the second half of the reign of Ramesses II (KRP8, 1-3; KRP18, 10-12; KRP2,

22, 23).[141] There is one pre-New Kingdom exception, perhaps the single most important inscription in the corpus and the only 'royal' example, that of a named ruler of Kush (KRP14), a monument which surely asserts territorial hegemony during a period (Middle Kingdom/late Middle Kingdom?) of growing Kushite ascendancy in the Middle Nile Valley and beyond. It seems clear that the Egyptian exploitation of the area began in earnest after the conquest of Kush under Thutmose I of the early 18th Dynasty. It was well advanced by the period of co-regency and fully established by the sole reign of Thutmose III, when substantial quantities of the 'gold of Wawat' were secured over a period of years, as recorded in the Annals.[142] While Eastern Desert routes were certainly traversed during the New Kingdom for military purposes,[143] there is no indication from the corpus that the 'Korosko Road' caravan route, linking Korosko and Abu Hamed (and thereafter Kurgus), was used, as has been suggested, during the Thutmoside campaigns of conquest.[144] The only military presence on the route so far definitely attested, by *in situ* inscription, is of the Ramesside Period, namely that of the troop from Aniba under the command of General Hornakht (KRP8), the troop's primary brief, as suggested above, almost certainly one of protection of the mines, their product and personnel, though allied no doubt to punitive action, possibly far-reaching, when necessary.

To achieve an up-to-date detailed picture of inscriptional distribution and prosopographical content, relating to the administration and development of the colonial gold-industry,

---

[135] See Vercoutter 1959, 146-7, noting the wide range of gold-workers attested from tombs at Aniba; cf. Näser 2017, 562-3; Spencer 2019b, 113. It is suggested that expeditions from Aniba might have departed from the east bank in the region of Toshka, cutting across the desert, along the Wadi Hamid, to join a major east-west track at roughly the point marked by Hekanefer's shelter, CeRDO A, with the option of proceeding south-eastwards to the Khashm el-Bab and thence south to Umm Nabari; see Castiglioni *et al.* 1995, 112, Map [itinerario C], and 120; Damiano-Appia 1999, 513-514, fig. 1.

[136] The seat of the 'Deputy of Wawat' for most of the New Kingdom, Aniba was also the location, from at least the early Ramesside period, of the Nubian Treasury (Müller 2013, 12, 44, 50, 55-56, 91; cf. Zibelius 1972, 122; Hein 1991, 27-29; Hikade 2001, 71; Raedler 2003, 161-162; Zibelius-Chen 2013, 142-3; Thill 2013-2015; Budka 2015, 73; Spencer *et al.* 2017, 28; Spencer 2019a, 446). A list of Deputies is included in Müller 2013, 197-206, nos 1-30, from which no. 1, Hori (Müller 2013, 169, 2.2.2. A 10), should be deleted (see Davies 2014, 41-42, pl. 25; 2017b, 66-67, fig. 5, pl. 13). To be added to the list is Djehutymose, Deputy under Viceroy Merymose (Piotrovsky 1983, 52, no. 81; Klotz and Brown 2016, 293-296), and possibly Py, probably a near-contemporary (Piotrovsky 1983, 52, no. 85; Mahfouz 2005, 69).

[137] Zibelius 1972, 111-112; Hein 1991, 12-16; Giddy 1998, 35; Klemm and Klemm 2013, 294-295; 2017, 267.

[138] Vercoutter 1959, 128-130, map 2; Zibelius-Chen 1988, 76-77; Hikade 2001, 92-3; Klemm and Klemm 2013, 24-5; Klemm and Klemm 2017, 260-261, fig. 1; cf. Müller 2013, 75-6 and 354.

[139] Klemm and Klemm 2013, 556-579; 2017, 261-2, fig. 1; cf. Edwards 2004, 106-107; Spence *et al.* 2009; Minault-Gout and Thill 2012, 417-418; Edwards and Mills 2013, 8, fig. 1, 10-11, fig. 3, 16; Budka 2015, 65; P. Spencer 1997, 106, pl. 81, d; Spencer 2015, 202, n. 34; McLean 2017; Spencer *et al.* 2017, 32; Budka 2019, 21; Spencer 2019a, 453; Edwards and Mills 2020, 398-407.

[140] Klemm and Klemm 2017, 266; cf. Vieth 2018. For the attestation of gold-working officials at Soleb, Sai and Amara West, see the prosopographical overview, Auenmüller 2018, 242-243, Table 1, T 26 (Sai), 245, 247, Table 2, Doc. 2.39, and 255 (Sai), 247-248, Table 3, T 38 (Soleb), and 251-254, Table 7, Doc. 7.7, and 255 (Amara West), the first and third officials dated to the mid-to later 18th Dynasty, the second and fourth to the 19th Dynasty; see, further on Sai, Budka 2018a, 113, 123; 2018b, 189-191, fig. 6, 193; on Amara West, Spencer 2019b, 101, 112-113, 120-121, cat. no. 2, fig. 17; for an 18th Dynasty attestation from Tombos, see references above (KRP8, no. 4, with n. 30). Note also that gold-personnel and the transport of gold by ship are mentioned in the Nauri stela of Sety I (KRI I, 50, l.14, 52, l. 8, and 56, l. 8; KRITA I, 44, 45, and 48; cf. Vercoutter 1959, 137, 142-143, 147; Brand 2000, 295; Müller 2013, 77-78). It is possible that the Batn el-Hajar gold-workings operated under the purview of Wawat officialdom, at least during the Thutmoside period. The Djehutyhotep family of treasury officials is well attested in the region (see KRP18, no. 5, comment), with the father, Sen-Djehuty, a 'Scribe reckoner of Wawat' (Hintze 1989, I, 37, no. 62), recorded as far south as the Dal Cataract (Davies 2018, 52-53, fig. 10, pls 11-12).

[141] By comparison, on current datable evidence, the earliest New Kingdom inscriptions in the Wadi Allaki are those of Merymose, viceroy of Amenhotep III (Piotrovsky 1983, 51, 153, no. 74, 51, no 82, 52, no. 81 [for the reading, Klotz and Brown 2016, 293-295, with n. 170]; 64, no. 180, 65, no. 189; cf. Hikade 2001, 69-71, 259-260, nos 224-269: '*Die Inschriften aus dem Wadi Allaki … umspannen einen Zeitraum von der Regierungzeit Amenophis' III. bis in die 19./20. Dynastie*'. On the military motives for Merymose's presence in Wadi Allaki, see Zibelius-Chen 1994, 413; Klotz and Brown 2016, 295-296; cf. Cooper 2020, 129. There is no reason to doubt that the exploitation of the Umm Nabari region, like that of the Wadi Allaki, continued beyond the 19th Dynasty, though, as already noted above, with apparently diminishing returns (see n. 113).

[142] See *Urk.* iv, 709, 6; 721,3; 728, 12; 734,3; Hikade 2001, 71, 92-3, Table 3; cf. Spalinger 2006, 365; Klemm and Klemm 2013, 11, 23-25, 608-609, fig. 7.4, 610; 2017, 260-261, fig. 1; 2018, 61-62; Spencer *et al.*, 2017, 30, 32. On the further general intensification of Eastern Desert gold exploitation under Amenhotep III, directed by Merymose, see Zibelius-Chen 1994, 415-417; Darnell 2013, 828; Morkot 2013, 938; Zibelius-Chen 2013, 148; Brown 2017, 178ff.

[143] See Zibelius-Chen 1994, 412-417, 2007, 404-405; 2014, 294-295, on campaigns against the desert regions of Ibhet, Ikyt and Irem; cf. Raedler 2009, 334; Davies 2017a, 73-75, 97; and recently on the toponyms, Cooper 2020, 125-136, and 383.

[144] On the mainly riverine route of the Thutmose I campaign on its way to Kurgus, south of Abu Hamed (in the land of Miu), see Davies 2017a, 93-6, fig. 36. Note that New Kingdom inscriptions have yet to be identified anywhere along the northernmost section of the caravan route (about 100km in length) between Korosko and the Khashm el-Bab. For rock-inscriptions of Middle Kingdom travellers located on the route 'about 16 kilometres south of Korosko', see Žába 1974, 117-119, nos 78-80, and Malek 1984, 50, who cautions: 'they do not necessarily prove that the caravan route was used by them at that time'; cf. Berg 1987, 8, n. 11; Cooper 2020, 133, n. 122. The route or routes by which the much-discussed military drummer Emhab of Edfu, dating from the late Second Intermediate Period, reached Miu, while on campaign, remain a matter of speculation, though the possibility that a desert-crossing (surely not the entire length of the Korosko Road) occurred at some point (perhaps from Buhen) should not be discounted (for bibliography, see Davies 2017a, 94, n. 80, adding Cooper 2018b, 146; 2020, 381-2).

as well as to military and related matters, including the acquisition of other kinds of resource, it remains to integrate these data with those obtained from similar work elsewhere, in the adjacent Batn el-Hajar and other such areas, where epigraphic survey has recently resumed and is making positive progress in documenting the records of itinerant parties.[145] Ideally, the Wadi Allaki corpus and archive should also be revisited in detail, not to mention the Wadi itself (and its tributaries), the south-eastern reaches of which remain above water and potentially accessible.[146] With regard to the Sudanese Eastern Desert routes, one might suggest that in such a vast area there is certainly more to be discovered.[147] Although the current mining activity is creating serious difficulties, it is to be hoped that, with the co-operation of NCAM, additional desert surveys (both epigraphic and archaeological), further building on the pioneering efforts of CeRDO, and those of Klemm and Klemm, might take to the field sometime in the near future. Such work is needed now more than ever.

Bibliography

Al-Ayedi, A. R. 2006. *Index of Egyptian Administrative, Religious and Military Titles of the New Kingdom*. Ismailia.

Anderson, J. R. and D. A. Welsby (eds) 2014. *The Fourth Cataract and Beyond. Proceedings of the 12th International Conference for Nubian Studies*. British Museum Publications on Egypt and Sudan 1. Leuven – Paris – Walpole, MA.

Andrassy, P. 2002. 'Zu einigen neuen expedition inschriften aus der nubischen Ostwüste', *Göttinger Miszellen* 186, 7-16.

Arpagaus, D. 2015. 'Fuzzy Boundaries in Nubien? Eine merkwürdige Art zur Angabe von Ackerflachen im Grab des Penniut von Aniba', in H. Amstutz, A. Dorn, M. Müller, M. Ronsdorf and S. Uljas (eds), *Fuzzy Boundaries: Festschrift für Antonio Loprieno*. Hamburg, 463-493.

Auenmüller, J. 2013. *Die Territorialität der Ägyptischen Elite(n) des Neuen Reiches. Eine Studie zum Raum und räumlichen Relationen im textlichen Diskurs, anhand prosografischer Daten und im archäologischen Record*. Unpublished PhD dissertation. Berlin.

Auenmüller, J. 2018. 'New Kingdom Towns in Upper Nubia: Sai, Soleb and Amara West in prosopographical perspective', in Budka and Auenmüller (eds), 239-260.

Auenmüller, J. 2019a. 'Topography and Regional Geography of Nubia: River, Cataract and Desert Landscapes', in Raue (ed.), I, 39-61.

Auenmüller, J. 2019b. 'Pharaonic Rock Inscriptions in Nubia – The 3rd and 2nd Millennia BC', in Raue (ed.), I, 393-412.

Auenmüller, J. 2019c. 'Epigraphical Dialogues with the Landscape – New Kingdom rock inscriptions in Upper Nubia', in N. Staring, H. Twiston Davies and L. Weiss (eds), *Perspectives on Lived Religion. Practices – Transmission – Landscape*. PALMA: Papers on Archaeology of the Leiden Museum of Antiquities 21. Leiden, 191-206.

Berengeur, F. 2003. 'Estela', in *Fundación "la Caixa"* (ed.), *Nubia: los reinos del Nilo en Sudán*. Barcelona, 187, no. 105.

Berg, D. A. 1987. 'Early 18th Dynasty expansion into Nubia', *Journal of the Society for the Study of Egyptian Antiquities* 17, 1-14.

Bierbrier, M. L. (ed.) 1982. *The British Museum. Hieroglyphic Texts from Egyptian Stelae etc, Part 10*. London.

Bonnet, C., avec la collaboration de D. Valbelle 2000. *Edifices et rites funéraires à Kerma*. Mission archéologique de l'Université de Genève à Kerma (Soudan). Paris.

Bonnet, C. 2007. 'Kerma et l'exploitation des mines d'or', *Bulletin de la Société Française d'Égyptologie* 169-170, 59-61.

Bonnet, C. 2014. 'Forty years research on Kerma cultures', in Anderson and Welsby (eds), 81-93.

Bonnet, C. and D. Valebelle 2018. *Les Temples Égyptiens de Panébès "Le Jujubier" à Doukki Gel – Soudan*. Paris.

Borla, M. 2010. 'Le iscrizioni di epoca faraonica', in S. Curto (ed.), *Lo Speos di Ellesija. Un Tempio della Nubia salvato dale Acque del Lago Nasser*. Turin, 69-104.

Brand, P. J. 2000. *The Monuments of Seti I: epigraphic, historical and art historical analysis*. Probleme der Ägyptologie 16. Leiden.

Brown, M. W. 2017. 'Agents of Construction: Ancient Egyptian Rock Inscriptions as Tools of Site Formation and Modern Functional Parallels', *Journal of Egyptian History* 10, 153-211.

Brown, M. W. and J. C. Darnell 2013. 'Review of *Pharaonic Inscriptions from the Southern Eastern Desert of Egypt* by R. D. Rothe, W. K. Miller and G. Rapp (Winona Lake, 2008)', *Journal of Near Eastern Studies* 72, 125-137.

Budka, J. 2015. 'The Egyptian "Re-conquest of Nubia" in the New Kingdom – Some Thoughts on the Legitimization of Pharaonic Power in the South', in F. Coppens, J. Janák, and H. Vymazalová (eds), *7. Symposion zur ägyptischen Konigsideologie, Royal versus Divine Authority: Acquisition, Legitimization and Renewal of Power, Prague, June 26-28, 2013*. Wiesbaden, 63-81.

Budka, J. 2018a. 'AcrossBorders: five seasons of work in the Pharaonic town, Sai Island', in Budka and Auenmüller (eds), 113-126.

Budka, J. 2018b. 'Tomb 26 in Cemetery SAC5 on Sai Island', in Budka and Auenmüller (eds), 185-196.

Budka, J. and J. Auenmüller (eds) 2018. *From Microcosm to Macrocosm: Individual households and cities in Ancient Egypt and Nubia*. Leiden.

Budka, J., with contributions by G. D'Ercole, C. Geiger, V. Hinterhuber and M. Scheiblecker 2019. 'Towards Middle Nile Biographies: the Munich University Attab to Ferka Survey Project 2018/2019', *Sudan & Nubia* 23, 13-26.

Caminos, R. A. 1968. *The Shrines and Rock-Inscriptions of Ibrim*. Egypt Exploration Society, Archaeological Survey of Egypt 32. London.

Caminos, R. A. 1974. *The New-Kingdom Temples of Buhen*. Vol. I. Egypt Exploration Society, Archaeological Survey of Egypt 33. London.

Cannyuer, C. 2010. *La girafe dans l'Égypte ancienne et le verbe sr: Étude de lexicographie et de symbolique animalière*. Acta Orientalia Belgica - Subsidia IV. Belgian Society of Oriental Studies. Bruxelles.

Castiglioni, A. and A. Castiglioni 1994. 'Discovering Berenice Panchrysos', *Egyptian Archaeology* 4, 19-22.

Castiglioni, A. and A. Castiglioni 2003, 'Pharaonic Inscriptions along the Eastern Desert Routes in Sudan', *Sudan & Nubia* 7, 47-51.

Castiglioni, A. and A. Castiglioni 2006a. 'The new discoveries along the route Korosko-Kurgus', in I. Caneva and A. Roccati (eds), *Acta Nubica: Proceedings of the X International Conference of Nubian Studies, Rome, 9-14 September 2002*. Rome, 401-410.

Castiglioni, A. and A. Castiglioni 2006b. *Nubia, Magica Terra Millenaria*. Firenze.

Castiglioni, A. and A. Castiglioni 2007. 'Les pistes millénaires du désert oriental de Nubie', *Bulletin de la Société Française d'Égyptologie* 169-170, 17-49.

---

[145] Davies 2008; 2009; 2012; 2014, 39-42; 2017a; 2017b; 2018; 2019; Auenmüller 2019b, 395; Davies in Edwards and Mills 2020, 352-354, 358-363.

[146] Giddy 1998; Klemm and Klemm 2013, 294-339; Klemm, Klemm and Murr 2019, 25-26, fig. 4.

[147] See already Cooper 2019; Cooper and Vanhulle 2019, 3: 'New fieldwork in this desert has the potential to expose many new sites and change our view on both the ancient indigenous nomads of the region as well as their relationship with the urban sites of Egypt and Nubia'.

Castiglioni, A., A. Castiglioni and J. Vercoutter 1995. *L'Eldorado dei Faraoni.* Novara.

Castiglioni, A., A. Castiglioni and G. Negro 1999. 'The ancient gold route from Buhen to Berenice Panchrysos', in S. Wenig (ed.), *Studien zum antiken Sudan. Akten der 7. Internationalen Tagung für meroitistische Forschungen von 14. bis 19. September 1992 in Gosen/ bei Berlin.* Meroitica 15. Wiesbaden, 501-510.

Castiglioni, A., A. Castiglioni, and C. Bonnet 2010. 'The gold mines of the Kingdom of Kerma', in W. Godlewski and A. Łajtar (eds), *Between the Cataracts. Proceedings of the 11ᵗʰ Conference for Nubian Studies. Vol. 2.* Warsaw, 263-70.

Černý, J. 1947. 'Graffiti at the Wādi El-'Allāḳi', *Journal of Egyptian Archaeology* 33, 52-57.

Chaix, L. 2000. 'La faune des peintures murales du temple K XI', in Bonnet, 163-175.

Chevereau, P.-M. 1994. *Prosopographie des cadres militaires égyptiens du Nouvel Empire.* Études et Mémoires d'Égyptologie 3. Paris.

Connor, S. 2019. 'Killing or "De-activating" Egyptian statues: who mutilated them, when, and why?', in Masson-Berghoff (ed.), 281-302.

Cooper, J. 2018a. 'The African Topographical Lists of the New Kingdom and the Historical Geography of Nubia in the Second Millennium BCE', in M. Honneger (ed.), *Nubian archaeology in the XX1ˢᵗ century: Proceedings of the Thirteenth International Conference for Nubian Studies, Neuchâtel, 1ˢᵗ -6ᵗʰ September 2014.* Publications de la Mission Archéologique Suisse à Kerma I. Orientalia Lovaniensia Analecta 273. Leuven-Paris-Bristol, CT, 669-680.

Cooper, J. 2018b. 'Kushites expressing "Egyptian" kingship: Nubian dynasties in hieroglyphic texts and a phantom Kushite king', *Ägypten und Levante* 28, 143-167.

Cooper, J. 2019. 'Into the desert', *Current World Archaeology* 98, 10-11.

Cooper, J. 2020. *Toponymy on the periphery: Placenames of the Eastern Desert, Red Sea, and South Sinai in Egyptian documents from the Early Dynastic until the end of the New Kingdom.* Probleme der Ägyptologie 39. Leiden.

Cooper, J. and D. Vanhulle 2019. 'Boats and Routes: New Rock Art in the Atbai Desert', *Sudan & Nubia* 23, 3-12.

Damiano-Appia, M. 1999. 'Inscriptions along the Tracks from Kubban, Buhen and Kumma to "Berenice Panchrysos" and to the South', in S. Wenig (ed.), *Studien zum antiken Sudan. Akten der 7. Internationalen Tagung für meroitistische Forschungen von 14. bis 19. September 1992 in Gosen/ bei Berlin.* Meroitica 15. Wiesbaden, 511-542.

Darnell, J. C. 2013. 'A bureaucratic challenge? Archaeology and administration in a desert environment (Second millennium B.C.E.)', in Moreno García (ed.), 787-830.

Davies, W. V. 2003a. 'Sobeknakht of Elkab and the coming of Kush', *Egyptian Archaeology* 23, 3-6.

Davies, W. V. 2003b. 'Kush in Egypt: a new historical inscription', *Sudan & Nubia* 7, 52-54.

Davies, W. V. 2004a. 'Stone Vessel', in Welsby and Anderson (eds), 101, no. 75.

Davies, W. V. 2004b. 'Statuette of Amenemhat'. 'Stela of Amenemhat', in Welsby and Anderson (eds), 104-105, nos. 77-78.

Davies, W. V. 2005. 'Egypt and Nubia. Conflict with the Kingdom of Kush', in C. R. Roehrig with R. Dreyfus and C. A. Keller (eds), *Hatshepsut from Queen to Pharaoh.* New York, 49-56.

Davies, W. V. 2008. 'Tombos and the Viceroy Inebny/Amenemnekhu', *Sudan & Nubia* 12, 25-33.

Davies, W. V. 2009. 'The British Museum epigraphic survey at Tombos: the stela of Usersatet and Hekaemsasen', *Sudan & Nubia* 13, 21-29.

Davies, W. V. 2010. 'Renseneb and Sobeknakht of Elkab: the genealogical data', in M. Marée (ed.), *The Second Intermediate Period (Thirteenth-Seventeenth Dynasties): Current Research, Future Prospects.* Orientalia Lovaniensia Analecta 192. Leuven – Paris – Walpole, MA, 223-240.

Davies, W. V. 2012. 'Merymose and others at Tombos', *Sudan & Nubia* 16, 29-36.

Davies, W. V. 2014. 'The Korosko Road Project: Recording Egyptian inscriptions in the Eastern Desert and elsewhere', *Sudan & Nubia* 18, 30-44.

Davies, W. V. 2017a. 'Nubia in the New Kingdom: the Egyptians at Kurgus', in N. Spencer, A. Stevens and M. Binder (eds), *Nubia in the New Kingdom: Lived experience, pharaonic control and indigenous traditions.* British Museum Publications on Egypt and Sudan 3. Leuven – Paris – Bristol, CT, 65-105.

Davies, W. V. 2017b. 'Recording Egyptian rock-inscriptions at Jebel Dosha and in the Batn el-Hajar, the 2016 season', *Sudan & Nubia* 21, 59-70.

Davies, W. V. 2018. 'Egyptian rock-inscriptions at Tombos and the Dal Cataract: the epigraphic survey, season 2017', *Sudan & Nubia* 22, 46-54.

Davies, W. V. 2019. 'Egyptian rock-inscriptions at Tombos, Debba and Sabu: the epigraphic survey, season 2018', *Sudan & Nubia* 23, 33-45.

Davies, W. V. and I. Welsby Sjöström 2016. 'Recording Jebel Dosha: the Chapel of Thutmose III', *Sudan & Nubia* 20, 18-27.

De Bruyn, P. 1956. 'A graffito of the scribe DÓutÓotpe, reckoner of gold, in the south-eastern desert', *Journal of Egyptian Archaeology* 42, 121-122.

De Morgan, J., U. Bouriant, G. Legrain, G. Jéquier, and A. Barsanti 1894. *Catalogue des monuments et inscriptions de l'Égypte Antique. Première Série: Haute Égypte, I. De la frontière de Nubie à Kom Ombo.* Vienne.

Dewachter, M. 1971. 'Nubie – Notes Diverses', *Bulletin de l'Institut français d'archéologie orientale* 70, 83-117.

Dewachter, M. 1978. *Repertoire des monuments des vice-rois de Kouch (De la reconquête ahmoside à la mort de Ramsès II).* 2 vols. Unpublished doctoral thesis, Paris IV-Sorbonne. Paris.

Doyen, F. and L. Gabolde 2017. 'Egyptians versus Kushites: the cultural question of writing or not', in Spencer *et al.* (eds), 149-158.

Dziobek, E. 1992. *Das Grab des Ineni: Theben Nr. 81.* Archäologische Veröffentlichungen 68. Mainz am Rhein.

Edel, E., K.-J. Seyfried, and G. Vieler 2008. *Die Felsgräbernekropole der Qubbet el-Hawa bei Assuan, I. Abteilung, Band 2. Architektur, Darstellungen, Texte, archäologischer Befund und Funde der Gräber QH 35l.* Paderborn – München – Wien – Zurich.

Edwards, D. N. 2004. *The Nubian Past. An Archaeology of the Sudan.* London; New York.

Edwards, D. N. 2006. 'Drawings on rocks, the most enduring monuments of Middle Nubia', *Sudan & Nubia* 10, 55-63.

Edwards, D. N. and A. J. Mills 2013. '"Pharaonic" Sites in the Batn el-Hajar—"the Archaeological Survey of Sudanese Nubia" Revisited', *Sudan & Nubia* 17, 8-17.

Edwards, D. N. and A. J. Mills 2020. Edited by D. N. Edwards. *The Archaeological Survey of Sudanese Nubia 1963-69. The Pharaonic sites.* Sudan Archaeological Research Society Publication Number 23. Oxford

El-Sayed, R. 2004. ''r' n Md3.iw – lingua blemmyica – tu-beḏawiɛ. Ein Sprachkontinuum im Areal der nubischen Ostwüste und seine (sprach-) historischen Implikationen', *Studien zur Altägyptischen Kultur* 32, 351-362.

El-Sayed, R. 2011. *Afrikanischstämmiger Lehnwortschatz im älteren Ägyptisch. Untersuchungen zur ägyptisch-afrikanischen lexikalischen Interferenz im dritten und zweiten Jahrtausend v. Chr.* Orientalia Lovaniensia Analecta 211. Leuven – Paris – Walpole, MA.

Espinel, A. D. 2012. 'Gods in the Red Land: Development of Cults and Religious Activities in the Eastern Desert', in H. Barnard and K. Duistermaat (eds), *The History of the Peoples of the Eastern Desert.* University of California, Cotsen Institute of Archaeology, Monograph 73. Los Angeles, 91-102.

Faulkner, R. O. 1962. *Concise Dictionary of Middle Egyptian.* Oxford.

Firth, C. M. 1927. *The Archaeological Survey of Nubia: Report for 1910-1911.* Survey of Egypt. Cairo.

Fitzenreiter, M. 2004. 'Identität als Bekenntnis und Anspruch – Notizien zum Grab des Pennut (Teil IV)', *Der antike Sudan: Mitteilungen der Sudanarchäologischen Gesellschaft zu Berlin e.V.* 15, 169-193.

Fitzenreiter, M. 2012. 'Ein Siegelstempel aus Elephantine', *Mitteilungen des Deutschen Archäologischen Instituts Abteilung Kairo* 68, 43-54.

Förster, F. 2007. 'With donkeys, jars and water bags into the Libyan Desert: the Abu Ballas trail in the late Old Kingdom/First Intermediate Period', *British Museum Studies in Ancient Egypt and Sudan* 7, 1-36.

Förster, F. 2013. 'Beyond Dakhla: The Abu Ballas Trail in the Libyan Desert (SW Egypt)', in Förster and Riemer (eds), 297-337.

Förster, F. and H. Riemer (eds) 2013. *Desert Road Archaeology in Ancient Egypt and Beyond.* Africa Praehistorica 27. Köln.

Förster, F., H. Riemer and M. Mahir 2013. 'Donkeys to El-Fasher or how the present informs the past', in Förster and Riemer (eds), 193-218.

Forstner-Müller, I. and N. Moeller (eds) 2018. *The Hyksos Ruler Khyan and the Early Second Intermediate Period in Egypt: Problems and Priorities of Current Research. Proceedings of the Workshop of the Austrian Archaeological Institute and the Oriental Institute of the University of Chicago, Vienna, July 4-5, 2014.* Ergänzungshefte zu den Jahresheften des Österreichischen Archäologischen Institutes, 17. Vienna.

Franke, D. 2010. '"When the sun goes down …" – early solar hymns on a pyramidion stela from the reign of Sekhemra-shedtawy Sobekemsaf', in M. Marée (ed.), *The Second Intermediate Period (Thirteenth-Seventeenth Dynasties): Current Research, Future Prospects.* Orientalia Lovaniensia Analecta 192. Leuven – Paris – Walpole, MA, 283-302.

Gabolde, L. 2018. 'Insight into the perception of royal and divine powers among Kushites and Egyptians', in Honneger (ed.), 91-103.

Gardiner, A. H. 1937. *Late Egyptian Miscellanies.* Bibliotheca Aegyptiaca VII. Bruxelles.

Gasse, A. and V. Rondot 2007. *Les inscriptions de Séhel.* Mémoires publiés par les membres de l'Institut français d' archéologie orientale du Caire 126. Cairo.

Giddy, L. 1998. 'The 1998 survey of the Wadi Allaqi and its tributaries', *Bulletin of the Australian Centre for Egyptology* 9, 35-41.

Gnirs, A. M. 1996. *Militär und Gesellschaft: Ein Beitrag zur Sozialgeschichte des Neuen Reiches.* Studien zur Archäologie und Geschichte Altägyptens, 21. Heidelberg.

Gnirs, A. 2009. 'Ägyptische Militärgeschichte als Kultur- und Sozialgeschichte', in Gundlach and Vogel (eds), 67-141.

Gnirs, A. M. 2013. 'Coping with the army: the Military and the State in the New Kingdom', in Moreno García (ed.), 639-717.

Gratien, B. 2019. *Mirgissa V. Les empreintes de sceaux: Aperçu sur l'administration de la Basse Nubie au Moyen Empire.* Fouilles de l'Ifao 80. Cairo.

Griffith, F. Ll. 1929. 'Oxford Excavations in Nubia', *Liverpool Annals of Archaeology and Anthropology* 8, 1-104.

Gundlach, R. and C. Vogel (eds) 2009. *Militärgeschichte des pharaonischen Ägypten. Altägypten und seine Nachbarkulturen im Spiegel aktueller Forschung.* KRiG 34. Paderborn-München-Wien-Zürich.

Hall, H. R. H. 1925. *Hieroglyphic Texts from Egyptian Stelae etc in the British Museum, Part 7.* London.

Hannig, R. 2006. *Grosses Handwörterbuch Ägyptisch-Deutsch (2800-950 v. Chr.).* Marburger Edition. Mainz.

Hein, I. 1991. *Die Ramessidische Bautätigkeit in Nubien.* Göttinger Orientforschungen IV. Reihe: Ägypten. Band 22. Wiesbaden.

Helck, W. 1967. 'Eine Briefsammlung aus der Verwaltung des Amuntempels', *Journal of the American Research Center in Egypt* 6, 135-151.

Hendrickx, S., F. Förster and M. Eyckerman 2013. 'The Pharaonic pottery of the Abu Ballas Trail: "Filling stations" along a desert highway in southwestern Egypt', in Förster and Riemer (eds), 339-379.

Hikade, T. 2001. *Das Expeditionswesen im ägyptischen Neuen Reich. Ein Beitrag zu Rohstoffversorgung und Aussenhandel.* Studien zur Archäologie und Geschichte Altägyptens 21. Heidelberg.

Hintze, F. and W. F. Reineke 1989. *Felsinschriften aus dem sudanesischen Nubien.* Publikation der Nubien-expedition 1961-1963, Band 1. 2 parts. Berlin.

Honneger, M. (ed.) 2018. *Nubian archaeology in the XXIst century: Proceedings of the Thirteenth International Conference for Nubian Studies, Neuchâtel, 1st-6th September 2014.* Publications de la Mission Archéologique Suisse à Kerma 1. Orientalia Lovaniensia Analecta 273. Leuven – Paris – Bristol, CT.

Ilin-Tomich, I. 2014. 'The Theban kingdom of Dynasty 16: Its rise, administration and politics', *Journal of Egyptian History* 7, 143-193.

Ilin-Tomich, A. 2016. 'Second Intermediate Period', *UCLA Encyclopedia of Egyptology.* http://escholarship.org/uc/item/72q561r2

Jacquet-Gordon, H. 1981. 'Graffiti from the region of Gerf Hussein', *Mitteilungen des Deutschen Archäologischen Instituts Abteilung Kairo* 37, 227-240.

Kawai, N. 2015. 'The Administrators and Notables in Nubia under Tutankhamun', in R. Jasnow and K. M. Cooney (eds), *Joyful in Thebes: Egyptological Studies in Honor of Betsy M. Bryan.* Material and Visual Culture of Ancient Egypt 1. Atlanta, 309-322.

Kleinitz, C. 2013. 'Bilder der Vergangenheit: Die Felskunst des Mittleren Niltals', in S. Wenig and K. Zibelius-Chen (eds), *Die Kulturen Nubiens – ein afrikanisches Vermächtnis.* Dettelbach, 341-359.

Klemm, R. and D. Klemm 2013. *Gold and Gold Mining in Ancient Egypt and Nubia. Geoarchaeology of the Ancient Gold Mining Sites in the Egyptian and Sudanese Eastern Deserts.* Berlin; Heidelberg.

Klemm, D. and R. Klemm 2017. 'New Kingdom and Early Kushite Gold Mining in Nubia', in Spencer *et al.* (eds), 259-270.

Klemm, D. and R. Klemm 2018. 'Ancient Gold Mining Settlements in the Eastern Deserts of Egypt and Nubia', in Budka and Auenmüller (eds), 59-66.

Klemm, D., R. Klemm and A. Murr 2019. 'Geologically induced raw materials stimulating the development of Nubian culture', in Raue (ed.), I, 15-38.

Klotz, D. and M. W. Brown 2016. 'The enigmatic statuette of Djehutymose (MFA 24.743): Deputy of Wawat and Viceroy of Kush', *Journal of the American Research Center in Egypt* 52, 269-302.

Knoblauch, C. 2012. 'The Ruler of Kush (Kerma) at Buhen during the Second Intermediate Period: A Reinterpretation of Buhen

Stela 691 and related Objects', in C. M. Knoblauch and J. C. Gill (eds), *Egyptology in Australia and New Zealand 2009. Proceedings of the Conference held in Melbourne, September 4th-6th*. BAR International Series 2355. Oxford.

Knoblauch, C. 2019. 'Middle Kingdom Fortresses', in Raue (ed.), I, 367-391.

Koenig, Y. 1990. 'Les textes d'envoûtement de Mirgissa', *Revue d'Égyptologie* 41, 101-125.

Köpp, H. 2013. 'Desert travel and transport in ancient Egypt. An overview based on epigraphic, pictorial and archaeological evidence', in Förster and Riemer (eds), 107-132.

Köpp-Junk, H. 2015. *Reisen im Alten Ägypten: Reisekultur, Fortbewegungs- und Transportmittel in pharaonischer Zeit*. Göttinger Orientforschungen IV. Reihe: Ägypten 55. Wiesbaden.

Köpp-Junk, H., H. Riemer and F. Förster 2017. 'Mobility in Ancient Egypt – Roads and Travel in the Nile Valley and Adjacent Deserts', in S. Scharl and B. Gehlen (eds), *Mobility in Prehistoric Sedentary Societies. Papers of the CRC 806 Workshop in Cologne 26-27 June 2015*. Kölner Studien zur Prähistorischen Archäologie 8. Rahden/Westf.

Kormysheva, E. 1996. 'Kulte der ägyptischen Götter des Neuen Reiches in Kusch', in M. Schade-Busch (ed.), *Wege öffnen: Festschrift für Rolf Gundlach zum 65. Geburtstag*. Wiesbaden, 133-148.

Kormysheva, E. 2013. 'Der Gott Horus in den nubischen Tempeln der 18. Dynastie', in H. Beinlich (ed.), *9. Ägyptologische Tempeltagung Kultabbildung und Kultrealitat. Hamburg, 27. September – 1.Oktober 2011*. Wiesbaden, 147-174.

Kuckertz, J. and A. Lohwasser 2016. *Einführung in die Religion von Kusch*. Dettelbach.

Lakomy, K. C. 2016. *"Der Löwe auf dem Schlachtfeld". Das Grab KV 36 und die Bestattung des Maiherperi im Tal der Könige*. Wiesbaden.

Lazaridis, N. 2015. 'Amun-Ra, lord of the sky: A deity for travellers of the western desert', *British Museum Studies in Ancient Egypt and Sudan* 22, 43-60.

Lazaridis, N. 2017. 'Carving out identities in the Egyptian desert: self-presentation styles adopted by the ancient travelers of Kharga Oasis', in G. Rosati and M. C. Guidotti (eds), *Proceedings of the XI International Congress of Egyptologists, Florence Egyptian Museum, Florence, 23-30 August 2015*. Archaeopress Egyptology 19. Oxford, 328-332.

Lazaridis, N. 2019. 'Carving the deserts: ancient travellers' epigraphic uses of Kharga Oasis rock surfaces', in M. Brose, P. Dils, F. Naether, L. Popko and D. Raue (eds), *En détail – Philologie und Archäologie im Diskurs: Festschrift für Hans-Werner Fischer-Elfert, Band 1*. Zeitschrift fur ägyptische Sprache und Altertumskunde, Beihefte 7/1. Berlin/Boston, 587-600.

Leclant, J. 1963. 'Rapport préliminaire sur la mission de l'université de Strasbourg à Tomâs (1961)', in Service des Antiquites de l'Egypte, Campagne international de l'UNESCO pour la sauvegarde des monuments de la Nubie, *Fouilles en Nubie (1959-1961)*. Cairo, 17-25.

Leclant, J. 1965. 'Recherches archeologiques à Tomas en 1961 et 1964', *Bulletin de la Société Française d'Égyptologie* 42, 6-14.

Leitz, C. (ed.) 2002. *Lexikon der ägyptischen Götter und Götterbezeichnungen*. 7 vols. Orientalia Lovaniensia Analecta 110-116. Leuven-Paris-Dudley, MA.

Liszka, K. 2015. 'Are the bearers of the Pan-Grave archaeological culture identical to the Medjay-people in the Egyptian textual record?', *Journal of Ancient Egyptian Interconnections* 7:2, 42-60.

Liszka, K. and B. Kraemer 2016. 'Evidence for Administration of the Nubian Fortresses in the Late Middle Kingdom: P. Ramesseum 18', *Journal of Egyptian History* 9, 151-208.

López, J. 1966. *Las Inscripciones rupestres faraonicas entre Korosko y Kasr Ibrim (Orilla oriental del Nilo)*. Madrid.

Mahfouz, El-S. 2005. 'Les directeurs des désert auriféres d'Amon', *Revue d'Égyptologie* 56, 55-78.

Malek, J. 1984. 'The date of the water-cisterns discovered along the desert crossing from Korosko to Abu Hamed in 1963', *Göttinger Miszellen* 83, 47-50.

Manzo, A. 2012. 'From the sea to the deserts and back: New research in Eastern Sudan', *British Museum Studies in Ancient Egypt and Sudan* 18, 75-106.

Manzo, A. 2014. 'Beyond the Fourth Cataract. Perspectives for research in Eastern Sudan', in Anderson and Welsby (eds), 1149-1157.

Manzo, A. 2016. 'Weapons, Ideology and Identity at Kerma (Upper Nubia, 2500-1500 BC)', *Annali, Sezione Orientali* 76, 3-29.

Manzo, A. 2017. 'The Territorial Expanse of the Pan-Grave culture thirty years later', *Sudan & Nubia* 21, 98-112.

Masson-Berghoff, A. (ed.) 2019. *Statues in Context: Production, meaning and (re)uses*. British Museum Publications on Egypt and Sudan 10. Leuven – Paris – Bristol, CT.

McLean, I. 2017. 'Human intervention in the landscape through ancient mining: a regional study applying satellite imagery', *Sudan & Nubia* 21, 82-97.

Minault-Gout, A. 2011-2012. 'La figurine funéraire Saï inv. S. 964 (*SNM* 23424) et un groupe de quatre chaouabtis de la XVIIIe dynastie de même type', *Cahiers de recherches de l'Institut de Papyrologie et d'Égyptologie de Lille* 29, 189–200.

Minault-Gout, A. and F. Thill 2012. *Saï II. Les cimetière des tombes hypogées du Nouvel Empire SAC5*. Fouilles de l'Institut français d'archéologie orientale 69. Cairo.

Möller, G. 1927. *Hieratische Paläographie. Die Aegyptische Buchschrift in ihrer Entwicklung von der Fünften Dynastie bis zur Römischen Kaiserzeit*. 3 Vols. Leipzig.

Moeller, N. and Forstner-Müller, I. 2018. 'Introduction', in Forstner-Müller and Moeller (eds), 7-13.

Moreno García, J. C. (ed.) 2013. *Ancient Egyptian Administration*. Handbook of Oriental Studies, Section 1, Ancient Near East, 104. Leiden; Boston.

Morkot, R. 2013. 'From conquered to conqueror: the organization of Nubia in the New Kingdom and the Kushite administration of Egypt', in Moreno García (ed.), 911-963.

Morris, E. F. 2005. *The Architecture of Imperialism: military bases and the evolution of foreign policy in Egypt's New Kingdom*. Probleme der Ägyptologie 22. Leiden – Boston.

Müller, I. 2013. *Die Verwaltung Nubiens im Neuen Reich*. Meroitica 18. Wiesbaden.

Müller, V. 2018. 'Chronological concepts for the Second Intermediate Period and their implications for the evaluation of its material culture', in Forstner-Müller and Moeller (eds), 199-216.

Näser, C. 2013. 'Structures and Realities of Egyptian-Nubian Interactions from the Late Old Kingdom to the Early New Kingdom', in D. Raue, S. J. Seidlmayer and P. Speiser (eds), *The First Cataract of the Nile: one region – diverse perspectives*. Deutsches Archäologisches Institut Abteilung Kairo, Sonderschrift 36. Berlin – Boston, 135-148.

Näser, C. 2017. 'Structures and realities of the Egyptian presence in Lower Nubia from the Middle Kingdom to the New Kingdom: the Egyptian cemetery S/SA at Aniba', in Spencer *et al.* (eds), 557-574.

Pamminger, P. 1997. 'Contributions à la prosopographie militaire du Nouvel Empire', *Bibliotheca Orientalis* 54, 5-31.

Pamminger, P. 2003. 'Contributions à la prosopographie militaire du Nouvel Empire II', *Bibliotheca Orientalis* 60, 25-40.

Peden, A. J. 2001. *The Graffiti of Pharaonic Egypt. Scope and Roles of Informal Writings (c. 3100-332 B.C.)*. Probleme der Ägyptologie 17. Leiden – Boston – Köln.

Pilgrim, C. von. 2015. 'An authentication sealing of the "Ruler of Kush" from Elephantine', in A. Jiménez-Serrano and C. von Pilgrim (eds), *From the Delta to the Cataract: studies dedicated to Mohamed el-Bialy*. Leiden and Boston, 218-226.

Piotrovsky, B. 1967. 'The Early Dynasty settlement of Khor-Daoud and Wadi-Allaki the ancient route of the Gold Mines', in Service des Antiquités de l'Égypte, Campagne Internationale de l'UNESCO pour la Sauvegarde des Monuments de la Nubie, *Fouilles en Nubie (1961-1963)*. Cairo, 127-140.

Piotrovsky, B. B. 1983. *Wadi Allaki, the road to the gold of Nubia* (in Russian). Moscow.

Polz, D. 2018. 'The territorial claim and the political role of the Theban State at the end of the Second Intermediate Period: a case study', in Forstner-Müller and Moeller (eds), 217-233.

Raedler, C. 2003. 'Zur Repräsentation und Verwirklichung pharaonischer Macht in Nubien: Der Vizekönig Setau', in R. Gundlach and U. Rössler-Köhler (eds), *Das Königtum der Ramessidenzeit. Voraussetzungen – Verwirklichung – Vermächtnis*. Ägypten und Altes Testament 36, 3. Wiesbaden, 129-173.

Raedler, C. 2009. 'Zur Prosopographie von altägyptischen Militärangehörigen', in R. Gundlach and C. Vogel (eds*)*, 309-343.

Ragazzoli, C. 2017. 'L'hommage au patron en Égypte ancienne: sur la présentation de soi du scribe compatible du grain Amenemhat (TT 82) et d'autres administrateurs intermédiaires à la XVIIIe Dynastie', in N. Favry, C. Ragazzoli, C. Somaglino, and P. Tallet (eds), *Du Sinaï au Soudan: itinéraires d'une égyptologue. Melanges offerts au Professeur Dominique Valbelle*. Orient & Méditerranée: archéologie 23. Paris, 195-217.

Raue, D. 2019a. 'Cultural Diversity of Nubia in the Later 3rd – Mid 2nd millennium BC', in Raue (ed.), I, 293-334.

Raue, D. 2019b. 'Nubians in Egypt in the 3rd and 2nd Millennium BC', in Raue (ed.), I, 567-588.

Raue, D. (ed.). 2019. *Handbook of Ancient Nubia*. 2 Vols. De Gruyter Reference. Berlin – Boston.

Régen, I. and G. Soukoussian 2008. *Gebel el-Zeit II. Le material inscrit. Moyen Empire-Nouvel Empire*. Fouilles de l'IFAO 57. Cairo.

Reineke, W. F. 2017. 'Sechs Felsinschriften aus der Festung Askut in Nubien', in F. Feder, G. Sperveslage and F. Steinborn (eds), *Ägypten begreifen: Erika Endesfelder in memoriam*. Internet-Beiträge zur Ägyptologie und Sudanarchäologie 19. Berlin/London.

Rilly, C. 2017. 'Histoire du Soudan: des origins à la chute du sultanat Fung', in O. Cabon, V. Francigny, F. Bernard, B. François, M. Maillot, M. M. Ibrahim, O. Nicoloso, C. Rilly and O. Rolin, *Histoire et civilization du Soudan de la préhistoire à nos jours*. Saint-Pourçain-sur-Sioule, 26-445.

Ritner, R. K. 1993. *The Mechanics of Ancient Egyptian Magical Practice*. Studies in Ancient Oriental Civilization 54. Chicago.

Roccati, A. 2007. 'Arpenter le désert autrefois et aujourd'hui', *Bulletin de la Société Française d'Égyptologie* 169-170, 51-58.

Roeder, G. 1911. *Les temples immergés de la Nubie. Debod bis Bab Kalabsche, I*. Cairo.

Rothe, R. D., W. K. Miller, and G. Rapp 2008. *Pharaonic Inscriptions from the Southern Eastern Desert of Egypt*. Winona Lake, Indiana.

Ruffieux, P. and M. S. Bashir 2014. 'Preliminary report on some New Kingdom amphorae from the Korosko Road', *Sudan & Nubia* 18, 44-46.

Ryholt, K. S. B. 1997. *The Political Situation in Egypt during the Second Intermediate Period c. 1800-1550 B.C.* Carsten Niebuhr Institute Publications 20. Copenhagen.

Sadr, K., A. Castiglioni, and A. Castiglioni 1995. 'Nubian desert archaeology: a preliminary view', *Archéologie du Nil Moyen* 7, 203-235.

Säve-Söderbergh, T. and L. Troy 1991. *New Kingdom Pharaonic Sites. The Finds and the Sites*. SJE 5:2. Uppsala.

Schweinfurth, G. 1903. 'Die Wiederaufnahme des alten Goldminenbetriebs in Ägypten und Nubien', *Annales du Service des Antiquités de l' Egypte* 4, 268-280.

Seidlmayer, S. J. 2013. 'Rock Inscriptions in the Area of Aswan: from epigraphy to landscape archaeology', in D. Raue, S. J. Seidlmayer and P. Speiser (eds), *The First Cataract of the Nile: one region – diverse perspectives*. Deutsches Archäologisches Institut Abteilung Kairo, Sonderschrift 36. Berlin – Boston, 205-210.

Shirley, J. J. 2013. 'Crisis and restructuring of the state: from the Second Intermediate Period to the advent of the Ramesses', in Moreno Garcia (ed.), 521-606.

Sidebotham, S. E., M. Hense and H. M. Nouwens 2008. *The Red Land: The illustrated archaeology of Egypt's Eastern Desert*. Cairo – New York.

Simpson, W. K. 1963. *Heka-nefer and the Dynastic Material from Toshka and Arminna*. New Haven; Philadelphia.

Smith, H. S. 1976. *The Fortress of Buhen: The Inscriptions*. Egypt Exploration Society, Excavation Memoir 48. London.

Smith, S. T. 2015. 'Hekanefer and the Lower Nubian Princes: Entanglement, Double Identity or Topos and Mimesis?', in H. Amstutz, A. Dorn, M. Müller, M. Ronsdorf, and S. Ulias (eds), *Fuzzy Boundaries: Festschrift fur Antonio Loprieno, II*. Hamburg, 768-779.

Smith, S. T. 2018. 'Colonial entanglements, immigration, acculturation and hybridity in New Kingdom Nubia (Tombos)', in M. Honneger (ed.), 71-89.

Smith, S. T. and M. R. Buzon 2017. 'Colonial encounters at New Kingdom Tombos: cultural entanglements and hybrid identity', in N. Spencer *et al.* (eds), 615-630.

Smith, S. T. and M. R. Buzon 2018. 'The fortified settlement at Tombos and Egyptian colonial strategy in New Kingdom Nubia', in Budka and Auenmüller (eds), 205-225.

Spalinger, A. J. 2006. 'Covetous eyes south: the background to Egypt's domination over Nubia by the reign of Thutmose III', in E. H. Cline and D. O'Connor (eds), *Thutmose III: a new biography*. Michigan, 344-369.

Spence, K. 2019. 'New Kingdom tombs in Lower and Upper Nubia', in Raue (ed.), I, 541-565.

Spence, K., P. Rose, J. Bunbury, A. Clapham, P. Collet, G. Smith and N. Soderbergh 2009. 'Fieldwork at Sesebi, 2009', *Sudan & Nubia* 13, 38-46.

Spencer, N. 2015. 'Creating a neighborhood within a changing town: household and other agencies at Amara West in Nubia', in M. Müller (ed.), *Household studies in complex societies: (micro) archaeological and textual approaches*. Oriental Institute Seminars 10. Chicago, 169-209.

Spencer, N. 2019a. 'Settlements of the Second Intermediate Period and New Kingdom', in Raue (ed.), I, 433-464.

Spencer, N. 2019b. 'In temple and home: statuary in the town of Amara West, Upper Nubia', in Masson-Berghoff (ed.), 95-130.

Spencer, N., A. Stevens, and M. Binder 2017. 'Introduction', in Spencer *et al.* (eds), 1-61.

Spencer, N., A. Stevens and M. Binder (eds) 2017. *Nubia in the New Kingdom: Lived experience, pharaonic control and indigenous traditions*. British Museum Publications on Egypt and Sudan 3. Leuven – Paris – Bristol, CT.

Spencer, P. 1997. *Amara West, I: The Architectural Report*. Egypt Exploration Society Excavation Memoir 63. London.

Steindorff, G. 1937. *Aniba II*. Mission Archéologique de Nubie 1929-1934. Glückstadt – Hamburg – New York.

Streit, K. 2017. 'A maximalist interpretation of the Execration Texts – archaeological and historical implications of a High Chronology',

Journal of Ancient Egyptian Interconnections 13, 59-69.

Thill, F. 2011-2012. 'Statuaire privée égyptienne de Sai', *Cahiers de recherches de l'Institut de Papyrologie et d'Égyptologie de Lille* 29, 253-284.

Thill, F. 2013-2015. 'Sai et Aniba: deux centres administratifs du vice-roi Nehy sous Thoutmosis III', *Cahiers de recherches de l'Institut de Papyrologie et d'Égyptologie de Lille* 30, 263-304.

Thum, J. 2016. 'When Pharaoh turned the landscape into a stela: royal living rock-monuments at the edges of the Egyptian world', *Near Eastern Archaeology* 79:2, 68-77.

Török, L. 2009. *Between Two Worlds. The Frontier Region between Ancient Nubia and Egypt 3700 BC – 500 AD*. Probleme der Ägyptologie 29. Leiden; Boston.

Trigger, B. C. 1996. 'Toshka and Arminna in the New Kingdom', in P. Der Manuelian (ed.), *Studies in Honor of William Kelly Simpson*, vol. 2. Boston, 801-817.

Ullmann, M. 2009. 'Überlegungen zur kultischen Strukurierung Nubiens im Neuen Reich', in R. Preys (ed.), *7. Ägyptologische Tempeltagung Structuring Religion. Leuven, 28. September – 1.Oktober 2005*. Wiesbaden, 245-266.

Ullmann, M. 2019. 'Egyptian Temples in Nubia during the Middle and the New Kingdom', in Raue (ed.), I, 511-540.

Valbelle, D. 2012. 'Comment les Égyptiens du début de la XVIIIe dynastie désignaient les Kouchites et leur alliés', *Bulletin de l'Institut français d'archéologie orientale* 112, 447-464.

Valbelle, D. 2014. 'International Relations between Kerma and Egypt', in Anderson and Welsby (eds), 103-109.

Valbelle, D. 2015. 'Où et comment les Égyptiens ont-ils commémoré leurs campagnes militaires contre Kerma?', *Bulletin de l'Institut français d'archéologie orientale* 115, 471-486.

Valbelle, D. 2018. 'Egyptian usage of Nubian Toponyms: Iam, Kush and Pnubs', in T. A. Bács, A. Bollók and T. Vida (eds), *Across the Mediterranean – Along the Nile: Studies in Egyptology, Nubiology and Late Antiquity dedicated to László Török on the occasion of his 75th birthday, 1*. Budapest, 445-453.

Van der Perre, A. 2017. 'The Egyptian Execration Statuettes (EES) Project', in G. Rosati and M. C. Guidotti (eds), *Proceedings of the XI International Congress of Egyptologists, Florence Egyptian Museum, Florence, 23-30 August 2015*. Archaeopress Egyptology 19. Oxford, 667-670.

Vercoutter, J. 1959. 'The Gold of Kush: two gold-washing stations at Faras East', *Kush* 7, 120-153.

Vercoutter, J. 1966. 'Semna South Fort and the Records of Nile Levels at Kumma', *Kush* 14, 125-164.

Vieth, J. 2018. 'Urbanism in Nubia and the New Kingdom Temple Towns', in Budka and Auenmüller (eds), 227-238.

Vogel, C. 2004. *Ägyptische Festungen und Garnisonen bis zum Ende des Mittleren Reiches*. Hildesheimer Ägyptologische Beiträge 46. Hildesheim.

Vogel, C. 2009. 'Das ägyptische Festungssystem bis zum Ende des Neuen Reiches', in R. Gundlach and C. Vogel (eds), 165-185.

Vogel, C. 2011. 'This far and not a step further! The ideological concept of Ancient Egyptian boundary stelae', in S. Bar, D. Kahn and J. J. Shirley (eds), *Egypt, Canaan and Israel: History, Imperialism, Ideology and Literature: Proceedings of a conference at the University of Haifa, 3-7 May 2009*. Leiden – Boston, 320-341.

Vogel, C. 2013. 'Keeping the Enemy Out - Egyptian Fortifications of the Third and Second Millennium BC', in F. Jesse and C. Vogel (eds), *The Power of Walls – Fortifications in Ancient Northeastern Africa. Proceedings of the International Workshop held at the University of Cologne, 4th -7th August 2011*. Köln, 73-100.

Weigall, A. E. P. 1907. *A Report on the Antiquities of Lower Nubia (the First Cataract to the Sudan Frontier) and their condition in 1906-7*. Oxford.

Wegner, J. W. 1995. 'Regional control in Middle Kingdom Lower Nubia: the function and history of the site of Areika', *Journal of the American Research Center in Egypt* 32, 127-160.

Welsby, D. A. and J. R. Anderson (eds) 2004. *Sudan, Ancient Treasures: An exhibition of recent discoveries from the Sudan National Museum*. London.

Wente, E. 1990. *Letters from Ancient Egypt*. Society of Biblical Literature Writings from the Ancient World 1. Atlanta.

Wildung, D. 1997. 'Stela', in D. Wildung (ed.), *Sudan: Ancient Kingdoms of the Nile*. Paris-New York, 84-85, no. 92.

Williams, B. 2006. 'The Cave-shrine and the *Gebel*', in E. Czerny, I. Hein, H. Hunger, D. Melman, and A. Schwab (eds), *Timelines: Studies in Honour of Manfred Bietak, Vol III*. Orientalia Lovaniensia Analecta 149. Leuven – Paris – Dudley, MA, 149-158.

Williams, B. B. 2013. 'Some geographical and political aspects to relations between Egypt and Nubia in C-Group and Kerma times, ca. 2500-1500 BC', *Journal of Ancient Egyptian Interconnections* 6, 62-75.

Williams, B. 2017. 'The New Kingdom town at Serra East and its cemetery', in Spencer *et al.* (eds), 309-321.

Williams, B. 2018. 'Egyptians and Nubians in the Early New Kingdom and the Kushite Background', in Budka and Auenmüller (eds), 99-112.

Woodward, J., M. Macklin, N. Spencer, M. Binder, M. Dalton, S. Hay, and A. Hardy 2017. 'Living with a changing river and desert landscape at Amara West', in Spencer *et al.* (eds), 229-257.

Žába, Z. 1974. *The Rock Inscriptions of Lower Nubia (Czechoslovak Concession)*. Prague.

Zibelius, K. 1972. *Afrikanische Orts- und Völkernamen in hieroglyphischen und hieratischen Texten*. TAVO/B1. Wiesbaden.

Zibelius-Chen, K. 1988. *Die ägyptische Expansion nach Nubien: Eine Darlegung der Grundfaktoren*. Beihefte zum Tübinger Atlas des Vorderen Orients, Reihe B, no. 78. Wiesbaden.

Zibelius-Chen, K. 1994. 'Die Kubanstele Ramses' II. und die nubischen Goldregion', in C. Berger, G. Clerc and N. Grimal (eds), *Hommages à Jean Leclant, 2. Nubie, Soudan, Éthiope*. Bibliothèque d'Étude 106/2. Cairo, 411-417.

Zibelius-Chen, K. 2007. 'Die Medja in altägyptischen Quellen', *Studien zur Altägyptischen Kultur* 36, 391-405.

Zibelius-Chen, K. 2011. *"Nubisches" Sprachmaterial in hieroglyphischen und hieratischen Texten: Personennamen, Appellativa, Phrasen von Neuen Reich bis in die napatanische und meroitische Zeit. Mit einem demotischen Anhang*. Meroitica 25. Wiesbaden.

Zibelius-Chen, K. 2013. 'Nubien wird ägyptische Kolonie', in S. Wenig and K. Zibelius-Chen (eds), *Die Kulturen Nubiens – ein afrikanisches Vermächtnis*. Dettelbach, 135-155.

Zibelius-Chen, K. 2014. 'Sprachen Nubiens in pharaonischer Zeit', *Lingua Aegyptia. Journal of Egyptian Language Studies* 22, 267-309.

Abbreviations

KRI I: Kitchen, K. A. 1969-1975. *Ramesside Inscriptions, Historical and Biographical, I. Ramesses I, Sethos I, and Contemporaries*. Oxford.

KRI II: Kitchen, K. A. 1969-79. *Ramesside Inscriptions, Historical and Biographical II. Ramesses II, Royal Inscriptions*. Oxford.

KRI III: Kitchen, K. A. 1978-1980. *Ramesside Inscriptions Historical and Biographical, III. Ramesses II, his Contemporaries*. Oxford.

KRI IV: Kitchen, K. A. 1982. *Ramesside Inscriptions, Historical and Biographical, IV. Merenptah and the Late Nineteenth Dynasty.* Oxford.

KRI VI: Kitchen, K. A. 1983. *Ramesside Inscriptions, Historical and Biographical VI. Ramesses IV to XI and Contemporaries.* Oxford.

KRI VII: Kitchen, K. A. 1989. *Ramesside Inscriptions, Historical and Biographical VII: Addenda to I-VI.*

KRITA I: Kitchen, K. A. 1993. *Ramesside Inscriptions, Translated and Annotated: Translations I. Ramesses I, Sethos I and Contemporaries.* Oxford.

KRITA II: Kitchen, K. A. 1996. *Ramesside Inscriptions, Translated and Annotated: Translations II. Ramesses II, Royal Inscriptions.* Oxford.

KRITA III: Kitchen, K. A. 2000. *Ramesside Inscriptions, Translated and Annotated. Translations III. Ramesses II, his Contemporaries.* Oxford.

KRITA IV: Kitchen, K. A. 2003. *Ramesside Inscriptions, Historical and Biographical, Translated and Annotated: Translations, IV. Merenptah and the Late Nineteenth Dynasty.* Oxford.

KRITA VI: Kitchen, K. A. 2012. *Ramesside Inscriptions, Historical and Biographical, Translated and Annotated: Translations VI. Ramesses IV to XI and Contemporaries.* Oxford.

KRITA VII: Kitchen, K. A. 2014. *Ramesside Inscriptions, Translated and Annotated: Translations VII. Addenda to I-VI.* Chichester.

KRITANC I: Kitchen, K. A. 1993. *Ramesside Inscriptions, Translated and Annotated: Notes and Comments, I. Ramesses I, Sethos I and Contemporaries.* Oxford.

KRITANC II: Kitchen, K. A. 1999. *Ramesside Inscriptions, Translated and Annotated: Notes and Comments, II. Ramesses II, Royal Inscriptions.* Oxford.

DRITANC III: Davies, B. G. 2013. *Ramesside Inscriptions, Translated and Annotated: Notes and Comments, III. Ramesses II, his Contemporaries.* Chichester.

DRITANC IV: Davies, B. G. 2014. *Ramesside Inscriptions, Translated and Annotated: Notes and Comments, IV. Merenptah and the Late Nineteenth Dynasty.* Chichester.

PM vii: Porter, B. and R. L. B. Moss (eds), 1951. *Topographical Bibliography of Ancient Egyptian Hieroglyphic Texts, Reliefs and Paintings, VII. Nubia, the Deserts, and Outside Egypt.* Oxford.

PN i: Ranke, H. 1935. *Die ägyptischen Personennamen, Band I. Verzeichnis der Namen.* Glückstadt.

Urk. iv: Sethe, K. (ed.) 1906-1909. *Urkunden der 18. Dynastie.* Leipzig.

Wb: Erman, A. and H. Grapow (eds) 1925-1950. *Wörterbuch der ägyptischen Sprache*, 7 vols. Leipzig.